One for All

One for All

THE LOGIC OF GROUP CONFLICT

Russell Hardin

PRINCETON UNIVERSITY PRESS
PRINCETON, NEW JERSEY

Library of Congress Cataloging-in-Publication Data
Hardin, Russell, 1940–
One for all : the logic of group conflict / Russell Hardin.
p.   cm.
Includes bibliographical references and index.
ISBN 0-691-04350-7
ISBN 0-691-04825-8 (pbk.)
1. Social groups.   2. Social conflict.   I. Title.
HM131.H239   1995
305—dc20   94-23626

This book has been composed in Adobe Sabon

Princeton University Press books are printed
on acid-free paper and meet the guidelines
for permanence and durability of the Committee
on Production Guidelines for Book Longevity
of the Council on Library Resources

Second printing, and first paperback printing, 1997

Printed in the United States of America

10 9 8 7 6 5 4 3 2

For James S. Coleman, wonderful colleague

Contents

Preface

SEVERAL years ago, I attended a conference on nationalism and ethnic identification. At the beginning, we all introduced ourselves. I was early in line and I told my story of academic affiliation and interest and why I was writing on this topic. The next person told the story of *his own ethnic identity* and he suggested we all do likewise because we must all have strong identifications. Of one thing he was virtually certain—none of us was merely American, which he said was an empty category. Everyone after him then gave an ethnic identity. As he suspected, all had very strong identifications as French-American, Armenian-American, South-African-white-reluctantly-sliding-into-American, Jewish-American, and emigré Russian. Many, maybe most, were born outside North America or were first-generation North Americans. At the completion of the circle, I was asked to divulge my story. The best I could do was say I was American—I was in the empty category. Everything else in my past and heritage had blended into nothing distinctively recognizable or *motivating*. The nearest thing to an identity I would really claim was roughly the academic identity I had given. Even that one is fractured—I am almost always engaged in bringing the normative and the positive together against the best intentions of virtually all my colleagues. But at that conference I was twice over an outsider—I was not even in the group of those who took pleasure and strength from membership in some ethnic group.

In our ethnic biographies, one might think we were doing different things. Most of the group were genuinely telling who they were. I was telling what I identified with. Erik Erikson supposed the central problem of identity is identification, what motivates you, not what characteristics you have. I shared Erikson's view of identity. And at bottom, what I identified with was what Gananath Obeyesekere characterized as Buddhist self lessness or absence of self (the empty category, in other words?), at least insofar as self was culturally or ethnically determined. The others, some people might say, were really telling who they were, they were only giving objective understandings. I think that is wrong. They were also, and quite genuinely, telling what they identified with. They *just did identify* with ethnic aspects of their lives.

One for All is an effort to understand the sway of groups in our time. Because of their weight in actual politics, the principal groups of interest are ethnic groups of an astonishing variety and complexity, involved in conflicts that dominate the lives of whole societies. The practical interest in this problem is probably self-evident. The theoretical interest comes from the kind of theory that superficially seems to say that such group organization should not happen, that individuals should renege on doing their share of the group labor. I think that this superficial conclusion is just that: superficial. The trick is to show how it is that individuals can so readily, voluntarily assume their share of the group burden, so that the group takes on a life above the individual members.

While presenting part of this work to the Gary Becker–James Coleman seminar at the University of Chicago, I reputedly slipped and mentioned the previously unknown conflict between Croats and Azeris. A colleague, David Laitin, corrected me, saying they were about a thousand miles apart. Another colleague, Stephen Stigler, then interjected, "But, David, you're just in the quarter-finals of ethnic conflict. Russell is already looking to the superbowl." Stigler's quick wit betrays a dark side. Alas, group identification often justifies a dark view.

Acknowledgments

I OWE special thanks to Gary S. Becker, James S. Coleman, and Robert K. Merton, who have influenced arguments throughout, including many arguments that they might not recognize as anything they've seen before. Perhaps their greatest influence is the model of constant questing and questioning that they present. With one of his questions, Bob Merton forced a massive reorganization and refocusing of my central arguments on norms when, at the idle end of a Wednesday lunch at Russell Sage, he challenged me to think of how to explain the fact that blacks had turned the opprobrious "nigger" into a term of endearment. It was an epiphantic moment that worked itself out over revisions of chapters 4 and 5. Those two chapters also generally benefited from the wonderful institution of daily lunch at the Russell Sage Foundation, a lunch that was my chief source of ethnographic data, which seem to weigh about five pounds. As is true for all my work of recent years, the book has benefited from the creative research assistance of Paul Bullen, some of it long after I left Chicago.

For discussions of various arguments, some here, some mercifully forgotten, I thank Richard Arneson, Robert Bonazzi, Albert Breton, Youseff Cohen, Annie Cohen-Solal, David Copp, Ingrid Creppell, Nancy Cuniff, Deborah Diamond, Gerald Dworkin, Haskell Fain, George Fletcher, Wendy Gordon, Gilbert Harman, the late Gregory Kavka, Patricia Fernandez Kelly, Lewis A. Kornhauser, Mary Clare Lennon, Alejandro Portes, Sherwin Rosen, Sarah Rosenfield, Saskia Sassen, John Scholz, Bart Schultz, Richard Sennett, Milton Singer, Fritz Stern, Charles Taylor, Ron Wintrobe, and Eric Wanner, as well as numerous participants in several conferences. For written commentaries, I am grateful to Andrew Austin, Gary Becker, Jean-Pierre Benoit, Paul Bullen, Joe Carens, Josep Colomer, Fernando Coronil, Jim Fearon, James W. Fernandez, Robert Goodin, Carol Heimer, Will Kymlicka, David Laitin, Margaret Levi, Robert Merton, Donald Moon, Bart Schultz, Duncan Snidal, and Paul Stern.

Parts of the work were presented at colloquia at the Universities of Michigan, Washington at Seattle, Colorado, and Melbourne; the Australian National University; the California Institute of Technology; the University of Southern California Law Center; the Centre de Recherche en Epistemologie Appliquée (CREA); Ecole Polytechnique, Paris; the Becker-Coleman seminar, the Center for Ethics, Rationality, and Society, the Transcultura Conference, and the perennial Wednesday evening seminar, all at the University of Chicago; conferences of the Pacific Division of the American Philosophical Association, the Public Choice Society, the National Academy of Sciences, the Villa Colombella Group (Italian University for Foreigners, Perugia, Italy), and the University of Siena; and the Princeton University Little Lecture series. I thank the organizers of all of these events for their generosity and the participants in them for their collegiality and critical comments. It is perhaps unconscionable that I found so much pleasure in discussing such often grim problems.

This work was supported at various stages by the Andrew W. Mellon Foundation, the Russell Sage Foundation, the University of Chicago, New York University, and IRIS. I thank all of these participants in the universalistic norm of social research.

One for All is dedicated to Jim Coleman of the Department of Sociology at the University of Chicago. Jim has been a wonderful colleague and a superb example. He causes many good things to happen in the lives of colleagues and students. Perhaps the most important of his influences is to show how fruitful it is to be resolute in applying a theory to a problem or a class of problems. He is one of the individuals who make the University of Chicago a great institution.

Chapter 2, "Group Power," was originally written for presentation as a Henry Stafford Little Lecture, Princeton University, April 10, 1986. An earlier version appeared in Karen Cook and Margaret Levi, eds., *The Limits of Rationality* (Chicago: University of Chicago Press, 1990), pp. 358–78.

One for All

CHAPTER ONE

Individuals and Groups

> Jewish mother in despair upon hearing her son will marry the
> Chinese woman sitting as a guest at her dinner table: "But
> how can you give up 5000 years of culture?"
> "Ma," he said, "she has 6000."
>
> —Jewish folk anecdote

EXTRAORDINARY ACTION

Damian Williams, then a teenager, while participating in the 1992 riots
in Los Angeles, threw a brick at the head of a white truck driver, Regi-
nald Denny, who had been dragged from his truck. The riots were a
response to a seemingly racist verdict of not guilty that freed four white
police officers who had been videotaped in the act of wantonly beating
a black man arrested for speeding. Williams was in turn videotaped in
his own racist act. Williams explained his action: "I was just caught up
in the rapture."[1] In essence, he was carried away by the spirit of the riot
and lost touch with rational sense, arguably doing something that was
not consistent with his usual character.

Perhaps most of us could be similarly carried away by "the rapture,"
enough to do things not in our interest, even if not enough to lead us to
hit anonymously selected people with bricks. For example, many liberal
young women of Teheran likely participated in the demonstrations that
brought the Ayatollah Khomeini to power. Khomeini then predictably
wrecked their hopes for their lives as they saw them. Although venality
and ordinary self-interest may have played a large part in the Children's
Crusade of the thirteenth century, something like rapture and belief in
doing something wonderful for god must have been central motivaters
for many people, especially for the children themselves. The Children's
Crusade resulted in slavery and disease for its many enraptured children.
As has often been true of intense religious beliefs, theirs led them to
disaster. The young liberal women of Teheran may have a lifetime to rue
their rapture. Williams will likely have about three and a half years in jail
and then decades to rue his moment of rapture.

A striking characteristic of Williams in his moment of rapture and of
many other people involved in group-oriented actions is that, in a compelling sense, he knew who he was. Even more important than that, he

identified with who he was. Most of us do not identify with most of the groups we know, but we might identify with one or more of them. Some boosters of identification with a particular group seem to hold that membership can be objectively determined. But clearly it often cannot. For example, siblings with objectively similar lives can identify with different groups. There is, especially, a popular tradition that ethnic group membership is objective and it is often supposed that such membership is easily determined.[2] Even if this were true nothing would follow for identification.

As a case in point, consider Ota Benga, the central African pygmy who was displayed at the St. Louis World's Fair, the Bronx Zoo, and other places in the early twentieth century. He eventually settled at a seminary in Virginia, went briefly back to Africa, then returned to the United States, where he soon committed suicide.[3] With likely better reason than in most cases, anthropologists thought they knew Ota Benga's objective identity. He was, after all, physically very distinctive. Nevertheless, not much followed for his identification. He clearly ceased to identify with his community of origin. In the end, he may have been able to identify with nothing at all.

This book is an effort to understand the motivations of those who act on behalf of groups and to understand how they come to identify with the groups for which they act. This has long been a central problem for social theory. In this moment in history, it has also become an urgent practical problem.

COLLECTIVE ACTION

In recent years, Serbs and Croats, Serbs and Muslims, and Croats and Muslims have fought each other in brutal wars that have given no quarter to civilians; Hutu and Tutsi faced each other with murderous hostility that, for a few days, may have transcended anything known before; Northern Irish Catholics mobilized extraordinary actions against the British and the Northern Irish Protestants; Québécois rallied behind claims for French-Canadian culture; and so forth. Over the centuries, kin-groups and others have mobilized in enduring, bloody vendettas, individuals have fought astonishingly many duels ostensibly for the sake of honor, and groups of many kinds have closed themselves off from larger societies in which they were embedded. All of these odd behaviors have at times been explained as the collective action of many individuals to provide a benefit to some larger group: kin, ethnic group, nation, or class.

The argument of "the logic of collective action" is that self-interest typically runs counter to group interest.[4] This is commonly thought to be a distressing conclusion: Because we are self-seeking, we fail collectively and, therefore, individually. Hence, the claim that the groups above have solved the problem of matching individual to collective interests seems odd to many observers who conclude that something else must motivate these actions. The argument of this book is that self-interest can often successfully be matched with group interest. And when it is, the result is often appalling. The world might be a far less bloody place, and less ugly in many other ways, if many groups failed in relevant moments.

Why should opposite conclusions *both* seem bad? The first conclusion—that individuals typically fail to act collectively—follows specifically with reference only to a group all of whose members share an interest in having a collective benefit provided to them. The second conclusion—that when individuals succeed in acting collectively, the result is bad—is typically applicable to a group whose benefit comes from the suppression of another group's interest. The full story in many cases of successful individual identification with a group involves such an alter group. Something about the natures of the members of the group and its alter group makes group identification workable and therefore overcomes the logic of collective action at least for the first group.

Adam Smith's argument for why the untrammeled market is likely to be better than a system in which various groups gain political control over production, distribution, or whatever was essentially an argument that successful collective action about such matters would typically be harmful. The happy fact that collective action is hard to motivate if it is not organized by government was the back of Smith's invisible hand that leads individuals to prosper. The back of that hand blocks groups from wrecking individual prospects. Individuals are led to prosper; groups are swatted away.

The task of this book is to understand certain classes of collective action that somehow overcome the usual logic. The focus is on how collective action can be successful with little more than the kinds of self-interest motivations that underlie the logic of collective action. The argument also has a back of the hand, because the characteristics that make for group success often, although not always, lead to perverse results, just as the mercantilist's protectionism and monopoly led to perverse results in Smith's time. But the group actions of interest here do not depend on government backing to work their harm. They can succeed with ordinary incentives of self-interest to motivate individuals to act for the group. With success, the groups sometimes gain control of government and then they may do even more grievous harm than they could with spontaneous actions, but they can do massive harm even without controlling government.

The happenstance that acting on a norm or for a collective interest is congruent with self-interest plays a substantial role in determining which norms and collective interests prevail and which fail. Yet it is a common move in social theory to infer normative claims from whether people display strong commitments to their norms and collective enterprises. The contemporary communitarian movement in political and legal philosophy sometimes includes a strand of normative communitarianism, as distinct from what might be called the epistemological communitarianism that merely claims that our knowledge is heavily influenced by our community or communities. Normative communitarianism assumes that communal commitment determines, or at least substantially infects, what is good for the community.

Despite the commonplace inference, we can understand the odd fact that ethnic and other group commitments can be rabidly stronger than commitments that are universalistic. The reason for the relative strength of such group commitments is largely a function of individual self-interest and of epistemological flaws, which do not correlate with goodness or rightness. Hence, group commitments are unlikely to be good *per se*. Given that their effect is often appalling, we might as soon conclude of a particular commitment that it is bad as that it is good.

Identification is the central concern and the driving force for the arguments of this book, and I will here briefly discuss its relation to identity. Then I will canvass several difficult issues that stand behind virtually all the arguments of the book. Each of these could itself be the subject of a book—indeed, each is the subject of a substantial literature—but they must be addressed only briefly here. Consider three large issues: the claim that our theoretical accounts may be justified even though they may violate our subjects' self-understandings, as they typically do; the problem of multiple motivations for individual action; and the nature of commonsense epistemology. Each of these is a matter of central theoretical importance in the explanations and normative inferences that follow. Next, I will very briefly note a miscellany of philosophical issues and stances that are often raised or considered fundamentally important in the analysis of group identification. Finally, I will outline the chapters that follow in a general overview of the arguments.

Identity and Identification

The literatures on personal and ethnic identity commonly run two matters together: *identity in some objective sense* and *subjective identification*. I could be objectively blue but subjectively committed to the greens. I will generally speak of identification rather than of identity. Many of the people in the kinds of group of concern here speak rather of identity. If we are to explain actions, we typically will wish to address subjective identification, which entails motivation, and not some putative identity, which may entail no motivation. Although he uses the word "identity" far more often than "identification," it is commonly the latter that concerns Erik Erikson in his many writings on the development of identity over the life cycle, as when he speaks of "a sense of inner identity."[5]

Those who tout the identity of members of some group often seem to intend a normative assertion about the rightness or goodness of identification on the part of those who share the identity. Identity, however, is often not at all objective. Or, rather, one should say, what objectively defines membership in some group is not the proclaimed ethnicity or other characteristic of its members, because this characteristic is often not objectively definable. For example, most of the so-called Muslims, Serbs, and Croats of Yugoslavia have little to distinguish themselves from each other, other than that they use two different alphabets for their joint language and those who are religious belong to three different faiths (for further discussion, see chap. 6). The Tutsi and the Hutu, however, are sufficiently distinctive physically that their tribal identifications correlate roughly, though not completely, with objective features.

If we did not have identifications, that is, commitments, it would not matter so much that we have the quasi objective identities we have—I as an Anglo-Saxon-Celtic-Huguenot-Hillbilly-Texas-American, you as a Tutsi, Serb, or whatever. Even the person who is a Serb has roots that branch out in many directions as we trace them back through history. Such identities also branch forward in time. The five thousand years of Jewish culture have produced an extraordinary variety of peoples; the six thousand years of Chinese culture may have produced even more. Ivan Karp tells of a traditionalist Kenyan village and tribal elder who is Presbyterian and who is strongly committed to each of his identities.[6]

As nations are imagined communities,[7] so too are individual identities in very large part only imagined. A distant colleague asserts her strong identification with the culture of the place where she was born. She left that place as a small child and has never returned. Her grandparents represent four different ethnic groups who were blended to create her parents and then her. None of them was from the culture with which my colleague identifies. I might as well have declared myself a hillbilly, although I left the hills as a child and never expect to return to live there again. The hills and their culture do not motivate me. In some sense, I have stronger objective grounds for identifying with the hills than my colleague has for identifying with the culture of her birth—my parents before me and theirs before them were also hillbillies. Yet, I have the thinnest of commitments to most of my objective identities—the strongest is probably to the life of trying to understand such issues and to teaching, which involve an identity that I acquired rather than inherited.

I have so little commitment to my putative ethnic identities that I know anything about some of them only from casual hearsay, and I may have got some of them wrong. Many Serbs must share my lack of ethnic identification; many others are willing to kill for theirs. Objective identity tells almost none of the story—indeed, it may only tell the victim's story, as many groups have suffered horrendous abuse because they were objectively identified as worthy of suppression or extinction.

There are two important questions for identification. First, why and how do we come to have the identifications that we have? Second, how might our identification matter? We tend to *assume* people have identifications—or identities, in Erikson's inner sense—that match their somehow definable objective identities. This is not merely to be assumed but to be *explained*. Its explanation is a natural project for anthropology, but it is also a central project for political philosophy and political science, and it was a—perhaps the—central project of Erikson's psychological theory. This book presents an explanation of certain kinds of identification that people develop that is largely a rational choice explanation. Or, one might wish to argue, what it explains is the maintenance of certain kinds of identification as principally the result of the powerful force of individual incentives.

Incidentally, explaining how someone gets or maintains an identification may say a lot about the morality of the identification or of action from it. One of the peculiarities of identity talk is the tendency to suppose that the mere *fact* of an identity makes certain actions *right*. This popular move is an instance of the derivation of a moral from a descriptive fact, of an "ought" from an "is." (This move may be related to the tendency to suppose that, because "self" is a noun, it must be a thing.[8]) There is solipsism in the implication that my identity justifies actions and, analogously, there is what one can call group-solipsism in the implication that our identification with a group justifies actions by us on behalf of our group.

What difference does identification make? Consider two ways in which identification might matter. First, it could matter simply at the individual level, so that the individual reacts with openness or hostility to every other, depending on whether the other is in the individual's group. If evidence is of any value, this seems not to be at work for most people most of the time. Bosnian Croats, Muslims, and Serbs have usually lived in relative harmony. In the early 1990s they happened to be murdering each other.

Second, identification might matter when structural constraints of whatever kind make it potentially beneficial to be a member of the prevailing group. If our former Soviet Republic is going to have its own independent government, I will want my group to be in power and you will want yours to be. While the Russians were in power we might have been able to compete relatively evenly with each other for positions in the economy and government. With one of our groups in power, the other group may suffer and we have good collective reason to fight. We are suddenly in a somewhat structured variant of Hobbes's state of nature with no powerful authority over us to secure for us the benefits of peace.

Once we start fighting there may then be no endogenous (or self-help) solution for our conflict other than gross suppression of one group or the other, up to and including genocide if we fear the future and wish to preempt future possibilities. Yet we are the same peoples who might have lived splendidly together for the entire lifetimes of all of us. Brutality, ethnic cleansing, and so forth are not part of our ethnic identification. They are merely a means to the protection of that identification. If this is true, then probing the psychology of ethnic violence is likely to be less helpful than trying to regulate the conditions that give incentive for it. Seen this way, the problem is game theoretic and institutional and it requires structural resolutions, resolutions that change incentives. For the short run we must agree with Ruth Benedict that our task is to make the world, or various bits of it, safe for cultural differences.

In this account, identification with a group matters because it can lead to coordination for great power. That power might then be used more for destruction than for creation just because destruction is easier and more readily focused on specific, extant objects, such as a Turkish bridge at Mostar in Bosnia, or an extant regime, such as that of the Shah in Iran. Its most typical positive uses are merely to take over a going institution, such as the apparatus of a state, and to defend against attack. An entire polity, with its diverse economic and other interests, cannot readily be coordinated as thoroughly on positive policies as it might have been on overthrowing a particular prior government.

In characterizing recent events in Yugoslavia, many people associate the carnage with "taking the lid off." This is the wrong way to view the problem if it is meant to imply that the violence is natural and will come out if not controlled. The violence is merely potential until the incentive structure is right (or wrong, one should say). The incentive structure might change quickly if leaders opt to mobilize violence or if economic opportunities change in the face of limits to growth, economic malaise, or attempted transition from one economic system to another.

The Indian anthropologist Ashis Nandy worries that we try to overcome our cultural differences at our peril, that we somehow need the mystery of these differences.[9] Ota Benga, the so-called pygmy in the zoo, was an extreme example of many people who have tried to bridge the gap between isolated, relatively primitive cultures and the world of modern civilizations. Despite such cases, it is not clear how forceful Nandy's worry is for broader cases of overcoming cultural differences between peoples. Is it really at their peril that people have mixed throughout history? Neither Nandy nor one who might disagree with him knows enough to argue compellingly—the range of cases is too vast and variegated. In any event, it seems likely that *some* aspects of cultural differences should be understood well—their mystery should be cracked—in order for us to prevent the carnage and other forms of shackling of life prospects that they drive. And many of the problems of cultural mixing that we know are like that of Ishi, the so-called last wild Indian of North America, whose peril was that he *had* to overcome some of his cultural differences in order merely to survive.[10]

Finally, note that there is a vast literature that uses identity and identification in very different ways. Perhaps the best known of these follows Sigmund Freud in using identification with someone to mean adopting that person as a role model in a particularly strong sense. For example, he characterized one type of homosexual as having identified so strongly with his mother that he wished to be like her.[11] There is a more recent literature in sociology and psychology in which identification has a less complex meaning. Much of that literature focuses on the phenomenon in which you might choose to identify with, say, a parent or Harry Truman or Bessie Smith—you take the other as a role model.[12] But there need not be deeper psychological motors at work.

In the notion of identification in this book, identification is with a group, not with an individual. The issue is not the adoption of a role model, but merely the concern that a person has with the interests of a particular group or concern to be included within the group. No Serb might identify with Slobodan Milosevic, but many might identify with fellow Serbs or with Serbia. Freud's homosexual might identify with the larger group of homosexuals whose interests he shares and, for that reason, would identify with the group. Clearly, Freud's notion of identification is rich in theoretical ways that, whether right or wrong, are not relevant to the simple concern with an individual's seeming acceptance of a group's interests as his or her own.

Whose Choices, Whose Theory?

Anthropologists are sometimes bothered by what they call the dilemma of the cultural broker, which is essentially what an anthropologist, who describes or explains one society to another, is. This is a specific instance of the more general problem of the theorist trying to explain actors.[13] Consider, for example, the problem of the rational choice theorist. Seemingly the harshest criticism of rational choice theory is that it is unrealistic. People are not like that, people do not calculate, they are not overwhelmingly self-interested. Just ask them. Maybe Machiavelli and Hobbes were overwhelmingly self-seeking, but not Hume, Mill, and the rest of us. Rational choice may be for theorists, but it is not for people.

This is a strange criticism because it is, in fact, not specific to rational choice theory. For example, contemporary anthropologists speak a language virtually no one else speaks—certainly the peoples they study do not speak it. Many sociologists cannot even understand their own vocabulary—the people who are their subjects have no chance. Psychology is almost entirely about ununderstood influences on the self and unperceived motivations. Economists also speak a rarefied language. The subjects of their inquiry often can understand and do even use much of the economists' vocabulary, especially in advanced industrial states in which economists have played large roles in setting the public agenda. But it would be egregious to claim that ordinary people regularly, consciously use economic reasoning for matters outside the money market realm. And maybe they do not even use it much within that realm.

If we finally construct a rational choice theory of something, we will often want to claim we have an understanding or an explanation of real people's behavior. Yet we will come to that understanding only through a great deal of hard work by a lot of people. Those whose rational behavior we think we explain have generally not gone through any such analytical effort. Moreover, many of them might deny the relevance of our accounts to *their* behavior and motivations. This may be the biggest thorn in all of social theory, whether normative or positive, whether rational choice or other.

How can we justify an intentionalist account of behavior when the actor claims not to have the relevant intention or, even worse, seems not to understand such an intention? This is an issue that should bother most social scientists in almost all of their work. In many contexts we simply reduce motivations to instincts, but such a move would not be pleasing in our major theories. For example, rational choice often seems to require conscious reasoning, even calculation, well beyond instincts. Acting according to symbols whose meanings are unconscious, as in the anthropological theories of Claude Lévi-Strauss, also must often require conscious attention to the symbols. Or following a primordial attachment to one's own group would require conscious attention, perhaps always, but certainly in cases in which ethnicity is not instantly discernible.

Systems theorists might seem to escape the problem by asserting that phenomena at the system level need not be deduced from phenomena at the individual level. But even the systems theorist will commonly suppose there are psychological implications of system-level phenomena that lead to actions that comprise the system-level results. For example, Anatol Rapoport supposes that people in mobs behave differently, irrationally, according to a specifically mob psychology.[14] The explanation of these psychological phenomena, perhaps especially when they seem to be individually irrational, is still as problematic as it is in the individual-level theories.

We could go on with virtually every theory worthy of any of the complexity of the lives of those it covers. Even accounts of the seeming irrationality or inconsistency of behavior face the same problem. For example, consider Jon Elster's account of adaptive preference formation, as when I change my preferences to match my possibilities in such phenomena as sour grapes.[15] Because I fail to attain the grapes, I conclude that they are probably sour anyway, as in Aesop's fable of the fox and the grapes. This is an account that I, the actor, am unlikely to share as an explanation of my behavior.

Hence, virtually all social and psychological theorists are together in their problem of using theories and vocabularies that defy the thoughts of those whose actions they are supposed to explain. The theories of Lévi-Strauss and other structuralists preemptively elevate this apparent problem to central dogma while the theories of most other schools do not. This move does not resolve our explanatory problem. We still must wonder how it works even if we might agree with the structuralist that it works.

The question here is not always perplexing. For example, as Michael Polanyi has forcefully argued, there can be knowledge that is tacit in the sense that one can know things one cannot say. For example, in some behavioral experiments, shock treatments were administered whenever a particular nonsense syllable appeared in a string of nonsense syllables. Subjects began to anticipate the shocks quite accurately, but they could not explain why—evidently, they were not conscious of the association.[16] Action to avoid the imminent shock would seem rational, but it would not be consciously justified. The psychologist George S. Klein says, "It requires no experimental demonstration to say confidently that we are not aware of all the stimuli we use in behavior."[17] We might even model various learning modes as functions of different parts of the brain. Then, to say that an individual is rational is to say that all the various parts of the brain perform relatively well in securing the interests of the individual. But such a move might spiral our theory out of control.

Even at the common sense level of discussion of people's actions, we often find it perspicuous to suppose someone acts from unrecognized motives. Consider an extreme example. In the novel, *The Remains of the Day*, Kazuo Ishiguro lets his lead character, Stevens, reminisce on his long life as butler to Lord Darlington. The assemblage of his facts, as presented by Stevens himself, gives an overwhelming picture of Stevens's character, his sadly lost opportunities, and his major failings. Yet Stevens seldom has more than glimmerings of what the reader perceives. To a strange, astonishing, and enchanting degree, Stevens is able to tell us everything while hearing almost none of it himself. There is magic on the page. Dignity, the attribute of a great butler, Stevens muses, "has to do crucially with a butler's ability not to abandon the professional being he inhabits."[18] Stevens's quest for professional dignity has blocked his chance for inhabiting his personal being. It is sad, incidentally, that the movie of this novel cannot visually portray this central, captivating feature of the book, which is a subtle variant of the perplexing problem of the theorist whose theory its subject would not recognize.

It may be true that most of our seemingly rational actions are themselves not fully consciously justifiable. Psychologists and rational choice theorists cannot even explain themselves to themselves. It should not be surprising that those who have given no thought to the psychology or rationality of their actions might reject or fail to comprehend theorists' explanations of their behavior. In the case of shock treatments and certain apparent instincts, we might suppose genetically developed mechanisms handle the phenomenon. That is much harder to suppose for very complex choice contexts, such as voting for one's interests or identifying with an ethnic group.

Plausibly every social and psychological theory worth thinking about violates agents' understandings of their behavior and motivations. Part of the difference may simply be tacit knowledge, as analyzed by Michael Polanyi, who has a relatively sanguine view of the role of such knowledge. I sympathize too much with Ishiguro's woeful butler, Stevens, to have so sanguine a view. And perhaps part of the problem is that agents often require knowledge from their own experience to have it be psychologically motivating enough to guide further actions and judgments. As Jessica Anderson says, "impersonal knowledge has not much cutting edge."[19] But the major part of the difference is presumably that any theory that has had serious work put into it must have transcended the already known or common sense understanding. That is the role of theory and explanation. Our problem is not that theory and explanation are wrong because they fail to represent what agents consciously intend or understand. Our problem is that we do not have a good account of how to justify a claim that some theory or explanation trumps the agent's vision in a particular case or class of cases.

Suppose we have a reasonable account of individuals' knowledge and of their motivations. How do we then give a rational-choice or self-interest account of some aggregate result, some institution, or some collective choice? It will generally be complex. It will almost never be of the simple form: Doing x is in our interest, therefore we do x. It will generally include at least one intermediate step: Doing x is in my interest, your interest, and so on, and therefore we each do x, with the collective result that y is produced. Even then it will often require some analysis of why doing x is in anyone's interest. In the norms of exclusion discussed in chapter 4, feedback from successful group identification makes it the interest of individuals to identify.

MULTIPLICITY OF MOTIVATIONS

Most people probably would claim to act from many kinds of motivation. Most social theorists would likely agree that people are motivated by many things, ranging from instincts, to self-interest, to moral concerns. Rational choice theorists are often accused of ignoring motivations other than self-interest. Their answer, when they bother to answer, is commonly that self-interest tells the bulk of the story for the phenomena they study in the market and politics. Increasingly, they even seem to think that it tells the bulk of the story in relationships outside the market and formal politics, that it is the motor even in biological evolution. It is a fundamentally important part of the story for group identification and for the group action that follows from such identification, as is argued in the following chapters.

The importance of self-interest in the story of group identification is the extent to which it can be mobilized to support or reinforce other motivations, especially to support particular norms. If you are a nationalist, for example, you may be radically stronger in your nationalism and in your actions if your career prospects can be tied to the national prospects. Individuals' nationalist sentiments rise during wartime in part because the individuals' fates become more closely tied to the national fate and, for many people perhaps, because wartime mobilization opens individual opportunities. Nationalist sentiments may go far beyond what self-interest would stimulate, but self-interest is there. Once the norm of nationalism takes over the field of play, it begins to reinforce itself. Under wartime conditions of nationalism, individuals begin to have reduced knowledge of alternatives and become less able to judge their own state. And, more generally, individuals who do not share the same views may find each other less appealing to be with. For example, the socialist social critic Kurt Tucholsky fled Germany for Switzerland after Hitler's election. Asked to write editorials for publication in Germany, he declined. He wrote that, since his fellow Germans seemed overwhelmingly willing to go along with Hitler, German politics was no longer his affair.[20]

There is an implicit functionalism in much of normative argument in the social sciences. The assumption seems to be that, if things are done from certain motivations, they will serve society well. No matter what the class of motivations, this assumption is clearly false in general. The most benign motivations can be coupled with perverse understanding to produce dreadful results. And the most grasping, self-seeking motivations can produce massive, wonderful social benefits. *Motivations may explain but, because they need not correlate with the goodness or rightness of their effects, they do not justify.* In Smith's view, as noted above, crude self-interest was collectively good for economic relations so long as certain group interests could be blocked.

Smith's view is not a general claim that self-interest is a motivation with necessarily good consequences—it can also have dreadful consequences, as any motivation can. For example, consider the non-self-interested motivation that affected Damian Williams during the Los Angeles riots. Literature is full of moments of rapture that is portrayed as good. But the rapture that overtook Williams led him into disgraceful action. Even less dramatic motivations need not correlate with the goodness of their outcomes. Self-interest can produce prosperity for an aggregate society—or it can produce special treatment for small groups at the cost of an aggregate society. In severe conflicts, it can produce mayhem. Even beneficence, one of the sweetest of motivations, provokes critics of socialism, who suppose that universal beneficence leads to poverty for all. It has also provoked many major thinkers, such as Samuel Johnson, John Stuart Mill, Joseph Townsend, and Alexis de Tocqueville.[21] The important fact is that it is apparently true of all motivations of any significance that they can have grossly harmful effects. Hence, any claim that a particular class of motivations is good is simply wrong unless the notion "good" is somehow abstracted from the world in which the motivations play out. For many of the groups considered here, their defining group-oriented motivations and norms cannot morally be seen as good.

COMMONSENSE EPISTEMOLOGY

Economics and rational choice are commonly thought to be focused on the narrow concern of what the actor calculates is best to do. Sociology is commonly thought to be about matters in which individuals do not have choices, cannot calculate, and often are guided or directed by various institutional structures that may have arisen for odd or even rational reasons. Although this contrast makes for a seemingly neat disciplinary dividing line, both of these views are too pristine.

There is a third alternative that falls between these categories that seems to make sense of many individual choices. We have knowledge that we apply when we calculate or choose, but often our knowledge is limited by past experiences and gaining relevant new knowledge may be very costly. We make investments in much of our knowledge before we know how we might use it. When we face a decision, we are stuck to a variably large extent with the prior knowledge. We may act rationally from the perspective of our available knowledge even though, with more time to work out the facts, we might retrospectively conclude that our action was not in our interest. It would be odd, however, to conclude that the action was *irrational when taken* if *it was fully rational given the available knowledge.*

A rational choice explanation of behavior must often therefore take individual-specific knowledge into account. Such knowledge may edge into norms or normative beliefs, although one might wish to avoid such considerations in calling behavior rational. Perhaps this is only a matter of taste. The pragmatic epistemology of ordinary people may often not differentiate well between factual and normative claims, but a rational choice theorist may nevertheless want to exclude apparently normatively motivated behavior even when people assert (contrary to objective measures) that such behavior is in their interest. Still, rational action can only be sensibly related to the best knowledge one has rather than to some objective truth of the matter that one does not know—maybe cannot know.

Clearly, much of one's knowledge comes from the rest of society, as when one looks something up in a dictionary or encyclopedia or when one merely relies on custom or institutional guidance. It is through their role in our knowledge and their role in establishing constraints and opportunities for us that institutions enter into a rational-choice account. Sometimes these considerations are so trivially obvious that they are not even analyzed as involving anything more complex than a simple calculus of costs and benefits, as when we take account of the likelihood and severity of punishment in the deterrence of crime. But often, they are much more complex and subtle in their working. On this view, a full account of rational behavior must include the rationality of the construction of one's knowledge set. Costs and benefits of gaining particular bits and categories of knowledge may be related to one's circumstances, as argued in chapter 3 on group identification.

In this study, I propose to go as far as possible with a rational choice account of the reputedly primordial, moral, and irrational phenomena of ethnic and nationalist identification and action. Primordialists and moralists attempt to establish their cases by arguing against the plausibility that the actors in many contexts could be choosing rationally on the spot. They seem to win the argument easily if we cannot go back in time to the rationality of the knowledge actors have and the benefits that follow from it now that the actors have it. But if we can rely on the actors' knowledge to determine what it is rational for them to do, we may often find apparently group-oriented action intelligible without the mystification of primordialism and without strong claims of moralism either.

Contrary to the sometime quip that sunk costs are bygones, there is a sense in which *our sunk costs are us* (chap. 3). In particular, we are largely stuck with the knowledge we have gained in the past and used enough to keep actively in mind. I want to try to make sense of the further claim that, whatever accidents produced who we are, our partially socially-constructed interests and preferences may be well defined and rationally sought. One may go even further and argue that our interests are morally defensible despite the accidental nature of their formation— although a morally defensible interest of mine might be trumped by other considerations, such as your conflicting moral interests. It would be perfectly moral for the Serbs to rule over all of Yugoslavia—if there were no Croats, Muslims, or others to contest their dominance.

One central thesis is that what it is rational (in one's interest) to do depends on who one is in the sense that it depends on what knowledge one has. This thesis is explicitly at issue in a commonsense epistemology; it plays a large role in the formation of particular identifications in chapter 3, the force of norms of exclusion in chapters 4 and 5, the maintenance of astonishingly violent conflicts in chapter 6, and the grounding of epistemological communitarianism in chapter 7. Bringing this subjective focus into rational choice theory helps to resolve major problems in many areas.

It is ironic that insisting on the subjective focus seems like little more than common sense, yet rational choice theorists often fail to do it and sometimes even dismiss the effort as though it were a murky, because irrational, move. In part the hostility may come from another sense in which the term "subjective" is often used. It is used to assert the authority of subjects' knowledge or understanding of their actions. In general, subjects may have something of interest to say about their intentions, but their claims do not trump other sources of such understanding. We know too much even to believe everything we ourselves think, let alone everything everyone else thinks.

PHILOSOPHICAL MISCELLANY

In academic life, remarkably much of the discussion in social thought is about *how we discuss things*. Outsiders would want to spend more of the time actually discussing things. Even then they might cut discussion short by asking what difference any of our understanding of these things makes and how our understanding can affect these things for the better. Greater understanding need not, for example, end violence. As Hervé Varenne said, discussion can clarify, but not alter, the fact that there is no wine in the cafeteria of Woodward Court dormitory.[22] And in Yugoslavia and in the focus-group marketing of the American president, understanding can even worsen violence and conflict by revealing how the conflict might be exploited. A similar point can be made against Habermasian claims for the beneficial value of political discourse. Discourse need not help.

A growing literature contends that the state-centered view of our world is inadequate to the current problems of civil society.[23] This literature sometimes notes the efflorescence of civil society in parts of central Europe, as though the East Europeans could show the rest of us the way. This view is a gross misreading. The extensive political participation of civil society receives enthusiastic expression only in moments of state collapse or other great crisis. It cannot be maintained at a perpetually high level—how many people want to be ardently political all the time? The years 1989 and 1787–88 were extraordinary moments that made relatively ordinary men such as Vàclav Havel and James Madison seem like intellectual giants or, at least, almost political philosophers. Madison lasted nearly fifty years longer as a political leader; Havel cannot last so long. But their initial successes are about all we can expect of civil society until the next crisis comes. Indeed, they are all we should want of it. The best of all worlds in the interim would have good government at a much less fevered pitch.

Finally, at the Transcultura conference and in many contemporary academic discussions, few multisyllabic words are used more frequently than "deconstruction" and its variants. Insofar as I understand deconstruction I am—forgive this outrage—a deconstructionist. A deconstructionist takes conventional notions—icons, myths, and so forth—apart and demystifies them. Remarkably, with slightly different wording that is more a matter of disciplinary tastes than of meanings, that is what analytic philosophers do. Bertrand Russell, the early Wittgenstein, and many of their forebears from Hobbes and Locke to Hume and Mill were analysts: They analyzed evidently complex terms into simpler components to make clearer, less mystified sense of the wholes. It is a widely held view that philosophical analysis is now in decline in the Anglo-Saxon world. It would be ironic if it were to be displaced by a more nihilistic and vitriolic variant. The early analysts seemed to suppose that, when they analyzed, say, the map of Oakland, they would find the there there. Deconstructionists seem to know there can be no there there even without paying it the courtesy of a visit.

One area in which traditional analysis is still being productively put to work is in ethics and social philosophy. Partly that is just because ethics was long dominated by intuitionism. In intuitionism, there are no principles to apply, no deductions to make. I know some action or something is good or right, bad or wrong when I see it—or at least I would know such things if I had gone to the right elite boys school in England at about the turn of the twentieth century. This was one of the emptiest movements in all the history of philosophy. It was finally displaced by metaethics—the study of the role and meaning of ethical terms and judgments—and finally in the past few decades by ordinary analysis. Upon thorough analysis or deconstruction, intuitionism has turned into nothing.

AN OVERVIEW OF THE BOOK

After a preliminary account of the structure of the social problems under discussion (chap. 2), I will address four issues. First is the problem of personal identification with a group (the topic of chap. 3). Second is the way certain norms benefit from reinforcement through self-interest incentives (chaps. 4 and 5). Third is the way group identification can lead to violence that is commonly misread as simply reflecting elemental hatred (chap. 6). And fourth is the way these arguments undercut the normative claims of communitarianism and of other group-solipsist moralities. Normative communitarianism is the political theorists' variant of ethnic identification (chap. 7). Chapter 8 concludes with a brief retrospective. A summary overview of these parts should help to keep their relations clear.

One could say this is a study of norms or of conflict, especially ethnic conflict. But its actual focus is more specific than either of these. It is about how individual self-interest is or is not consistent with group identification and action on behalf of the group. Norms and conflict are of concern only incidentally, because they have large roles in the molding of self-interest into group identification. The norms of concern here are those that motivate strong behaviors that seem in the abstract contrary to interest. The conflicts of concern are those that divide one group from another and sometimes lead to violence. In both cases, the focus is on the apparent failure of the logic of collective action in manifold cases of spontaneous and organized individual actions on behalf of often large collectives. And throughout there is concern with the normative implications of group identification and action.

Chapter Two: Group Power

Widespread identification with a group, such as an ethnic group, can be the source of great power. Power is often discussed as though it were primarily a matter of control over resources, such as weapons and money. Revolutionary groups, who would not deny themselves such resources if they could get them, often prevail despite their poverty of such resources. Similarly, groups that are spontaneously organized by individual identification often prevail without an excess of standard resources. Their power comes primarily from coordination of many people, not from resources.

Groups that depend on *coordination power* can accomplish things that are very different from what groups and institutions that depend on resource or *exchange power* commonly accomplish. The former are inherently less flexible just because they depend on the commitments of their individual members. And they must be quite focused if they are to maintain commitments. Typically, this means they can be more readily mobilized by hostilities to extant institutions, practices, or statuses than by commitment to practical programs or policies for development. They are more likely to be important in times of crisis and loss than in times of relative prosperity and progress.

For example, identification with the union movement tends to be strongest when unions are weakest because the economy is faltering; identification falls off as the economy does better at employing people. To some extent, then, union commitment is less about the issues of exploitation, hierarchy, and so forth that concern academic and other analysts of the union movement. It is much more directly about jobs and wages. Ideology may help to mobilize, but it may do so primarily by helping to focus coordination, partly by moralizing the conflict between wage earners and wage payers but especially by making clear that there is a group conflict, not merely an individual worker-by-worker conflict.[24]

Chapter Three: Group Identification

Identification with a group clearly can matter. Then how does it happen? Much of the writing on it assumes that it is a primordial, moral, or irrational matter. Irrationality sounds like a large category but may be a nearly empty category, unless it is merely the category of insanity plus that of instinct. Instinct seems to be the primordial, so that we are left with insanity. Relentless commitment to a group that is against one's interest and that is not morally determined sounds incredible. The extraordinary religious cults, with their personal abuse and suicidal tendencies, as at Jonestown and Waco, might be instances of induced insanity.

The thesis that group identification is primordial could merely be a basic sociobiological claim that we are programmed to blame others for our harms and our lacks. Such an instinct might have been selected by evolution. If that is the primordialist thesis, however, it leaves open most of what we wish to explain, which is why Croat and Serb, Tutsi and Hutu, German and Jew, and many others have had such violent conflicts while, for example, the Swiss have been pacific. The primordialist thesis seems rather to be that specific groups have a primordial antipathy or hatred for specific other groups. This last thesis could be that, somehow, individuals are programmed to identify with a particular group and to be hostile to particular groups. But this is a silly and implausible thesis, which evokes the specter of Lamarckian learning that is inherited, and which sweeps the problem under a provocative word. Alternatively, this thesis might be a claim that group identification develops sociologically—but then the invocation of the provocative term "primordial" is out of place. If identification does develop in ordinary sociological ways, there must be a large role for rational, self-interest considerations.

A standard view of self-interest and rational choice is that it is overwhelmingly present- and future-oriented—after all, choices generally are made about what is to come. Bygones are bygones.[25] But there are at least two important ways in which the past comes into rational choice.

First, the rationality of our choice when we now face a decision is relative to what we already know or can choose to find out. If you and I are hiking the Appalachian Trail far from anyone else, and you collapse with a heart attack, I might be able to save you immediately if I am a doctor, or I might be able to do little more than comfort you as you die if I am not. In either case, *at that moment*, I act rationally. We face far less dramatic versions of this problem daily, even hourly. When I have to act in this moment, I must act from commonsense epistemology, not from ideally correct understanding. Suppose I do act from my best understanding. To say that I am irrational in my action is implicitly to say I should have come to know something other than what I do know, that I should have had the foresight to make better investments in knowledge—which is to say I was irrational earlier. But earlier I made choices about investments in knowledge and ability that were trade-offs with alternative investments and I made them in a state of overwhelming ignorance about such things as whether I would one day be in the odd position to save someone from death by heart failure. My earlier choices must have depended heavily on relative costs of gaining various bits of knowledge with especially low costs for bits of knowledge that came coincidentally through activities that were attractive apart from what they might teach. Until very late in life, for example, I made no choices about what language to speak, but it is eminently rational of me now to speak English in most contexts.

Second, my interests are the product in large part of my past history. For example, I may derive great pleasure from listening to a particular kind of music, which I have come to know so well that I resonate with it. If I am making a choice of what to do this evening, my tastes, as developed by past activities, should matter. Members of a community or culture similarly are likely to have strong preferences for doing things the way they have learned to do them from their community. Such preferences can constitute a strong commitment to the epistemological comforts of home, which help to define a group with which they identify.

Chapter Four: Norms of Exclusion

An important fact about many norms is that the behaviors they guide may be strongly reinforced by incentives of self-interest. Therefore, these norms have both whatever normative force they carry and the force of interest to make them seem to work and to give them greater stability. The thesis of chapters 4 and 5 is that certain group norms—norms of exclusion and difference—are especially likely to be reinforced by self-interest. Hence, these norms, whose implication might be thought to be some kind of collective benefit, work to get individuals to cooperate in the provision of that benefit. In this way, these norms overcome the standard logic of collective action, which typically predicts failure of individual action to produce collective benefits.

One of the most fantastic of all widely effective social norms was the norm of honor in the duel among aristocrats during several centuries in Europe. Individuals faced the prospect of being killed or of murdering an adversary over what were often very slight offenses that would not even trouble most people today. This norm seems likely to have had the general collective effect of reinforcing the status of the aristocracy as separate and somehow superior to nonaristocrats. Yet, it might seem that the individual had no incentive of self-interest to risk death merely for honor, sometimes for trivial honor, such as to settle a dispute over which of two dead poets was the better one. But, in fact, the norm seems to have worked almost coercively, leaving many aristocrats without realistic alternatives to following the norm.

Dueling was merely an extreme case of a host of norms which function to support some group against the rest of society or against some specific other group and which benefit from strong reinforcement from self-interest. The incentive structure of these norms is that of simple functional (not functionalist) explanation. Following the norm helps to reinforce it and to make others follow it by raising the costs to them of not following it.

Chapter Five: Universalistic Norms

More nearly universalistic norms—those not directed at another group but merely directed at the direct service of the actor's group or society—do not benefit from reinforcement through incentives of self-interest.

The latter are generally much weaker than norms of exclusion and difference. Two categories of such norms, however, seem to be quite strong. First, those norms that are specifically relevant to dyadic and small-number interactions—such as promise-keeping, truth-telling, and fidelity—are very strong. They are so strong primarily because they can be reinforced through the self-interest that people typically have in maintaining the relations they have with those with whom they interact enough ever to develop and require reliability in keeping their promises, telling the truth, and remaining faithful. As David Hume says, the first motive to keeping promises is interest.[26]

The second category of strong universalistic norms is those that can be distorted by mechanisms of self-interest that then reinforce the distorted norm. For example, in a society without government, we might all benefit from having a system of decentralized vengeance for wrongdoing, such as stealing, injuring, killing, or otherwise harming. Such systems may tend to develop into structured vengeance relations of vendetta or feud. In vendetta, one group—typically a kin group—is in continuous conflict with another group. Hence, each group stands to benefit from the harms it does to the other group and each group may mobilize its members to the defense of the group's interests by using, in effect, the mechanisms of norms of exclusion. Once the universalistic norm is distorted in this way, it can become very strong.

Chapter Six: Violent Conflicts

The most extraordinary result of strong identification with a group, especially with an ethnic group or nation, but also with certain other groups, such as the aristocracy during the age of the duel, is willingness to run grotesque risks of personal harm for a meager group benefit. Benedict Anderson asks of the deaths of millions of people for the sake of relatively trivial national interests: "What makes the shrunken imaginings of recent history [scarcely more than two centuries] generate such colossal sacrifices?"[27] A large part of the answer is that there is a stepwise progression from identification with a group, to mobilization of still stronger identification, to implicit conflict with another group, and finally to violence, particularly when both the group and the other group are faced with increasing incentives for preemptive action. People who would not have put themselves at risk at early stages take great risks at later stages, when they are more subject to group commitments and less subject to extra-group connections and when there are fewer opportunities for doing anything other than joining in the group violence. In an extreme case, such as in many communities in Yugoslavia in the 1990s, it may become virtually impossible to stay in the community without joining in the violence.

Chapter Seven: Einstein's Dictum and Communitarianism

Until quite recently, there was one value that was central to every major western moral or political theory: universalism. In the past two decades, western political theorists have proposed their first genuinely anti-universalist theory: communitarianism. Or rather, one should say, they have proposed the first widely accepted criticism of universalist theories—they have yet to propose a constructive theory. Communitarianism is sometimes strongly touted as a theory that makes the views of particular societies right—at least for their own members. But it is an oddity of communitarian thought that it is something philosophers may believe although it is not what particularistic communitarians of actual communities believe. The latter do not believe that what communities establish is therefore right. Rather, they believe *their* views are right, even to the point of justifying the suppression of others.

Philosophical communitarianism has two strands: epistemological and normative. The general thesis that our society informs our individual understanding is essentially an epistemological thesis that is acceptable to virtually all theorists, but it has no fundamentally normative communitarian implication. If it is to have normative bite, the communitarian criticism must eventually yield a principle or theory of the good in which at least some of the good is constituted by groups for their members.

Clearly, our preferences and interests are partially produced by our social experiences. Are they therefore communitarian and anti-universalist? Again, they are communitarian in an epistemological sense. I have the tastes and values I have in part because I am a citizen of my time and place—although my neighbor may have dramatically different tastes and values. Are my values and tastes somehow right? Insofar as their fulfillment conflicts with the lives of others, they may not be right at all. But, otherwise, their fulfillment could clearly be good on a utilitarian or other welfarist account because their fulfillment would be pleasing to me. Hence, communities may produce goods which are not communitarian in the sense that they are even acceptable to the methodologically individualist economist or other theorist. But it is not clear that communities produce any good that is inherently communal or that a community can be inherently good.

Chapter Eight: Whither Difference?

Special moral claims for community are suspect on their face, although a particular actual community might be morally splendid. But community as demanding or considerable as what the communitarian philoso-

phers and many political movements in the world want is arguably impossible in any case. Unless a community is merely one of many to which
I belong, none of which makes very great demands on my life, there
cannot be genuine communities in the modern world. Utopian thinkers
might wish to conjure up visions of community that might suggest to us
better ways of organizing our societies. But no one can sensibly com-
mend very strong community, with its central demand for loyalty and
for exclusion, as a possible way to organize. Very far short of the utopian project, we are sorely in need of practical understanding of the actual and the possible. Our task is to live well with difference, not to
enshrine sameness and obeisance to limited groups.

CHAPTER TWO

Group Power

> Without a prince, the Baganda do not rebel.
> —Bagandan proverb, in Max Gluckman,
> *Politics, Law and Ritual in Tribal Society*

THE STRUCTURES OF SOCIAL INTERACTION

There are three great categories of strategic interaction: conflict, coordination, and cooperation. If your actions affect my outcome, we are in one of these three kinds of interaction. *Pure conflict interactions* are typified by such games as poker and chess and to some extent by such social interactions as primitive wars of annihilation and the scramble for natural resources. In a pure conflict one party can gain only if another loses. *Coordination interactions* are the virtual opposite of this. In such interactions each party can gain only if others also gain. The most striking example of such interactions is the rule of the road, according to which we all want to drive by the same convention. In many countries we drive on the right; in many others, on the left. No one really cares whether we all drive right or left—but we all care whether we *all* drive by the same convention in any given place. *Cooperation interactions* involve elements of both conflict and coordination. The central example of cooperation interactions is exchange: I have something you want and you have something I want. I'd rather have what you have than what I have and you'd rather have what I have. We can both benefit by exchanging. There is conflict because each of us has to give up something in order for the other to gain. And there is coordination because we can both be made better off at once by exchanging.

Much of the discussion of cooperation, both in ordinary language and in political theory, runs together the latter two categories that I have called coordination and cooperation. It is silly to quibble about vocabulary here but it is useful to keep the interactions straight, because the distinction between them is clearly very important in explanations of many social processes and institutions. To avoid the confusion of the vernacular that runs these two categories together, I will often refer to cooperation interactions as exchange, although the category of exchange is not as extensive as that of cooperation.

What we exchange may be objects: you give me a book, I give you one.

Or it can be actions: you do something for me and I do something for you. This sounds like the very stuff of politics. Or what we exchange can even be abstentions: during the Cold War, the United States might have abstained from building a new weapons system if the Soviet Union also abstained from building it. Exchanges can be perverse in the sense that the element of conflict, of loss, may dominate that of coordination, of gain. For example, you give me the book you wrote and I retort by giving you the book I wrote.

Coordination problems are commonly resolved by conventions. We somehow happen on a way of coordinating that might be one of many plausible ways of coordinating well. Once we have done so, there is little or no incentive to do anything but go along with the convention. This is an account that is given by Hume and articulated in game theoretic terms by David Lewis.[1] For example, the driving convention in the United States may have arisen spontaneously without legal backing, although it is now backed by the force of law. The very orderly convention for time that we now follow arose almost spontaneously only last century. The morass of diverse local sun times, which were the norm in the United States until 1883, was too confusing to keep sensible railway schedules. The railways coordinated on standard railway time and eventually cities, states, and—in living memory—the nation adopted laws to mandate standard time.[2] One can see the problem from the fact that in the 1960s there was a thirty-five-mile bus trip from Steubenville, Ohio, to Moundsville, West Virginia, that required seven time changes.[3]

Coordination is often a causally and morally confusing matter. Charles Taylor argues that traffic signals are a restriction of freedom but not in a serious political sense. Why not? Because it is too trivial a restriction, Taylor writes.[4] This misses the structure of the issue. Traffic signals, if sensibly used, are not a restriction, though trivial, of freedom. They are no restriction at all. They enable activity, they do not block it. A sensible objection to a particular traffic signal would be that it generally interferes with our activities. Well-placed traffic signals do not do this but, rather, generally expedite our activities by coordinating our movements. Part of the problem in understanding coordination problems is that the resolution of the problem is often systematic, not piecemeal. There is no problem of my having or not having a traffic signal in this moment; there is typically only the problem of having one in general or not having one at all. To try to reason about the resolution at the level of whether there is to be a signal *in this moment* as I personally approach the intersection is to reason about a virtually impossible world.[5]

Coordination is also confusing when it is only partial, when some would rather not have it. The coordinations involved in the driving and time conventions are essentially harmonious across a whole society.

Other coordinations, many of central importance, are harmonious across some group in a larger society but conflictual across the whole society. Among the most important of these is coordination that constitutes power.

COORDINATION AND POWER

Successful social coordination, whether intended or not, can create extraordinary power. Even the driving convention carries with it great power to sanction those who violate it, as many who are accustomed to one convention learn to their sorrow when they drive in nations that follow a different one. Each of us may go along with a particular coordination merely because it would be individually costly not to. But because each of us goes along, the resulting convention may elevate someone to a station of power. This realization is at the core of the nascent theory of the state in Adam Smith, who—I have it on the authority of certain of my former colleagues at the University of Chicago—is every economist's favorite political theorist.

The usual concern with Smith's theory of the state is with his apparent theory of stages of development, from the state of nature through pastoral societies to, eventually, the England of his own time. That account is of no concern here. But the way in which Smith implicitly explains the power of government is of central interest. For example, in a pastoral society he supposes that an individual shepherd will find it in his interest to be part of a group of shepherds because the group or tribe can better protect each individual against various depredations.[6] In a competitive world of pastoralists, one benefits best from association with the most powerful tribe. Hence, if someone rises to capable leadership within a tribe, others will be attracted to join with it. The result eventually will be remarkable power in the control of the leader of the tribe.[7] Combination for the sake of survival then makes it possible not merely to survive but to thrive and even to plunder.

This is essentially an argument from coordination. We coalesce because it is individually in our interest to do so so long as others cooperate as well. What we need to guide us in coalescing with others is merely the evidence of sufficient leadership and sufficient numbers to make our joining them clearly beneficial. If others were coalescing around a different leader or a different group, we would be as pleased to join with them. On this evolutionary theory of the growth of power, fitness leads not merely to survival but also to increasing fitness. Power may not simply be a resource that can be expended until it is gone; rather, it may derive from coordination that re-creates itself.[8]

Incidentally, coordination can radically exaggerate the significance of minor differences. For example, for several decades, Bosnians, Croatians, and Serbs commonly married each other, lived as neighbors, and worked as colleagues. Coordination for group advantage has now made such harmony unimaginable. It would be foolish to say that the coordination is the product of the ethnic hatred and violence that we have seen recently. It is rather the provocation of that hatred and violence. Of course, the violence reinforces the separation into groups that compete with each other for land and other resources while it also breaks down the previous opportunities for individual achievement in the multicultural society that is now nearly gone.

That power from coordination is a central part of the power of even modern states can be shown by the answer to an apparent conundrum in John Austin's theory of law, according to which obedience to law is based on the threat of sanction.[9] We may call this the "gunman theory" of law.[10] The conundrum is that, if we are to be made to obey the law by threat of force, then the state will be unable to mount adequate mechanisms of enforcement. Hume says, "No man would have any reason to *fear* the fury of a tyrant, if he had no authority over any but from fear; since, as a single man, his bodily force can reach but a small way, and all the farther power he possesses must be founded either on our own opinion, or on the presumed opinion of others."[11] As a contemporary lawyer puts this argument: "No state could possibly compel people to obey all these rules at gun point; there would not be enough soldiers and policemen to hold the guns (a sort of Orwellian vision of society), they would have to sleep sooner or later, and then anarchy might break out."[12]

Anarchy *might* indeed break out, but as we all know it generally does not even under far less massively controlled circumstances. Why? It is commonly assumed that norms of cooperation and obedience are necessary to keep us in our places. Talcott Parsons wrote that the "problem of order . . . cannot be solved without a common normative system."[13] This does not follow, however. To wreck the state, it is not enough that anarchy break out a little bit at a time. If it is to prevail against threatened sanctions, it must break out all at once. It must be pervasive. A moderately organized state can typically keep its citizens under control without going to Orwellian extremes. The Videla regime in Argentina, the Nazi occupation in Czechoslovakia, the Ceausescu regime in Romania, and many others have kept large populations under control with little more than force simply because it was not actually necessary to invoke the force against everyone at once. Those who would oppose such a regime must coordinate their actions in opposition or be weaker than their numbers. Gaetano Mosca notes that minorities rule majorities because "each single individual in the majority . . . stands alone before the totality of the organized minority."[14]

In a relatively orderly state, most individuals cannot expect to benefit from seriously transgressing the law, because the police, as weak as they may be, can be expected to apprehend a significant proportion of transgressors. That, remarkably, may be all that the gunman theory of the state requires for its success. The gunman theory might well be called the coordination theory of state power or even the *dual-coordination theory*. It depends on coordination at the level of government and on lack of coordination at the level of any potential popular opposition. The state need not compel everyone at gunpoint, it need merely make it in virtually everyone's clear interest *individually* to comply with the law even though collectively it might be their interest to oppose the law.

Note the way coordination works here. It creates power because it makes certain behaviors on the part of relevant others less rewarding than they would be against an uncoordinated group. In turn, this means that the coordinated, powerful group can now do many things at far less cost than doing these things would otherwise have exacted. Hence, coordination not only creates power, it also reduces the need to use power. Therefore, few police are necessary for maintaining order until order is cracked by a tipping event or signal that coordinates an opposition. Then individuals may be able to demonstrate or riot with impunity.

On the dual-coordination theory of state power and of obedience to law it is relatively easy to understand the remarkable change in allegiance of a populace under certain radical changes in government. For example, we are often treated to agonizing questions about the nature of the German people that they could have given their allegiance to Hitler on short notice and then could quickly have switched their allegiance from him to the puppet governments of the western allies and the Soviet Union. Throughout, most Germans seem to have been model citizens. Most of us would similarly be model citizens under the coercive circumstances of the Germans during and after Hitler's rule. If there were as many genuinely loyal Nazis as we sometimes suspect, it would be odd that they submitted so readily to the postwar governments if obedience really turned on a civic norm of cooperation or a shared commitment to a particular set of values.

On the dual coordination theory it is also easy to grasp the power of passive disobedience, as in the Indian independence movement or the American Civil Rights movement. Passive disobedience depends on the power of popular coordination against the limited capacity of a normal state to control its population. That there is differential capacity for coordination is clear. The large population often cannot coordinate except by careful, covert conspiracy while the minions of the state can conspire openly. What makes passive disobedience a rare device is that it too requires open conspiracy, hence widespread moral agreement. But passive disobedience is not anarchy, or at least not chaos. It is generally quite orderly. If there is great disorder, it is often introduced by the state in the effort to rout the orderly resisters.

A striking example of dual coordination and its eventual failure is the collapse of the regime of Nicolae Ceausescu in Romania in four days in December 1989 in the wake of the passing of other autocratic Communist regimes in East Europe. The tipping events were a demonstration on 17 December in Timisoara that started in support of a Hungarian Protestant minister. As the small demonstration attracted others, it grew out of control, with chants of "Down with Ceausescu." Ceausescu ordered the army to quell the disturbance and the soldiers killed many demonstrators. Ceausescu ordered a huge turnout in Palace Square in Bucharest on 21 December. Since he had been unanimously reelected general secretary of the Romanian Communist Party on 25 November at the XIV Party Congress, he presumably expected the usually obeisant turnout to confirm his authority.[15]

In the protection of the mass, some people began to shout that Ceausescu was a dictator. When no reprisal followed, the crowd joined the chant. Ceausescu left the balcony of the Central Committee headquarters and fled Bucharest. He was soon captured by the army and, four days later, he and his wife were tried and executed. Reputedly, three hundred soldiers volunteered to serve in his firing squad.[16] The Securitate—essentially Ceausescu's personal police force—could no longer contain the population or the army. Days earlier Ceausescu and his Securitate had the power of life and death over virtually the entire Romanian population. The coordinations that made for their power collapsed almost instantaneously—and together. The mass of people were ironically coordinated in the fatal moment by Ceausescu himself in Palace Square. They might never have brought themselves successfully together without his signal.

As a rule, successful revolutions are similar to the so-called constructive veto in the German parliamentary government. In Germany, a chancellor can be unseated only by a majority vote in favor of an alternative chancellor. This avoids the chaotic possibility of removing one government without having another to replace it, as happens in the Italian parliamentary system. As in the Bagandan proverb that the Baganda do not rebel without a prince to take over, revolutions generally organize behind a particular potential governor. It is plausible that the Romanian rejection of Ceausescu was the relatively rare instance of popular veto of a government without any clear alternative in mind to replace it. Perhaps some of those who demonstrated against the Shah in Iran similarly saw their purpose as the wholly negative one of removing the Shah. But, as is typical, in their case the way to mobilize the population was behind an alternative leader, Khomeini. Many of those, such as liberal women, who anarchically marched against the Shah might have acted differently if they had understood that they were most likely involved not in anarchy but in constructive veto.

The constructive veto and most revolutions require that both sides of the dual coordination theory be met: The current leadership must suffer falling coordination while the alternative leadership is backed by increasing coordination. Political order can often survive if only one of these conditions is met. The effectiveness of power depends on the obstacles to be moved with it.

EXCHANGE

Perhaps the interaction that most commonly underlies what, in ordinary discourse, we call cooperation is that of the game theorist's favorite game, the prisoner's dilemma. This game was discovered or invented—it is not clear which is the more apt term here—by Merrill Flood and Melvin Dresher, two early game theorists who were trying to test bargaining theories with experimental games.[17] Oddly, two of the games with which Flood experimented before the prisoner's dilemma involved simple exchanges—of old cars for money. He seems not to have seen that his prisoner's dilemma game was a simplification and generalization of such exchanges. Unfortunately, this association got lost in the later naming of the game by A. W. Tucker, who saw in the game a perverse analog of American criminal justice, in which prosecutors extract confessions on the promise of reduced sentences.[18] Social theorists have come to see prisoner's dilemmas everywhere in social interaction and many have been surprised by the ubiquity of the game.[19] Had the game originally been named "exchange," we would have *expected* it to be ubiquitous.

Ordinarily we think of exchange as essentially a two-party affair, as in Flood's games over the sale of used cars in California. But the strategic structure of exchange can be generalized to any number of players. In its many-person or collective guise, exchange is a very interesting problem at the core of the issue of social order. It is in some ways less tractable than the ordinary two-party problem and, indeed, it entails the perversity of the logic of collective action.[20] Under this logic, a group of people with a common interest that requires common action may share an interest collectively but not individually. You and I both want cleaner air and we can both contribute to cleaning it up by not burning our leaves or grilling our dinners over charcoal and by paying more for cars that pollute less. Unfortunately, it is in my interest for everyone else to behave well in these ways, but it is not in my interest for *me* to behave well. The best of all worlds for me, egocentric as I am, is that in which you all behave well while I barbecue and otherwise pollute to my heart's content and my pocketbook's benefit.

This is not unlike the motivations in Flood's and Dresher's original, still unnamed, prisoner's dilemma or in any ordinary exchange. In the best of all worlds for Flood in one of his car buying games, he would have got the car without having to pay for it. At the level of two-person exchange in our actual world, that would amount to theft. But if I pollute the air of thousands of asthma sufferers in order to gain a slight pleasure, that is not theft—it is just the dismal logic of collective action. When we want benefits from collective exchange, we are swatted by the back of the invisible hand that coddles us to success in dyadic exchanges on the market.

The problem of pollution is a perverse and in some degree a modern variant of the central problem of collective action in social life. The collective problem of pollution results from the failure to control destructive impulses that are individually beneficial. The more urgent problem at the base of social life is that of motivating constructive actions to create order and prosperity. The order we enjoy in a well-ordered state is in part the product of large-number exchanges or collective actions in which we individually contribute to the provision of a collective good. Collectively we may create resources that give us collective power. But generally we cannot count on individual generosity to contribute to collective endeavors. We need the motivations of direct benefit to individuals that made Flood's game of buying and selling a used car an easy problem. It was easy because neither the buyer nor the seller could get the benefits of the exchange without paying the cost of giving up the money or giving up the car. Often the only way to tie the benefits and costs of *collective* action so directly together is through legal sanctions. Our cars do not pollute as much as they once did because the state forces us to buy cars with pollution control devices. While many people might pay extra for optional safety equipment such as airbags or seatbelts on their cars, presumably few would pay extra for optional pollution control equipment.

Traditional political philosophers suppose that voluntary collective action is hard to motivate. They have commonly argued that we therefore create states with the power to sanction people individually. Not surprisingly, this move is ridiculed as circular because it supposes that we solve the grievous problem of collective action by *collectively* acting to solve it. This would not be a helpful explanatory move. Yet it does seem true that much of the source of a society's power to motivate collective action comes from mutual cooperation. If this is so, must people not finally be motivated primarily by normative concerns rather than by interests when they are concerned with social order? Surely to some extent people *are* normatively motivated. But much of modern social life seems much more heavily to depend on motivations from interest. The extraor-

dinary wealth of industrial societies would be hard to explain if normative concerns were thought to be the central motivaters of workers on
the job. Then do we partition ourselves and act normatively in politics
and from interests in economics? That seems to be the central division
for many scholarly accounts and, on the apparent views of some people,
it underlies our division into academic disciplines.

Against this way of viewing social cooperation, a large part of the
answer to our seeming paradox is that much of the cooperation that is
needed to create central power to regulate further cooperation grows out
of a substantially different form of collective interaction: it grows out of
games of coordination, not out of games of exchange. *Coordination produces power that produces sanctions that motivate collective exchange.*
Of course, the causal chain of social life will not typically be so simple
and pristine as this. Indeed, there will be no beginning for the chain. In
any actual institution we will see an amalgam of resources that are sometimes created by coordination, sometimes by voluntary collective exchange, and sometimes by the use of prior resources to compel further
contributions to the collective stores. There may be elements of norm-
guided behavior in any of these, especially in voluntary collective exchange. But for many institutions the clear structure of motivations is
individual incentives derived largely from the power of coordination.

Confusions between Coordination and Exchange

Is the distinction between coordination and exchange important for our
further understanding of political theory? To see that it is, let us briefly
consider several issues. First, let us consider the central conceptual issue
in the understanding of political power. Debates on power are often confused by the failure to distinguish the sources of it. Then let us turn to
three instances of confusion in important political theories that are also
based in this failure. These theories are Hobbes's theory of political society, Marx's optimistic theory of revolution, and contemporary explanations of the common law that base the law in arguments from efficiency.
Keeping straight the different strategic sources of power in the nature of
power and in such theories as these is crucial to political theory.

Power

Game theoretically, mobilizing a group or populace around any purpose
is easier if they all share that purpose. We may then say the group or
populace faces a coordination problem. But what purpose can be served
by mobilization? In general, massive coordination produces great power
that can be used for varied ends. In a particular case, it may be used only

insofar as it is directed at the purpose around which the populace has coordinated. If we have coordinated around leaders in a demand for nationhood, those leaders might instantly lose our support if they try to compromise or change the goal.

There are at least two forms in which collectivities produce power. First, they produce resources that can be converted to use in coercing or influencing others to act in varied ways. Second, they coordinate behind a leadership to give the leaders capacity to act. Power therefore has at least two forms: the amassment of ordinary economic resources and the massive coordination of individual actions. We may distinguish these two forms as *exchange power* and *coordination power*.

Coordination power is especially important in stimulating nationalist and ethnic identification and action on behalf of the nation or people. My joining in a coordination of group X contributes to the power of group X, thereby increasing the likelihood of the group's gaining its objectives, which will benefit me along with all other members of X. Coordination power is conceptually prior to exchange power in that we must at least coordinate to create order with which we may then create resources. This is essentially Hobbes's theory of government: Order precedes production.

If success turns on prevailing over another group or nation, then the prospects for success do not derive merely from an internal calculus of participation. There may be little incentive to mobilize behind ethnic or nationalist leadership if there is little to gain or scant chance of success. Therefore we may see remarkably little political activity from an ethnic group as such for long periods of time. The ethnic minorities of the Soviet Union were largely quiescent for two generations. Now, with the failure of hopes for greater individual economic success and with the prospect of central incapacity to respond to groups' political moves, they have burst into almost instant activity.

In similar fashion, in keeping with the dual-coordination theory, revolutionary movements have often taken the field with success only when the central regime was severely weakened, especially by military defeat, as in Russia in 1917 and Iraq in 1991, or by the decline or death of a powerful leader without whom continued coordination of the regime was difficult, as at the end of the Shah's Iran or Haile Selassie's Ethiopia. The difference between ethnic activity in the Soviet Union in, say, 1960 and the early 1990s is overtly associated with perceived, dramatic changes in the payoffs from such activity. In addition to changes in activity levels, ethnic groups also may become more loyal to group ideals or interests as the prospects for group success rise. Improving prospects may heighten attention and therefore commitment. This is particularly true if success is a matter of finally tipping the scales, so that loyalty rises as the tipping point nears just because the marginal benefit of increasing loyalty rises.

When national or ethnic loyalties are conjoined with institutional bases of power, they become forceful and articulate in moving many people. National governments may mobilize populations; religious leaders may mobilize ethnic groups. By their act of coordinating masses behind them, national, religious, and other leaders become powerful (or more powerful).

From this account, consider conceptual confusions in the notion of power. All too often discussions of power are concerned too soon with what power is rather than with how it comes to be, how it is created. As noted above, political power can be based *directly* in successful coordination of many people. Such coordination may sensibly be called a form of power. Power can also be based *indirectly* in collective exchange, which can produce resources, such as money. People can cooperate in such exchanges either spontaneously or under threat of sanctions. The force of the sanctions may derive from the power of a coordinated body or from the availability of resources to the state or other sanctioner. These resources can be used to manipulate or coerce people to do things unrelated to the original exchange that produced the resources.

It follows that power derived from resources can be used to augment the resources. It can also be expended as the resources are expended, as in war; and, if it is not adequately augmented, it can be exhausted. Power based in coordination can increase as it attracts further people to the coordination. For example, Smith's pastoral leader may be so powerful as to attract others to his following because they seek his protection. Power based in coordination can be destroyed very quickly by recoordination behind a different leader or on a different convention, or even by the collapse of coordination. For example, on Xenophon's account, Cyrus's upstart army was on the verge of victory over the army of Artaxerxes II and might soon have routed the latter when Cyrus charged into battle against the king and was slain in 401 B.C. As the news spread, his army collapsed before an alternative leader could be elevated to its head. Although it had taken months to mold that army, its extraordinary power was dissipated in hours once it lost its prince.[21] Artaxerxes seemed correctly to infer that victory went to the survivor even if the survivor may have lost most of the battle.

Power based in coordination may be harder to manipulate than that based in resources. It may be more fragile, as the Greeks fighting on the side of Cyrus learned, and it may be more resistant to changes in the uses to which it is put. It is often associated with charisma. Whether it requires charisma, it requires a focus. Among the Baganda (on Lake Victoria in what is now Uganda) there was a saying that "without a prince the

Baganda do not rebel."[22] There must be a relevant candidate for kingship behind whom rebels can organize. Power based in resources extracted from collective exchange or from coerced contributions will be far more fungible. It can often be seized, as in coups.

Power based in coordination is rather more like the money system than like exchange. We generally can rely on the intrinsically worthless paper money in our pockets just because virtually everyone else relies on it. If, however, enough of us suddenly were to coordinate in running on our banks to convert our currency into something else—silver, gold, or yen—our currency would suddenly lose its value. Coordination power is similarly a function of reinforcing expectations about behavior of others. Exchange power is more nearly like the actual goods that are in exchange, either for money or for other goods. It takes the form of deployable resources.

It is this dual nature of the sources of power and therefore of the workings of power that make efforts to define it generally unsatisfactory in the vast and vastly disagreeable "power is . . ." literature. For example, contrary to the view of Parsons, there is no "generalized medium" of power analogous to the medium of money in exchange.[23] Coordination power shares the characteristic of money that it depends on mutually reinforcing expectations. And exchange power shares the sometime characteristic of money that it is backed by real resources.

It is on the coordination view of power that we should analyze many aspects of political life, as for example, political participation. When one is a voter, Brian Barry asks, "Is it better to be powerful or lucky?"[24] He rightly concludes that it is better to be lucky in the sense that what one wants is simply to have one's views be the majority views. If, on the resource view of power, we were to analyze the resources of individual voters to determine their power, these would seem paltry. On the coordination view, it is not the individual voter who is powerful; rather, it is the coordinated mass of voters who vote together that is powerful. Similarly, it is not the individual herder in Smith's pastoral society who is powerful; rather, it is the coordinated collective of herders under unified leadership. When the coordination breaks, the power dissipates, as it did for Cyrus's army. In game theoretical language, power based in coordination is superadditive, it adds up to more than the sum of the individual contributions to it.

Again, as noted above, successful coordination of a group may radically reduce the group's costs of action in important ways simply because its coordination induces others not to oppose it. Individual or small groups of herders, for example, might have to be constantly on the alert to protect their herds. The members of a large pastoral tribe might rest relatively content in the same environment.

Leviathan

It is sometimes supposed that Hobbes represents the central problem of political order as a general prisoner's dilemma. If we all voluntarily cooperate in leaving each other's goods and persons alone, we all prosper better than if we all plunder one another's goods and threaten one another's safety. But so long as everyone else is cooperating, I would benefit from taking advantage of them and plundering for my benefit. Indeed, no matter what anyone else does, my interest is better served by my plundering than by my abstinence. This is the structure of the prisoner's dilemma.

Smith's account of the rise of powerful leaders in pastoral societies seems far more plausible than this account, which, in any case, is a misreading of Hobbes.[25] Smith supposes that before the rise of herding there could have been little advantage in going after another's property because there could be little property of value.[26] This is not the conceptual point that without a state to define ownership there can be no property but merely the economic point that before herding there could have been little of value to plunder from anyone. The potential benefits of plundering would therefore have been negligible. Moreover, if a plunderer ran some risk of personal harm, then plundering would be worse than not plundering.

That is to say, in the rudest state of economic and political development—not to speak of what philosophers call a "state of nature"—plundering no matter what others did was plausibly not the dominant strategy it would be in the supposed prisoner's dilemma of Hobbes. Since the harm that could come from being attacked was likely greater than the gains to be made from attacking, the strategic structure of a rude society is that of a coordination game *if only* it is true that coordination of the many gives protection against attack, as surely it often must. Hence, the problem that Hobbes had to resolve is not a prisoner's dilemma or exchange but a coordination game. The rudimentary state precedes the rise of wealth that would make plundering worthwhile.

The resolution of such a game might seem similar to Hobbes's resolution of his problem in that it might well involve the elevation of someone to a position of powerful leadership. The elevation will not follow by a variant version of a contract to regulate an exchange, however, but will happen merely by coordination, perhaps spontaneously without direction from anyone. And the leader's power can fade as quickly as did the power of Cyrus's army.

Consider an earlier version of the justification of government to overcome prisoner's dilemma interactions, that posed by Glaucon in Plato's *Republic*. Glaucon says that if I could have the ring of Gyges, which would allow me to become invisible at will, I would plunder and rape at will. His theory of obedience to law is simply an early variant of the gunman theory.[27] The problem of the possibility of freely committing crimes and escaping punishment *under the law* poses a prisoner's dilemma and not merely a coordination problem. It requires the general cooperation of others for me to gain advantage from my own uncooperative behavior. Hence, Glaucon's problem is a problem of incentives *after* order has been established to make production and accumulation of wealth possible. Hobbes's problem in the so-called state of nature is a problem *before* or about the establishment of order. If the order that is established can successfully punish all transgressors, that is, if there is no working equivalent of the ring of Gyges, there will be no sense to the notion of freeriding on that order.

The Socialist Revolution

The hope of a socialist revolution in Marx and in latter-day Marxists is also commonly seen as the resolution of what appears to be a prisoner's dilemma. But if this is the strategic structure of the problem, then, as Mancur Olson concludes, *"class-oriented action will not occur if the individuals that make up a class act rationally."*[28] This is merely a specific instance of the more general logic of collective action: all of those who would benefit from a revolution will choose to let others take the risks of fighting it, but then it will not be fought. Marx is commonly thought to see social change as driven by interests, not ideas. Hence, he should agree with Olson.

On this account, Marx is thought simply to have misunderstood the strategic structure of the problem of revolution and to have founded his historicist theory of the coming of socialism on flawed reasoning.[29] One defense of Marx on this point is to suppose that he did not think that class action would be based on narrowly rational or self-interested motivations but would follow from class-oriented motivations. Such an explanation elevates normative or altruistic motivations over self-interest motivations in this context. At first it sounds odd to think that what motivates an individual to act against the interest of the individual is the interest of the individual's class. But it is possible that the self-seeking that drives much of our lives retires momentarily in the face of certain opportunities, as it does when we see someone in danger, when we work for the benefit of a child or others, or when we become great patriots in times of national crisis.

What is wanted in an explanation of revolution that relies on such a motivation is an account of how individuals come to identify the interests of their class as their own interest. Without this latter explanation, the contemporary efforts to refurbish Marx's prediction of socialist revolution in industrial societies seem like wish fulfillment. They recall the popular Sidney Harris cartoon in which two mathematicians are standing before a blackboard. On the left and right sides of the board are complicated formulations that look very different but that one of the mathematicians seems to think equivalent. The other mathematician has doubts: he is pointing at the middle of the board and saying, "I think you should be more explicit here in step two." Step two simply says, "THEN A MIRACLE OCCURS."

An alternative, less miraculous defense of Marx's view of the possibility of socialist revolution is to suppose that he did not see the problem as merely a prisoner's dilemma, but also in part as a simple problem of coordination. In particular, the mobilization of large enough numbers on certain occasions reduces the costs of acting against state power. On the actual evidence of earlier events of his lifetime, this would not have been a perverse way to view the problem, although it may later have come to seem implausible. It would be tendentious to claim that Marx held a clear view of the strategic structure of the problem of revolutionary action. But on the evidence of the French Revolution and of the revolutionary events of 1848, it is not implausible to suppose that revolution would be relatively easy *if* it could get coordinated.[30] Once coordinated, it was on these occasions almost a matter of orderly, focused rioting or mutiny. Once enough people were participating, the costs of participating fell to almost negligible levels.

There was always some chance of harm, as there was for street demonstrators in Teheran during the events leading to the abdication of the Shah, but it was slight once the crowds at, say, the Bastille were large. Technically it might typically be true on these occasions that the order of payoffs in the matrix of the game of revolution was strictly that of the prisoner's dilemma, as it may also be for voting in, say, American elections. But successful coordination may so greatly reduce costs that the latter are almost negligible, so that the slightest moral commitment may tip the scales toward action. Just as it would be odd for many Americans in communities in which voting is easy to balk at the minor cost in inconvenience, so it might seem odd for many workers or soldiers or others to balk at joining a crowd to march on the palace or the Bastille. This is not identical to a multiple coordination problem, such as that in the driving convention, in which one simply wants to go with the flow. In the revolutionary coordination, one has an active preference between the outcome of full attack and that of no attack. Still, one prefers to attack if enough others do and not to attack if enough others do not.

This argument would seem to fit well with Marx's analysis. Richard Arneson, however, argues that in his expectations of revolution Marx was really "the German Romantic, not the sober Victorian political economist."[31] Marx characterizes the problem of modern proletarian revolutions as one in which the proletariat "recoil ever and anon from the indefinite prodigiousness of their own aims, until the situation has been created which makes all turning back impossible."[32] Arneson supposes this cannot mean that the proletariat reach a point at which individual benefits from revolutionary action outweigh individual risks. Rather, he says, "a point is reached at which turning back would renege on a commitment to one's most ideal self-image, to be realized in the attainment of the most prodigious aims by heroic means."[33] The florid style of Marx's rhetoric makes it hard to call his account sober rather than romantic.

Against Arneson's view, what seems to make "all turning back impossible" is not romantic attachment to one's "most ideal self-image." Rather, it is the eventual development of the necessary class consciousness to know what to do with the state once it has been taken. The revolution will succeed when the proletariat has been prepared for its mission of rule and when it then has momentary opportunity to grasp control in a *coup de main*, an unexpected stroke, such as that of 1848.[34] Coordination without clear enough purpose will soon collapse, as it did in 1848. Turning back from a coordination once there is clear purpose then is impossible in part because opposing forces cannot naturally regain control after those forces collapse in the face of the revolutionary move.

It was perhaps the startling ease with which spontaneous revolutions took control in cities that led the French under Thiers to put down the Paris Commune with such thoroughgoing brutality as to make it seem more nearly like murder than warfare. The answer to the coordination explanation of revolutionary action is draconian force. This lesson of the Commune has been learned well by many later regimes and leaders in various places, such as the Nazis in Czechoslovakia, Stalin in the Soviet Union, Pinochet in Chile, and Videla in Argentina, with their harsh, blanket suppression of dissenters and potential dissenters. *They raise the likely costs of revolutionary activity enough to change its strategic structure.*

Since the time of the Commune, no one can any longer suppose that revolution can be simply a matter of spontaneous coordination in an industrial state. It can occur relatively easily, if at all, only when the state has lost its resources for self defense, as in Russia in 1917 at the end of a disastrous war or in Iran during the death agony of the Shah, or in societies with far poorer resources in the state's control. It was this realization that long gave the chill to our expectations for South Africa.

If the old state raises the costs enough to individuals for revolutionary activity, it overcomes the power of coordination to reduce the costs of revolutionary activity. It forces potential revolutionaries to see their problem overwhelmingly as a prisoner's dilemma in which free-riding is in the individual's interest. Indeed, in recent decades it is hard in many settings to view the prospect of revolution as even a prisoner's dilemma. States often especially and effectively target the leadership of revolutionary groups, so that early leaders cannot sensibly see their cause as one in which they have any hope of benefiting from the collective action even if it eventually succeeds. A well-organized state can use the very resources that Marx thinks the revolutionaries want to seize to stop them in their tracks. Then the conflict aspect in the collective interaction of insurgency may severely override its coordination aspect and we should not expect much further revolutionary activity.

The Common Law

One of the most innovative and interesting scholarly endeavors of the past decade or so has been the renewed effort to give economic interpretations of the nature and content of law. The chief omission in this endeavor to date has been the relative neglect of strategic considerations in the focus on efficiency and wealth maximization.[35] In much of this work, the concern is with the global efficiency of a given state of affairs as compared to some other. This is a relatively static view of the problem, not unlike the predominant mode of economic analysis more generally, which focuses on static equilibrium. A major difficulty in a static understanding of efficiency is that our major concern is often with policy, with how to get from the state of affairs in which we find ourselves to another that seems ideally better. This is fundamentally a strategic and dynamic problem.[36] If such dynamic considerations are important in economics, they are crucial in the law.

In general the greatest barrier to achieving ideally efficient outcomes in a system of common law, and plausibly also in a system of legislated law, is the weight of what we have already decided and of the institutions we have already created. These structure expectations and overwhelmingly determine the general cast of outcomes. Once they have been in place long enough to do this, they are conventions in the strong game theoretic sense that they resolve coordination problems. Although we can change conventions—that is typically the purpose of legislation that alters part of a regime of common law—we may not be able to do it easily. Moreover, if our concern is with efficiency, it should be partly with dynamic efficiency, with the costs and benefits of making changes—not only with static efficiency, with the costs and benefits of living under one legal regime rather than another.

Once we have a particular legal rule in place, it acquires political force, but it also acquires moral force. Neither of these may be sufficient to block revision of the rule, but they are likely to be serious considerations if the rule is important. One of the important aspects of passive disobedience to a particular law is the demonstration that the moral force of that law is in serious question. Voiding the Jim Crow laws of the American South and passing laws against the Jim Crow practices of much of the nation clearly affected many expectations, no doubt to the detriment of many interests. Some of these expectations may have been moral on any reasonable account. Blocking them was part of the cost of changing the laws.

More fundamentally, we may ask why have a system of common law at all? The answer is a grand version of the doctrine of *stare decisis*: because we already have it. At various early times in the history of the development of any particular legal system, we have opted for various systems. At early enough stages when it might be possible to choose a system, it might be hard to put forth a compelling argument for the general superiority of any one system, whether codified or common law. The choice of *which* system to adopt might have been virtually a matter of indifference. But choosing *some* system was not a matter of indifference: We need some system of law to give us decisive resolutions of issues so that we may get on with our lives. Hence, the central problem is to get everyone coordinated on some workable system. If historically we did not come around to choosing a system, that may not have been a serious loss. A system of common law based on precedents is a system that could simply grow up over time even without active creative efforts to devise the best possible system.

THE NORMATIVE QUESTION

It would be out of place here to go very extensively into the answers to the normative question of how to justify the state's working the way it does. But consider the implications for that question of the explanatory analysis here. According to a well-known dictum of Hume, objective facts cannot imply values. One who was convinced of this dictum might readily conclude that the foregoing analysis cannot imply anything about the justification of the state's working. To some extent this conclusion would be wrong, for two reasons.

First, there is a related, contrary dictum that "ought" implies "can." If it is not possible for me to do something then it cannot be the case that I morally ought to do it. At the level of a society, this dictum would suggest that if the requisite institutional structure for accomplishing some end cannot be created out of the stuff of actual humans, then it cannot be true that that end ought to be achieved. This is the limited lesson that Bernard Williams thinks we may draw from sociobiology. "The most that sociobiology might do for ethics," he says, is "to suggest that certain institutions or patterns of behavior are not realistic options for human societies."[37]

Second, one answer to the normative question is that, in a narrow sense, might may sometimes make right.[38] For example, once we have successfully coordinated in the same way on a particular, recurring problem, we may have established a convention, as in the discussion of the common law above. Thereafter, we individually have very strong incentive to follow the convention. Moreover, and more important here, we have very strong moral reason to do so to the extent that violating the convention would bring harm to others, as my driving on the left in North America would likely do.[39] On this account, efforts to find *a priori* normative justification for many laws and for the system of common law are often wrongheaded. What justifies them is a combination of historicist explanation of their origin and consideration of whether they are reasonably, not ideally, workable.

Apart from these two considerations, however, Hume's dictum seems compelling—we cannot derive an ought from an is. We may explain the state's power as the results of coordination and the creation of resources through collective exchange, but this explanation yields us no immediate proof of the rightness of what the state may do. Indeed, we may reasonably suppose that resources generated for general purposes may well be corruptly used for particular purposes. This is, of course, the traditional liberal's great fear: that the state will abuse its power. Indeed, no sooner does Smith lay out the nascent theory of the pastoral state discussed above than he notes that the system in which the sovereign dispensed justice for a fee "could scarce fail to be productive of several very gross abuses."[40]

CONCLUSION

The major forms of cooperation that we see in social and political contexts have their origins in two distinctively different kinds of strategic interaction: coordination and exchange. These typically come together in important institutional arrangements. But in many contexts, such as in Smith's account of the organization of a pastoral society and in many problems of international relations, coordination seems to come first. Is it in fact prior to exchange in explaining widespread social cooperation and institutions? In an explanatory sense it probably is, although in a historical sense it might be impossible to show that it was in actual cases. It is prior because coordination creates a convention—an institution, a norm, or power—and that convention then promotes further coordination and also exchange.

Although it may sound circular, this explanation is valid. As noted earlier, the problem of collective action cannot sensibly be resolved in the seemingly similar circular manner of supposing we should act collectively in order to resolve our problem of collective action. That just is our problem of collective action. But coordination can come about without intent, without overcoming contrary incentives. It can just happen. And if it just happens the same way a few times the result may be a forceful convention that then governs future behavior by giving us specific incentives for action.

In recent years we have been given very clever evolutionary explanations of cooperation and of altruism. This is an important effort just because an evolutionary perspective would seem to predict a very strong trait of looking out for one's own interest. This trait and any trait for altruism clearly conflict in many contexts and we might commonly think interest would dominate in determining much behavior. An alternative to biological evolution is social evolution in the rise of institutions and norms. On an explanation from social evolution we account for strong institutions for cooperation even on the assumption that, biologically, we are wired to be strongly self-seeking. Hence we have cooperation that is consistent with our biologically determined egoism.

Through social evolution we build complex institutional structures out of simpler ones. In the end we have an inextricable mixing of exchange and coordination, of power from resources based in exchange and power that is coordination. In this book, the focus is on explaining successful group coordinations that constitute extraordinary power, often but not always to be used for massive harms. In many—but not all—instances, the coordinations will depend on the use of institutions to manipulate identification of individuals with relevant groups. Chapter 3 addresses how coordination leads to identification with a group by making it in one's interest to attach oneself to the group.

CHAPTER THREE

Group Identification

You are what you know.
—Epistemological variation on a theme

SELF-INTEREST

How far can ethnic and nationalist identification in politics be understood to result from essentially self-interested behavior? At first thought, plausibly not very far. Nationalism and ethnic loyalty are commonly viewed as inherently irrational or extra-rational in the sense that they supposedly violate or transcend considerations of self-interest. Surely this common view is correct to some extent. Still, it is useful to draw out the self-interest incentives for such commitments and behaviors. There is yet another category of motivations—those that are a-rational. For example, you want only to sit on the beach and watch seagulls. This is not strictly a matter of your interest but of your pleasure or whatever in consuming your time and energy that way. Similarly, we all have a-rational drives that make us want things. When we act from those drives, we may lack reasons that could define our actions as rational. These four terms—rational, irrational, extra-rational, and a-rational—are not strictly parallel.

Throughout this book I use the term "rational" to mean to have narrowly self-interested intentions and I do not constantly restate this qualification. Rationality is, of course, typically a subjective or intentional notion, not a purely objective notion. You act rationally if you do what you believe serves your interest. Self-interest might better be seen as an objective notion. Its service is the object of rational action, although one may fail to understand what is in one's interest. George Washington presumably acted rationally, but mistakenly, when he allowed himself to be bled by doctors, perhaps with fatal consequences. I will refer to primordial, atavistic, inconsistent, and other motivations not intended to serve either the individual or the group interest as "irrational"; and I will refer to individual motivations to serve the group- or national-level interest more or less independently of immediate individual costs and benefits as extra-rational. It is possible, of course, that rational and extra-rational motivations will lead to similar actions in some contexts. The rational choice account of ethnic, nationalist, or other group loyalty will be compelling if (1) *it often happens that self-interest and group identification are congruent* and if (2) actions that are costly to the individual but beneficial to the group or nation are increasingly less likely the higher the individual costs.

Although it may not be necessary for many readers, I should note that these terms are used in varied ways in different disciplines and literatures. For example, rationality is often given a substantive content. It is said that to be rational is to be a certain kind of person or to have certain desires. In other literatures rationality is taken to apply only to instrumental considerations, to means rather than to ends. Whatever desires I have, I should act in ways that will fulfill them. In the standard rational choice literature from the Scottish Enlightenment through to contemporary writings, rationality is taken to combine one quasi substantive concern, self-interest, with concern for selection of means to the end of self-interest. Self-interest is only quasi-substantive because it is concerned with means for consumption, not with consumption *per se*. For example, I have an interest in having more money, but money is not a substantive good for me, it is only a means to obtaining various goods. If the proximate end in view is self-interest, we can even compare the choice of means to that end by focusing on the relative efficiency of various means.

In some ways, it would be more assertively clear to speak of self-interest rather than of rationality. But there is no simple equivalent of the range of terms we want here: rational, irrational, and extra-rational. Moreover, we may often accommodate extra-rational concern for the well-being of others by speaking of it as a concern for others' interests, and we can then rationally choose best means to fulfill those interests. You may be an altruist or an ethnic loyalist who has a group interest as well as a self-interest. Finally, and most important, self-interest is not generally treated as a subjective notion—even if I like the taste of some poison, it may not be in my interest to eat it and, if I knew enough about it, I would actively prefer not to eat it. Limits to knowledge lead all of us to mistaken beliefs about our interests even when it would be silly to say we had mistaken intentions. George Washington had mistaken beliefs about the benefits of bleeding to treat a bad cold. This fundamental problem of subjectivity often complicates any account of intentional action, as it will complicate our account of group identification.

Much of the work on nationalism is primarily concerned with will, interests, and identity. It is about the cognitive aspects of actors' being nationalist. Writings on ethnicity may more commonly invoke primordial and other emotional motivations. There are many other identities that might underlie conflict as nationalism and ethnicity seem to do.

Many of these, however, do not seem to be of much concern to us in explaining major conflicts up to and including war and internal war. Indeed, many of them seem to be trumped by nationalism in times of war, as identification with class in the Socialist International was, to Lenin's disgust, widely trumped by nationalist identities at the advent of World War I. In a multiethnic state, nationalist and ethnic identities may clash even while the state goes to war.

Often it is claimed that there is something natural about ethnic identification. As there are arguably genetic grounds for physical identification *of* a particular ethnic group, so there might be genetic grounds for psychological identification *with* the group by those who have the relevant physical characteristics.[1] I will take for granted that this presumptive genetic basis of the psychological identification *with one's particular group* is most likely false. Surely it is not merely false but also preposterous for, say, the nationalist identification with the United States, such as was displayed at impressive levels during the Gulf crisis and war against Iraq.

Whatever genetic basis we might find for ethnic and nationalist identification is at most a genetic basis for the propensity to identify with *some* larger group.[2] How we might select a group for identification or how identification may just grow up for some group of which we are part is likely still to be a cognitive problem of making choices. Those choices may be about matters other than direct identification with the particular group or nation. But they will have implications for such identification, which may be an unintended by-product. It is such choices and their grounding in self-interest that are of concern here. One might go further than I wish to go to say that even the basic urge to identify is itself a cognitive result. At the very least, the data on such identification may not readily differentiate biological from cognitive explanations.

Throughout the discussion of this chapter, there will be two partly separable issues: the role of interest in an individual's coming to identify with a particular group, and the interest an individual has in supporting that group as a beneficiary of the group's successes. The second issue may seem more readily than the first to be about deliberate action. Of course, one could see that membership in a particular group would be beneficial and could therefore develop an apparent or even real identification with it. But for very many identifications, it would be odd to suppose the individuals had deliberately set out to develop or adopt the relevant identity. Hence, the explanatory concern must be with the rationality of various choices they make that eventually lead them to identification with a particular group, identification that, again, may be an unintended consequence of many rational actions.

There are three main moves in the arguments that follow. First, I consider the rationality of an action given one's available knowledge, theory, and so forth at the time of choosing. Second, I consider the rationality of *coming to have* the knowledge and theory one now has. And third, I consider the possibility of confusing moral and factual knowledge as seen from the epistemological stance of the person whose knowledge (or belief) it is. These three moves are independent and one may reject one while accepting the others. I think the third of the moves is the most troublesome for a rational choice account. The first two moves seem too sensible to be objectionable, but they are also commonly not overtly made by rational choice theorists or their critics. All three moves enormously increase the demand for data in trying to assess the rationality of actions.

Group Identification from Coordination

How can we plausibly associate nationalist, ethnic, or other strong group identification with self-interest? Surely, it seems, such commitment is beyond the self, it is a commitment to a community of some kind. To get beneath this superficial appearance, first note that many national and ethnic group conflicts are likely to have outcomes that will favor or disfavor members of the relevant group. Contributing to the potential success of the group to which one belongs therefore benefits oneself. Unfortunately, as we well know from the logic of collective action, such considerations are typically outweighed by the costs of contributing.[3] For example, by voting in an election, I may help my candidate win. But to do so, I have to go to the trouble of voting, trouble that can be substantial in many locations. Unless the probability that my vote will make a real difference in the outcome is extremely high, I cannot justify, from my own interest alone, taking the trouble to vote. Then how can I justify contributing to the collective purpose of my nation or ethnic group?

The first answer is that there may be no costs of my joining in the relevant activities of my group. The second answer is that, even if there are costs, I may also expect specific rewards or punishments that will be tailored to whether I contribute. The first answer will apply to many contexts that essentially involve coordination but no expenditure of resources by many of us. The second answer will apply to many contexts in which there are real costs of contributing—so that the problem is not simply one of coordination—but in which rewards of leadership or spontaneous punishments by one's peers are possible.

Of course, a nationalist or ethnic commitment might be purely ideal or normative in that it might involve only ideal-regarding and other-regarding motivations. But it might also be strongly correlated with individual interests. Suppose the commitment is to a nation or ethnic group in conflict with others and with a prospect of success in that conflict. Then it is likely that the nationals or the ethnic group members will jointly benefit from that success. The benefit is often likely to be collectively provided but individually distributed. The group wins or loses together, but winning means that each member or many members of the group benefit individually. Indeed, one need not be committed to the group in any normative or additional psychological sense to see one's interests served by its success.

There are generally two forms that collective, mutually beneficial endeavors may take. These may be represented game theoretically by the prisoner's dilemma and coordination games, as shown in games 1 and 2. The prisoner's dilemma is perhaps the best-known game in all of the massive game theory literature, especially in the discursive applied literature in the social sciences. In this game, I as the Row player face a choice between two strategies, didactically labeled cooperate and defect. You as the Column player face a similar choice. In the end, we will each receive the payoff determined by our simultaneous choice of joint strategies. Our payoffs in the various outcomes are listed ordinally, with 1 as the most-preferred and 4 the least-preferred outcome; and the first payoff in each cell goes to the Row player, the second to Column. If we both defect, we each receive our third-best payoff. If we both cooperate, we each receive our second-best payoff. If I cooperate while you defect, I receive my worst payoff while you receive your best; and vice versa. Hence, there is incentive for both of us to try to cheat the other by defecting while the other cooperates.

Game 1: Prisoner's Dilemma or Exchange

		Column	
		Cooperate	*Defect*
	Cooperate	2,2	4,1
Row			
	Defect	1,4	3,3

Game 2: Coordination

		Column	
		I	II
	I	1,1	2,2
Row			
	II	2,2	1,1

In the coordination game of game 2, you and I have harmonious interests. We wish either to coordinate on both choosing our strategy I or on both choosing our strategy II. There is no conflict. In the prisoner's dilemma there is both a coordination interest in choosing the (2,2) over the (3,3) outcome and a conflict of interests in which I prefer the outcome (1,4) while you prefer (4,1).

Many of the standard problems of political mobilization are generalizations of the prisoner's dilemma strategic structure. Each of us has an interest in not contributing a personal share to, say, a political campaign, because each of us will benefit from all others' contributions while our own contribution may cost us more than it is worth to us alone. Hence, each of us has incentive to try to be a freerider. (This is what Mancur Olson calls the logic of collective action.[4])

Many other problems of political mobilization are more nearly generalizations of the structure of the simple two-person coordination game represented here. In such problems, all that is needed to achieve successful mobilization is relevant communication to coordinate on doing what we would all want to do if only we were sure others were also doing it. In what follows, *most of my account of group identification, as opposed to action on behalf of a group, will argue or assume that the central strategic problem is merely one of coordination.*

There is something objective and something subjective in the idea of an ethnic group or a nationality.[5] This is true in general of coordination points. There are good objective reasons for me to coordinate on X rather than fail to coordinate by choosing Y. But there may be no a priori objective reason for the choice of X rather than of Y apart from knowledge of how you and others are choosing. Hence, group coordination is an achievement that likely turns on highly subjective considerations such as the psychological prominence of particular points in the set of all possible coordination points.[6]

A peculiarity of explanations from coordination is that they often have an important chance element. We might have coordinated on driving on the left, as the English do, or on the right, as North Americans do. There might be no rational ground for the original selection or, rather, for the early pattern of order that turns into a hard coordination. Similarly, we might coordinate on linguistic, religious, or ethnic affinity. If all of these come together to define our group, we may be much more likely to succeed in adopting a strong commitment to the group. If they do not come together, some of us may nevertheless define ourselves as a group on the basis of some attribute that excludes others with whom we might have associated. But the chance element may be more fundamental than this. We might simply fail to coordinate at all in any active sense, even if we have language, religion, and ethnicity in common. Whether we coordinate might turn in part on whether there is someone urging us to recognize our identity and coordinate on it. I may fully identify with my group but take no action on its and my behalf until an Alexander Herzen, Adolf Hitler, Martin Luther King, or Ruhollah Khomeini mobilizes those of us with similar identifications.

Moreover, successful mobilization may be a tipping phenomenon in large part. What would not make sense for a self-interested individual when very few are acting might begin to make sense when many others are acting.[7] At that point the relationship changes from a potentially risky prisoner's dilemma to a virtual coordination involving very nearly no risk. Both before and after tipping, the interaction might be successful in providing the group with a collective good whose benefit is distributed among group members. It is such distributed collective goods that give individuals direct interest in identifying with the relevant group.

A prisoner's dilemma can tip into a coordination problem in at least two ways. First, when the number acting on behalf of the group interest becomes large enough, the possibilities of punishment and suppression of individual coordinators may dwindle. When too few are acting, the prospects of punishment may be great enough to make participation costly, as in the logic of collective action. If enough are acting, however, the state's capacity to respond might be swamped and the state might let the crowd go while its police or military concentrate their attentions on channeling the crowd rather than suppressing it outright.

Second, an interaction might tip when those who are cooperating can impose retribution on those not cooperating by inflicting harm on them. It might be supposed that the costs of punishment are somehow closely related to the disvalue of the punishment, as though the act of punishing were potentially a constant-sum game. For example, to impose a ten-dollar sanction on you might cost me about ten dollars. This relationship might hold in some cases, but there is no reason to suppose it holds generally. Sanctions can be radically cheaper than the harm they cause. The costs of producing a sanction and the costs of suffering one need not be in any way logically related. The story of Lebanon and Somalia is one of the trivially cheap production of dreadful harms. William Rees-Mogg wrote that, in an Irish Republican Army bombing in the City of London, a hundred pounds of Semtex did a billion pounds of damage.[8] One of the threats—seldom actualized—of antiwar groups in the United States during the Vietnam War was to do grievous damage to corporate and university installations. The people who did or threatened the harms in Lebanon and the United States arguably could not have done as much good for their efforts as they did harms. This may be typically true of virtually all of us. Indeed, if there is a very important element of seeming irrationality or extra-rationality (other than that of the is-ought fallacy, as discussed below) in nationalist and ethnic commitments, it is the fact that many people derive great pleasure from inflicting harms on certain others, including those of their own group who seem treacherously not committed to the group's ends.

This insight, that harming can be cheap, is a central underpinning for Hobbes's theory of government and its great value.[9] It also undergirds Robert Axelrod's theory of meta-norms for punishing those who fail to punish defectors in collective actions.[10] Indeed, one might suppose Axelrod's punishment schedule of bearing a cost of 2 units for 9 units of punishment inflicted is not steep enough for many contexts. *When harm-*

ing is intended to be deterrent, so that it need not be coherently related in kind to the action it is to punish, the form it takes can be specifically selected for its effectiveness and cheapness. The nuclear deterrent of the cold war era was ridiculously cheap in comparison to the harms it could have inflicted, and that is a major reason for our resorting to nuclear deterrence: We could afford it. Moreover, in collective action contexts, effective punishment can be decentralized to one-on-one and small-group actions, often more easily than effective rewards can be.

Information through Coordination

Joining a coordination with a group of people who share one's interests in some way can also produce information that makes further identification rational. To see this most clearly, we should consider a case in which there can hardly be any argument that the coordination or identification is somehow intrinsically related to the group or the object of its identification. Let us therefore consider loyalty to a sports team, which afflicts remarkably many people but seldom afflicts all those it might.

Why is anyone loyal to any sports team, such as the Chicago Cubs baseball team? Clearly, this is not a biological or in any sense native or primordial identification. Perhaps the urge to identify, to put us against them, is biological. Still, however, there remains the difficult question: Why identify with this *particular* group? We could ask this question of any group: the Cubs boosters, Armenians, or whatever. But let us focus on the Cubs boosters.

The local community of sports fans has an easy time coordinating on the local team. News media, neighborhood banter, and on-the-job talk can all focus on the Cubs. Circles of friends and other groups in the local community could not so easily sustain diverse attachments. This is not to say that people sit back and select the local team for these reasons but only that these factors are real constraints that affect the pleasures fans get from their game. They also affect how much a potential fan is likely to know about any team. The local team has privileged access, fans can know more about it, they can see and come to like its star players. Fans who go to games are virtually bound to know the local team better than they could know any other. In the end, many might become critics rather than boosters, but still they may focus their concern on the local team. Again, the reason for such a focus is that the local team is in a privileged position with respect to local loyalties.

Locally there may be claims for why the home team is special and therefore merits support. This result may be a case of the is-ought fallacy: What is is taken to be good. Fans in Chicago used to say that, among basketball players, Michael Jordan was the most beautiful to watch. Fans in Los Angeles said Magic Johnson was most beautiful. One suspects that both judgments were at least as much derivative from local loyalties as they were causes of such loyalties. Much of their substantive basis is similar to that of the views of the ethnic loyalist. The loyalist's experience of knowing her own ethnic group gives her special entree to the pleasures of its practices and customs. From these comes the sense of comfort and well-being that seems to recommend the superiority of that group over others.

For the present discussion, the example of identification with a sports team has the odd advantage that it is purely a consumption good, it is not sensibly seen as an interest one has in the way one has an interest in a higher salary or a windfall profit. Ethnic identification might, in many contexts, actually be in one's interest. I may reasonably be said to have an interest in the resources necessary to get the daily pleasures of fans of the home team, just as I have an interest in the money necessary for satisfaction of other desires, such as those for food and shelter. In a sense, then, it is in my interest that others around me are also followers of the home team so that I may have a context in which to enjoy my own commitment to the team. Here, my interest is directly in the availability of others with similar pleasures and in successful coordination with them.

In a similar way, I might have an interest in the workings of my national or ethnic group, with which I might be especially comfortable for the simple reason that I know it well. (This issue of the epistemological comforts of home will be discussed more fully in chap. 7.) But there is also a quite different way in which I have an interest in the workings of my national or ethnic group. From the fact that, say, my ethnic group prevails politically, I may personally benefit because I may get a better job. Hence, I have an interest in the participation of others not because that participation directly gratifies me, as it does in the case of a sports team. I have that interest because I have an interest in what can be accomplished by substantial coordination. I share with others of my ethnic group in the benefits that may flow from our achieving greater political power. In this latter case, the coordination is itself a means to an end. Therefore, as is typically true of means, it may turn out finally not to lead to the benefits that the members of the group hope to get—it may fail. Coordination around the home team, on the contrary, is immediately beneficial to the individual who joins in the coordination. We may therefore expect coordinated action for ethnic or national interests will be harder to motivate than coordination on support for the local sports team.

Indeed, we may even go further to suppose recoordination around a new team will often be easy for one who moves from one city to another.

This seems especially likely if the role of the particular team is merely as a coordination point as a means to the pleasure of being a sports fan. The role of a particular ethnic identification is clearly much stronger, it is constitutive of the collective good that will benefit the loyal individual. And it cannot easily be replaced for the individual by coordination on participation in some other group that might provide an alternative route to distributed collective benefits.

Nationalism is intermediate between identification with a sports team and identification with an ethnic group. For example, French, German, and Japanese national identifications might continue to motivate those who migrate from France, Germany, and Japan; they might even be hard to give up after a generation away from home. That may in large part turn on the facts that these identifications involve ethnic as well as nationalist coordinations and that family members may still be in their original home countries. But clearly many people find it relatively easy to become American nationalists, not to say superpatriots, when they migrate to the United States. They can do so because they can plausibly see their personal interests as now associated with the successes of the United States.

One of the most important ways information affects groups is in giving group members an understanding of their common interests. This is one half of Marx's theory of revolution, which requires the development of class consciousness before there can be class-oriented action. Workers in a factory share so much time together that they begin to understand their common fate much better, not least because each can benefit from the insights of all. Peasants scattered across the countryside cannot spend enough time together to gain a comparable sense of class identity. Hence, they are unlikely to become a class for themselves.[11] They are, Marx says, like potatoes in a sack without benefit of manifold relations.[12] Hence, even when given opportunity to act for their interests, French peasants failed to do so and voted for Louis Napoleon out of failure to understand their own interests. The mothers of the Plaza de Mayo movement in Argentina had very nearly the factory experience of Marx's workers. They encountered one another repeatedly in the same revealing contexts as they went to bureaucrat after bureaucrat trying to locate their "disappeared" children. Through this experience of each other's experience, they discovered the real nature of their problem and soon mobilized to help topple the military regime that had murdered their children.[13] Part of the cause of the explosion of ethnic identification and ethnic political agitation in parts of the former Soviet Union now may be the sudden openness of the society that lets groups openly discuss and pool their knowledge and views and openly organize for political action.

CONFLICT FROM GROUP COORDINATION

Explanations of ethnic conflict often invoke emotions. Unfortunately, explaining ethnically oriented behavior as emotional may not be explaining it at all or may be explaining only aspects of it given that it happens. The part we most need to explain is why the behavior happens, why such behavior is ethnically oriented. And we need to explain why one group falls into conflict with another. Why these groups? In the preceding discussion, the process of group identification seems to be sanguine. But we know that it often leads to deep enmity, bloodshed, and even genocide and ethnic cleansing. Benign phenomena apparently produce the conditions for malign phenomena.

The benign phenomena are well understood. Among the benign sources of group coordination are language, religion, local community, mores, customs, and so forth. All of these affect individual's costs of transactions with one another and stabilize expectations. They may also affect the development and maintenance of group consciousness and, hence, identification. Characterizing these influences as economic is not standard in much of the literature on ethnicity and ethnic and other group politics. For example, it is sometimes contended that Québécois sentiment for secession derives from a non-economic fear of loss of language.[14] But loss of language is clearly an economic concern in the sense that it affects the interests of most people in the two or three current generations of Québécois. Not everything that greatly affects our interests falls into standard business accounts of monetary income and expenditure.

What is the source of conflict? Suppose two groups have formed different ethnic identifications in a society. Each of their coordinations may be innocuous and fully beneficial to their group's members. But coordination of each group provides the basis on which to build many things, including political action against the other group. To a political conflict over allocations, a coordinated group brings advantages of reduced transaction costs and, often, strong identification and agreement. Hence, *coordination of a group is potentially political*. If two groups seek to achieve collective resolutions of various issues, they may come directly into conflict with each other. My group wants its language adopted as the official language, your group wants its language adopted. My group wants more access to land and jobs for its members, and so does your group, although the supply of each might be relatively fixed. Within each group, the initial problem was one of coordination on common interests; in the larger society the eventual problem is often grim conflict of interest made grimmer by the fact that one of our groups may defeat the other.

To keep the nature of the conflicts clearer, note that there are three classes of issues. There are *positional goods*, such as public office, *distributional goods*, such as income and welfare benefits, and *interactions between these two*.[15] The Tutsi might wish to hold power in Burundi because a large percentage of available jobs—positional goods—are government jobs that must be filled but that are likely to be filled by the winners in the political conflict. They might also wish to receive certain benefits—distributional goods—from government, such as support for the expenses of maintaining cattle. And, finally, they might wish to hold power and to fill many government positions because the government has control over certain distributional goods.

Consider positional goods of public office. When Rwanda gained independence, it was to begin with a majority Hutu government. Prior to that moment, Tutsi had favored access to native offices under the colonial administration, just as they had dominated control of the nation before colonial domination. Tutsi seemingly spontaneously rose to attempt to block the transfer of power to Hutu, and Rwanda had a bloody civil war that ended with the expulsion of many Tutsi and the dominance of Hutu. The response might not have been spontaneous, however, because among those whose positions were threatened were many in positions to organize and lead a rebellion. When, a generation later, Burundi had its first democratically elected majoritarian government, thereby switching central power from Tutsi to Hutu, Tutsi again rebelled under the leadership of the Tutsi-dominated military. There have been many similar explosions in other states. For example, majority Buddhist Sinhalese governments in Sri Lanka adopted many preferences for Sinhalese. When a later government began to reverse these policies in order to equalize opportunities for Tamils in state-controlled jobs, Sinhalese rioted against the slight reduction in their status.[16] All of these actions were focused on control of positional goods.

Conflict over distributional goods is a commonplace of political life. The standard example in American politics for most of United States national history is conflict over tariffs. Agrarian interests (especially in the south and west) long wanted low tariffs on industrial goods (which they needed to buy and for which they naturally preferred to pay low prices), while industrial interests (especially in the north) wanted high tariffs to protect their domestic markets. In Nigeria, Yoruba from the northern region benefited from regional control of agricultural (especially cocoa) revenues and state control of mineral (especially oil) revenues, while the Igbo from the eastern region would have benefited from the opposite arrangements.[17] The Igbo attempted to secede as Biafra, but were crushed in the ensuing civil war.

In Yugoslavia, disproportionately many of the positional goods of military and governmental leadership have gone to Serbians, who have also done well in receiving distributional goods allocated by the government. The latter have reputedly been disproportionately funded by the more productive Croatians and Slovenians, who therefore subsidized Serbia. That the distributional result follows in part from the positional advantages of the Serbs is a natural inference. In any case, when the Serbs under Slobodan Milosevic changed the rules and expectations on the sharing of positions, the Yugoslav civil war and break-up were virtually secured. Similarly, when the Croats chose to change the status of Serbs in Croatia, removing them from positions in the police force and reducing their status to "protected minority" rather than full citizens, the Serbo-Croatian war over Krajina was virtually secured.[18]

Note that in good economic times, state-managed distributional goods matter less because private opportunities are very good. Indeed, in very good times, even the positional goods of government may be far less attractive. But in harsh times, when the prospects of individual achievement are dim, the possibility of using government to transfer goods from others to one's own group may offer better hope of improving one's position. Failing to provide an economy that generated private opportunities, one of the great failures of socialist governments in the former Soviet Union and Eastern Europe, was almost ordained by definition. But it helped to set the stage for massive ethnic conflict upon the end of the Soviet Union. Giving a former republic autonomy opens opportunity to fill extant positions—hence, to offer positional goods. From the Baltics to the Urals to the Steppes, ethnic groups have wanted to seize government in order to allocate positions.

A similar malaise befell many, perhaps most, newly decolonized states, as in Africa. In an act of gross cynicism or stupidity, the Portuguese government transferred power in Angola to the Angolan people rather than to a government.[19] They thereby invited the three main groups to fight out the definition of that people. Many formerly colonial states have chosen to follow the statist path to economic and political development and have therefore made their populations too dependent on government for their own opportunities. The statist path might have been almost unavoidable in underdeveloped nations, because it immediately offered positions to enough people to build support for the new native governments. Alas, it may also be a sad accident of history that many of these states gained independence at the apex of belief that the Soviet Union had a better way.

Ethnic conflict often cannot be defused through control over complementary functions. The members of one group might be virtually perfect substitutes for the members of another. Hence, they may benefit best from the group's achieving full control over allocation of positions. In general, when benefits are provided through government, they can have a strongly conflictual quality. Any policy that benefits one group through a general tax or regulatory scheme typically harms some other group relative to its position before or without the policy. Consider two forms of discrimination on the basis of group identity, one that is quite deliberate and one that is largely accidental. Both, however, are conflictual.

First, on Gary Becker's account of its economics, ethnic discrimination in employment and sales can only occur where markets are not fully competitive because discrimination is not efficient and is costly to firms that practice it.[20] Ethnic conflict in parts of the former Soviet Union is in areas from which the market is nearly absent. In some of these there may be active opposition to the market for ethnic reasons. If the opportunities from market reorganization were believed to be great enough, dominant groups and their leaders might relax their grip and let the market allocate positions, thus undercutting discrimination. If the gains from market organization do not seem compelling, then the economy offers a straight conflict between two groups, each of which would be best served by having its members given preference by government. Giving preference to members of my group reduces prospects for members of your group.

Second, when two groups speak different languages, they have in fact each coordinated on a language. If one of the groups gains a dominant position in politics or in the economy, it may discriminate against those who speak any language other than its own. This discrimination need not be economically inefficient, as straight racial discrimination typically may be. Indeed, it could be driven chiefly by concern with productivity, which is likely to be greater if members of the firm can coordinate more easily with each other and if they can communicate better with the principal clientele of the firm. Letting the two languages be used without any government regulation in favor of either may lead to the disadvantage of the speakers of the minority language. Their job opportunities may turn heavily on whether they master the majority language.

To impose rules against racial discrimination can enhance economic productivity. This may not typically be true for rules against language discrimination. To impose such rules might benefit the current generation or two of the minority language speakers. But it is likely to reduce economic efficiency. Language policy is inherently conflictual because different policies differentially affect relevant parties. The current two or three generations of speakers of the minority language will be losers if their language loses its utility. The present generations of speakers of the majority language will be losers if the minority language is kept viable.

THE IS-OUGHT FALLACY

Most people probably know from experience what anthropologists have established very generally: People have strong community-specific beliefs about what is right and wrong and about the special goodness and rightness of their own communities. Perhaps we all occasionally share the sensibility of a letter writer to the *London Times*, who wrote, "Sir, I wonder if I am alone in being mildly irritated by people who say 'Good afternoon' in reply to my greeting of 'Good morning' during the hour between midday and lunchtime?"[21] We suppose our way is not merely our way but also the right way.

In a discussion of Melville Herskovits's views on cultural pluralism, James Fernandez writes, "Within cultures, with some interesting variations between cultures, one finds people accepting and agreeing to abide by certain norms and values to which they have been enculturated. Why they do this, Herskovits would often say, is difficult to understand."[22] Anthropologists have been read to say more than merely that different cultures have different values; they are accused of holding a brief for moral relativism, as though they claim that the different values are right for the relevant communities. Fernandez argues that Herskovits has been widely misread, perhaps especially by philosophers, as a moral relativist, an advocate of the ipso facto moral rightness of ethnocentric values for the group or society that generates them. Indeed, Bernard Williams calls this "the anthropologists' heresy, possibly the most absurd view to have been advanced even in moral philosophy."[23] On the contrary, Herskovits argues only that people do feel bound by their culture's values, not that they ought to.[24]

Without claiming finally to understand ethnocentric moral beliefs, I wish to argue that there are at least two elements to the explanation of them. First, as argued above, such beliefs grow in part from the way in which individuals gain any knowledge at all, including moral knowledge. Here, interest and rational choice play an important role in producing identification. Again, the argument is not the simplistic one that it is directly rational to adopt a particular identification with its associated community beliefs. Such an argument would often be patently false and beside the point. Rather, *the argument is that it may be rational to do what produces a particular identification and, once one has that identification, it is commonly rational to further the interests determined by that identification.*

The second element in explaining Herskovits's problem is the following. There seems to be a very nearly universal tendency of people to move from what is to what ought to be in the strong sense of concluding that what is is right or good. In this commonsense move, people deduce an "ought" from an "is." Any such deduction is generally rejected by theorists since Hume's brilliant paragraph on the tendency in the works of moral philosophers.[25] Hume's concern was with writers who describe a state of affairs and then smuggle in an unstated moral principle from which it follows that there is something morally wrong with the state of affairs. Leaving the relevant moral principle unstated makes it superficially seem that the conclusion of moral wrongness is merely a descriptive matter of fact about the state of affairs rather than an evaluative judgment of it.

In popular versions of deducing rightness from what is, people tend to think their own way of doing something is not merely one of many possible—and arguably comparably good—ways of doing it but is the only right way to do it. The hidden assumption that is smuggled into many normative judgments is that what is is good or, more commonly, what *we* do is good. Our custom is to shake hands upon meeting, theirs is to hug and kiss. Our custom is good, theirs is bad—and also a bit funny. (The tendency to succumb to the is-ought fallacy may be radically reinforced when there are also religious differences at stake.)

Herskovits argues that "Ethnocentrism is the point of view that one's own way of life is to be preferred above all others. Flowing logically from the process of early enculturation it characterizes the way most individuals feel about their own culture, whether or not they verbalize their feeling."[26] The relevant jump from "is" to "ought" is a "simple kind of reasoning," a "natural bias." Herskovits further supposes that identification with one's own group is important for strengthening the ego. For this reason, one might conclude that ethnocentrism is good, because it is good for us. However, it may turn militant with a program of action against others, as in modern Europe and America, in which case it need no longer be benevolent, as it commonly has been in anthropological societies.[27] A Soviet journalist remarked of ethnocentric upsurges in the last days of the Soviet Union that the various groups "espouse the superiority of their own nationality" and champion "the rights of nations at the expense of the rights of the individual."[28] He clearly thought some of these groups were militant and often malign.

The move from "is" to "ought" has both an irrational and an extrarational aspect. It is typically irrational in that there is no justifiable reason for the move, so that it may be unrelated to interest. At best it is merely a fallacy of reasoning. But it may also lead to extra-rational behavior in that one may be morally motivated by the fallacious deduction even when acting on its dictates is against one's own personal interests. One acts for a presumed greater good, perhaps the greater good of one's group or nation, but perhaps merely the greater good of others without expectation of benefits to oneself.

It seems clear that the is-ought fallacy plays a central role in much of ethnic and nationalist identification. For example, many Germans in the first half of this century did not merely think it in their people's interest to prevail in war, they thought it right for Germany to dominate other nations, they even thought they had a moral duty to do so. American leaders regularly refer to the moral duty of the United States and its citizens to act for good, a good that is often virtually defined as replication of the form of government and economy the United States has. In such a case there may be independent moral grounds for the conclusion, so that it need not follow from the is-ought fallacy. Even then, however, it seems often to be strongly reinforced by reasoning from this fallacy.

Hobsbawm wryly notes that "nationalism requires too much belief in what is patently not so."[29] This helps to achieve and maybe to justify coordination on the interests of the group as one's own interests. If the group is winning and if in victory it will allocate positions and rewards to group members, potential members may have reasons of self-interest to coordinate with the group.[30] Still, it is the belief in what is patently not so that may make nationalism possible in many cases. The core of that belief is plausibly the is-ought fallacy. The way in which such a belief is patently not so is the way a scientific or factual belief may often be called into question by the evidence of overwhelming contrary beliefs that one cannot wave aside. The nationalist who speaks of the rightness of her nation's claims cannot finally produce any argument to convince anyone other than another fellow citizen. *That the belief is not convincing, even patently not so in the sense that it would not stand serious scrutiny, however, does not entail that people cannot believe it.*

One might say that the supposed knowledge of ethnic or national superiority is corrupt at its foundations. Unfortunately, this is true also of other knowledge, perhaps of almost all knowledge of factual matters.[31] (One might insist that knowledge of mathematical and logical relations can be free of such corruption at its base.) Hence, at their foundations there is little to distinguish supposed knowledge of normative from that of factual matters. In ordinary thought the two categories may be very nearly one. Should we say that anyone who acts on such knowledge is irrational? We could, but then we would be saying that virtually everyone's actions are always irrational. It seems more natural to say that one's beliefs may have corrupt foundations but that, given those beliefs, it is reasonable to act in certain ways rather than others if one wishes to achieve particular goals. For example, much of my factual knowledge about some aspect of the world, such as geography, is in the form of collectively aggregated knowledge, much of which may be false or inaccurate,[32] but all of which together is much better than no knowledge if I wish to make my way in the world. Therefore it is rational of me to act on my poorly grounded knowledge.

But if this is true, then it may also be rational of me to act on my supposed knowledge of normative matters. In my case, because I agree with Hume's dismissal of the slide from "is" to "ought" and have made that a part of my general understanding, it would not be rational to act from some of my supposed normative knowledge even to the degree to which it is rational for me to use my likely corrupt knowledge of geography. Someone who carries through on an ethnic commitment on the claim that her ethnic group is in fact superior, even normatively superior, to others, may not be any more irrational than I am in following my geographical knowledge. She merely follows the aggregated wisdom of her ethnic group.

While I may eventually come to challenge some of my corrupt geographical knowledge when I run up against the real world, the member of the ethnic minority may never encounter anything resembling a test of her knowledge of her community's moral superiority. Nevertheless, the world may give her some confirmation of her beliefs. In daily life she comes to know far more about her group than about any other, she is naturally comfortable in it, and she is uncomfortable in strange groups. Her comfort becomes associated with the rightness of what makes for the comfort and her discomfort with the wrongness of what makes for the discomfort. In fact, however, the only substantive difference she can claim between the two groups is her greater familiarity with one than with the other.

A psychological reason for the appeal of the simplistic move of the is-ought fallacy in ethnocentric views is that it is analogous to a less inclusive variant whose conclusion, although perhaps reached by fallacious reasoning, is often correct. The variant might be expressed as follows. This is our way of doing things and therefore it is good for us. In its individual-level version, this conclusion may be true of, for example, tastes. Once I have my tastes, it is likely then good for me to have food or whatever that fits those tastes. This conclusion need not follow, because it is contingent and not simply logical. I might follow the ancient Roman aristocracy in developing a taste for wine tempered with harmful lead. But the fact of my tastes makes a difference for the goodness for me of various consumptions. The fact that a community has developed tastes or preferences for doing things in certain ways similarly makes a difference for the goodness to that community of doing things their way.

Hence, while reasoning strictly to a normative claim of the goodness or rightness of a group's mores may justify commitment to the group and even some action on its behalf, it may still be true that action will typically turn on interest. It is partly because others in the group have a vision of its normative superiority that members can expect to benefit from the successes of the group. The threatened loss of benefits from failure of action by some provides compelling justification for their punishment. And coordination with others in the group behind strong leadership is especially of value when such coordination creates power that may be put to successful use in providing the group its collective benefit and distributing it to members. *The way we should attend to group commitments is the way we should attend to interests.* Your interests should be a consideration in social decisions, but they need not trump other considerations, such as my interests. Similarly, your group's commitments need not trump the conflicting commitments of other groups.

Note that this argument is not conceptually circular. It is not of the form: We value our group and therefore we have an interest in its success. Rather, for historical personal reasons of the particularity of our experience, our interests are causally associated with our group's interest (as in the argument above on information through coordination).

Leaders who want the masses behind them may provoke ethnic or nationalist sentiments. But perhaps it must be true that there is something already latent that can be provoked.[33] What is typically at least latent is the shared interest in the group's fate if it is to have a fate as a group. But recognition of the interest may remain latent even when the group is activated. Leaders may provoke that latent interest; but they may also, and perhaps rather more likely, provoke ethnic or nationalist sentiments grounded in an is-ought fallacy. As Lord Acton, foreshadowing Hobsbawm's remark on the patently incredible beliefs grounding nationalism, notes, "The few have not strength to achieve great changes unaided; the many have not wisdom to be moved by truth unmixed."[34]

Until recently, moral and political philosophy were almost entirely universalist in their principles. Various traditional theories, from utilitarian to Kantian to rights theories, were applied to everyone identically. There were occasional claims by Hegel and others for the rightness of a particular community's values, but moral and political theorists usually insisted on universality. For example, moral theorists, apparently misreading his positive claims about the prevalence of ethnocentric views as a moral claim for their rightness, criticized Herskovits's anthropology. Over the past decade or two, however, there has arisen a strong and articulate camp of communitarian moral thinkers who claim that the source of values is necessarily in the community and that communal values are generally good for the relevant community.

Note that the philosophers' communitarianism is not the people's. The popular moral claim for community and its values is likely to be very specifically about *this* community. It is an instance of Herskovits's ethnocentrism. It is not a moral principle about communities as such and it may therefore be a claim that stands outside any contemporary moral or political theory. In particular, it is not itself a communitarian view. The communitarian political philosopher argues for the good of community, not for the exclusive good of *this* community. Hence, we may distinguish *philosophical* and *particularistic* communitarianisms. Philosophical communitarianism is an oddly universalistic theory about communities; particularistic communitarianism is the set of beliefs of a specific community, perhaps especially if these beliefs are restrictive. The discussions of chapters 4 through 6 are largely about particularistic communitarianism; that of chapter 7 is about philosophical communitarianism.

Herskovits claims that holding ethnocentric views helps to construct a successful ego. That is an argument that may elevate particular ethnocentric views, to make them good for those members of the relevant community whose egos benefit from the views. But this "good" is the relatively bland functional good of serving the interests of those who hold the views. It is not good in any intrinsic sense, as the ethnocentrist might think it is. Hence, our external judgment of the goodness of the ethnocentric view turns on considerations utterly unlike those that move the internal judgment of members of the ethnic group.

A striking aspect of the is-ought fallacy is the extraordinary range of concerns to which it is applied. Nationalist and ethnic identification are merely two categories of these. And there is nothing special about them that moralizes them or that suggests we ought to take the moralization of them very seriously as a moral matter. We should take the moralization seriously only in the descriptive and causal sense that we should take massive causal effects into consideration. Insofar as the is-ought moralization of nationalism and ethnicity is the only moral claim on their behalf, they have no moral claim on us. Oddly, therefore, *it may be the fact of the particular interest a nationalist or ethnic identification and action may serve, the distributed collective good it may help supply, that gives it some potential moral claim on us.* An interest account of the phenomena may therefore be the foundation of a moral account. Without interest to justify the identification, there is little more than morally accidental facts.

IRREDUCIBLY SOCIAL GOODS

Many of the contemporary communitarian critics of universalist moral and political theories argue against the methodological individualist assumptions of many of such theories. They note that human identity is socially, not individually, constituted. One must readily grant that much of human identity is socially constituted. Indeed, the view that we might individually bootstrap ourselves into our identities is ludicrous, and evidently no one argues for such a view.[35] To be made cogent, the communitarian criticism must eventually yield a principle or theory of the good in which at least some of the good is constituted by groups for their members. Charles Taylor makes a direct attempt to do just that in his argument for "irreducibly social goods."

Taylor sets up his discussion by first noting that there are many collective goods but that he is concerned with a class of goods that are not like these.[36] Military forces for national defense and a local dam against a rampaging river are collective goods. If they are provided to you, they may readily be provided to me as well without additional cost. These material goods are instrumentally good. They protect us against attack from enemies or floodwaters. The goods we derive from them are not themselves—only the military are apt to love the weapons they use, and only the Army Corps of Engineers may love an actual dam. The goods we derive are peace and unflooded homes. The material goods of military forces and dams causally produce these goods and are only therefore good themselves. If we could get peace and no floods some other way, we might dispense with the instrumental goods of military force and dams.

Taylor argues that it is quite otherwise with such goods as those of community and culture. The culture that we value is essentially linked to the good that we get from it. It is not merely a means to that good, it constitutes the good. Furthermore, he says of certain virtue-theory conceptions of particular virtues that, if these virtues are good, then the culture which makes them possible must also be good.[37] But these virtues may be goods only in a functional sense, as most of them seem to be in Aristotle, who saw different virtues for different roles. The virtues conduce to running a state well, to a good life, or even to pleasure or whatever. They do so in contingent ways. What might be a very important virtue in a hunter-gatherer society might be of little or no significance in the society of Taylor's university world. Hence, these virtues are not *per se* goods, they are only contingently goods. It does not follow that the culture that produced them is a good at all, either intrinsically or instrumentally. Driving on the right produces the intrinsic good of less dangerous and more enjoyable life in Taylor's Montreal and many other places. But driving on the right is not a good *per se*, any more than driving on the left is.

We might therefore suppose the culture of a particular people is worth fostering and preserving independently of that people's benefit from it. Is that so? Well, plausibly, no. It might be worth preserving in order to protect the current members of the society from suffering the painful fate of surviving past their culture, as Ishi, the last Yahi Indian did in early twentieth-century California.[38] But if there were no Ishis to care for, there need be no value in preserving a Yahi culture. (There might be social scientific value in preserving it for study, but this is not relevant to Taylor's thesis.) Yet Taylor says that a particular culture is "intrinsically good."[39] Either this is an odd use of "intrinsically" or the claim is false. If the thousands of vanished cultures were intrinsically good, one might think effort should have been put into preserving them or should now be put into re-creating them. But many of those cultures were ill-suited to providing good lives to their members. Many of the cultures died from within, as individuals abandoned them for other opportunities.

Of six thousand languages currently spoken in the world, comparative linguists estimate about half will disappear within a century. This is not a mere guess or trend-line projection. There are no longer any children speaking these languages. Some linguists evidently think this is a great loss and they think something should be done to give new life to these languages. One proposed solution is to establish "centers where children are taught and encouraged to use the threatened tongues."[40] For linguists and others interested in linguistic theory, perhaps three thousand dying languages is a great loss. But it cannot be a great loss for the next generation of children from the cultures in which those languages are spoken. Children who grow up speaking, as principal language, a language spoken by only hundreds or a few thousands might reasonably feel cheated by their culture. And that culture would be intrinsically good?

Language, incidentally, is one of Taylor's irreducibly social goods. All languages may be irreducibly social, but none is intrinsically good. They are good only contingently. What makes one of them good is the contingent facts of who speaks it, what has been written in it, and what opportunities for personal growth and well-being it offers its speakers. Note that we need not argue against Taylor's claim for intrinsic goodness by asserting that the good of a particular language or culture is merely instrumental. It may actually be good. But it is only contingently good. Remarkably, we may show it is good by giving an account of how *it serves and affects individuals who consume it*. It is individuals who are beneficiaries of a culture or of membership in a language community. Hence, methodological individualists are not prima facie precluded from arguing for the goodness of cultures.

Nevertheless, it is true, as Taylor wishes to show, that such goods as language and culture are irreducibly social in important respects. An individual cannot produce a serious language. Not even a sterling committee may be able to do so, as the doleful experience with Esperanto suggests. We cannot compromise on a blend of several languages to avoid giving unfair advantage to the natives of an actual language if we are to have an international lingua franca. A worthy language must be richly, socially produced.

But here again, we can agree with Taylor only in part. Language and many other good aspects of culture are produced collectively, they are in this sense irreducibly social. Even the possibility of enjoying many of the pleasures of the sports fan in boosting the local team is socially produced. But it does not follow from the way it is produced that the *enjoyment* of such a good is irreducibly social. The benefit I get from my culture is my benefit even though it may be constituted in part by my actions and beliefs as inculcated by that very culture. Just as with material goods, collective production or provision does not entail collective consumption. Indeed, it is hard to imagine what collective consumption would be. We can speak of collective provision of some particular thing. I pay taxes, you pay taxes, it adds up to enough to provide a new highway. I participate in the use of the English language and help to determine its drift toward new forms just as you do. But when our cultural creations are *consumed*, they are consumed by us individually. I sit in my study and read Taylor, he sits in his study and reads Hegel. Despite the individual creativity of our authors, the learning that goes into our readings and the meanings of our texts are irreducibly social. Still, our reading is highly individual.

Philosophical communitarianism is clearly an appealing theory to many people, especially including academics at world class, extremely universalistic and uncommunitarian universities, including at least one university that is renowned as a wonderful collection of idiosyncratic individuals who could not possibly constitute a community. What is the core of truth that makes philosophical communitarianism plausible enough to be appealing? Perhaps it is simply that a group may coordinate on any one of several possible ways of satisfying its members, any of which would be good for them. Once it has coordinated on a particular way, that way may then be not merely good (as many alternative ways would be) but even better than any other way for the group. That way becomes better because it can mobilize members in their interest more readily than any alternative then can.

Typically, such coordination has advantages of better communal information and understanding and of common expectations that make continued coordination easy, even effortless, and that enhance particular tastes and preferences that are satisfied by continued coordination. There is nothing more to the community good, no consideration over and above the benefits of coordination in general, including Herskovits's concern with the benefits to the individual ego, to justify any particular coordination.

Could there be any scope for irreducibly social consumption of a good? Perhaps there could be. Love or friendship as a mutual relationship seems to depend not only on having two separate people contribute to creating and maintaining the relationship but also on having those two benefit from the relationship. That may suggest an opening to thinking of irreducibly social consumption on the larger scale of a whole polity rather than of a mere couple. So far, however, Taylor and other contemporary communitarians have not led us through that opening to anything grander.

Anthropologists often note there are different values in different societies. Communitarian theorists moralize this observation into the odd claim that each group's or society's values are right for it. I want to understand the anthropologists' finding in rational-choice terms. If it is successful, this move blocks the communitarian move to justify the content of the diverse values. But it still leaves what one might call a communitarian residue: the sunk costs of each person's upbringing and cultural knowledge. Economists sometimes consider sunk costs as merely bygones. For the communitarian residue, however, this view would be wrong to a large extent. Our sunk costs are us. Our cultural sunk costs have been transmuted into information and putative knowledge that is not merely gone. Much of it is a resource to us in our further actions—although much of it is perhaps an unfortunate resource, more nearly an obstacle, and we might wish it were gone.

Much of our sunk costs also informs our preferences. Ishi lost almost all of what mattered in his life with the disappearance of his culture. He lived through his loss in later years with seeming equanimity. Consider a very different case of loss of self through the destruction of all of a person's sunk costs. Kurt Tucholsky fled Germany when Hitler rose to power and famously said that what happened in Germany no longer was his affair. Indeed, he wrote a friend, "The world for which we have worked and to which we belonged exists no more."[41] Just how much did it exist no more? Tucholsky wrote further, "I am a writer and *how* I say my stuff is often better than *what* I say."[42] Furthermore, his adult life had been spent in social, art, and literary criticism—of the German society, arts, and literature of his time. Now that, too, was dead as was his language. In Sweden he could read books, often only in translation, and could see that many writers were dead in translation, as he thought he was. He had worked with the intensely pacifist weekly, *Die Weltbühne*, from before the time Carl von Ossietzky joined the journal. With the rise of Hitler, even his pacifism was irrelevant, as he remarked that the pacifism of the Czechs would only let the Germans roll them under that much more easily.

Tucholsky evidently craved contact with people who were part of the culture they had lost, but most of those people were struggling to survive or were not yet sensible enough to face what Tucholsky saw—he could not understand the hundreds of thousands of Jews who stayed on in Germany or the Russians who sought good trade relations with a government that openly asserted it would as soon destroy them. Ossietzky was in a concentration camp for his writings on German rearmament and would die soon after the announcement that he had been awarded the Nobel Prize for peace. Tucholsky's brother fled via Czechoslovakia to London to the United States. Tucholsky's life dissipated before his eyes. Even in Switzerland he found himself leaving restaurants in revulsion when German Swiss commented approvingly on Hitler's actions (on his account, Tucholsky would say, "Oh pardon me—you, I thought you were a Mensch"[43]). Like Ota Benga in similar straits, cut off from himself, Tucholsky finally committed suicide at a young age.

Surely there were moral values at stake in Tucholsky's suffering through his final three years. But the desperate loss of the sunk costs of his self, of his tastes, his commitments, and his life, screams through his protestations that Germany and his past life no longer matter to him. They were almost all that he was and he was therefore almost all gone, destroyed by Hitler and by those Germans who accepted Hitler. Nothing must have mattered more to his daily existence than that Kurt Tucholsky was no longer .

Conclusion

In sum, individual identification with such groups as ethnic groups is not primordial or somehow extra-rational in its ascendancy of group over individual interests but is rational. Individuals identify with such groups because it is in their interest to do so. Individuals may find identification with their group beneficial because those who identify strongly may gain access to positions under the control of the group and because the group provides a relatively secure and comfortable environment. Individuals create their own identification with the group through the information and capacities they gain from life in the group. A group gains power from coordination of its members, power that may enable it to take action against other groups. Hence, the group may genuinely be instrumentally good for its members, who may tend, without foundation, to think it is inherently, not merely contingently, good.

Much of the detail of human nature is a social construction in each case. But this means primarily that opportunities and their costs and benefits are largely a function of what others have done or are doing. A North American can become a wealthy lawyer or entrepreneur because the relevant opportunities are there. Such options are far less readily available to a typical Kenyan or Bangladeshi, or in the early 1990s to a typical Bosnian. But there are constraints that seem even more perversely the product of social interaction. For example, people in different societies are seemingly constrained by different norms. Such constraints seem to play a large role in defining the groups to which individuals become committed. The rise and maintenance of group identification in many and diverse groups is the subject of the next two chapters, in which the role of socially constructed norms is central. The argument for many of these norms, and especially for those that help to motivate loyalty to groups, is that they work as well as they do because they serve relevant interests, even if often in complicated ways that may be opaque to the participants.

CHAPTER FOUR

Norms of Exclusion

> You stayed with the balija for eighteen months. Okay, let's see
> how you feel about the balija now. You can go to the front
> lines and kill a balija, then maybe we'll let you go.
> —Serbian officer to a Serbian civilian fleeing Sarajevo
> (*New York Times*, 14 Nov. 1993)

NORMS OF DIFFERENCE AND UNIVERSALISTIC NORMS

To understand communal norms, we can best put them into comparison with more broadly directed norms. I wish to discuss norms in two quite general categories: those that redound to the benefit of members of a more or less well-defined subgroup within a larger society, and those that seem to apply universalistically to more or less all members of a society. In general, comparison of these two classes suggests that norms of difference and exclusion are especially tractable to rational choice analysis and that universalistic norms are less tractable. This conclusion is the reverse of what may be the common view in the literature that norms of difference and exclusion—sometimes called communal norms—are especially intractable to a rational-choice account, that they are perhaps primordial or, in the view of communitarians, that they are extra-rational commitments to something beyond the self or to community sources of the self.

Norms of great social interest are those that enforce something that might go otherwise. For example, an ethnic group might simply assimilate, as many have done in the United States over the past couple of centuries, or aristocrats might join the larger society. Norms for behavior against such assimilation might have a significant impact on the rate of assimilation. Subgroup norms typically reinforce individual identification with the group and enhance the separation of the group from the larger society or from another specific group in the society. They commonly work by changing the interests of marginal group members to get them to act in conformity with the interests of the core of the group. This is not to say that they are somehow "intended" to do that, but only that they happen to do so. Universalistic norms tend to reinforce behavior that may be collectively beneficial but contrary to individual interest or even contrary to a subgroup's interests. Norms of difference and exclusion might be said to make good use of self-interest. But self-interest might also be said to make good use of norms of difference and exclusion. In either case, such norms may gain enormous force from their congruence with interests.

Many norms appear to have the strategic structure of coordination. In David Lewis's term, they are conventions or, rather, they govern conventional resolutions of coordination problems.[1] For example, driving on the right in North America is merely a convention. But it benefits us all to follow the convention rather than to violate it. Oddly, however, it would be wrong to claim we have that *particular* convention *because* it is in our interest. What is in our interest is merely that we have *some* convention that makes driving safe. For example, driving on the left would be as good as driving on the right, as suggested by the experience of England, Japan, and many other nations. What is rational for me is to follow the extant convention when I drive. Hence, it is rational for me to follow whatever convention prevails where I am—on the right in North America and on the left in Australia.

The convention of driving on the right (as in North America) or the left (as in the United Kingdom and Japan) might be seen as an ideal type of the category of universalistic norms. Having everyone in the relevant society follow that norm is beneficial to all. However, the driving convention is not a norm of great social interest in the sense above. There is very little or no need to enforce it against anyone other than those who enjoy the risks of violating the convention; there is only rare need to instruct people of what they would immediately acknowledge to be erroneous, self-destructive behavior. We are apt to accuse someone of stupidity rather than of cupidity when they drive on the wrong side of the street. If we call following the convention a norm, it is a norm whose function is almost wholly epistemological rather than to affect motivations by affecting incentives.[2] I will restrict the term "norm" to those cases that are motivational and will therefore not count the driving convention as a norm here. Still, many norms have much of the coordination quality of the driving convention. We would all be better off if everyone followed a certain norm just as we would all be better off if everyone drove either on the left or right. Hence, we can coordinate on following that norm in preference to not following it.

The norm of truth-telling might similarly be of universal appeal, but the incentive for it is not already built into the situations in which it might be invoked, as the incentive for driving according to the local convention is built into the situation on the road. Hence, the norm of truth-telling is not always redundant, it can potentially add to the incentive for relevant behavior. Such norms are universal in a given society. I will refer to them as *universalistic norms*.

The ethnic norm that supports identification with a particular community is also not redundant. There is likely to be some mixing and intermarriage. Without the norm, there might be far more. Those who are most comfortable in their group are most likely to find their norms of community redundant for themselves but not for others. But the norm is likely to be of interest to people in the community precisely because it can be invoked against certain behaviors that are attractive to at least some members of the community. If everyone in our community shared identical interests in sticking with the community, we might not need a community norm. Some of us benefit from having such a norm merely because the community's boundaries are not well defined, there is no clear dividing line or step function between those who identify with the community and those who do not. The functional role of community norms is typically to establish difference. Indeed, they might most instructively be called *norms of particularism, difference, or exclusion* rather than of community. They often have some variant of the content of the Vietnam-era norm expressed in the slogan "Love it or leave it," where "it" was the United States.

Note that the terminology for these two classes of norms is not parallel. One might refer to universalistic norms as norms of universality or similarity, but that would be misleading. Kantians, utilitarians, egalitarians, and other universalistic moral theorists may follow their own norms of universality or similarity. But their more specific norms, such as norms of altruism, reciprocity, or veracity, are universalistic in the sense that they apply to everyone.

The central difference between the two classes, universalistic norms and norms of difference, is that the latter require a sense of group separation or even an outside, typically adversary, group to give them any value. Difference is a relative value that depends on an external referent. There is obviously no point in difference if there is no alternative to the group that is to be different. A norm of exclusion is, by implication, also a norm of inclusion for the relevant group. The ideal for norms of difference would be individual submission through acceptance of the value of identification with the group.

At the fringes of the group, however, there may be people who are tempted by the alternative benefits of weaker identification with the group, even of defection from it. I might wish to benefit from membership in a group without being really committed because I have competing commitments. Compared to those with much stronger commitments to the group, I am at the fringe. If the group did not react, full defection would not be necessary, but the group might react to even partial defection by excluding me. For an individual case, the incentive structure might be essentially prisoner's dilemma, with both the individual and the group better off with partial defection than with full defection or exclusion. But there might be a strategic benefit to the group from full exclusion, which raises the costs of partial defection and therefore, plausibly, reduces its incidence. An effect of the group norm is to raise these costs and thereby to reduce the size of *the prisoner's dilemma fringe*.

Interethnic marriage rates might suffice as a rough proxy measure of the sizes of prisoner's dilemma fringes. Some groups appear headed for mixing quickly, others only slowly. In particular, blacks in the United States may now have stronger norms of difference and a narrower prisoner's dilemma fringe than in earlier decades, while Jews may be going through a dramatic widening of their fringe and the rapid breakdown of their separateness. Among American Jews married before 1965, 9 percent had married outside the Jewish community; among those married after 1985, 52 percent married outside.[3] For eliminating the force of norms of difference between two groups, both groups must be open, perhaps because each has a very large prisoner's dilemma fringe. When enough mixing in the fringes happens, others in the groups have less to gain from difference, and they fall into a still wider fringe.

Norms of difference typically have a prisoner's dilemma fringe of more weakly identified group members. The size of the fringe is a function of the relative benefits of membership and defection. Universalistic norms typically have prisoner's dilemma strains throughout the relevant society. The function of these norms is to raise the cost of certain individually rewarding behaviors, such as lying and cheating, to reduce their incidence. But, since there is no group boundary for the universalistic norm, there is no relevant sense in which those who violate the norm are at the margins of the group. The incentive to lie or cheat may affect any member of the society, not merely fringe members. In both classes of norms, the general norm has enforcement value if it can block prisoner's dilemma incentives to defect from the relevant social order and the content of the norm itself is a matter of coordination.[4]

There are many other ways to categorize norms. For example, Edna Ullmann-Margalit divides them into prisoner's dilemma, pure coordination, and unequal coordination categories. Ullmann-Margalit speaks of "norms of partiality," which are norms that permanently ensconce two groups in a coordination that benefits one of them more than the other.[5] For example, one might suppose it the interest of humans that some group, such as women, should specialize in procreation and rearing of the species, which just happens to redound to the special advantage of men.[6] As it happens, a statable norm may fit one of these categories quite clearly in one period of its history, and then fit another category in a later period, or the same statement of a norm might be pure coordination in one context and unequal coordination in another. For example, the norm of truth-telling might be of generally beneficial quality in a benign community but of divisive quality in a malign society such as that in which some might hide Jewish or other refugees from a genocidal government. Many of the norms in a given society may be residual norms, they may be norms gone awry, left over from prior conditions in which they made sense and still invoked in contexts that lack the relevant strategic structure. They may be survivals past their time. Marx said that the norm of dueling was "a relic of a past stage of culture."[7] Others may be over-generalized norms that cover more than they should if they were thought to have a simple strategic structure.

Norms of universality may fall into either prisoner's dilemma or nearly pure coordination strategic structures or, perhaps more typically, they may fall into a mixed strategic structure, if only because they govern ongoing relationships. Many of us might not need a norm to get us to go along with the community principle because we might see ourselves as benefiting directly from going along. Hence, application of the norm to us is little different from application of the driving "norm." But we might see the value of having the norm to regulate the behavior of those more nearly marginal to the community, those for whom weaker identification with the community has its more than compensating rewards.

Norms of Difference

Ethnic and other groups commonly have norms that differentiate their members from the larger community in which they live, and those of the larger society may have related norms to reinforce the separation. This is most conspicuous, perhaps, in religious contexts. For example, the Jewish biblical injunction that one could lend money at interest but not to a brother was interpreted to mean that Jews could not lend at interest to other Jews but only to non-Jews.[8] Although Thomas Aquinas held it sinful for a Christian to lend at interest, he conveniently supposed it not sinful to borrow at interest.[9] The separate merchants' and lenders' role for Jews in medieval and later European society was therefore the strategic implication of the combination of Jewish and Christian norms.

Why would members of a group wish to be different, to exclude non-members? Often because there might be benefits of membership. Benefits can take at least two quite different forms.[10] First, there might be *conflict of interest over limited resources* that make it the interest of one group to gain control of those resources on behalf of its members. For example, land and other resources in fixed supply might not be expandable to make them more widely available. Also, jobs under the control of a group or of the state might be in relatively fixed supply in the short run. In a conflict in what is roughly a constant-sum game, at least for the short run, some subgroup or coalition can benefit its members most quickly by excluding others from access to the limited resources. Here the group is a means to other goods.

Second, there may be straightforward *benefits of comfort, familiarity, and easy communication in one's group*. We might call these epistemological benefits, because they take the form of reducing the need for knowledge beyond what one may have just from growing up in a community or being part of it. Here the group is virtually a consumption good itself—living much of our lives in the ambiance of the group is what we want.

The two kinds of benefit might often work together. For example, members of a group might have easy access to jobs through community networks of information and assistance. Dealing with an outsider who comes to a group might require more effort from group members than dealing with an insider would. For example, if I marry outside my community, my fellow community members might find my spouse to be more trouble to deal with, less predictable, and generally much less enjoyable than they find the neighbor whom I might have married. As a result, my spouse may feel relatively ill at ease in my community and we might together have far poorer opportunities for social intercourse than other couples of our age and milieu would have.

Not every apparent group member need share in either of the two forms of benefit to membership. Some may see better opportunities outside than inside the group. And some might bridle at the limits of the familiar. Such people are, in the discussions here, members at the fringes of their groups. Much of what we must understand about norms of difference and exclusion will depend on the mix of people at the fringes and people in what might be called the core of relevant groups.

Universalistic Norms

Universalistic norms apply indifferently to everyone. Such a norm may be held in a specific community without necessary reference to or ongoing effect on any other community. In general, such norms take one of at least two distinct forms. First, they may be theoretically deduced, as for example by Immanuel Kant, by a religious leader, or more or less by everyone through some principle of universality. Second, they may be socially constructed with, perhaps, unknown origin. Generally, norms in the second category are likely to be community-specific. One might argue that all norms, even those ostensibly in the first category, are in the second category in that they are community-based, although it is at least conceivable that some norm or set of norms would someday be literally universal for humans in whatever community. *Because all or nearly all norms are community-based, it would be misleading to refer to norms of difference and exclusion as community norms as though this were a distinguishing mark for them.*

There is a class of important universalistic norms which are virtually self-enforcing in many contexts. These are norms such as those for telling the truth, keeping promises, and maintaining fidelity to spouses and friends. They are self-enforcing when they govern ongoing relationships between pairs or very small numbers of people. In brief, I will refer to these as *dyadic norms.* The enforcement of these norms comes naturally from the fact that *the relationships that they govern are of value to the participants* beyond the instant interaction on which someone must keep the relevant norm or violate it. These characteristics of the relationship suggest that it is an iterated prisoner's dilemma in its incentive structure. Each participant in the dyad sometimes has a short-term interest in violating the norm but a long-term interest in maintaining the relationship. If the latter is great enough, it can trump the short-term interest and make it worthwhile to forego short-term gains in the interest of longer-term gains.[11]

One might tell the truth out of strict moral scruples, but one also has an interest in telling the truth to one's ongoing relations. Even if you are bound by moral scruples, you may nevertheless depend on the incentives of self-interest that keep others honest enough to make dealing with them worth your while. The usual resolution of an iterated prisoner's dilemma in which one party fails to cooperate often enough is not to join that party in cheating but simply to withdraw from the relationship. If others have an interest in cooperation with you, you have better prospects from cooperating than from withdrawing or cheating. In general, you have better life prospects if those around you recognize their interest in maintaining cooperative relations with you.[12] Being cooperative loses much of its value if too few others are cooperative and it may finally even become disvalued. Similarly, truth-telling may often seem to serve perverse purposes for many relationships in a Nazi or other totalitarian society.

Typically, then, these dyadic norms are straightforwardly self-enforcing. Such a norm may govern a very large population, all of whom are involved with various others in dyadic relationships. But there is no large-number equivalent of the dyadic norms. A norm that governs relationships that are inherently large-number rather than dyadic cannot be reinforced merely by the withdrawal of cooperative parties from interactions with uncooperative parties.[13] The norms of difference and exclusion discussed below govern large-number relationships of identification of a whole community and exclusion of others from it. They are reinforced through the mechanism implicit in their functional structure, not directly through the iterated incentive offered by the fellow group members in a large-number prisoner's dilemma. The explanation of large-number norms in general cannot turn on a rational regulation of the problem of collective action in enforcing the norm, although there may be some cases that can be regulated through somewhat unstable conventions.[14]

Incidentally, modern nationalism has often turned into the analog of a subgroup norm of difference, but, of course, at the whole-nation level. It has the function of differentiating the nation and its people from other nations and their peoples. There can be a universalistic, non-adversarial nationalism, and no doubt many nationalisms have been. For example, a particular nationalism could be directed at stimulating economic activity and productivity and artistic and other efforts, at lifting the condition of the nation's citizens without onus to anyone else. Lovers of blood sports might think such a nationalism uninteresting and might prefer the nationalism that tends to war. Nationalism that is a norm of difference often has bellicose tendencies. The general category of seemingly universalistic norms will be discussed in chapter 5.

EXPLAINING NORMS OF EXCLUSION

Norms of exclusion and difference take many forms. For example, there can be quite local norms that elevate my town over other towns, my club over other clubs, or my company over other companies. In most societies, there are norms of dress that differentiate men and women. Some Canadians think there are norms that differentiate Canada from the United States, while other Canadians fear that no such norms survive. Two general types of norm of exclusion will be of special interest here: norms that define ethnic or racial groups and those that define social classes. In this section, I will call on many norms of the first type to explain how norms of exclusion work. Then, in the following section I will discuss an odd but uniquely important norm—the duel—that helped to maintain the definition and status of a social class that was of declining significance.

Consider an important category of non-religious norms that function to establish difference: norms for linguistic usage, especially for slang and specialized terms. Some community-specific slang may not be anything more than useful shorthand to relevant parties, as psychologists, plumbers, musicians, opinion pollsters, and others might develop terms to deal with matters of special interest to their groups. But some community-specific slang may have no such simple function, linguistically it may do no more than substitute for standard terminology. Its effective function is, rather, to distinguish its users as users, to signal their difference from those who do not use the special terminology.

For some group norms, such as that of the rapper, it is not necessary that those who most express and define the norm be of the community that adopts it. Some of the rappers, whom we might call the *bearers of the norm* of rap, which flouts the bourgeoisie, are from bourgeois backgrounds, not from inner cities. Yet it may still be true that the norm in which they participate is primarily the norm of the inner-city poor. The norm has been commercialized—that is, after all, how it was communicated with such rapidity. Anyone with the relevant commercial vision can see the benefits of bearing the norm of rap independently of whether they actually share in its values, even independently of whether they personally wish to flout the bourgeoisie for any reason other than profit. Even a convicted white racist can commercially exploit the norm as a bearer of it while posing in some of the whitest and most bourgeois of all underwear.

Among the possible terms for establishing difference and therefore special community are those that are, in the broader community, negative in their connotations, terms that are perhaps even epithets. For example, some blacks now call each other "nigger," pronounced "nigga."[15] This term was once despised by blacks and commonly used as an insult by white racists. The rap, "Sucka Nigga," by A Tribe Called Quest, says that, when used by whites, the word meant blacks would never grow. The rapper says, "Other niggas in the community think it's crummy, but I don't." The youth are with him, he says. They embrace adversity and the word nigga goes right to the race.[16]

While the term is still an epithet when used by most whites, it has become a term of affection and community for many blacks—mostly younger urban blacks, as the rapper notes. Blacks now can get away with such usage while most whites cannot, so that the term entails exclusion of most whites from at least the language community of blacks. On his account, a white professor in Chicago recently attempted to help students understand the power of racist language to do harm by saying to the only black student in his class: "We have a nigger student here." The student said afterwards that she couldn't move: "I wanted to run out but was afraid I didn't have the strength to make it to the door."[17] Yet that woman could well also have heard blacks calling their friends nigger, and she might have smiled at their communal jocularity.

That the term can so demean someone and yet also elevate may seem astonishing. Nevertheless, it may make sense to the relevant community. American blacks use many other terms that sound negative in strong positive senses. For example, a bad mutha is, in some sense, especially good, a bad outfit is a great outfit, and a bad meal is one you would go out of your way to eat. When the standard terms, such as great, terrific, and so forth, have been diminished by overuse, bad sounds very good.

Even more generally, for more than a century, American blacks have been "redefining race as an abiding source of pride rather than stigma."[18] This move, which was discouraged and deplored by Frederick Douglass, reached its height with the slogan "Black is beautiful." What much of American society has treated as a stigma for many centuries, has ceased to be a stigma in the vision of many blacks. It has even become a claim to special quality and a norm of exclusion.

What is in it for you? Why should you adopt the slang and manner of a group? Doing so allows you entree to the group and what rewards it has. These may be more attractive than what you lose from adopting the odd slang and manner. Refusing to adopt the slang or abandoning it later casts doubt on your commitments and your trustworthiness, making you less attractive to other members of the community. Indeed, it may even seem to other members of the group to be a rejection of them as persons, rather than merely of their style. And if you reject them, what are they to make of your hanging around them, what motives must they impute to you?

In the early seventies in New York, I was walking between a group of four or five young black men and a group of as many young black women. One of the men was imploring one of the women to do something with him but she repeatedly spurned him. He went up to her and put his arm around her waist, but she pushed his arm away. In disgust, he said, "You a motherfucker." She slowed and turned back to look at him with a beatific smile, saying, "No, I can't be no motherfucker—you must be thinking of yourself." The entire crowd laughed in appreciation of her sly put-down. Her target laughed hardest. Much of the rest of their conversation had been witty and extraordinarily overt. I would have liked to have such openness in my own community, but anyone who tried it there would have fallen out of favor and would have been spurned. The style of openness of much of the black community and the style of privacy and primness of much of the white community constitute norms of difference that reinforce the separateness of the two.[19] There may be nothing invidious in these norms, but their effects are de facto invidious and they virtually become norms of exclusion.

The slang and other linguistic devices of the rapper may be enhanced by the full panoply of the "cool pose" of young black men, especially in the inner city. Janet Mancini Billson and Richard Majors interpret that pose as a response to the exclusions of white or at least prosperous

American society.[20] But consider the range of plausible audiences for the pose. In addition to whites (who do not live in the ghetto), it could be directed at members of the group itself, older blacks who do not share the norm of the pose, or at young black women. It seems likely that the various behaviors are directed at different ones of these plausible audiences. The words of rap songs may have the widest audience, from the young inner-city black males themselves to whites. The pose, which is overwhelmingly visual and of therefore little effect unless it is seen, seems more likely to be directed only at an immediate, frequent audience, including the poseurs themselves, young women, and older blacks. As Billson and Majors read the pose, it is macho. Hence, its main audience could well be young black women, whose relative independence from men may provoke its swagger. Rap may be fundamentally political; the pose may not be very political at all.

Functional Explanation

What makes particular slang acceptable is not that it is deliberately chosen by someone but that, however it arises, it survives as a convention. Once the convention is in place, I can most readily show my identity by following it. The norm of using it becomes functional to identification with the group. Indeed, we may give a functional explanation of the survival of the norm once it is established, as follows:

> *An institution or a behavioral pattern X is explained by its function F for group G if and only if:*

1. F is an *effect* of X;
2. F is *beneficial* for G;
3. F maintains X by a causal *feedback* loop passing through G.[21]

In the present case, X is the norm of group slang or style; F is group identification; and G is the members of the relevant subgroup, such as certain blacks. The full explanation is as follows:

1. We might suppose that those who adopt the slang and style of the group are likely to identify more closely with the group thereafter because they will find the rewards of life in the group better than if they did not adopt the slang and style.
2. To show that group identification is beneficial for members of a group may seem difficult. But there are many reasons for this conclusion to follow (not necessarily, but contingently in many instances). Tight group affiliation can reduce the costs of requisite daily knowledge and thereby facilitate one's daily activities. It can give one access to benefits, such as jobs, controlled by the group.[22] For example, for both of these concerns, it can

provide readily available networks for discovering information and making connections. It can also be directly pleasurable for the relationships it underlies and the activities it organizes.[23]

3. Now we may see that group identification (F) maintains the norm of group slang or style (X) by a causal feedback loop passing through the members of the relevant group (G). Members who strongly identify with the group are likely to spend more of their time in it than members who identify more loosely. They will find it more natural to indulge, and hence to develop, the slang and style of the group. Hence, that slang and style may become more extreme as time passes, not because the group intends for it to do so but because that is the individual incentive of the most identified members of the group.

A cost of becoming closely associated with some subgroup in a society may be relative exclusion from other groups, including those that have better economic and social opportunities than the subgroup has. For some people this cost could outweigh the benefits under 2 above, in which case the relevant norms of difference are not beneficial. But these costs might be imposed by an alternative group that practices its own exclusions, so that one's own group may have norms of separation without fear of aggravating the losses from exclusion by others. In North American history, the exclusion of blacks by whites has been overwhelmingly important for black lack of opportunity. Today it is conceivable that the benefits of black norms of difference are finally rivaled for some by their costs in exacerbated exclusion by whites and even by bourgeois blacks.

The black teenager who dresses, walks, and gestures like a rapper or who adopts a cool pose may bear no costs for that style. But the later adult who has developed the language of the rapper and has adopted gestures that have since become second nature may bear substantial costs. The later adult may have to choose between cultivating a different image and language and continuing membership in the sub-community. The costs of the transition and the uncertainties of succeeding in the larger community weigh against making the change. The costs of the transition may typically include at least some loss of camaraderie in the rejected community. Shawn Hunt, a Brooklyn seventeen-year-old striving to get through high school and into college, says he talks to whites in "Regular, straight up and down English." But that would not go over well with his black friends, "They'd be like—that's not what they're used to. They wouldn't take too good to that. They'd think I was funny."[24]

Hunt's split might not work indefinitely. The novelist Kristin Hunter Lattany notes that "An individual in conflict with himself is only marginally functional, and if half his loyalty lies elsewhere, his community cannot trust him."[25] Molefi Asante of the African-American Studies Program at Temple University sharply criticizes Cornel West for his "assimilationist" orientation. "Our solutions are within ourselves, not outside of us," Asante says. West "finds his intellectual center in white tradition. He has been educated away from himself."[26] Both Lattany and Asante seem to intend moral criticisms. But there might be great psychological difficulties as well.

If there are great psychological difficulties in maintaining a dual personality, note that one of the values of ghetto slang is that it can be used successfully only in the community. Hence, any ghetto teenager who cannot maintain a dual language personality such as Shawn Hunt does in order to maintain his dual existence, is virtually trapped in the ghetto community of teenage males. As Michael Hechter argues, communities that have their own private language within a larger society are more readily able to maintain solidarity because they have greater opportunity for cheap monitoring of each other's actions and even attitudes.[27]

Once, at a barbecue party, I was one of the few whites among the black friends of my neighbors. The husband was a brilliant gardener who produced miracles from a six-foot square carved out of the pavement of our back alley and who filled his house with thriving plants. Someone complimented the wife for all her plants, and she declined the praise. "I have nothing to do with those. Jim does them all—and he tells *me* to stay away. I have a white thumb." I laughed because the phrase was completely new to me but was wonderfully evocative. In part, I was enchanted by the phrase the way one might be on reading or hearing a figure of speech in a second language. It then comes across vividly, even though one's own language might use the equivalent figure of speech. "Catch fire" in English is mundane to me; the first time I read it in German, it evoked an instant image of a hand reaching up to catch a ball of fire and it turned into the usual mundane meaning only after interpretation. But in the case of my neighbor's white thumb, of course, the phrase was especially powerful because it said something in a new and novel way. It was slave traders with white thumbs who killed most of the blacks shipped across the Atlantic, it was plantation owners with white thumbs who ruled over the survivors and their progeny, and white thumbs may still press heavily on black lives in America. My neighbor's "white thumb" evoked all of that.

At my laughter one of the women in the group gave my neighbor a look of disdain. She was up to the occasion; she grinned and said to me, "That's okay, that's just what *we* say." Clearly, *their* phrase was apt. But the phrase was not one that could readily be shared; it was *their* phrase.

There was therefore a mild jolt to both communities when my neighbor spoke her language in my presence. We might generalize the look of disdain one of her black friends gave my neighbor. Like Shawn Hunt she was expected to talk regular, straight up and down English in the presence of whites. Clearly it would be strenuous to do that if one's ordinary catch phrases are going to turn into balls of fire, so that one must constantly monitor every statement. There must be evenings, days, weeks, and even longer times, when one would rather not bother.

At the extreme of trying to fit in two communities at once is a San Francisco taxi driver who recently told me of his life as a heavy drug user. He had stopped all of the harder stuff and now consumed only marijuana. But it had taken him a couple of years to realize he would never successfully leave the more insidious drugs behind if he did not sever contacts with his drug-using friends, who could not stand to have him around while they shot up and snorted various things if he was not going to join in. At another extreme is the case of the Serbian refugee from Sarajevo in the epigraph for this chapter. That Serb was impressed into military service in one of the units besieging the Muslim-majority city and was challenged to kill a Muslim from his former community in order to demonstrate his loyalty to his fellow Serbs.[28] Eighteen months of consorting with Muslims evidently put that refugee off into the dubious fringe of the Serbian community, where the hard-core of that community could not trust him.

In his definition of functional explanation, Jon Elster includes two other conditions:

i. F is *unintended* by the actors producing X; and
ii. F (or at least the causal relationship between X and F) is *unrecognized* by the actors in G.

In this era of the instant sociology of everything,[29] it would be surprising if the second of these conditions would hold universally for a norm that has been established for even a short while and eventually, therefore, even the first of these conditions might fail to hold. But, even though some of the supporters of the norm might fully understand its functional role and might deliberately work to maintain it, many of the followers of the norm would typically still fit Elster's conditions.[30]

In fact, these two conditions are merely the extra conditions that distinguish "latent" from "manifest" functions. This distinction may be important, because some feedbacks that work well when they are latent might fail once they become manifest. Other feedbacks work very well even when they are fully manifest. Indeed, organizations commonly have feedback intentionally designed in to enhance organizational effectiveness. The workings of such devices often clearly fit the model of functional explanation. For the present discussion, the important concern is that feedback is functional in that it reinforces the relevant norm, not whether it is latent or manifest.[31]

It can be dysfunctional to recognize a functional relationship for what it is. We may be members of a group that has been identified by others and that has faced constrained opportunities. We might finally get better opportunities primarily by improving the status of the group, and this claim is one we could make to help motivate actions by fellow group members. But members might also benefit from having members reject aspects of the identification foisted on them by others or by having them transform those aspects into good rather than bad things. Here it could be counterproductive to argue overtly that this is why we should think these things good. We are more likely to motivate each other successfully if we can convincingly argue that somehow these things *are* good. Blacks might say black is beautiful and that might energize many blacks and lead them to be more stalwart in seeking opportunities and overcoming racial barriers. We could then fit the slogan to a functional explanation of improved black status. But blacks could not very well assert that this is all they mean when they say black is beautiful. Hence, making this particular functional relationship work may depend on keeping it unstated and latent.

Finally, also note that the form that functional feedback takes can be quite varied. It can work through biological mechanisms, through structural impacts on environment, or through effects on incentives for various behaviors. When it works through incentive effects, then functional explanation is a part of rational choice explanation. And if the feedback produces important incentive effects, functional explanation is inherently an important part of rational choice explanation. In the discussion here, the functional feedback relations all work through effects on incentives and they yield rational choice explanations of behaviors that superficially might not seem consistent with self-interest. It is only when unpacked functionally that the rational incentives for the relevant behaviors can be comprehended.

Origin and Development

Note that the issue in the preceding discussion is how the norm of calling each other nigger works. The norm contributes to establishing or asserting identity by seemingly abasing oneself, one's ways, or one's appearance. This may seem odd. Hence, one may wish to ask the prior question of how an individual could think to do such a thing *before the establishment of such a norm in her community*. If no one did so, the norm could not arise. This seems likely to be a much harder psychological trick than merely following a well-supported norm. But it is also a trick that need not be turned by very many people. After a few have done it, the norm may be on its way. For example, an early rapper might merely have accentuated gestures that are commonly used in stylized, dismissive argument, indeed, in intrafamilial, not interracial, argument. Giving the object of the rap the back of the hand, dramatically pointing at the imagined object, waving it away, dismissing it with egocentric posturing— these were all daily fare long before rap, probably in many communities other than the black inner city.

Competition in distinctiveness has the odd result of producing such extreme gestures that they become stylized and no longer distinctive from one rapper to another—any eight-year-old can do them with ease. Flouting the bourgeoisie has a long tradition (in France it is even a standard phrase: *épater le bourgeois*), with the cultivated belch, the up-yours swagger, the I-am-all-that-matters bearing. In the United States, being bourgeois correlates fairly strongly with being white. Flouting the bourgeoisie and flouting whites are not easily kept separate for many American blacks.

The term "nigger" is one of the harshest racist epithets in the United States. Those who have used it may largely, as Irving Lewis Allen asserts, have used it to distinguish themselves as not black.[32] Now, however, it is used to distinguish oneself as black.[33] How does someone turn "nigger" into a term of honor when used by blacks? Again, it is hard to answer the individual-level question before the norm is established. At that level, the move was a seemingly strange trick. But at that level there are millions of strange tricks turned daily. The basic question for us, therefore, is how this particular trick came out of the millions to become a norm. To a large extent, the issue must be roughly parallel to questions of how certain products make it in the market. Competition kills many and lets some through. In such competition, oddity or distinctiveness may be an advantage, it helps to make a slogan or product memorable.

When the vocabulary and politics of race changed at the height of the Civil Rights movement in the late fifties and the sixties, elderly Toms sometimes admonished the young: "You're nothing but a nigger and don't you forget it," just as many whites had regularly done for generations. A stump speaker might naturally appropriate this slogan, not to admonish, but to incense. "You ain't nothin' but niggers in this country, and don't you forget it."[34] Earlier, the term had been used, especially by white racists, to distinguish and separate blacks to keep them "in their place."[35] On the political stump it was also used to distinguish blacks and to acknowledge the separation imposed on them, but then to galvanize them as a political group. The old, ugly slogan turned positive; what was formerly derogatory had become hortatory. The step to making "nigger" an honorific term was presumably easy after that because the ground was fully prepared for treating it as a positive identification.[36]

To establish how the convention of using nigger honorifically arose, we would have to investigate millions of actions by vast numbers of people over several years. We might have to determine not only who drifted into such usage when, but also why alternative norms did not get more widely adopted. No matter whether we are clear on how the convention specifically arose, however, we can still understand how that convention works as a norm. In general, the latter is the more interesting task for social scientific understanding. Perhaps this realization underlies or at least is taken to support theories of cultural determination.

But it would be wrong to conclude from the competitive generation of norms that they are inherently irrational. They may often be no more irrational than driving on the right in North America: They often coordinate for common ends, especially common ends that are group-specific. If we had an authoritative leader with many exclusive options for coordinating us, all reasonably acceptable and functional for achieving our common end, it would be merely rational for the leader to pick one and benefit from it.[37] But we can evidently sometimes also "pick" one without the help of an authoritative leader, as we did in the original adoption of the driving convention.

There may be other instances of the elevation of a derogatory term for a group into a term of approbation and distinction that are more easily traced through. For example, during the hegemony of Spain over the Netherlands, the Dutch revolutionary movement became known as *les Gueux*, after the French word for beggars (*Geuzen* in Dutch). The term plausibly arose when one of Philip's counselors used the word *gueux* to express contempt for the group of Netherlands nobles who presented a list of political demands to the Spanish regent in April 1566. To defy the Spanish or to goad themselves or to do both, the Dutch then called themselves beggars and went on to rally themselves to rise against Spanish rule. Victory went to the *les Gueux*, who were not begging but demanding. The insult became their rallying cry.[38] In the end there were beggars of many varieties, designated by region, by leadership (such as that of William of Orange, the eventual monarch), and by kind (such as the beggar navy).

Maintenance

An obvious question for the development of a norm of exclusion or difference that is to be enforced against community members is how the enforcement is done. In part it is done merely by misfit, as in the discussion of the rapper turned quasi-bourgeois. The deviant is no longer a source of pleasure to the community. Consider the cases of John Howard Griffin and Thomas Wolfe.

After publishing *Black Like Me*, an account of his passing for black and suffering the discriminations of Southern racism,[39] John Howard Griffin (who was white) was treated to shunning by many in his small hometown of Mansfield, Texas. Perhaps some of the shunning was morally or politically motivated rather than merely an expression of his misfit with the community.

Many people have had the experience of returning home after going off for education or for job opportunities and of finding themselves not very welcome. Indeed, this is one of a related pair of general theses in the title of Thomas Wolfe's *You Can't Go Home Again* and throughout his work.[40] Wolfe clearly appreciated the benefits, the comforts of home. He characterized a town as "coiling in a thousand fumes of homely smoke, now winking into a thousand points of friendly light its glorious small design, its aching passionate assurances of walls, warmth, comfort, food, and love."[41] Hence, on his view, the costs of separation were real and potentially large.

The other thesis in Wolfe's pair is that, upon return, one may not find the comforts of home as pleasing as they once were because one may have learned or changed too much.[42] Wolfe saw that the comforts of home may be as appealing as they are in part because of ignorance of what alternatives there are. The full story is as follows. *The comforts induce staying at home, which secures ignorance by pruning vistas, which maintains tastes for the comforts of home.* That is a demoralizing chain of relationships. Those like Wolfe can break that chain only at the price of permanent disquiet.

Incidentally, the epistemological comforts of home feed back to reinforce themselves. But this may work for many people only if the feedback is latent, not evident. To make it evident is almost by definition to violate it. The ignorance implicit in settling for the epistemological comforts of home might be actively opposed by some if they came to understand its functional role in reinforcing belief in the goodness of their community. Most of the other norms discussed here would be effective even if they became fully manifest.

As noted earlier, the epistemological comforts of home are something that a person consumes, they give pleasure. They are therefore not directly part of a person's interests. Rather, if one enjoys them, it is in one's interest to be able to enjoy them, to have relevant resources for their provision. The epistemological comforts of home are in a category with chocolate ice cream rather than with money. If your presence, with your hostilities to our local tastes and ways of doing things, is discomforting to me, I have an interest in excluding you. I may have other interests, such as having you as a contact for job opportunities, that trumps my interest in excluding you. If not, however, my excluding you is not sensibly seen as my punishing you but merely as my benefiting myself.

It is sometimes supposed that the costs of shunning or otherwise sanctioning those who deviate from a norm cannot be in the interest of the sanctioner, so that a norm that requires sanctioning for its enforcement cannot be rationally sustained. For some norms, this conclusion may follow. But for norms of difference and exclusion, there may be no costs to some sanctioners. They are not sanctioning per se; rather, they are merely acting in the interests of their comfort in familiarity or whatever and excluding those who are unfamiliar. For whites in Mansfield to shun Griffin was no harder than for them to shun blacks. Both actions fit into their world of the separation of whites and blacks with its apparent advantage to whites, who controlled most of the economic and other opportunities of the community.

Furthermore, the success of a norm of exclusion must typically depend on how widely supported it is. In the American South before the Civil Rights movement, the norm of white supremacy was apparently very widely held.[43] Yet, as soon as blacks mobilized and the laws began to change, many whites joined the cause of racial equality. Were people's views so quickly changed? Probably not. Many of them were people who might not have spoken their true feelings before because the costs of bucking the apparent norm were too great.[44] Even those who were not racially prejudiced therefore may have participated in racial discrimination—because it seemed costly not to do so. The core of those who strongly held the norm of racial prejudice had succeeded in coordinating others behind the norm even when the others did not literally support the norm or even benefit from it. As is generally true of norms of exclusion and difference, southern racism was enforced on the—perhaps large—fringe of those whose identification with the community was weak. The Civil Rights movement finally enabled these people to join blacks to attempt a new coordination on a norm of racial equality.[45] That norm too is enforced against those who do not share it.

Let us anticipate the discussion of chapter 6 to see how this account of norms of difference fits the sudden efflorescence of often violent ethnic conflict in former republics of the Soviet Union. Many commentators attribute this explosion to the end of Soviet suppression of conflicts that, while suppressed, remained latent. This analysis seems to be fundamentally wrong. During the era of Soviet hegemony, the ethnic groups were not in control of opportunities, which were more nearly universalistically open to all independently of their ethnic identification.[46] There was, during that era, almost no call to suppress the conflicts because ethnic identification had little to offer besides the epistemological comforts of home.

A sustained burst of economic growth that made opportunities less a matter of taking or withholding from others and more a matter of individual (not group) opportunism would similarly undermine the power of extremist ethnic groups. Alas, the transition from central control of the economy to market control entailed immediate loss of productivity and earnings, not least because it made a large fraction of the work force (the bureaucrats and others involved in control, both in the government and in firms) irrelevant while only slowly conjuring a new class of entrepreneurs into being. Hence, at the end of the Soviet hegemony over various republics, immediate economic prospects were grim and the quickest way to hold the ground was likely by excluding others, which required group efforts to gain political control.

THE DUEL

The duel as a matter of honor began in Italy, spread to France in the early sixteenth century, and to England later in the century, where duels remained rare until the seventeenth century. It spread to Germany, Poland, and Russia, and was stopped early in Scandinavia, the Netherlands, and Portugal. It was strictly for Christians—Turks, Persians, and Abyssinians thought it ridiculous. The right of the duel was like the right to kill game: It was reserved to the gentry. When Voltaire had the effrontery to challenge the Chevalier de Rohan to a duel, the Chevalier had his servants beat him up.[47]

The duel and the vendetta seem to have similar points: vengeance and, perhaps, the defense of honor. But the explanation of the norm of dueling depends very clearly on its association with a single class, the aristocracy, in a time when aristocrats were slowly being displaced in economic and political importance by the rising bourgeoisie. The duel arose and became a remarkably powerful institution because it "set the gentry class above all others, as possessing a courage and resolution no other could emulate, and a code of conduct none but it could live up to."[48] Contrary to the basic rule of law of Coke that "revenge belongeth to the magistrate," the nobility could take revenge and could virtually stand above the law. In England, killing someone in a duel was tantamount to murder, the penalty for which was capital punishment. But peers could be tried for capital crimes only in the House of Lords, where there was no lack of sympathy for duelists. Giving the Lords exclusive jurisdiction over duels by the peerage gave the peerage exclusive opportunity to resort to duels.

Although seemingly similar to the duel in its focus on vengeance, the vendetta does not have the role of separating one group from others or of excluding other groups. It is potentially universally appealing if it appeals at all. Let us try to make sense of the greater complexity of the duel. At its height, "the duel was one of the most fantastical things in human annals."[49] Sir Francis Bacon, while he was attorney general of England, asserted simply that the blemishes of honor that led to duels were too inconsequential to exact such a price as the risk of murder or death. These blemishes, after all, were merely lies and slurs of kinds that had not motivated Greeks, Romans, and others to such drastic responses.[50] As Adam Smith argued, where the law of honor was revered, it was wholly from this new notion of honor that the injury of the relevant affronts arose. He, too, acknowledged "that formerly those actions and words which we think the greatest affront were little thought of."[51]

It was sometimes recommended that government could best stop dueling by taking over the punishment of the provocations to duel.[52] Bacon supposed these should not be punished at all, unless they reached the level of slander or assault, for which law already existed. Against the complaint that the law provided no remedy for lying, he asserted that this was only right. He denied there is an effect of lies and insults on honor. "Any law-giver, if hee had beene asked the question, would have made Solons answer, *that he had not ordained any punishment for it, because he never imagined the world would have been so fantasticall as to take it so highly.*" If the gentleman's honor was so fragile as to be torn by petty lies and contumely, it was cut from flimsy cloth.[53] To gild the lunacy, the nineteenth-century Polish poet and nationalist Adam Mickiewicz noted, "It is the custom of men of honor, before proceeding to murder, first to exchange greetings."[54]

Rather than punish lying and contumely, Bacon held, government should punish dueling. To do the latter, he proposed to stop the duel by responding to the thing it supposedly responded to: honor. He wished the King to banish duelers from his court and his service "for certaine years." And he proposed that the law punish all the actions that are part of the organization of the duel: appointing a field, making a challenge, delivery of a challenge, accepting or returning a challenge, agreeing to be a second, leaving the country in order to duel, reviving a quarrel contrary to a proclamation by the King.[55]

Although he failed to grasp the urge to duel, characterizing it as "noe better then a sorcery that enchanteth the spirits of young men," Bacon seemed to catch its core in another observation. "Nay I should thinke," he wrote, "that men of birth and quality will leave the practice, when it begins to bee vilified and come so lowe as to Barbers-surgeons and Butchers, and such base mechanicall persons."[56] Had it come so low, with aristocrats called out by any tradesman, the norm would have lost its distinguishing power. Or, alternatively, if Hobbes's injunction that honor be ordained for those who refused to duel and ignominy for those who made the challenge, the practice would have failed.[57]

What was at stake in the duel was maintenance of one's status in the dueling class and, by implication, of most others' exclusion from that class. Dueling over frivolous insults that could not plausibly rank in importance with the risk of killing or dying was at least as effective for this purpose as dueling over grievous assaults. Indeed, the functional account which follows is consistent with a tendency over the years to make the standards for provocation *less* grievous. The more grievous an affront is, the less dueling depends on assertion of status and the more it begins to seem fitted to the actual affront of the moment. It was frivolous duels that would balk non-aristocrats. *Therefore, it was frivolous duels that best served the function of defining aristocrats as a separate class.*

If the dueling norm set boundaries for a group, there is the obvious question how individuals in the group could be motivated to act by it, especially if these motivations reinforced and were reinforced by the role of the duel in excluding others from the aristocratic class. If the duel functioned as a norm of exclusion, it fit the form of functional explanation for such norms above (in "Explaining norms of exclusion"): X is the norm of dueling, F is identification with the class of aristocrats, and G is the class of aristocrats. These fit our functional model:

1. Identification was an effect of the norm. Aristocrats held their status by acting on the norm and non-aristocrats, who could not readily be admitted to the class, also identified the aristocrats by that "ultimate hallmark of gentility" : "the right of gentlemen to kill each other."[58] Even non-aristocrats have often admired the apparent courage and vigor of the dueling class, although many of them might not have been willing to pay the price of membership in that class.
2. Identification as a separate class was beneficial for members of the class of aristocrats. They were rewarded with jobs by the state, in government and in the officer corps of the standing armies that arose after Napoleon's havoc. And they were rewarded with the comforts and joys of their odd community, with its privileges.
3. As with conventions, the successful following of the norm of dueling by many aristocrats raised the costs of not following it, therefore likely increasing its support. Indeed, the norm contributed to its own reinforcement in especially frivolous contexts.

Costs of Not Dueling

One of the first conclusions from the functional account is that, for the individual facing a situation that called for giving or accepting a challenge, the duel was rational, that is to say, *it was in the interests of the dueler.* Against this claim, V. G. Kiernan says the duel "cannot be made to look rational in terms of the individual, but only as an institution from which a *class,* a social order, benefited."[59] Similarly, Warren F.

Schwartz, Keith Baxter, and David Ryan argue that conformity to the code of honor of which the duel was a large part in the pre–Civil-War South of the United States required the imposition of "a moral cost on cheating."[60] At the level of the dueler, it is not clear that Kiernan, Schwartz, and others are right. They assert more than argue the case and, indeed, Kiernan's rich survey of dueling in Europe commends the contrary view that dueling must commonly have been individually rational.

A century after Bacon, Montesquieu wrote of the dilemma potentially faced by a French *gentilhomme* (aristocrat): "If he obeys the laws of honor, he perishes on the scaffold; if those of justice, he is banished forever from the society of men."[61] Bacon had deplored the invocation of "laws" outside the national law, scornfully asking whether the French and Italian manuals on dueling should be incorporated in the laws of England in order to prevent such dilemmas as Montesquieu's *gentilhomme* might face.[62] But Bacon's view did not prevail. Two centuries after him, a duelist in Scotland in 1822 was acquitted of a murder charge. The justification of his acquittal, in the tutored opinion of the celebrated Judge Cockburn, was "the *necessity*, according to the existing law of society, of acting as he did."[63]

The sense of the necessity to abide by a strong social norm might be spelled out in at least two ways. First, it might be something in the range from Sartrean or Nietzschean declaration of self, as it seems to be in the words of many a fictional dueler, to the mere flaunting of personal bravery or the quest for glory.[64] Second, it might be a recognition that one's life must be shattered by failure to live up to the norm and face the risk of dueling. For the second ground of necessity, the failure to take on a duel, either to deliver a challenge when requisite or to accept a challenge, would dearly cost a member of the small caste of the odd, selective society of which the duelers were part.[65] The losses from shunning or merely shaming by that society were serious to those who enjoyed the benefits of living as members of it. As Kiernan remarks, the "penalty for rejecting a challenge was far more severe than any condemnation by the elite of its members' lapses from the morality of parsons."[66] In his apologia before his fatal duel, Alexander Hamilton wrote, "The ability to be in future useful, whether in resisting mischief or effecting good, in those crises of our public affairs which seem likely to happen, would probably be inseparable from a conformity to the prejudice in this particular."[67]

In some contexts the costs of balking at a duel could be quite explicit and even imposed by the state or by other powerful institutions. In the nineteenth-century French army it was virtually compulsory to accept a challenge. In 1900, a Habsburg officer was demoted in rank "for failing to resent an insult." Between 1871 and 1914, when German officers had little other reason for fighting, one who balked at dueling was compelled to resign on a vote of two-thirds majority of his regiment's fellow officers. This position was ratified as executive policy by Chancellor Prince Bernhard von Bülow in 1906. Bülow's statement, possibly an oversight in a time when he was too busy to note what was being said for him, declared that the officer corps could not tolerate in its ranks anyone too cowardly to defend his honor in a duel. In eighteenth-century England, King George II held a similar position.[68]

Costs of Dueling

By comparison, consider the costs of participating in a duel. A writer in the early nineteenth century did experiments using the relatively primitive guns used for duels and found them quite inaccurate at the typical dueling distance. He tallied results of two hundred duels, and estimated that about one in fourteen duelers was killed.[69] Many duels without casualties may not have been registered. In four hundred duels at Leipzig in one year during the 1840s while he was a student there, Max Muller reported only two deaths. In Georges Clemenceau's reputed twenty-two duels, "only one of his opponents seems to have been wounded at all seriously." Hence, the costs of risking loss of life may not have overwhelmed the costs of risking loss of society. If that was true, participating honorably in the duel was merely part of the price of being in the society. Much of the practice of the duel suggests that public reputation and face-saving were centrally important. For example, the seconds at a duel were "delegates of the class to which all concerned belonged, and whose standards of conduct all of them were taking the field to vindicate."[70]

Finally, consider the possibility that dueling was a good for some.[71] It was perhaps a variant of current thrills such as hang-gliding, skiing down mountains that are deadly dangerous to climb, auto racing on public roads, and other reckless joys. For many people, dueling may have been more nearly a consumption good than a means. Therefore, we cannot say it was irrational merely because it failed to further someone's interests. Consuming a vacation in a ski resort also may fail to further someone's interests. But the only reason we are concerned with interests is as means to consumption and to fulfillment of various desires. Those who especially enjoyed dueling and who were good at it may have had a tendency to offer more challenges than others did. They more readily crossed the threshold of acting in their own interests. But then the stakes of interest were drastically raised for one who faced a challenge. Hence, differences in tastes for dueling may have increased the likelihood that participants were rational, contrary to the view of Kiernan noted above.

The Force of the Dueling Norm

Superficially, dueling appears to be a decentralized device for regulating aberrant behavior, such as insulting women or, perhaps more typically, insulting a fellow aristocrat by, for example, calling him a liar or striking him during an argument. Dueling may function rather as an aberrant behavior that signifies and reinforces who is and who is not in the relevant group.[72] An aristocrat would not offer a challenge to a workman who insulted a woman but could use devices of shunning and economic exclusion to exact punishment (or might even resort to violence without the protections of a code of behavior). Nor would an aristocrat be obliged to accept a challenge from a commoner.[73] Moreover, the norms of dueling were themselves enforced by shunning and exclusion. Perhaps that would have been at least as effective for enforcing the norms that dueling regulated, since the usual incentives to violate those norms might seem to be far less compelling than the incentive to avoid a duel.

There is, however, perhaps one important way in which regulation of dueling was especially easy, and this fact might go far to explain its prevalence. Violations of the norms of dueling were on fairly conspicuous public display with well-defined actions that might not be misinterpreted. Early on, seconds were introduced to attest that any dueling fatality was not the product of ambush and murder and to protect against such ambush. This public witness was in keeping with the notion of the aristocrat, who was "noble," that is, noteworthy. "What is implied," Kiernan writes, "is a neurotic sense of being always under observation, by a man's peers and by an alien humankind staring from a distance, ready to jeer or mutiny at any hint of weakness."[74] Hence, there was plausibly less wide divergence of opinion on whether someone violated a dueling norm than on whether someone violated another norm. This characteristic of dueling might also help to explain why duelers who were jointly unsuccessful could commonly shake hands and let their original conflict pass once their duel failed to kill either of them.[75] The greater motive to duel was not to inflict punishment or vengeance but to maintain personal status.

In one context, the role of the functional reinforcement of the dueling norm is elegantly clear. Kiernan notes of the officers in the eighteenth-century Prussian army of Frederick the Great that they were largely aristocratic landowners "with more ancestors than acres," and they depended on their military role for their livelihood. They freely dueled and thereby deterred non-nobles from entering or staying in the officer corps, where they faced the fear of having to duel or being disgraced.[76]

The duel at the center of Ivan Turgenev's *Spring Torrents* displays the social costs and benefits to the individual dueler. Sanin is fond of Miss

Gemma,[77] who is expected to marry the older, wealthier Herr Klueber, and who is insulted by Baron Doenhof. Klueber fails to offer a challenge to Doenhof, thereby losing status and face in this ridiculous community of the parasitic and idle bourgeoisie and emigres, and Sanin offers a challenge. Sanin and Doenhof go through the usual ritual, procuring a doctor who is essentially a specialist at overseeing duels (he has a standard fee for the service) and arranging knowledgeable seconds to keep the duelers to the letter of the code. They meet in an isolated clearing in the woods. Sanin fires and misses (as must have been typical). Now Doenhof could coldly, carefully take aim to kill Sanin for his challenge. But Doenhof fires deliberately into the air, opening himself to another attempt by Sanin. Sanin then can honorably renounce his right to fire again and the duel is over, and Doenhof can finally admit he was churlish to Gemma. Sanin and Doenhof are now both honorably elevated and secured in their status in the community of the frivolous. They have handled the minor dishonor in the best of all possible ways. Of course, Gemma is evidently delighted at Sanin's survival, to Sanin's great pleasure.[78]

In Turgenev's tale, it is only Klueber, with his independent source of status in the world of economic achievement, who might be thought to benefit from violating the norms of dueling for a lady's honor. Even one chance in fourteen of dying to protect his status in Turgenev's unstable resort community was too great a price to pay. Klueber is emblematic of the commercial society that eventually destroyed the incentive to duel for even many aristocrats. With the sweeping success of that society, the norm has virtually died. Similar success, progressively maintained, might finally undercut the appeal of loyalty to divisive groups, such as the ethnic groups of chapter 6.

Once the duel was established as a norm within a group, it could become a major incentive for behavior even for one who thought it a stupid norm, as a doltish American might think it stupid for a society to drive on the left but would nevertheless do so as an individual while in England. Indeed, Bazerov, one of the sons in *Fathers and Sons*, argues theoretically that dueling is absurd but that "from the practical standpoint—well, that's another matter altogether."[79] This subtle observation, distorted by Pavel Petrovich's moralistic retort, is often the sad conclusion one must reach in the face of a convention that is not optimal but that nevertheless governs enough behavior to make it costly to violate it. The church elder Father Zossima in *The Brothers Karamazov* tells of his youthful duel and his realization of its foolishness. But he was unable to break it off, "it was almost impossible to do that, for it was only after I had faced his shot at a distance of twelve paces that my words could have any meaning for him."[80] That is to say, he could have broken off the duel, but only at unacceptable cost in lost status in his group of young military officers. Like Turgenev's Sanin, he could act sensibly only after securing his status by braving at least one shot. This is probably all there is behind the pompously worded and otherwise silly conclusion of Von Koren, the opinionated zoologist in Anton Chekhov's "The Duel," that "it follows that there is a force, if not higher, at any rate stronger, than us and our philosophy."[81] That force is merely the quotidian, often corrosive force of incentives, incentives that in this case are the product of an unfortunate convention—not anything grand or mysterious, not even to a Russian.

Father Zossima notes that "although duels were forbidden and severely punished in those days, they were rather in fashion among the military."[82] Perhaps its being forbidden by the dull, bureaucratic, legalistic government enhanced the appeal of the duel to a group that wished to see itself as distinctly separate and superior. The duel was the aristocrats' nigger or *gueux*, it marked their separateness and distinctiveness by flouting the rest of society for its duller behavior.

If one were choosing whether to enter the society with the dueling norm, one might rightly suppose one's chances of ever having to duel were low and that therefore the odds of dying or being badly hurt were also low. Hence, the cost of joining the society would be very low insofar as joining entailed risks from dueling. At the moment of being challenged or of being in a situation in which one had to challenge, the relative costs would be loss of society versus the risks of the particular duel, the latter no longer discounted by the improbability of getting into a duel. Even then, loss of society might have seemed catastrophic to many aristocrats, who might sooner have risked death than have suffered exclusion.[83]

Collapse of the Dueling Norm

We are familiar with the duel after it had lost its attachment to the aristocracy, after the thesis of Kiernan no longer fits it. As discussed below, by the late nineteenth century, there was too much general hostility to the duel for it to be as compelling as it evidently once was. Moreover, the aristocratic class that the duel had once helped to define had lost much of its definition in the face of radical economic and political changes. Aleksander Pushkin wrote of one of the most frivolous duels, which killed one participant and grievously damaged the life of the other, and then Pushkin died in a duel of his own, as did the younger writer Mikhail Lermontov soon afterwards. Both of Pushkin's duels seem more squalid than honorable. (Indeed, virtually all the duels of major works in Russian literature seem squalid, including duels from Turgenev, Chekhov, and Dostoevsky discussed here and two from Tolstoy.[84]) Alexander Hamilton may have concluded that he could only lose once he was challenged to a duel by Aaron Burr: His career would fail whether he refused or won the duel (as Burr's career did fail despite his winning the duel) and he might die if he lost it. He died perhaps without trying to win and hoping Burr would also not try.[85]

The duel eventually lost its compelling quality when the aristocracy, whose separate status it had served, became weakened, infiltrated, and dissipated.[86] Indeed, as do many norms, the norm of dueling undercut itself by being an implicit source of entree to aristocratic status for men who were, in a standard pun, "not to the manner born." By challenging an established aristocrat and having the challenge taken up, a parvenu could seem to be included in the class of those set off as distinct and separate by the norm of dueling.[87] The nearly total dissolution of the original functional justification of the aristocratic norm came in the United States, where egalitarian and parvenu visions gave virtually every white man status to challenge any other to a duel. The prize of proving one's membership in the class of all white men was not enough to motivate strong attachment to the norm of dueling.

The duel finally died perhaps more by ridicule than by law.[88] It had long survived against the law, but it did not long survive widespread ridicule that ill-fit the honor that dueling was supposed to bring or protect. At last we have realized Bacon's clever insight that the way to defeat the hold of the duel was to dissociate it from honor. Clemenceau, with his laughable record of almost no harm done in twenty-two encounters, could hardly be taken seriously. The Russian and other novelists and playwrights who portrayed squalid duels unworthy of any class cannot have helped the norm.

And, finally, the frivolity of the grounds for many duels cast doubt on the practice. For example, one challenge ensued in France when a husband accused another man of looking at his wife through opera glasses while at the opera, another followed a point of musical criticism, another was fought over a cat, one in England over the question which duelist had more game on his estate, and one in Italy followed a debate over the rival merits of the poets Tasso and Ariosto.[89] The mortally wounded loser of the last of these confessed he had never even read the poet he defended. A late sixteenth-century writer remarked that seconds, to the number of three, four, or more on each side, would join in a duel "*par gayeté de coeur*," from sheer lightheartedness.[90] Prosper Mérimée's fictional duel in "The Etruscan Vase" followed a minor insult when Auguste Saint-Clair, in pain and fury on coming to believe his beloved had an affair with a troglodyte, carelessly rebuffed the man who'd told him of her supposed affair.[91] For equivalent events of greater severity, half the men of New York would be dead of duels in any given year, even at the poor odds of one in fourteen.

Perhaps the apparent aloofness of Frenchmen and the seemingly greater care with which they walk the streets of Paris are the residue of the duel. Bernard de Mandeville noted that refinement of the sense of honor went so far that "barely looking upon a Man was often taken for an Affront."[92] If one dared not glance at another, one must also have suppressed overt humor that might be taken amiss by the slow-witted. Dueling may have flourished less from stupidity than stupidity flourished from dueling. Hence, the society of aristocrats must have been impoverished in many ways by the norm of dueling. The duel was finally gutted when its benefits collapsed and when the function it might once have served, of distinguishing the aristocracy, could no longer be served by it.

Understanding the duel may be especially relevant for understanding ethnic and nationalist identification. The duel serves to demarcate a particular group and to motivate identification with that group in its conflict with other groups. The dueling norm is a norm of honor, as are norms of ethnic purity and nationalism. T. V. Smith argues that "whatever social entity can best foster hostile impulse can most easily appropriate the honor motif. The national state has a peculiar advantage here."[93] That the honor in each of these cases may be determined by interest perhaps sullies it.

The Epistemology of Norms

One way to understand norms might simply be to suppose that, for idiosyncratic or communal epistemological reasons, people in a relevant community just do believe them to be right. In general, however, it is far more interesting to attempt to construct the epistemology that leads to a particular norm. Moreover, much of the time, a critical element will be such strategic considerations as whether certain others are also regulated by a particular norm. It may actually be in my immediate interest to follow a norm even though it would be better for me if the norm had collapsed or had been displaced by a quite different norm. A full account of a particular norm might explain how it arose and why it survives. In the best of circumstances, this could be done comparatively.

Hereward, one of Sir Walter Scott's blustery soldiers, says that to be called a liar is "the same as a blow, and a blow degrades him into a slave and a beast of burden, if endured without retaliation."[94] For him, this is evidently a simple fact that he apprehends directly. That it is stupid beyond measure and that it could not be supposed true outside a peculiar cultural context never occurs to him. But if challenging someone to a duel provoked ridicule, contempt, and horror from everyone in the relevant society, one could not easily sustain Hereward's view, and one could not well sustain the view that dueling brought honor. If dueling brought exclusion from society rather than inclusion in it, dueling could hardly be supported.

In a widely known desert island joke, a Jewish man is cast ashore where he remains for five years. One day, the captain of a passing ship notices two impressive buildings on what is supposed to be an uninhabited desert island. He anchors and goes ashore. There are two beautiful synagogues on the beach, about half a mile apart, but no one is to be seen. The captain and his crew enter one of the synagogues, where they find the lone man. Told that the man built the two synagogues himself, the captain is in awe. "But they're so beautiful. How did you do it?" The man shrugs that, after all, he's been there with nothing else to do for five years. "But why did you build two?" the captain asks. "In this one, I worship," the Jew says. "That one I wouldn't go near." This forlorn castaway is so committed to the norm of supporting his branch of Judaism that he cannot escape the conventions of the society in which he grew up even when shipwrecked alone on a desert island.

Hereward and the Jewish castaway seem incredible. That is their fascination, they are not like anyone we can genuinely say we know. Others are too subject to common sense to have their commitments in such extreme contexts. Yet members of groups with strong norms of exclusion seem often to generate such extreme commitments. How do they do this? At least three processes play a role, the first two of which have been noted already. First, a norm of separation and exclusion may evolve to be increasingly strenuous. As fringe members leave, the harder core becomes more nearly the average. The process of out-migration may be much of the explanation of the increasing extremism of, for example, the Lubavitchers in Brooklyn's Crown Heights.[95]

Second, the test of membership may become more demanding as the most stalwart members perform at a level that casts doubt on the commitments of the less stalwart (as in gang challenges). For example, the dueling norm was subject to the excess discussed earlier, in which one could take offense at trivia, one could risk death or murder for a whim. If the demonstration of personal courage and status of membership in the group was the point of the exercise, then dueling for trivial grounds may have given the most effective demonstration.

The third and final process is that, if separation really works, it constrains the group's epistemology, perhaps disastrously.[96] A group may become ignorant at a level that would be appalling in an individual. We would judge an individual who set out to be that ignorant as stupid and plausibly self-destructive. But members of a group that achieves such self-enforced ignorance need not typically intend for it to do so. It merely produces ignorance as a function of the success of its norm of separation, and that ignorance reinforces the norm. Cults, chiliastic movements, and rigidly fundamentalist sects cause their own ignorance, without which their odd beliefs would not be credible. This is an example of why functional explanation is not inherently subject to the perverse claim that the explained function is somehow good. A clearly self-reinforcing norm can be destructive, both for the affected individuals and, eventually, for the group in which it arises, as in the perverse religious communities at Jonestown and Waco. Functional explanation does not entail a commitment to any of the various brands of functionalism.

The Enforcement of Norms

If norms are to be significant, they must affect behavior, which typically means they must be enforced. How are norms successfully enforced? There are at least two relatively straightforward ways they can be nearly self-enforcing through incentives created by the norms. Group norms are commonly enforceable through the strong incentive they offer to members of the group: the implicit threat of exclusion from the group. This device is not typically available for universalistic norms, although shunning might be effective in some cases, for example, in response to violations of strong parenting or religious norms. Dueling and other norms of exclusion are self-enforcing because they reinforce separation and difference, not because that is necessarily anyone's intention.

A device that seems readily available and attractive for many of the most important universalistic norms (truth-telling, marital fidelity, fair dealing) is directly inherent in the iterated quality of many of the relationships in which these norms have a role. If you and I are to interact repeatedly, my telling you the truth even when it is mildly against my immediate interest to do so may be in my longer-term interest, because it helps secure further valued interaction with you and it contributes to my reputation for honesty.[97] The value of the continued iteration of our interaction may override my momentary prisoner's dilemma interest in defecting from our cooperative relationship. This incentive from hopes for iteration works only in dyadic and very small-number contexts; it typically fails for norms that govern actions on behalf of a large group. Hence, it may work for truth-telling and promise-keeping but not for voting, contributing to large-scale charities, obedience to law, paying taxes without cheating, and many other important but not dyadic concerns.

The norm of serving in the military in time of war may work as a norm of exclusion.[98] One who refuses to serve, even if there is no severe penalty, might still lose substantially from shunning. This would be true, however, only when the general sense of the relevant war is to unite us as a group, merely a whole-nation group. If the war does not motivate many of us, this norm is weakened, as it was during the Vietnam War in the United States, when very many people opposed the war as wrong and many more doubted that it was really their war.

Many universalistic norms typically cannot be motivated by such considerations, however, since they govern relationships that are not ongoing or that are, under some norm, slated for termination. Unlike the norm of truth-telling, the norm of vendetta cannot be maintained through dyadic iteration. But if it also cannot be maintained through exclusion, then it is seemingly less supported by rational constraints than are dyadic universalistic norms or norms of exclusion. Many such norms, however, can be distorted to fit them with interests, so that they then are self-enforcing.[99]

With rapidly rising prosperity, individual hopes for advancement are less tied to group fate. Thus, the hold of the group is likely to be weakened. Oddly, this implies that the introduction of opportunity for great inequality for individuals can break down inequality between groups and can wreck group efforts to achieve for the group.

Functional explanation seems especially apt for interests, that is, for motivating individual actions on behalf of collective benefits, especially when there is the possibility of exclusion of those who fail to abide by the norm. The possibility of exclusion is what makes it possible to motivate contributions to collectively provided goods. For example, toll barriers on some public roads can be used to extract payments enough to cover the cost of amortizing and maintaining the roads. The possibility of exclusion is typically part of the nature of norms of difference. But there is a striking and important difference between the standard resolution of the incentive problem in ordinary collective provision of roads and other goods and in the incentive problem in regulation of behavior through norms of exclusion. In the former, there is a state that can mobilize resources to set up mechanisms to enforce individual contributions to the collective good. In the world of norms there is often no independently empowered enforcement authority—enforcement comes directly from the relevant group members. One might think this could be normatively motivated or even that it must be. Obviously, it could be and probably often is. But it is not necessarily normatively motivated. The members, as described and argued above, may have more mundane incentives to enforce the norm by excluding or shunning those who violate it, or merely by being less responsive and welcoming to them.

Non-dyadic universalistic norms typically do not include devices for exclusion. Individual followers of a norm might shun violators from strictly normative motivations. But this means the norm is not self-enforcing merely through individual incentives. Universalistic norms may therefore require strong inculcation or, alternatively, oversight by the state or other strong enforcement agency, such as a hegemonic religious body. In their incentive structure, they have more in common with ordinary collective goods than with typical norms of difference or they get displaced by or distorted into misfit norms of difference.

Stability and Fragility of Norms

Walter Pater, the nineteenth-century English essayist, held that "nothing that has stirred men deeply can ever altogether lose its meaning for us."[100] Kiernan seems to think this claim applies to the duel. But consider the opposite view, that we may not only no longer feel the force of dead norms, but we may not even understand the force they once had. Perhaps I can still imagine the sensations of anticipation of a duel, but I cannot imagine holding with Sir Walter Scott's Hereward, cited above, that to be called a liar degrades me "into a slave and a beast of burden"—that is preposterous and not motivating, not even comprehensible, to me. Hence, Pater's view seems to be a theorist's idle thought that has not been brought to ground in experience. He could say such a thing because the words could be strung together, not because he was actually moved by experience to recognize that his view was evidently true.

We are left with the question, Why can a norm motivate in one context and be utterly dead in another?

Let us approach an answer by first considering a simple convention rather than a strong norm. Abiding by a norm can pass from being in our interest to being not in our interest, even to being strongly contrary to our interest just as a coordination can tip from one of the possible points of coordination to another. If the latter actually happened, say, for the driving convention, it would be odd for very many people years later to say, "Still, it's wrong to drive on the left, we should go back to driving on the right." People did react that way in the immediate aftermath of the government-sponsored change in the driving convention in Sweden in 1967.[101] Someone who was too slow-witted to change old habits might complain for much longer. But the vast bulk of the population must soon have grown accustomed to the new convention and, if they believed the arguments in favor of the change, they must have considered it morally acceptable. Jane Austen says of Woodhouse, a widowed father whose daughter, who is half his life, wishes to marry, "He began to think it was to be, and that he could not prevent it—a very promising step of the mind on its way to resignation."[102] Many Swedes of 1967 and European aristocrats not very long before may have understood Woodhouse's change of heart, step by step.[103]

Now suppose we have a dueling norm and the state effectively intervenes to stop and to punish duels. The self-interest reinforcement of the norm now fails in general, although one might still expect to confirm one's status if one successfully dueled without punishment. Very soon, there will be no duels for the trivial offenses to honor, perhaps there will even be none for very serious offenses. Shunning might soon take the place of dueling for many offenses, although perhaps not for debates over the relative merits of Tasso and Ariosto, which will simply be reduced to the ordinary insignificance they have outside aristocratic circles. There might therefore still be an effective norm of community and exclusion for the aristocratic class, but not one so dramatic or so effective as the duel. Although it might take frequent and severe punishment of duelers to stop the practice initially, it might soon take only infrequent and less severe punishment to keep it stopped. Soon, decades might pass without a single duel or punishment.

Alternatively—and perhaps this is more nearly what happened to the duel in Europe—the duelist might begin to be more the subject of ridicule than of respect or admiration from others. As with forcible suppression, the duelist might therefore see it as no longer in his interest to duel.

Apart from behavior, what will change in either of these developments? Our knowledge and expectations might also dramatically change. Our children might know that the effective response to an offense is disdain, where we once knew the effective response was a challenge to duel. And, reading an "ought" from an "is," they might come to suppose it is *right* to offer only disdain. While we once thought the right way to confirm our status was by dueling, our children might think the right way is to demonstrate a more perfect air of *je ne sais quoi*. Those who have never been governed by the dueling norm may be fascinated by what Bacon called a "fantasticall" practice. But that is virtually to say that they share none of the motivation of the norm. They share none of it because it gives them no incentive of self-interest.

CONCLUDING REMARKS

Norms in general inhabit the range between conventions and institutionally enforced rules, both of which work because they directly make it the individual's interest to go along. Conventions are spontaneous—the incentive is built into the aggregate practice, as in the driving convention. Institutional enforcement is rather more deliberate and methodical, although it might be capricious, as it is in traffic and criminal law enforcement. Typically, norms are spontaneously maintained and enforced rather than deliberately or organizationally. But they commonly also have the substantial backing of some larger community that, in effect, enforces them. It is this structure that gives norms of exclusion their sometimes remarkable power. They are backed by spontaneous acts that effectively enforce them.

The reasons for the two sides of the enforcement behavior—doing things that have the impact of sanctions and feeling those things as costs when borne—may often require careful deconstruction from what the actors suppose they are doing. But each side may be fully rational in the sense that it is the interest of individuals on that side to act and react in the relevant ways. The stimulus to exclude a violator of the norm may be nothing more substantial or difficult than the discomfort that comes from having a misfit around. And the cost of being excluded may be nothing more than the loss of comfortable relationships. There might also be losses of opportunities, such as economic opportunities of connections for getting jobs or goods, that compound the burden of being excluded.

Norms of exclusion are enforced when there is asymmetric demand for the benefits of membership in a group, as well as, perhaps, for alternatives. These asymmetries define a core and a periphery for a group. Those less dependent on the group may be in a fringe of those likely to be sanctioned or excluded. Of course, membership need not turn on objective characteristics of members other than their degree of commitment to the group. For those in the core, a strong norm of exclusion might never run against their interest—indeed, it might generally contribute to their interest to enforce it. Clearly, a norm that does not constantly run against interests for a committed membership has a better chance of surviving and seeming inviolate than one that constantly runs against interest. Chapter 5 turns to the discussion of norms that do inherently run against interests: large-number universalistic norms. Such norms are inclusive, not exclusive. Both kinds of norms exist because they serve a purpose: to overcome the hurdle of self-interest to act in collectively disadvantageous ways. But norms of exclusion succeed better in principle because they marshal self-interest to oppose self-interest, whereas universalistic norms depend wholly on collective or otherwise normative commitment to overcome self-interest.

CHAPTER FIVE

Universalistic Norms

> It's a cruel convention, not base cupidity, that has plunged
> them into the life they lead.
> —Prosper Mérimée, "Colomba," in Mérimée,
> *Carmen and Other Stories*

NORMS AND INTEREST

Norms of exclusion can evidently be powerful in motivating individuals to act for groups. The logical extreme for groups is the group of all. By definition, this is not a group from which some other group can be excluded. Can a universal norm then motivate individuals in the group of all? Obviously, the answer must be in part that it can. But the answer also seems to be in part that it cannot motivate very forcefully. Universalistic norms, except for those governing essentially dyadic, ongoing relationships such as promise-keeping, truth-telling, and fidelity among close associates, are generally weak. They are not well reinforced by incentives of self-interest.

Consider a standard example. Citizens in democracies are often thought to follow a norm of civic duty that requires voting in elections. Such a norm may play an important role in getting people to vote. It is, as Anthony Downs argues, not in most individuals' interests to vote.[1] Yet many do. Slightly over half of the eligible voters in the United States vote in quadrennial presidential elections. Somewhat higher percentages vote in comparably important elections in most other long-standing democracies. Hence, roughly half to three-fourths of all citizens vote in any given major election. Surely, in those same societies, far larger percentages of individuals tell the truth, keep their promises, and are faithful to close associates at each opportunity to do otherwise. The norm of voting is not a powerful one, although it is seemingly powerful enough to trump self-interest for many people, even if not by very much in most instances, in which the cost of voting is slight. If a quarter or half of all promises were broken, of all statements were false, or of all close relationships were heavily opportunistic, we would not much care about what happened in elections—our world would be too grim for government to do much good.

Why then are any universalistic norms effective at all? An immediate answer is that their followers might be normatively driven, as many voters may be. But normative concerns are not generally overwhelmingly compelling, although they may be for a particular person. Norms of exclusion and norms for dyadic relationships are typically self-reinforcing through incentives of self-interest. How do apparently strong, non-dyadic universalistic norms prevail? Surprisingly often the answer is that, as are norms of exclusion, they are based in groups with the possibility of strong reinforcement that makes following them rational.

Much of the apparent debate between those who think norm-following is necessarily not rational and those who think it is rational is therefore a misconceived debate. For norms of great force in actual social life, norm-following may well be both normatively and rationally motivated. When interest and norm push in the same direction, it may be hard to separate their effects to say which is dominant. But, as argued for such norms as vendetta below, the duel of chapter 4, and many others, the push of self-interest might determine very many features of norms, including their forcefulness and their form or structure. Their structure will be what fits interest, that is to say, what gives interest a strong role. One might wish to say that interest distorts many of the most important norms—but this is an odd way to describe what happens, because there was no pristine norm to be distorted other than in the vision of some norm follower or of some theorist.

ARE NORMS OUTCOME-ORIENTED?

It is commonly supposed that norms are not rational. In part, this is merely an error, as in the supposition that promise-keeping is not rational. As Hume grasped, promise-keeping is thoroughly a matter of self-interest in many contexts, perhaps in almost all contexts in which one would bother to make promises.[2] And in part, the supposition is merely a generalization from some norms that are not heavily self-interested—such as norms of beneficence and of voting in national elections. But in part, it turns on some variant of the claim that, as Jon Elster argues, norms are *not outcome-oriented*.[3] Elster poses this as a defining characteristic of norms. In essence, he supposes that norms are exclusively about classes of actions and not about outcomes. Hence, they are a part of a deontological morality and not of a consequentialist morality, about doing what is right rather than about causing good results.

Some norms apparently are not outcome-oriented. For example, consider the norm of civic duty to vote. This norm typically cannot be outcome-oriented in the sense that in a major election I cannot generally affect the outcome with my vote. Indeed, this norm is of value at all because the individual would not vote if the only consideration were her effect on the outcome of the action. But, as a rule, such definitional moves as Elster's are suspect if they are supposed to apply to the ordinary-language notion they govern. The usual terminology of norms is not exclusively deontological. Indeed, since the very categories of deontological and consequentialist moral theories are a very recent thesis or discovery, it would be odd to find that the language of norms already reflected this thesis while moral theories until recently generally ran the two categories together, as street-level morality still does.[4]

In defining norms to be not outcome-oriented we would be defining many common principles out of the realm of norms. Such a move might be reasonable for certain purposes. But then we would have to be consequential and drop the label "norm" from many of the norms Elster and we discuss. In the treatment of particular norms below, part of the issue will be whether abiding by them could depend heavily on self-interest—which would make them outcome-oriented by implication—or almost exclusively on moral or otherwise extra-rational motivations. On Elster's definitional principle, this is finally a question whether a putative norm really is a norm.

The view that norms are not outcome-oriented raises complex questions. Let us address four of these: whether norms are subject to rational assessment by their potential followers; the status of norms in our larger body of knowledge; the apparent association of norms with *homo sociologicus* and of outcome-oriented actions with *homo economicus*; and the complexity of the notion of outcome-orientation.

The Rational Assessment of Norms

It should be transparently clear that putative norms are commonly subject to rational assessment. For example, a young black may have to decide whether to give up the norm of rap or the cool pose in order to fit into an appealing job or university. Cardinal Richelieu and Francis Bacon decided that the norm of dueling brought more harm than good and they attempted to break it. In the Icelandic sagas, those engaged in vendettas endlessly debate the likely consequences of their various options. They often choose to take vendetta against one family member rather than another because doing so has better auxiliary consequences (see discussion below). When Slobodan Milosevic evidently saw the value to him of his leading Serbian nationalism, he readily abused history to generate extravagant xenophobic claims. Environmentalists, pacifists, and many other universalists attempt to establish new norms that would serve their goals. All of these people plausibly make straightforwardly rational assessments of the effectiveness and value of following particular norms.

Furthermore, the supposition that norm-following is not sensitive to outcomes is belied by the relatively quick passing of many norms that have become dysfunctional. The dueling norm of Europe passed in the lifetime of one of the most foolish duelers: Georges Clemenceau. It passed because it ceased to make sense in the changed world in which aristocrats as a class had lost control of most of society and had little reason to promote group identification. If the norm passed from the relevant group, it must have done so through its failure to motivate some, then still more, and finally virtually all individuals. These individuals must commonly have refused to follow the norm, one of the most fantastic of modern history, because it was not in their interest to do so. As soon as interest might go either way, it was taken into account and allowed to trump the norm when it went the wrong way. While the norm had reigned earlier, interest had been nearly perfectly, brutally congruent with following the norm.

Moreover, there is a large category of pragmatic norms that are obviously outcome-oriented. We could say these are not norms but are merely rules of thumb. For example, our village might follow a set of norms on when to plant, how to cultivate, and when to harvest. We may be lousy agronomists in theory, but we may succeed quite well in practice. Yet our norm-following need not be blind to outcomes. If we genuinely came to believe that other practices would produce better results, we would try them. Of course, we might not be easily persuaded, not least because, lacking experience and teaching in the scientific spirit, we would likely be poor scientists. In part, our norms raise issues of knowledge, as discussed immediately below, and of the complexity of motivations behind norms, as discussed under "Outcome-Orientation."

Norms in Our Knowledge

Much of my knowledge of how to get through life is merely borrowed knowledge: I take it on faith from others around me.[5] A sailor might have no understanding of astrophysics and very little of astronomy but might still navigate very well by the stars, using charts, maps, and navigational equipment that represent knowledge taken on faith. If I am not very good at calculating things on the spot but I want to do well, I might be served well by various norms. For example, I may be lousy at understanding the rationality of promise-keeping with my family and friends or I may be very nearly incapable of figuring out whether keeping *this* promise is beneficial to me. But I might summarize the knowledge of a large part of my society in a norm of promise-keeping. The rise and collapse of norms is merely part of the general effort to gain mastery over our lives.

But the issue for Elster and many others is not whether we can give a rational account of a norm but, rather, whether the individual in the moment of following a norm acts from a concern with outcomes. V. G. Kiernan refers in passing to "the proud indifference [of the dueler] to consequences."[6] Unfortunately, as argued in chapter 4, Kiernan's view seems to be wrong on his own account. Elster's issue may reduce to this question: Is my action blind to consequences if it is not based on a conscious calculation of costs and benefits? The account of the duel in chapter 4 is an attempt to make rational sense of the force of the convention, which affects expectations so heavily that the rationality of the individual faced with a duel is arguably not problematic. For example, even Sir Walter Scott's Hereward, who seems to have been an intuitionist about his norm of honor and dueling, put the matter in terms of the outcome. He could not live if he did not respond properly to an insult.[7] What he evidently meant was that he could not live in his society and that he knew no other. The choice was therefore straightforwardly outcome-oriented.

Yet, some promise-keepers, for example, surely do not think in these terms; they are not motivated by the force of social sanctions for violating the norm or by the expectation of reciprocal gains from fulfilling their own promises. Clearly their motivation is not self-interested even if the norm of promise-keeping serves interests well. That many people have such motivations seems plausible and may not be subject to rational explanation. Even for these people, however, we may still suppose they have many of the norms they do have because these norms, as serving interests, are inculcated by parents, teachers, and other associates from an early age. They may believe they have direct access to true norms through their own intuition, as Hereward evidently thinks he does, but this essentially solipsist belief (it is right because *I* think it is right) merits no respect from others. More likely, perhaps, they may merely believe the truth of some norm without having any sense of why they believe it or they believe it under a command theory of ethics, such as a religious theory or communitarianism, according to which there is no reason that they need beyond belief that they are commanded. Elster's definition restricts the use of the term norm to apply to such people: intuitionist deontologists and followers of various command theories.

Homo Sociologicus, Homo Economicus

These terms are commonly used as though to characterize the duality of the individual as part calculatingly rational, part uncalculatingly sociological.[8] The two are often treated as though they were somehow fundamentally different: The one is the alter ego of the other. Despite such grand but murky claims, it seems that the genuine difference between the two is essentially epistemological in the following sense. I am acting as a *homo economicus* when I act from fairly clear (perhaps wrong) knowledge about cause and effect and I make conscious assessment of costs and benefits of possible actions. I am acting as a *homo sociologicus* when I act from little such knowledge but merely follow my group or society or culture, as when I choose from a habit or a norm without much understanding of its rationale. In the former case, I have knowledge from deduction and from relatively direct measurement or assessment. In the latter, I have knowledge that is borrowed or taken on faith, as noted above.

On this view of the difference, what is economic and what is sociological may change with learning. One might at first suppose that the typical change will be the result of learning that moves us from sociological to economic motivation. But the change may go either way, from economic to sociological or from sociological to economic motivation. For example, there might be perverse learning that leads to greater ignorance and less understanding (the Ayatollahs and many fanatical ethnic leaders attempt to produce such learning and the success of their movements virtually assures it). But there is a more important class of examples. Alfred North Whitehead cleverly noted that civilization advances through the reduction of things that had to be thought through each time to matters of habit. Reduction of things to habit in complex society is often accomplished through the division of labor that lets most of us be radically ignorant of most of the things that matter to us. I once knew how to make a car work in the strong sense of repairing it if necessary. I no longer know that very well. In part the change has been technological, so that the mastery of current cars requires knowledge I never acquired. But in part the change is one of my giving up on doing that kind of thing and losing past knowledge. I am plausibly in the transitional generation between a generation in which very many or maybe even most American men knew how to tinker with cars to get them going again and a generation in which few people know how to do that.

On the learning account, one might think we must become less sociological, more economic over the generations. But increased beneficial learning over time may be offset by Whitehead's reduction of knowledge to habit that may be relatively poorly understood by most people. Note, however, that it would be silly to say that the deliberate, Whiteheadian reduction of the demand for detailed causal knowledge was not an economic effort. I want a computer to do most of its magic in the unseen (and largely ununderstood) background as I "write." I want to ride a bicycle by the seat of my pants without having to work through the physics of it or even to think much at all about it. There are days when I want to walk from my apartment to my office without planning or thinking about the route because I want to have my mind free of that clutter while I ponder what it means to be a *homo sociologicus*.

Finally, because all knowledge is partly on faith, the distinction between *homo economicus* and *homo sociologicus* is murky. All our knowledge—of facts, norms, theories—is both sociological and economic.

Outcome-Orientation

For Elster, "X is a norm" means X is not followed for the sake of the outcomes its following would produce. Here, outcome-orientation is apparently a subjective category. If *my* following of a norm is not outcome-oriented, that norm is not outcome-oriented *for me*. But you may follow the same norm because you think doing so will produce good outcomes for you or someone else. Virtually every significant norm may be backed by such dual motivation. At the subjective level of the individuals involved, every norm (and every other significant category of action or commitment) must be a mess. To load all of this complexity into the definition of the norm is to make the definition itself a relatively full explanation of the phenomena at issue. Contrary to the way of much argument in the social sciences, I think the definitions of our concepts are generally likely to be in contest so long as explanations are not settled. To impose a definition first and then look for explanations is generally backwards. Ostensive definitions of the form "that is a norm, and that, and that," are adequate for many of our categories until we understand them much better than we do.

Return to the agricultural norms of our village above (under "The Rational Assessment of Norms"). One of these norms is to plant three kernels of corn in each hole. I think this is a form of obeisance to the Holy Trinity. You think it is supposed to increase yields, although you have no direct knowledge whether one, two, three, or more kernels per hole would be best. In both cases, we follow the larger society, taking its supposed knowledge on faith. Hence, we both seem to belong in the *homo sociologicus* category, although you are also in the *homo economicus* category in the way you put your *homo sociologicus* knowledge to use. On the outcome-orientation view, our village planting norm is a norm for me but not for you. In a year when there is a shortage of seed corn, we might test our norm—out of necessity—and we might soon change it. We need not have an economic or scientific perspective that drives us to revalue the norm; we might simply stumble on a better practice, as Durkheim thought we merely stumbled into the division of labor. Is our norm then outcome-oriented? Or does it merely cease to be our norm in the face of greater knowledge and experience?

One day, you suggest to me that my association of the Holy Trinity with the number of kernels per hole is silly. You have been reading of the Azande who associate ringworm with bird droppings, because they look similar. Therefore, they conclude both that bird droppings cause ringworm *and* that they cure it. My association is just as silly. Or you point out to me that historical records show that our forebears planted three kernels per hole long before the Holy Trinity was introduced to our part of the world. Your arguments might seem immediately compelling to an outsider not committed to my belief. But I might have no difficulty continuing to believe that we should use three kernels because it is the will of our trinitarian god. What might eventually affect my beliefs would be the slow change in the beliefs of others in my community, especially a change toward some other number of kernels for reasons of productivity. I might then forget about the Trinity at planting time, but I might use a different rubric of justification that was also religious rather than outcome-oriented.

We are forced to an odd conclusion. *That my norm is not outcome-oriented is more a function of me than of the norm*—I attribute almost everything to the will of god. People like you, who question such beliefs and therefore undercut our useful norms, are a royal pain in such communities as ours. In any case, if a norm cannot be outcome-oriented, then norm is a poor category for most social science because the norm is in the eye of the norm-holder.

STRONG UNIVERSALISTIC NORMS

Consider several striking norms that govern sometimes extreme behavior, norms that might superficially seem irrational or extra-rational. Three pairs of norms highlight the issues. One norm in each pair is a sub-community norm and one is a universalistic or seemingly universalistic norm within its society. The real histories of these norms in any actual case are likely to be much messier than what I will describe, so that there may be an air of ideal types about the norms. The communal norms are specific norms of difference such as exclusionary labeling, dueling, and Jewish guilt; the universalistic norms are truth-telling and honor, the vendetta, and Catholic guilt. I have already discussed the labeling and dueling norms in chapter 4, and here I will compare honor and the vendetta to them, respectively. Then I will compare Jewish and Catholic guilt and, finally, I will look at a similar pair of what seem to be norms: the norm of *omertà* that supports the order of the Mafia against the larger society and the norm of law-abidingness that supports the order of the state.

There might be didactic value in choosing minor norms that are less fraught with the complexities of important social norms. But there is also didactic value in focusing discussion on these very important norms that seem to underlie the very possibilities of social order in modern societies. In any case, the first norm in each paired comparison is of special interest to the analysis of group identification. Division into subgroup and universalistic norms focuses on the alternative forms that control of individual deviance takes when the deviance is from universal principles and when it is from subgroup identification. It seems to be true that norms at the group level, norms that are adversarial, have stronger support from natural sources for enforcement, essentially, from incentives of self-interest. It further seems that even universalistic norms depend on such sources of enforcement if they are to be strong norms. That is to say, with perhaps rare exceptions, such as the Catholic guilt discussed below, if universalistic values are to be supported by norms, these norms must be distorted, group-enforced versions of those values.

Honor

Norms of honor that are not specific to a particular group may be commonplace, although they may more typically be tied to groups or they may have force only in relatively small, coherent communities, such as tribes and clans or, in larger societies, in such subcommunities as a military officer corps or an aristocracy. They seem to work especially well in smaller societies. T. V. Smith asserts that "the more generalized the ideal. . . , the less emotionally poignant and perhaps the less practically effective it is."[9] For Smith this may have been merely a summary of apparent facts, but the association seems likely to follow for sociological reasons. In small groups, norms of honor commonly have the appeal of norms of difference and even exclusion, and therefore they benefit from the self-interest reinforcement of such norms. The norms of the duel, as discussed in chapter 4, and the vendetta, as discussed below, are generally seen as norms of honor, and the norms of rap and the cool pose (chap. 4) are plausibly seen as norms of honor.

Seemingly universalistic norms of honor go berserk in Verdi's opera, *Ernani*.[10] Plots of great works of literature can often be summarized in a sentence or two. Opera often does not work that way. Ernani is a bandit in love with Elvira, niece of Don Ruy Gomez de Silva, who intends to marry her himself. Ernani enters Silva's home in disguise and is welcomed, so that when he reveals his identity, Silva is then bound by his code of hospitality to treat him as a guest, even to the point of protecting him from the King who wishes to capture him. After the King absconds with Elvira, Silva invites Ernani to duel outside. Ernani declines because it would be dishonorable to fight such an old man. He offers his life in trust to Silva while they go together to retrieve Elvira. He swears that he will kill himself at any time Silva signals to him by blowing on a hunting horn that Ernani gives him. (Ernani does this not merely on a whim but in order to let Silva off the demands of his own honor to duel the rascal.) Silva later offers to forgive the obligation to die on demand if Ernani will give him his winning lot in a drawing to determine who should kill the King. Ernani declines the dishonor. When the conspirators to kill the King are captured and the nobles among them are to be executed, Ernani declares that he is a noble, the son of a Duke who, he thinks, the King has murdered. It would be dishonorable to live by subterfuge, and the King agrees to have him executed with the others. Elvira pleads with the King for Ernani's life and the King, Charles V, recalls the glory of his namesake, Charlemagne, and relents, offering Elvira, whom he was going to marry, to Ernani. On their wedding day, Silva blows Ernani's hunting horn and, after forlornly pleading for enough mercy at least to enjoy his wedding night (was that honor?), Ernani kills himself as promised.

It is difficult to see how Ernani's action in his moment of suicide can make sense as a matter of self-interest. In his death, Ernani is not a dueler facing a *risk* of death for honor and for continuance in his society. He voluntarily *kills himself* for honor. Whatever loss of society he might suffer for repudiating Silva's demand for his death, it could not have outweighed certain death—after all, he has already been living as an outcast bandit. Many people regularly face slight to large risks of great harm and death in order merely to make a living or to enjoy a sport. None of them need ever be attracted to suicide in order to accept such risks. Ernani almost instantly accepts his doom when asked to do so. He seems to be motivated by a normative concern, not by interest.

Smith argued that "honor is an open acknowledgment of external demand but an acknowledgment which through pride has become enthroned in the very citadel of the self."[11] While this need not have been true for the prevalence of compliance with the dueling norm, it might seem to be true for Ernani and Silva in much of their behavior. Oddly, however, it may not be true that Ernani's norms were social or, in Smith's words, "of external demand." His two most striking moments of honor are in his suicide and in his insisting on his right to execution by the very King he wanted to assassinate for his wrongs. Neither of these can have been common enough situations to give force to a generally accepted norm. Ernani's commitments in these moments are the commitments of someone acting from intuition or invention, not from a clear, prior code. The only norm he has is the fairly vague norm of honor, whose entailments he thinks up as needed. Silva's most striking action is his protection of Ernani when Ernani is, even under subterfuge, his guest. He goes so far as *to let the King leave his home with his beloved Elvira* rather than with his hunted guest Ernani. Seat-of-the-pants intuitions about honor might have led him to such an action, but no genuine code could have.

The actions of Ernani and Silva therefore seem like perversions of the norm of honor. (Some of them are also perversions of a standard part of codes of Latin honor that would not permit such gross abuse of Elvira in the name of honor.) Nevertheless, their motivation seems overwhelmingly normative. These men are deontological intuitionists with badly flawed powers of intuition. *Ernani* suggests an odd conclusion. A code of honor or other normative code that is not articulate but, rather, leaves its content to seat-of-the-pants intuition is likely to be perverse, even though it might be clearly normative. A code that is articulate, with fairly explicit requirements on what to do when, is likely to be the construction of a society or sub-society. But then it is unlikely to provoke unambiguously normative commitments, because *there will typically be substantial social incentives at work to make it the interest of the followers of the code to abide by it.* It is only the corrupt code that will be a norm if norms are required not to be outcome-oriented.

Incidentally, Verdi seems to have followed his own code of honor in composing *Ernani*. First, he salvaged the romantic silliness with wonderful music. And second, while Wagner let Tristan take a whole hour to die, Ernani manages death, as Eduard Hanslick noted, "in a few modest bars."[12]

Vendetta

The vendetta is a norm of honor that might seem to be a generalized version of the duel. It is not tied to a particular class or group but may motivate people in varied status orders in a particular society. Vendetta is often described as a way of bringing order into a world without adequate law, as in Corsica and medieval Iceland.[13] It is "the vengeance of dead men."[14] Indeed, in the Corsica of the della Rebbia and the Barricini families, as discussed below, gaining control of the supposed institutions of law is merely one of the ways of gaining the upper hand in an ongoing family feud, because the local law is itself lawless. Vendetta may therefore bring some order to the anarchy. To this extent, then, the vendetta norm might seem to be a universalistic norm that works for the good of the larger society and not merely to the advantage, when it is invoked, of the person or family pursuing a vendetta.

The vendetta norm seems typically to arise in a society in which there is at best weak state enforcement. Vendetta then produces a collective benefit: enforcement of order. That enforcement could work to the advantage of virtually everyone in a society. The duel similarly produced a collective benefit (the demonstration of the special quality of the aristocracy), but the collective benefit was restricted to a small part of the society. Indeed, this benefit derived from the exclusion of other groups from the society and from the privileges of the aristocracy. As a substitute for the state, vendetta regulates relations between individuals. Although it may work within a class, it commonly does not work for one class against others, but only for individuals within that class against each other.[15]

How good a regulator is vendetta? The anthropologist Max Gluckman wrote of "the peace in the feud," by which he meant the relative success of the anarchic system of feud in maintaining peace. It does so, he supposed, because people tend to have cross-cutting relationships: We are enemies on one matter and allies on another. Among the Nuer of Africa, for example, a man may not marry a woman who is his close relative. That means he must be friendly enough with others for them to give him a wife. Gluckman noted that some African peoples say of groups other than their own: "They are our enemies; we marry them."[16] Gluckman therefore doubted the common view that feud invites incessant conflict.[17]

Against Gluckman's vision of vendetta in anarchic society, it is hard to read the Icelandic sagas, discussed below, without a dreadful sense of frequent, regularized killing—the peace of the feud is founded on pervasive violence and death. More nearly contemporary visions of life under the vendetta in Corsica, Montenegro, and Albania are also not appealing.[18] Moreover, the vendetta norm is typically directed onto groups, such as families, households, clans, or local communities, which severely distort the norm into a norm of exclusion for the protection of the relevant group's *interests* against the interests of others. The defense of my family, right or wrong, obtrudes on the collective interest in a just regulation of conflict through vendetta against wrongdoers. The vendetta as actually practiced tends toward fixed feud unmoored from an initial justification.

Contrary to the vision of vendetta as regulating individual relations, the vendetta typically works between families, clans, tribes, or other groups. In essence, vendetta turns into feuds. The reasons for this are essentially two, which are familiar from earlier discussions, such as in chapters 3 and 4. First, groups are apt to have better information about their members' actions than about the actions of people in other groups. Second, groups are apt to have fairly straightforward reasons for imposing order on their own members if they are to be held responsible for their fellow members' actions.

The result of the working of these two factors is a subtle mix of individual and collective responsibility. In my dealings with anyone in your group, I may take your entire group as responsible. In your dealings within your group, you take individuals as responsible. In actual fact, your entire group might be responsible for some of the actions of its members, as, for example, all the eligible males in a family might join in the plot to take bloody vengeance on another family. But I might treat all of you as responsible even if some of you did not participate in the plot or actions, perhaps even if one of you was away from our community at the time. Some of you may have only vicarious liability. There is, again, often a good reason to hold a group collectively responsible. The group, partly for epistemological reasons and partly for reasons of relations of interest, may be in a position to force a miscreant individual to change behavior.[19]

Unfortunately, as soon as two groups confront each other, they are apt to increase their prospects of mutual hostility. They fall prey to the incentive and epistemological structures of norms of exclusion. Because I am in my clan, depend on its members' good behavior toward others, and depend on their defense of me, I become even more narrowly constrained by my group's knowledge.

Moreover, because interest is in play when there is a norm of vendetta, that norm may become available for use and manipulation. The rules for vendetta can be used to legitimate political and personal actions that are not otherwise legitimate.[20]

Consider in some detail the vendetta relationship in Prosper Mérimée's "Colomba," set in nineteenth-century Corsica. Colomba manages to get her brother, Orso, who has largely left his Corsican community, to carry out the della Rebbia family vendetta against the Barricini family who murdered their father. Colomba would surely have shamed Orso and she might even have shunned him if he had not carried it out. Colomba is seemingly motivated by the vendetta norm, while Orso is motivated by Colomba. Indeed, Colomba leaves the community soon after the vendetta to accompany her brother and his English bride, yet, by chance, she continues the vendetta against the infirm old man who was originally responsible for her father's murder and whose sons were killed by Orso. She tells the old man to stop complaining at the murder of his sons because, unlike her when her father was murdered, he has not long to live with his suffering.[21] Her action in that moment is among the most chilling in literature. It is chilling just because it is evidently universalized, abstracted vendetta, hatred pure and simple, on the part of someone who has seemingly become a charming and delightful person, someone who has actually left the culture in which the vendetta made any sense.

Orso's English friend, Miss Nevil, is appalled at the ugliness and stupidity of the values of these people. Orso says, in the epigraph for this chapter, that the Corsican obeisance to the vendetta norm is not a matter of stupidity but of a cruel convention.[22] A Hobbesian would move one step further back to say it is a lack of adequate government that permits their cruel convention to have its force.

Vendetta often has in common with the duel, first, that, as Orso says, "people never murder one another unless a challenge has been issued in proper form."[23] It is an oddly civilized way to handle the brutality of revenge and murder. And second, failing to meet the vendetta norm might lead to loss of society, as failing to meet the dueling norm led to loss of society among the aristocracy of much of Europe until roughly the end of the nineteenth century or a bit later. To give the *rimbecco* was, in Orso's time, the worst insult one could offer a Corsican. The insult is merely to accuse some man of not taking his revenge.[24] There might also be condemnation for failure to adhere to the civilized niceties of letting the vendetta be known in advance in "proper form." But this is a minor part of the norm. The important issue is why the norm of vendetta would be compelling at all, why the *rimbecco* could be a mortal insult.

In part the answer is probably merely that people just do feel revenge toward those who harm them. The urge for punishment that often corrupts debates over law and order in modern societies is a real and felt urge. It seems to lie behind ancient views that even inanimate objects must be punished for harming people, a view that children often seem to share from their earliest ages. But the urge for vengeance that ate at Colomba vastly surpasses anything that ever afflicts most people in many modern societies. Clearly, Colomba's urge was the product of social context. Was it merely the product of social *ambiance and learning*? Or was her social context such as to give her strong *incentive* to seek vengeance? At least in part, it must have been mere ambiance, whose effect on Colomba and her peers might be causally understood with a relevant psychological theory.

Consider, however, the force of interest in Colomba's urge. In her relatively small community, families fought families for familial advantage. The vendetta that Colomba sought was against the family that she believed had murdered her father and that had been in conflict with her family for generations. If one were to assess who was most responsible for her father's murder, one would likely pick the patriarch of the Barricini family. But it was the sons of that family who could actually bring harm to Colomba's family and it was the sons whom she wanted destroyed. In successfully destroying them, she secured the safety of her own family's future. Had she then remained in Corsica and had she married and had children, their safety would have been increased by the elimination of the male line of the Barricini family.

The Capulets and the Montagues, the Hatfields and the McCoys, the della Rebbias and the Barricinis, the feuds of the Icelandic sagas, and other vendettas of history and literature typically involve the interests of two groups in conflict, often in conflict over limited local resources and offices. Hence, they are similar to ethnic and other groups that exclude each other and that conflict over resources. Vendetta often becomes serial warfare between two hostile families. Mérimée elegantly frames his tale of Corsican vendetta by having Miss Nevil's father be charmed by Orso, with the charm increasing as the retired English cavalry officer learns more about his past engagements on the battlefield against Orso's father and then Orso himself in two of Napoleon's battles with the English. Their former hostility makes them friends. But then they had no personal conflict over territories that brought the government of England into war against Napoleon.

Mérimée comments that "one is murdered by one's enemies; but the reason one has enemies is often very hard to ascertain."[25] Oddly, a della Rebbia and a Barricini while abroad became close friends when they joined in defense against a slur on their Corsican roots. Back in Corsica, they drifted apart and fell back into mortal enmity. They followed the opposite path of Colonel Nevil and Orso, former enemies who came together while no longer impersonally at war.

Why did the two Corsican families become enemies? This is probably not as interesting a question as that of how their enmity was maintained and what course it took. Once they were coordinated on enmity by some more-or-less random event, they were likely to continue in the convention of enmity because neither could trust the other to write off past behavior in their culture of the vendetta. The della Rebbia and Barricini families found themselves on opposite sides in greater national politics and therefore on opposite sides in local politics, in which the conflict over resources and powers was acute in their relatively impoverished subsistence society. Hence, they frequently found new causes for hostility and new reasons for preemptive murder to protect their interests.

On its face, the vendetta appears to be more universalistic than the duel. In general, the vendetta may in fact produce a general benefit of broader social order, but only as a consequence of the protection of group interests. Hence, its force is not from a universalistic norm, but from a norm of exclusion. Its prevalence merely reflects that kinship can be a dividing line for group difference, as religion, language, and race can be. The latter are all typically divisions that define very large groups, while kinship, even in the elaborate kinship systems of anthropological societies, typically defines small groups.

Why does vendetta finally work most forcefully—and perhaps therefore primarily—at the small-group level? Consider three factors. First, it is at that level that specific concern with particular possibilities of vengeance against oneself arise. Hence, it is at that level that preemption becomes a strong incentive. The Thjostarssons wanted Sam to kill Hrafnkel, not merely to torture him, because merely torturing him let him live to seek vengeance, as he did seven years later.[26]

Second, it is also at that level that the individual can see specific gains from a particular act of vengeance. Gudrun ranked the men against whom she wanted vengeance according to her degree of hostility to them more generally, not according to any assessment of their variable responsibility for killing her husband.[27] When the Njalssons wished to kill Thrain for a minor offense, their father counseled that they first should provoke insults that would justify lethal reprisal.[28] In her urges, Colomba coupled her desire to get vengeance with her future interest in seeing the elimination of the Barricini threat.

Third, once a vendetta is underway, it also gets reinforced by constrained epistemology. Hostility leads to or exacerbates limited human contact between the groups, hence to greater ignorance and greater suspicion.

Unfortunately, an actual reprisal may tend to be at a higher level than the original harm done, at least in the eyes of the initial miscreant. In a similar fashion, reprisal for the vengeance may go to a still higher level, at least in the eyes of the first avenger. Hence, an initial act of vengeance may tend to escalate, thereby creating an enduring family or other group feud.[29] In *Njáls saga*, a woman's objection to where she was seated at a feast led to the annihilation of the two factions.[30]

William Ian Miller reports a brilliant resolution of the problem of divergent valuations that underlie the potential for escalation. When a Norwegian merchant cut off the hand of Skæring, an Icelander, Gudmund, Skæring's kinsman, demanded a payment of thirty hundreds to settle the offense and ward off vendetta. The Norwegians balked at what they considered the high price of a middling Icelandic hand. After further failed bargaining, Gudmund then said he would pay Skæring the thirty hundreds, but then "I shall choose one man from amongst you who seems to me of equivalent standing with Skæring and chop off his hand. You may then compensate that man's hand as cheaply as you wish." Evidently the Norwegians then understood the value of a hand as generally that of one of their own hands, which they valued highly, and they paid the thirty hundreds.[31] In this showdown, Gudmund found a way of overcoming the normal epistemological bias of one group in conflict with another. Gudmund forced the Norwegians to frame the issue on nearly abstract, equal terms, treating the Icelander as like themselves.

None of the reinforcements in these four classes would play such strong roles if vendetta were strictly universalistically directed at particular offenses. Indeed, it is these factors that lead vendetta onto the path of enduring feud, turning it into a norm of exclusion. Self-interest and skewed epistemology finally determine the possible or workable content of the norm of vendetta. If this is true, then, contrary to Gluckman's view of the peace of the feud, we *should expect to see high levels of violence* in a society regulated by vendetta. In such a society, the interest in suppressing others and, therefore, the interest in suppressing them irrevocably is very strong. Sam was too dumb to see his interest in killing Hrafnkel. All Barricinis might want all della Rebbia men dead, and vice versa (the della Rebbias succeeded). All these people might have been much better off with a system of law that could constrain all. Their societies, with their peculiar suborders, were not as desperate as the state of nature in Hobbes's vision, but they were mean and murderous societies.

Incidentally, the Icelandic feuds may have been more suited to maintaining general order than were the Corsican feuds. In medieval Iceland, a vendetta could be terminated by the refusal of relevant others to help. This was an important constraint in a world in which the targets of a vendetta were likely to be surrounded by family to join them in their defense, so that an avenger also needed assistance to carry out a vendetta. In the individualistic context of Corsica, where murders were commonly carried out in ambushes with no extras on hand, support of relatives was not a necessary condition for vendetta. Since responsibility was collective, those who might be held vicariously liable for a vendetta had good reason not to join it if they were not convinced of its reasonableness. Sam sought support from the Thjostarssons to help him kill Hrafnkel after the latter killed Sam's brother in long-delayed vengeance. They, recalling their plea seven years earlier that Sam kill Hrafnkel rather than merely torture him, declined.[32]

A system of vendetta that requires mobilization of large numbers to carry out vengeance might be more stable and less bloody than a system that reduces acts of vengeance to the level of the most rabidly committed avenger. While it worked, the Icelandic system may have done a better job of elevating the role of interest, especially to tying individual to collective interests. It might also, however, have been more readily subject to the kind of broader political mobilization that brought the Icelandic civilization down in bloody civil war in the thirteenth century.

Catholic and Jewish Guilt

Feelings of guilt seem to play an enormous role in ordinary life. At first thought, one might suppose guilt is not a norm but is merely a motivation for abiding by particular norms. But the propensity to feel guilt seems itself to be highly variable, across both cultures and individuals. It is not merely variable correlatively with the norms that spark it. It is variable in its own right independently of the ranges of actions it motivates. We may plausibly see the generation of guilt feelings as the product of a norm of guilt. That norm must be created, instilled, and likely maintained by enforcement if it is to play a significant role. Then it may function to motivate behavior under various norms that are not self-enforcing and that require feelings of guilt or other incentives external to the norms themselves for their enforcement.

Ideal-typically, guilt may take two forms: group-specific and universalistic. While there may be no clear instances of real norms of guilt that coincide with these ideal types, as the driving convention coincides with an ideal type of the pure coordination convention, Jewish guilt and Catholic guilt have modal characteristics of group-specific and universalistic norms. The group-specific norm of guilt has the indirect effect of strongly reinforcing group identification. It therefore functions as a norm of difference or separation. At the risk of caricature, I will briefly characterize these two quite different norms of guilt.

Catholic guilt is, ideal-typically, between the individual and god or the priest. Anatole France, in *Le Livre de mon ami* (My Friend's Book), presents the problem of Catholic guilt in its most abstract, ideal-typical form.[33] The ten-year-old child Pierre, who is evidently France himself, faces a grim difficulty. He must go to confessional with his school chaplain every week—but he has nothing to confess. There is a book of sins for him to consult, but it is no help—it tells of sins he cannot even understand. The point of confession is to humiliate him for his sins, but he is humiliated that he has nothing to confess. Soon he has an inspiration: to abuse the cap of his schoolmate, Fontanet. Thereafter, with a bit of originality in his abuses from week to week, he has a deliberate sin to confess. All of this is evidently played out solely in the universalistic context of dealing with an official confessor, a representative of god. Pierre does not work out his problem in discussions with schoolmates or family.

Jewish guilt is managed without a confessor or formal representative of god. It is handled spontaneously by members of the community, especially members of the family. The most important single manager of a person's guilt is often that person's mother. But there are others who also take part in enforcement. Traditionally, Jewish guilt was bifurcated into focus on different matters for males and females. Boys were held accountable to the community, and their success in various occupations was in the interest of the community.[34] (This was a tough and perhaps impossible demand—one could never do enough for the community, especially a community in the Diaspora.) Girls were held responsible for maintaining family commitments and values. Today, in reaction to their feminist views, Jewish girls in some communities are burdened with a double norm: They are held accountable to the community and responsible for the family.

In the norm of Catholic guilt, insofar as it is universalistic, the Catholic's feeling of guilt is backed by present or childhood belief in punishment after death. The norm is made quasi-dyadic, between god and the individual, so that it can be quite strong despite its being universalistic. Even for a lapsed Catholic who does not really believe in punishment after death, the childhood belief might still motivate strong feelings. In the norm of Jewish guilt, individuals are punished or called to account in their own lifetimes, more or less immediately, for their transgressions. The sanctioners carry out their task with the backing of the implicit norm of exclusion that governs the community.

GROUNDS FOR GUILT

To say that one is guilty of a crime is generally to say that one caused some result that one should not have caused. To say in moral life that one is guilty of an immorality is to say either that one caused a bad result or that one broke a moral rule. One can analogously be guilty of merely breaking a legal rule without causing a bad result, as is particularly common in the civil law, especially in stochastic or probabilistic contexts. For example, in traffic law I can be guilty of speeding or of failing to stop at a stop sign even though I have caused no harm. (In some jurisdictions, the arresting officer must assert not only that I was, for example, speeding but that I was thereby putting others at increased risk of harm.)

There may be an important psychological difference between these two forms of guilt. If I am guilty of causing a harm, I may tend to think I was wrong even if I had no reason to think my actions wrong in advance of seeing the harm they cause. For example, I may think I am guilty not so much for my specific actions at the time but for my lack of preparation for that moment. If I am guilty of breaking a rule, I might readily assume my own guilt if I break the rule despite knowing it and knowing that my actions break it. Of course, I might think there are mitigating circumstances, such as conflict with another rule in the context of my actions. But if I break the rule out of ignorance or miscalculation, I am likely to feel little guilt, or perhaps a confused sense of guilt.

To moral theorists, this might sound like the beginning of a debate about the relative force of consequentialist (result-based) and deontological (rule-based) moral theories. But my purpose here is to explore the psychology of guilt and to try to understand its functioning as a norm for regulating social interaction. A central issue is the sometime mismatch between guilt assignments or feelings of guilt and causal responsibilities, or between guilt and deontological responsibilities. I am concerned with what one might call the reasonableness of guilt, both as felt by someone and as charged against another. The function of a successful norm is to make some reasonable pattern of behavior or the accomplishment of some reasonable kind of outcome happen. A norm of feeling guilty should help to induce better behavior in contexts in which guilt is reasonable. But a norm may go beyond the reasonable, it may induce unreasonable patterns of behavior.

EARLY TRAINING IN GUILT

Cultures teach guilt in two ways: intentionally and as a by-product of various practices and other values. Two distinctive cultures with strong norms of guilt are the Italian and Hispanic Catholic community and the Jewish community. Both Catholic and Jewish guilt often regulate behavior in good ways but both also can go far awry. Catholic guilt is typically deliberately instilled. In principle it seems likely that it would be hard to teach a universalistic norm about when to feel guilty if the grounds for guilt must be identified by the guilty rather than by a norm-enforcing community that gives quick feedback. Yet, to a substantial degree, that is how the ideal type of Catholic guilt is handled. When it is not reinforced by the confessional, one might expect it to fade or be transmuted into the parent-child form that Jewish guilt takes.

Jewish guilt appears often to be merely a by-product, although there may also be some masterful teachers. Guilt is often the by-product of seemingly or *prima facie* very good practices and values. Jewish cultivation of strong support for family members leads implicitly to strong expectations of reciprocal support and of censure for failure of support. But, at the extreme, the support syndrome may become almost self-reflexive: One must support the supportive structure or relationship. To seek a moment of privacy, as in the example below, or to hold part of one's life private might be seen as an affront to the support syndrome. Privacy or separateness, something the individual thinks of as good, then is criticized, and one feels guilty for *wanting* to do wrong, for intentional, not merely accidental wrongdoing. Jewish parents need not set out to use and cultivate feelings of guilt to get compliance with certain standards from their child, as Catholic parents, clerics, or teachers might readily do. But their actual ways of dealing with their child might nevertheless instill a strong sense of guilt.

Some cultures have relatively weak norms of guilt. For example, my own largely Anglo-Saxon, Irish, Huguenot, a-religious, migrant culture made little use of guilt. (Some might take that as evidence that mine was no culture at all.) In some now forgotten context over lunch with several colleagues from diverse disciplines, I said I didn't suffer much from guilt. An Irish Catholic stated her enthusiastic support for my "attitude" and then long discussions ensued on different cultural backgrounds. Later that day a Jewish colleague said, "Maybe you don't suffer guilt because you never do anything wrong." I laughed as though she was joking, as though this was merely Jewish guilt run amok, attributing both her burden of guilt feelings and my lack of such feelings to correct assessments of our objective guilt.

But she wasn't joking. Perhaps she is right in a peculiar way. Norms of wrongdoing are themselves socially defined. Perhaps what Jewish and Catholic cultures do is define many relatively ordinary and even unavoidable behaviors as wrong or define many standards for behavior that mortals cannot meet or, in their interest, should not meet. For an extreme example, perhaps very extreme, a Jewish colleague spoke of her sister who, as a child, sought privacy in her room behind closed doors. This was an offense to the child's mother, who clearly thought it a wrong. Yet in some degree it must have seemed to the young girl to be a good thing to do. At the very least it was good for her. It would be hard to find a more obvious generator of confused feelings of guilt than being told what one considered to be a good thing to do was in fact a wrong. The chief lesson to be learned from such an encounter is that one cannot successfully assess one's own guilt because one cannot assess what outcomes it is wrong to cause or what behaviors are wrong. The child might develop a sense of inadequacy and of generalized guilt rather than a causal sense of responsibility.

Strong concern with guilt may lead one to be almost constantly on the alert for one's own possible missteps, so that anticipated guilt, or the potential for eventual guilt, regulates and motivates action. Generalized guilt that is not moored in the perceived wrongness of particular actions cannot be used to motivate moral action. When guilt is too general, even invoked about things that are seemingly right, it becomes free of anchor, out of control. Or it becomes associated with the wrong objects, such as the parent who blames rather than the action for which the child is blamed. Thereafter, the parent's presence may provoke feelings of guilt without any action by the child or by the parent. Great concern with generalized guilt leads not to successful regulation of behavior but to constant anticipation of blame.

The Calvinist doctrine of preterition (that some are passed over for salvation before they are born while others are selected) implies that there is nothing about a particular individual that earns salvation. It is only the "grace" of god that turns the trick. Nothing the individual does matters. It seems to follow that salvation and morality are logically and causally unrelated. The doctrine of preterition is perhaps the iciest response to the notion of original sin, which is one of the stupidest of collective ideas. If original sin, why not racism and any other kind of prejudgment? Because it is not grounded in anything an individual does or could do, original sin cannot be rationally motivating for many Christians who assert it. It is like preterition, it is an abstract, intellectual matter, logically and causally unrelated to action and morality. But, grimly, it may still motivate feelings of guilt, which must be generalized guilt.

It is remarkable that such religious beliefs are moralized at all, that they can be a source of guilt. Plausibly, they gain their power by misguided association with genuine problems of action. And perhaps it is readily possible for them to survive such misguided association only if they are pushed onto people at very young ages, as G.E.M. Anscombe recommends for certain particularly implausible religious beliefs.[35] A young child might fail to notice the illogic of the putative connection between, say, original sin and personal grounds for guilt.

Punishment may follow from mere conflict of interests, as when a child cries and disturbs or embarrasses a parent. Here, again, feelings of guilt might be misplaced. But a child might not feel guilty for such an infraction and might treat the punishment for what it is, as powerful parent versus child in a conflict of interests. Perhaps the capacity to do that is affected by how much the child is normally freighted with feelings of guilt for other things. If the child suffers from generalized guilt, she might readily assimilate conflict of interest with parents (or others) as worthy of guilt feelings, as though it were wrong to have one's own different interests. A child not already heavily burdened with generalized guilt might more naturally treat conflicts of interest as not moralized.

PSYCHOLOGICAL RESIDUE OF EARLY GUILT

Suppose I believe the account above. Is it rational of me to continue to suffer feelings of generalized guilt? In some abstract sense, one might answer No. But this is really an epistemological question like that at the heart of chapter 3. Because my reaction of feeling guilty when I do and not at other times is learned from the past and may also be psychologically developmental to some extent, I cannot simply choose not to feel guilty when my interests are served by my acting in an immoral way or against your interests. Rather, I can only undertake a program of purging myself of such feelings generally. That program and the results of it might not be in my interest in general even though it might well be in my interest to be able to skip the burden of guilt in this moment.

My original development of my guilt syndrome may have been rational in the sense that it made sense of the data I had under the theory available to me. Coming to accept a different theory later in life does not automatically lead to revision of earlier interpretations, the data for many of which are long forgotten.[36] More generally, I cannot know enough and cannot have experienced enough to get to the right theory on my own, and if I try to ferret out better theories in the literature I may discover that they are all poor at best. If that is true, I will not be able to motivate myself to adopt a single knockdown theory as though it were a paragon. I am apt to be a Humean skeptic about more or less everything, including why anyone should have guilt feelings. Strangely, however, one thing about which I might come to be relatively certain is the comfort of my present social relationships. (Of course, I may alternatively become confident of their discomfort.) Much of that comfort has epistemological grounds in such facts as that I know the community and its members, its slang, its expectations, its bars where everyone knows my name. Hence, I may find that my community's views on guilt support me better than alternatives might be expected to do if my community's views seem reasonably to support the community. This seems to be the common conclusion of very many people, perhaps of most people.

CULTURAL RESIDUE OF THE GUILT SYNDROME

There may be a cultural residue of guilt after the larger cultural values on which it was based have decayed or after the things it once produced are no longer of such compelling value. Jewish guilt might no longer have survival value. It need not lead to extinction of the community, but it might work against the interests of virtually all individuals in the next generation. But the carriers of the norm of Jewish guilt do not reinforce it out of direct concern for its functional effects. Rather, they may reinforce it because they believe it to be morally or religiously right, because they have given virtually no thought to the matter beyond merely following communal norms, or because there is a real difficulty in coordinating on any alternative. The first of these is a normative constraint, the second an epistemological constraint, and the third a strategic constraint. Consider the last of these more extensively.

Communitywide following of a particular norm may produce a state of affairs in which many could not gain from unilateral departure even if the norm is destructive for them. For example, genuinely to break the hold of Jewish guilt might mean to break the hold of the Jewish community over oneself. For people in later life, breaking with Jewish guilt might not be worth this grievous cost. Even for a younger person who would like to break the hold of the community, it might still be very painful to damage or lose connections with particular people in the community. An eighteenth-century *gentilhomme* similarly could not break with the dueling norm without painful losses.

Breaking with Catholic guilt might have no such implication. The Catholic shared vision and the central norms that rule lives under Catholic faith are universalistic; they are not community- or even family-oriented. As communitarians sense, universalistic norms are corrosive of community, which is inherently particularistic. Italian and Hispanic Catholic communities have an additional norm that seems bound up in the religious norm but that could be independent of it. That norm, of reverence for one's mother and for the idea of motherhood, may directly reinforce community. Italian and Hispanic Catholic cultures may therefore be far more communal than French or German Catholic cultures. Still, the central *religious* norm of guilt is universalistic and its hold on an individual might be broken without catastrophic effects on the individual's further life in the community.

Regulation by Jewish guilt produces tight cohesion at the family level and perhaps also at the community level. Regulation by Catholic guilt may produce such cohesion, if at all, only through the common vision of the right and the wrong that Catholics typically share. To exaggerate only somewhat, the Catholic child is ideally brought up to be regulated through one-on-one contact with god and god's representatives. The Jewish child is brought up being regulated through one-on-one contact with her mother (and, peripherally, one-on-one contact with every adult who might be a surrogate mother, such as relatives, neighbors, and more distant associates). The Jewish guilt syndrome produces strong familial and, hence, communal cohesion, perhaps despite whatever conflict it stimulates. Strong communal cohesion may be the chief reason for the survival of variants of Jewish culture and community over roughly seventy generations of the Diaspora. A community without an analog of Jewish guilt might have been much more readily assimilated into the hegemonic culture of its time and place.

If we understand the psychological residue of early training in guilt, we can extrapolate to some degree of collective residue. Ruth Benedict speculated that western society is in transition from a culture regulated by guilt to one regulated by shame. That is an odd conclusion for an anthropologist, since she had studied isolated, traditional societies that typically used shame and honor rather than guilt to motivate proper behavior. In any case, it seems very unlikely that the role of shame comes close to that of guilt in its significance for social regulation in the West.

The actual weight of the transition is from regulation by guilt to regulation by interests and by various social norms, including shame. Some of these norms may serve interests. This transition may not uniformly involve the substitution of another form of regulation for regulation by guilt. Rather, in part, regulation by guilt may simply erode without replacement. Those things that regulation by guilt supported may be weakened or even destroyed as the norm of guilt degrades. For example, if guilt functions to support communal ties, these may be weakened with its passing and there need be no alternative norm to rise to support community, which may be weakened or may dissipate.

The Mafia and the State

Institutions commonly have incentive systems that can be explained in functional terms. The Mafia is a group-level analog of the state in this respect. But the Mafia is, of course, successful to the extent it defends its difference from the rest of society while the state is successful to the extent its power reaches virtually everyone in the society. A norm of obedience within the Mafia would therefore be a norm of difference, while a norm of obedience in a state would be more nearly universalistic. The Mafia and the state are both worth consideration here, however, not because they require norms to motivate obedience, but rather because it seems likely that they do not. In the moment when one comes to decide whether to cheat the Mafia or to break the law, one is also likely to face overwhelming, deliberately imposed incentives not to do so.

The Mafia seems to have arisen in response to the dreadful heavy hand of the Spanish rule of southern Italy. That rule was not generally directed at exploitation or incorporation but merely at suppression. It reduced the functions of government, making it unresponsive to the populace, with the general result that distrust became the modal principle for interpersonal relations beyond the family. In the context of so little order, the Mafia, through competitive evolution, rose to dominate large parts of Sicilian life.[37]

The Mafia has a seeming norm, *omertà*, that helps to maintain the power of the group. *Omertà*, perhaps a corruption of *humilità* or perhaps derivative from *omu* (man), means deference to the leadership of the Mafia, primarily through silence about its activities. Such silence is desirable because the society outside the Mafia would typically like to stop the organization from its exactions of tribute for so-called protection. Silence is especially desired when the police inquire into Mafia activities. *Omertà* is applied not merely to members of the Mafia, but to everyone in the vicinity. When officials of the state come to inquire about crimes in a village, the villagers must be silent or face reprisals.[38]

Omertà is a complex principle because the situations in which it would be invoked often involve powerful incentives to break silence. If I am in the Mafia and I keep silent, I may serve many years in prison for a crime, while if I talk I may get a very light sentence. The threat of mere exclusion from the Mafia community cannot be adequate to enforce *omertà* in such a case. Quick extinction is the more effective threat. If I am one of those in the village who are exploited by the Mafia, I would like the officials to know the truth. But I would sooner stay alive and be exploited than tell the truth and be assassinated. *Omertà* is straight-forwardly, deliberately enforced through the threat of harm to any individual who violates it. This threat is the more compelling the more people follow the principle of *omertà*.

If the effect of a norm is a collective good, such as the greater power of the group, there need be no incentive of individual self-interest to motivate contributing to this collective good for the usual reasons of the logic of collective action. The overwhelming force behind the norm might then be the threat of deliberate punishment of individuals for their violation of the norm. Sanctions for many norms are much more nearly spontaneous and part of the nature of the interaction. For example, people who will not go along with our way of talking may reduce the pleasure of our moments together and we might therefore tend to leave them out of our activities. We need not actively choose to punish them, we just do not get enough pleasure from their company to include them as often as we might. *Omertà* may be a norm for many in the Mafia roughly the way traffic laws are a norm for many people, who speed when they think they can get away with it but not when they think they are likely to be caught. To call this a norm is roughly comparable to saying that the weak follow a norm not to attack the strong. Only a stupid person among the weak would benefit from such a norm.

Omertà fits the paradigm for functional explanation in chapter 4. If F is the greater power of G, the Mafia, that follows from *omertà*, X, then *omertà* contributes to the power of the Mafia (condition 1), this greater power is beneficial for virtually all members of the Mafia (condition 2), which therefore becomes even more capable of enforcing *omertà* against the occasional miscreant (condition 3).[39] *Omertà* is similar to the norm of honor in Mérimée's story, "Mateo Falcone." Falcone's norm functions as a norm of exclusion that defends the Corsicans against officers of the state, who have often been "foreigners" from France or Italy. It requires a dreadful action from Falcone.[40]

The analysis of law-abiding is similar. The more a population is law-abiding, the greater power the police have vis-à-vis those who are not law-abiding. That the core population abides by law then gives the state greater capacity to deal with the prisoner's dilemma fringe of those who would free ride on the order by committing crimes. If too many become lawless, the police lose their power to control that fringe. Even at the peaceful gathering of people in Times Square in New York to celebrate the beginning of the new year, the crowds are at first successfully kept back from the barricades erected to keep them a block or more from the Square. Then the crowds become too large and finally push to the barricades, where the police finally stop insisting that individuals move on. Such moments must make the police feel as dumb as the citizens think they are, as though the police do not know what citizens instantly recognize: that making one person move on merely makes room for another person. Yet, the handful of police officers are able to keep thousands from crossing the barricades.

With enough disorder, we can explain the helplessness of the police before a full-scale breach of the barricades—or the sudden fall of Nicolae Ceausescu from power in Romania and of the Communist regimes in East Germany and Czechoslovakia in 1989.[41] This is, arguably, Hobbes's view of the state and its enforcement power: A bit of sedition, even a bit of mere reform, can bring the state down by wrecking the coordination that is its order.[42]

THE MORALITY OF NORMS

When Colomba invites Miss Nevil to visit Orso where he is hiding after killing the two sons of the family that had killed Orso's and Colomba's father, Miss Nevil replies, "But, Colomba, it would not be proper for me to do so." With her rapier tongue, Colomba retorts, "I see. You city women are always worried about what's proper. We village women think only of what is right."[43] At first hearing, Colomba's distinction may sound compelling: Miss Nevil is driven merely by social convention while she, Colomba, is driven by morality. Those who have rebelled against many of the nineteenth-century English sensibilities that Miss Nevil seems to honor may readily side with Colomba. Alas, her sly put-down is a verbal trick. Colomba's morality is merely a different society's conventions. Her morality includes the hideous vendetta into which she has pushed Orso. For her, that too is right, it is not merely a convention; indeed, it may be the most right thing she knows. But it is inconceivable outside the social context in which it evolved and holds sway.

As with Colomba's grotesque norm of vendetta, we may be able to explain a norm and to ground it in rational choices, but this may entail little or nothing for the morality of the norm. To judge the morality we would, of course, have to start from some moral theory or principle.[44] A norm that is moral on one theory may be immoral on another. A convention that resolves a pure coordination problem, such as the driving convention, may seem to be moral on any plausible moral theory. In the driving case, everyone's interests are harmonious with all others' interests and all are prima facie worthy of fulfillment. A utilitarian must readily conclude that the driving convention is good unless coordinated driving is bad. A contractarian might suppose we would have contracted to adopt a relevant convention so that, even if our actual convention arose some other way, we would judge the convention good or right. A rationalist contractarian, such as John Rawls or Thomas Scanlon, might suppose we could not do otherwise than rationally choose to have a driving convention. If any moral theory had difficulty with the rightness of a driving convention, we would wonder about that theory.

The norms discussed here, and most of the norms of any interest in actual societies, however, do not have the pristine quality of the driving convention. Many of them may seem dubious on one moral theory or another. For example, a norm of difference or exclusion typically functions to regulate conflict between the interests of a core and a periphery of members of a group. Such a norm sounds appealing (in a communitarian sense) in its voluntary fit with the values and interests of the core members whose life prospects most depend on the group's prosperity and cohesion. But the effective function of the norm is to change incentives for those at the fringe who might abandon the group in some or all respects. *The role of the norm when it is invoked to sanction anyone is to sanction one who does not fully share it, to crush the Salman Rushdies at the borders of the separate group.* No doubt, many people can give moral support to particular norms that function this way, but there is no easy acceptance of their morality from a simple assertion of the voluntariness of community. By contrast, there is no fringe for the driving convention—virtually everyone is likely to support it and follow it, everyone is in the core of the interested group.

Why is violation of a coordination norm wrong? Not for contractarian reasons—we need never have contracted, explicitly, implicitly, tacitly, or otherwise. And not for deontological-action reasons—there is nothing inherently right in one of the possible actions for us, there is only contingent reason for thinking one of them right. Violation is wrong for simple utilitarian reasons. Even an outsider who has never participated in a communal norm might be expected, rightly, to follow it because violating it would harm others and perhaps herself. A North American driving in Australia morally should drive on the left. Clearly, the driving convention is uniquely well defined on this matter. It is virtually an ideal type, an unusual ideal type in that it coincides with a concrete social reality. There are norms that approach it without being quite so perfectly in everyone's interest. For example, the value of money is almost a matter of pure coordination. It is not quite pure because one might second-guess its future value and act strategically. One might hedge against its decline, thereby contributing to its decline. Or one might gamble on its rise, thereby contributing to the rise by hoarding it and reducing the supply available to others, as in the former billionaire Hunts' effort to drive up the price of silver.

Actual communities may often elevate their conventions to the status of moral right as a mistaken inference of an "ought" from an "is," of a normative judgment from a pure matter of fact. They might therefore assert the wrongness of violating a communal norm, whatever it is. This is a simplistic move that is not valid, although it may be honestly made, perhaps from reasons of poor epistemology. It is sometimes asserted that communal norms are particularly strongly held and, seemingly therefore, especially worthy of respect. The subgroup norms canvassed here seem to be more nearly self-enforcing than the universalistic norms. In that sense, they may be stronger or have greater longevity (except that such a norm is as vulnerable as its group). But that would not make them somehow more moral. Unfortunately for any communitarian defense of such norms, they may be strongly held only because they are self-enforcing through their functional mechanism, as discussed earlier, which makes it the interest of everyone in the relevant community to abide by them.[45] This is not per se a moral consideration and *we need have no special moral respect for these norms on the ground of the strength with which they may be held.*

Although it may be good for the prevailing group, clearly there is nothing inherently moral in the prevailing of one group over another. Not even a communitarian moral theorist could make that a right or good result—communitarianism is, after all, anti-universalist.

Consider a superficially plausible defense of the duel. One might suppose that the right to duel depends only on both duelers participating voluntarily.[46] If they both really want to take such risks, that is their business. Against this view, we might immediately raise the objection that others depend on the actions, so that the duel cannot be a right if it harms third parties, as Auguste Saint-Clair's fatal duel destroyed the life of the woman he was to marry.[47] The position may face even more fundamental problems. If you challenge me to a duel today in the conditions of present norms, and I accept your challenge, and there are no other parties with a stake in the outcome, our duel seems to fit the condition of voluntariness. But if one French *gentilhomme* posed a challenge to another, especially in the presence of other people, during the heyday of the dueling norm, that challenge immediately had coercive effects on the challenged.[48] He then risked loss of face and society if he refused the challenge and he risked death if he accepted it. The choices for the person challenged could not be voluntary unless viewed as abstracted from the larger situation. Moreover, if there were strong sanctions for failing to offer a challenge in relevant circumstances, the challenger also might have felt coerced by the potential loss of society. The supposed right to enter voluntarily into a duel is therefore evidently incoherent in a time in which the norm of dueling is strong.[49] As is commonly true, we cannot ground rights strictly in the nature of the individual persons who hold them or are affected by them.[50]

What is coercive or not voluntary is the institution of dueling itself. If we had a state apparatus that enforced such a practice as dueling by sanctioning those who failed to join in, we would readily conclude that the state was coercive. Some libertarians would insist that there was no lack of voluntariness in the dueling norm if no one intentionally created it against the wishes of those who were affected by it.[51] So long as all the acts that were taken along the way to establishing the powerful norm were morally acceptable, then the institution that results is morally acceptable. But there is little saving grace in supposing past generations all acted voluntarily in perhaps unintentionally creating the norm that now threatens to destroy my life as a *gentilhomme*. The right to challenge me to a duel is the unilateral right to destroy my status quo. My situation as I face my challenger is not so different from Tosca's as she balks in the face of Scarpia's offer to release her lover from the firing squad in return for her sexual favor: "I do you no violence," Scarpia says, "You are free. Go."[52] You are free to choose whether merely to walk away from your entire life or to submit. Hence, outlawing the duel was a universalistic move and, if laws against the duel had been enforced earlier, it seems likely that the typical *gentilhomme* would have had increased, not reduced, freedom.

Norms beyond Interest

Many norms may have only coincidental effects on difference, and are focused rather on standard behavior that everyone ought to manifest. For example, norms of parenting, which may differ substantially from one community to another, are typically norms that everyone in a community would expect any parent to follow. They become a mark of differentiation only if one community has norms of parenting that differ from those of another community and if the difference gives grounds for judgment. Consider the norm of parenting or, rather, more broadly of family loyalty that drives the pair of films, *Jean de Florette* and *Manon of the Spring*.

On behalf of his nephew, his only heir, César (Papet) Soubeyran hounds Jean Cadoret into grim, soul-deadening failure and early death. (Cadoret might have been known as Jean de Florette in the village of Aubagne, had the villagers known Florette Camions was his mother.) In destroying Jean, Soubeyran is utterly vicious and careless. He has no actual feelings for the man, with whom he avoids contact, never seeing his face or his eyes, only seeing him from a distance, from which his hunchback was his defining personal feature. Soubeyran's only concern is that the man is in the way of his nephew, Ugolin (called Galinette), and he works to clear Jean from the way as he might lay a trap for a wolf that threatened his nephew.

When Soubeyran later discovers that Jean was evidently his own son by a former lover from whom he had been separated by military service, he then wants only to help his granddaughter, Manon, whom he has largely despised until then. He also mourns for his dead son, Jean de Florette, and he wants, for himself, only to die. It is not in his character to approach Manon to set things right, and he faces no reciprocal incentive with her. In any case, he probably thinks his wrong cannot be set right for Manon, for her that wrong will stand above anything he could possibly do.

Oddly, Soubeyran's actions would not have been, in his view, a wrong except for the horrible mistake that they were done to his own son. (In his death-letter to Manon, he even asserts that her father would defend Soubeyran's actions before god—it evidently does not occur to him that Jean might not have been motivated by the dreadful, solipsistic norms of Aubagne.) The norm that now drives his concern for Manon is the same as that which drove him when he set out to destroy the supposed interloper who was her father. Within the constraints of his available information, he is completely consistent in his commitments, both in wanting Jean destroyed and then in regretting Jean's destruction.

Norms of family loyalty might seem reciprocal and iterated, as truth-telling and promise-keeping are. But they may readily transcend the incentives built into reciprocal expectations, as when they are directed at a future generation that cannot reciprocate. Soubeyran declares that his efforts on behalf of his nephew are really on behalf of all Soubeyrans, past and future, and he later swears "by all the Soubeyrans" when he wants his nephew to trust him.[53] If there are reciprocal expectations, these are at least in part in the wider community. For example, I will be held to account by others for not being a responsible parent, child, or sibling. Soubeyran does not directly face any such accounting while he thinks there is none but his nephew left of the family line.

The dreadful fate of Jean de Florette depends heavily on another community norm. Against the possibility that the villagers will figure out the intentions of Soubeyran and his nephew and come to Jean's aid, Soubeyran notes that "the villagers here don't mix into other people's business." When villagers in a bar idly talk of the possibility that Soubeyran and his nephew have blocked Jean's spring, another villager breaks the discussion with the admonition that "we" do not meddle in the affairs of others. The villagers, indeed, are hateful in their attitude to Jean and his family—for no evident reason other than malice toward anyone said to be from Crespin.

Oddly, despite its intensely personal focus, the norm that drives Soubeyran seems to be a social construction. It is the norm of his southern French community. Parents and forebears in many communities have had no such norm, they have sold their children or have otherwise treated them as chattel or servants. The norm of familial loyalty in southern France seems similar to norms that drive people in southern Italy.[54] Both of these populations were politically and economically suppressed for long periods by external powers that took little or no account of their interests and that may have contributed to developing high levels of distrust between members of the local communities.[55] With local government under the control of foreigners who did not care much for the locals, the locals were forced into greater self-reliance than would have been necessary with a reasonable system of police and justice to protect relations. Literal self-reliance could not have been very successful for most people, who therefore benefited from the development of strong familial ties, including group familial responsibility for the actions of individual family members.

Soubeyran's actions are partly similar to those of Orso della Rebbia in his family's vendetta against the Barricini, except that the conflict is one-sided. Soubeyran sees Jean de Florette as his enemy, but Jean de Florette does not know Soubeyran is his enemy. Soubeyran's norm lacks the nicety of the Corsican vendetta: It is not announced but can be followed deviously. What Jean de Florette does that is against Soubeyran's interest is merely what is commonly done in societies with property relations: Jean owns something that Soubeyran wants.

There are many norms, such as that of familial loyalty in southern France, that drive people but that do not transparently fit the two large categories of norms that are governed by the interests of their followers. These other norms include both those that systematically drive individuals in the context of communities (which may be relatively fractured) and norms that overcome the perverse incentives of the logic of collective action, but without the device of functional feedback to reinforce them. The former category includes such norms as that of family loyalty in southern France. The latter includes such norms as those of fairness, voting, paying one's taxes, and so forth, norms that may be widespread. They may not be overpowering but they may motivate a lot of behavior that is not evidently self-interested.

Perhaps we may account for some of these norms as products of evolutionary selection. To say that a norm is selected for its communal survival value is to say that, among various communities subjected to relevant stresses, the community regulated by this norm held together over many generations while others disappeared, perhaps through assimilation. The Jewish norm of guilt may have played such a role. Subtle arguments have been offered for biological selection of some norm-following behaviors. Social selection is more fragile, because, unlike biological selection, it is subject to reversal. Social selection might work through the epistemology of comfort and the resultant restriction of knowledge that lets a norm seem objective. Socially selected norms may be epistemologically reinforced even when they are not reinforced by interests.

If that is the way social selection works, there may be an advantage in growing up in a culture that is transitional and whose comforts are not very fondly recalled. People from such a culture may have a relative lack of commitment to norms or beliefs that depend on being epistemologically reinforced. Similarly, education outside one's community has the effect of weakening such commitments. A leading youthful advocate of creationism in the Netherlands chose to get an education in geology in order to be able to match wits with scientists to show that creationism is correct. In four years at Princeton he received his doctorate and became apostate.[56] This story can probably be told in millions of variants. It may often be the brunt of W. B. Yeats's frequently quoted lines that

> The best lack all conviction, while the worst
> Are full of passionate intensity.[57]

Many of the convictions that the best lack are largely perverse convictions artificially made seemingly right by their grounding in a particular community, especially an ignorant one.

Finally, there are many behaviors that seem to be normatively driven but that do not clearly fall under a generally held norm. For example, revenge is a seeming near relative of vendetta, but it is much more idiosyncratically motivating than is the vendetta, which typically organizes a community.[58] Heathcliff, in *Wuthering Heights*, is driven by such vengeful bile that he spends his life gaining control of the property of his betrayers. Then, once all the principals are dead and cannot suffer from his wrath, he wants to tear down their family manor with his own hands.[59] Yasunari Kawabata gives us an instance of transverse revenge, a cousin of the Corsican *vendetta transversale*, which is vengeance visited upon a more or less distant relative of the perpetrator of the offense.[60] Kawabata's tale is told with gentle elegance and understatement, but no amount of overstatement could lead us into the mind of Keiko, the sly and beautiful avenger. Her action does, however, suggest a motivation for transverse revenge or vendetta: Killing a relative leaves the target of the vengeance to suffer.

CONCLUSION

Elster argues against the view that "what seems to be norm-oriented action is, in reality, a form of rational or, more generally, optimizing behaviour."[61] Given his move to define norms as not-outcome-oriented, this view follows automatically. If my accounts of the norms of rap, promise-keeping, the duel, the vendetta, and others, are correct, then these are not norms for Elster. One might read Elster's view as stronger than this, however, as saying that one should not attempt rational-choice explanations of these behaviors that we all somehow know are not rationally motivated. One might then wonder what is the error of such an *effort* as opposed to the error of a particular analysis.

Some norms seemingly cannot be characterized as in the interest of their followers in the act of following them. For example, the norms of honor that drove Ernani and Silva seem to reach beyond interest, as do the norms for voting in large-scale elections, the norm of being benefi-cent in various circumstances, and numerous norms of religious obei-sance. The effort to make various norms seem rational is not worthy of criticism, however. All that should be criticized or opposed is a bad ex-planation. But then bad explanations of particular norms as extra-ra-tional should also be criticized. It is unlikely that all of what we might call norms in the vernacular are rational or that all are normative. As noted above, it is also generally unlikely that any significant norm is a matter of rational choice for all its followers or of normative choice for all.

There are two striking facts of the pattern of many of the most impor-tant norms of contemporary and earlier societies. First, *norms that serve collective interests are stronger when they are consistent with individual interest, and they are weaker when they are not.* That should come as no surprise. Having the force of two motivations that are congruent is surely more effective than having the force of the same two motivations in opposition. This is not to say that the former norms are always stronger than the latter, individual by individual. The force of Ernani's norm of honor is among the greatest of any individual's norms in all of literature and history. The measure of its strength is that it trumped even life for a vibrant, energetic man on the threshold of marriage to the woman he loved, and that it trumped life almost instantly. The norm of beneficence similarly has led people to self-sacrifice. But the evident fact of Ernani's kind of norm is that it burdens relatively few people, while the norms of exclusion canvassed here and in chapter 4 afflict millions, leading many of them to extreme actions.

Second, *norms that are focused on groups are more forceful than those that are universalistic.* This partly follows from the previous claim.

Norms of exclusion commonly override universal norms. Indeed, as T. V. Smith argues, the honor that motivates criminals, such as members of the Mafia, "is a more hardy growth than the loyalty that citizens feel for the law set over against, but not therefore set over, the antisocial group."[62] This is essentially an implication of the first point that norms congruent with interests are especially strong. Groups can mobilize incentives to entice stronger commitments and can reduce opportunities for wider knowledge that would undercut their claims. Gananath Obeyesekere writes that the discourse of anthropologists must be about culture, not merely a culture. The anthropologist must see varied cultures in relation to each other. Yet, he ruefully grants that this view "cannot provide the energy, the blindness, and the passion that religious and political fundamentalism give to their adherents."[63] The latter may not be as blind as they seem; they may be given much of their energy and passion by their being harnessed to interests. Obeyesekere and I are academics and therefore fortunate to have it congruently in our interest to push the universalistic values of his anthropology and my political philosophy.

These conclusions raise two general questions: What are the consequences of strong group norms? and How are we to judge them? These are the topics of the next two chapters on violent conflicts and on communitarianism. Understanding the rational underpinnings of norms of exclusion, especially of the ethnic-group norms that drive many contemporary bouts of violent conflict, may finally affect our normative judgments of those norms.

CHAPTER SIX

Violent Conflicts

> In these quarrels [between supporters of France and of Germany at the time of World War I], the surest way of being convinced of the excellence of the cause of one party or the other is actually to be that party.
> —Marcel Proust, *Remembrance of Things Past*

FROM CONFLICT TO VIOLENCE

Suppose we face limited, relatively fixed resources. If some of us can form a group that gains hegemony over our society, we can extract a disproportionate share of total resources for members of our group. The remainder of the society has incentive to counter-organize against us to protect its welfare. If it does so, we are now two groups in manifest conflict. Any would-be political leader may find that asserting the predominance of a particular group is key to gaining substantial support. All that is required to make the conflict between the two groups manifest are plausible definitions of group and counter-group memberships. Slight differences might suffice. More dramatic differences, such as race or ethnicity, language, or religion, might allow for easy mobilization. No one in group A need be personally hostile to anyone in group B for the two groups to be politically hostile simply because they have a conflict of interest. Their conflict is one over which there may be perfect agreement: both groups want the same thing, namely, the available resources.

Shortly after Tito's death, Milovan Djilas reputedly said that the Yugoslav system could only be run by Tito. "Now that Tito is gone and our economic situation becomes critical, there will be a natural tendency for greater centralization of power. But this centralization will not succeed because it will run up against ethnic-political power bases in the republics. This is not classical nationalism but a more dangerous, bureaucratic nationalism built on economic self-interest. This is how the Yugoslav system will begin to collapse."[1]

Norms of difference and exclusion can establish in and out groups and thereby ground a conflict of interest between the groups. Having a conflict of interest is not, however, sufficient for producing violence. You and I may have a conflict of interest over a job that only one of us can get. One of us might attempt to prevail in that conflict by hiring a hit man to kill the other, but we might also simply compete to the best of our abilities and then let the loser make the best of other options. Ethnic conflicts commonly lead to mere competition, as they may have done to a large extent in the period of economic progress in Tito's Yugoslavia, when Slovenians and Croatians did relatively well, Bosnians did less well, and Serbs and Macedonians did relatively poorly, but no one turned to massive violence to change the results.

Why violence? Many reasons are proposed in varied literatures on ethnic conflict. The reason most commonly asserted for the travails in Yugoslavia since 1991 is ethnic hatred, which will be discussed more fully below. Another that was once high on the list of causes, especially among writers under the sway of Thomas Hobbes, is anarchy that leaves no institutional barrier to conflict so that we all tend to match the lowest common denominator established by the most violent among us. Of these two, that of Hobbes has the greater claim on our attention. On a Hobbesian view of political life, without institutions to help us stay orderly we take a preemptive view of all conflicts. If conflict can lead to violence, I can improve my prospects of surviving the conflict if I preemptively suppress those with whom I am in conflict. I sneak up on you before you sneak up on me.

Self-defense against possible (not even actual) attack suffices to motivate murderous conflict. Risk aversion is enough. And the risk, unfortunately, of not preemptively attacking may be heightened by the fact that the other side—such as an ethnic group—cannot commit to not attacking, and therefore cannot be trusted beyond what can be inferred from their interests. An ethnic group that depends on relatively spontaneous organization, as the Bosnian Serbs did at least in large part, cannot make credible guarantees about what it might do. Indeed, in the cases of the Irish Republican Army (IRA) and the Bosnian Serbs, discussed below, internal competition for leadership might make any commitment automatically the target of some faction among those supposedly making the commitment.

In 1991, virtually all political leaders in Yugoslavia must have seen the potential for the break-up of the Yugoslav regime in the morass of post-Tito and post-Communist politics. Many people in the two most prosperous republics, Slovenia and Croatia, wanted independence. Unfortunately, Croatia included within its borders a large Serbian community. If Croatia seceded from Yugoslavia, the resident Serbs could wonder about their minority status in the new nation. Since Serbs dominated the national government and the army, there was some prospect of Serbian intervention in a rebellious Croatia. But there could not soon have been a more propitious moment for Croatia to hope to secede successfully, because the central Yugoslav government and economy were weak. The Croatian government opted for secession and then it preemptively turned on the Serbs within Croatia. Croatians have paid dearly for attacking the Croatian Serbs, but they have also been made partner in the subsequent destruction and dismantling of Bosnia. The bloody collapse of Yugoslavia has been a product of this series of opportunistic grabs and preemptive violence.

The Hobbesian view seems to fit ethnic conflicts that have turned violent in Lebanon, Azerbaijan and Armenia, Rwanda and Burundi, Iraq, and many other societies, as it fits Yugoslavia. Destabilized governments, brought to weakness by war, economic failure, or fights over succession, cannot maintain adequate barriers to violence. Conflicts that are already well defined then escalate to violence. Once the violence is underway, as in Yugoslavia, preemption becomes an unavoidable urge. One need not hate members of another group, but one might still fear their potential hatred or even merely their threat. Hobbes's vision of the need of all to preempt lest they be the victims of the few who are murderous still fits even in the relatively organized state of ethnic conflict, *except that it applies at the group level.*

Incidentally, this modified Hobbesian view also fits the apparent results of the various rebellions: Almost all are worse off in the short run. Hobbes supposed that revolution against a going government is inherently harmful even to those who rebel, as seems to be true for the mass of people in, for example, Yugoslavia.[2] Only certain leaders (and perhaps occasional others) may have improved their lot and their prospects. Oddly, these leaders have improved their lot not by raising the level of welfare for their groups but through individually specific rewards of leadership. They are unlike the Jimmy Hoffas of the labor movement. Hoffa extracted wealth from his teamsters but he more than made up for his extractions by raising the level of welfare for the bulk of the members of his union (while lowering the welfare of some teamsters and of vast numbers of people not in his union). For the short run, at least, Franjo Tudjman, Slobodan Milosevic, and Radovan Karadzic lack Hoffa's saving grace. They are merely parasitic on their societies. They use ethnic differences to justify murder, mass rape, the destruction of cities, and even genocide while reducing the lives of their own ethnic compatriots. As Faoud Ajami and many others remark, they call on "brotherhood and faith and kin when it is in their interests to do so."[3]

For Hobbes's reason, it would be wrong to say, in the sloppy way some people talk about Yugoslav and other conflicts, that real-world conflicts are zero-sum. They might be fixed-sum in one limited sense or another. For example, when Croatians and Serbs have a conflict over some bit of land, there is a fixed supply of land available. But if they fight over control of the land, they destroy resources and people on both sides and the resulting outcome is one in which total gains are swamped by total losses. It is not fixed-sum, it is negative-sum. Latent conflicts may be zero-sum, but manifest conflicts must typically be negative sum, at least in the short run. In game theoretic language, all that we need say is that, in a pure conflict, any change that makes one party to a conflict better off must make the other party worse off. It is possible for both to become worse off in a pure conflict, but not possible for both to become better off or for one to become better off without harm to the other.

One could imagine a manifest, even violent, conflict that could lead to net gains in the somewhat longer run. For example, one state might seize part of another because the inhabitants are all of the nation of the first state. This is a pristine variant of the conflict between Romania and Hungary over the Hungarian nationals in Romania. If these Romanian Hungarians became part of Hungary, they might immediately become more productive and prosperous and the welfare of all three of the groups—Romanians, Romanian Hungarians, and the original Hungarians—might rise. The welfare of Romanians might rise only to the extent Romanian resources no longer were spent to keep the Romanian Hungarians under control. But for most of the violent conflicts of our time, it seems likely that the outcomes are severely negative-sum. And, if it would be mutually beneficial to all three groups to transfer part of formerly Hungarian Transylvania to Hungary, then the situation between Hungary and Romania is not conflictual but is misunderstood.

It is common in the literature on nationalism to assert that the underlying issues are not economic and that the events are not matters of rational choice.[4] As in the discussion of ethnic hatred below, the real motivators are metaphors and likely false beliefs that define the world. Many strong nationalists suffer the solipsistic and egotistical belief that they are *the* chosen people. This belief can coexist with reasoned understandings of its irrationality.[5] Although it might be a benign belief, it has a natural tendency to include the further belief that other peoples are inferior, even bad. It is very hard to disprove a metaphorical thesis, which in the end is at best a form of description of the matter we would like to understand. But even for one who accepts the metaphorical thesis, it merely pushes back the matter to be explained: How and why do people come to have such systematically odd beliefs?

Walker Connor seems to hold that it is nationalist beliefs which cause the behaviors associated with nationalist movements and that various economic explanations can be shown not to be "essential prerequisites for ethnonational conflict."[6] Unfortunately for showing their irrelevance, the way economic issues matter is not merely through a linear causal effect. Economic issues (in the broad sense that includes politicians' career incentives and citizens' comforts) merely construct the range of possibility of conflict. Violence is then a separate matter that very likely depends on tipping phenomena.

A typical tipping phenomenon is residential segregation by race.[7] In many urban areas of the United States, whites have evidently begun to leave their neighborhoods in growing percentages more or less in reaction to previous departures. One family leaves the neighborhood and their closest friends now have more reason to leave. When they leave, others follow, and soon the neighborhood has tipped from one of mixed race to one of, say, blacks only. (At the same time, black movement into the neighborhood may be a tipping phenomenon, with more blacks willing to move in the more there are already in the neighborhood.)

Similarly, when one cell of the IRA forms and begins to take action, another cell forms, then another and another, until there is virtual civil war. If the first few cells had been stopped, there might not have been twenty-five years of such violence. When Somalia's Siad Barre was suddenly deflated by the switch of Soviet support from him to Ethiopia in his attempted war to take a Somali section of Ethiopia, one or more clan leaders in Somalia saw opportunity for their own gains, others followed suit, and soon there were many warlords tearing Somalia apart. In Burundi, where initiation of the violence beginning in 1993 may have been deliberately planned, the scale of that violence might still be a tipping phenomenon, as also in Rwanda. In Yugoslavia several failed Communists attempted to hang onto power despite their demonstrated incapacity to rule the Yugoslav economy. Since their routes into political office were through the various republics, they used regional appeals, with the result that the leaders of four of the six republics soon preferred regional over national interests. Yugoslavia tipped from being a nation to being a fratricidal association of principalities. Serbia subverted Yugoslav government in the name of Serbian precedence, while Slovenia and Croatia seceded and Bosnia attempted to secede from Yugoslavia. With Slovenia and Croatia out, being in Yugoslavia could no longer be appealing to the Muslims and Croatians of Bosnia. After the destruction of Bosnia, being in Yugoslavia could also no longer be appealing to the non-Serbian majority populations of Kossovo and Macedonia. In the end, even Serbs may be uncomfortable in a Serbian Yugoslavia. Incidentally, the worst excrescences of ethnic hostility in Yugoslavia followed the initial tipping events—they did not precede or cause these events. Indeed, the worst excrescences followed only after a period of harsh warfare, as discussed further below under "Ethnic Hatred."

Not all instances of great violence are clearly tipping phenomena. For example, when Hitler deliberately massed forces to initiate his various wars, he was presumably not being tipped into violence by others' violence or threats. But World War I might be seen as a tipping event that followed from relatively trivial actions of the assassination of the Archduke Francis Ferdinand in Sarajevo and mobilizations that stimulated other mobilizations, which led to war that eventually tipped even North America and bits of Africa and Asia into the European fracas. It is plausible that spontaneous large-group conflicts that are not under the firm leadership of someone with intentions of violence are generally candidates for explanation from tipping. In these phenomena, accidents can play a very large role. In a particular case, one might insist that, despite the tipping, the end result was relatively sure to happen because, eventually, something would have provoked the initial tipping response, as one crazed person did in Sarajevo in 1914.

The order of beliefs and events is important because the content of the falsehoods of nationalism may be determined or manipulated by their fit with political agendas. Connor asks, "What is a nation?" He answers that it is "the largest group that can command a person's loyalty because of felt kinship ties." Emphasis is on *felt*, because I might be led to feel a tie that I cannot objectively claim to have. Connor speaks of intuitive, in contrast to objective, conviction.[8] The distortion of history, the distortion of reports from the battle zones, distortions of claimed ethnic and linguistic differences, and distortions of leaders' intentions can all be used, especially in a nation with centrally controlled television, to instill an intensity of nationalist commitment that did not cause the events that brought about such intensity but that may then be put to use in other events. It is because these odd beliefs must be manipulated into being that mass nationalism is a strictly modern phenomenon—it requires extensive communication, the very communication that also spreads the cosmopolitan vision of humanity. Perversely, we may see grotesquely violent assertions of ethnic superiority just because extensive communication has been laid onto the ignorance of village culture.

ETHNIC HATRED

Robert Kaplan quotes a 1920 story by the Bosnian Croat, Ivo Andric, the 1961 Nobel Prize winner in Literature: "Yes, Bosnia is a country of hatred. That is Bosnia. . . . [In] secret depths . . . hide burning hatreds, entire hurricanes of tethered and compressed hatreds. . . . Thus you are condemned to live on deep layers of explosive, which are lit from time to time by the very sparks of your loves and your fiery and violent emotion."[9] This sounds like Dostoevsky, Kafka, or Poe on a particular fictional person, a person worthy of fictional treatment just because the character is so dramatically unlike the normal. It does not sound like the characterization of a whole people. But Kaplan and Andric evidently take it as characterizing Bosnians in general, and Kaplan takes it as definitive of Yugoslav culture. Further, the view that "visceral hatred of the neighbors" is "the main ingredient" in violent ethnic conflict is a commonplace in journalistic accounts.[10]

The view that the peculiarities of Balkan hatred drives the Yugoslav horrors infuriates humane Yugoslavs who write on the sufferings of their compatriots.[11] The thesis of ethnic hatred cannot be established by anecdote, not even by the fictional musings of a Nobel laureate. If it systematically underlies history, it must be systematically evident. The overwhelming problem of the thesis that ethnic hatred motivates the ethnic conflict we see is that, for most of the groups in conflict, relations have generally been good through most of history. In the scale of history, the moments of catastrophic breakdown into violence are just that: moments. Between these episodes, there is often substantial mixing. For example, in Yugoslavia, Croatians and Bosnians have typically been next-door neighbors of Serbs; they have been cooperative with them in institutional and economic arrangements; and they have even heavily intermarried with them.

Moreover, many of the participants in the grisly Bosnian wars deny that they hate. One of the young killers in a brutal and merciless paramilitary force of several hundred Croatians at Mostar said, "I really don't hate Muslims—but because of the situation I want to kill them all."[12] He had intended to sit the war out, but the "situation in Mostar caught up with him, labeled him, made him choose: stand with your own or leave your city like a dog and a traitor."[13] Perversely, *he had either to leave his community altogether or he had to identify with it altogether.* He had grown up with Muslims and Serbs among his friends, but when he saw them after the conflict hardened, he had nothing to say to them. Rather than leave his community, he chose to identify altogether with it and soon became a systematic murderer of trapped civilians. He murdered men, women, and children, armed or not, because, after all, in this preemptive world, someone who is not dead might shoot you in the back as you leave. His method was to watch Muslims to determine their patterns of activity in order to know where to lie in ambush to murder them.

The Croatian killer's alternatives were grim and therefore his choice was grim. But he was not so different from the *gentilhomme* of centuries past in France who chose to risk committing murder in a duel rather than be banished from his community. The saving grace for the *gentilhomme* is that we know him primarily from literature, where he is often presented with style and even humanity. The killers have so far not been romanticized in the world at large.

The killer is striking in the extent to which he seems not to have needed to justify his actions morally by anything more than the grim situation. He does not seem to need to make his victims be deserving for wrongs they have done—he evidently knows they deserve none of it, they are merely unfortunately there. For many of the participants in such carnage, their own gruesome actions seem to lead to putative beliefs in the wrongs of the other group. Serbs, for example, begin to believe Croats or Muslims or Albanians are guilty of atrocities as a rationalization for their own barbarities. If the claim cannot be grounded in fact, it is simply grounded in myth. But the Croatian killer of Mostar does not need Milosevic's or Tudjman's lies and mythologies to give him license. He openly confesses to having nothing other than interests at stake.

Ethnic hatred might prevail in some contexts, such as those that involve a long history of overt subjugation of one race or ethnic group to another, as in South Africa, the United States, Guatemala, and many other places, such as Rwanda and Burundi after thirty years of ethnic slaughter. But a genuine hatred that is not reinforced by something from the hated, such as regularly occurring hostile actions, can hardly last over generations. The term "primordial" is often attached to such a seeming impossibility. By labeling it primordial, we seem to have explained something, when we have in fact only labeled it. Thereafter, we can proceed with a know-nothing stance that labels what we do not understand and cannot really believe when it is more fully spelled out.

Durkheim quotes a primordialist statement that is sufficiently lunatic as to be almost charming, especially since it is not invidious: "Woe to the scholar," writes the nineteenth-century historian of religions, J. Darmesteter, "who approaches divine matters without having in the depths of his consciousness, in the innermost indestructible regions of his being, where the souls of his ancestors sleep, an unknown sanctuary from which rises now and then the aroma of incense."[14]

Perhaps the fundamental supposition of the primordialists is an unstated Lamarckianism that attributes current human nature to what was *learned* in earlier generations. On such a theory, the Texan and the Serb, the Australian Aborigine and the Parisian dilettante, the Igbo and the Armenian, the Japanese and the Sri Lankan Sinhalese all have their independent human natures derived from the accidents of their history. Of course, on this theory, some of us are grotesque messes, with such diverse elements tossed together as to create a terribly overdone and botched salad. At least such messes are not likely to abound in adequate numbers of identical types to be capable of ethnic dominance over anyone else.

The quasi-Lamarckian vision of ethnic identification is patently silly, and its silliness pervades much of the commentary on ethnic conflict, both in the press and in more substantial works. Such identification is not primeval, original, primitive, or fundamental—in particular, it is not pre-social. Some things about us may reasonably be called primordial. For example, certain instincts, many of which we share with numerous other species, are surely primordial. But nothing that must first be socially learned can be primordial. Ethnic identification is a theoretical, not an instinctive notion. If you have it, you learned it in your own lifetime, you did not somehow learn it at the Battle of Kosovo in 1389. History that predates us may play a role in our concern with ethnic conflict because it may show a range of possibilities that might not have been intuitively obvious. History might well suggest that we have a potential interest in preemptively protecting ourselves.

Assuming they do not learn through Lamarckian mechanisms of genetic inheritance, how do young adult Bosnians come to hate Bosnians of other ethnicities? It is plausible that, say, Muslims could do so in the grim conditions of their civil war, with Serbian soldiers raping Muslim women in evidently well-organized and deliberate attacks condoned by Serbian leaders and with Muslim mosques and homes being systematically destroyed by Serbian and Croatian mortar and rocket fire and even by prosaic and methodical dynamite squads. But how do they do so during more than four decades of peace, cooperation, neighborliness, and intermarriage? Of course, it was this last that preceded the war of the 1990s and, in turn, it was the war that preceded whatever ethnic hatred there now is. It therefore seems likely a canard on humanity to assert that ethnic hatred played the leading causal role in the Yugoslav violence.

Group Identification and War

In relatively casual language, nationalism is associated with two very different phenomena involving war. First, it is often associated with national states that go to war against each other. Second, it is often associated with internal "nations" such as Irish Catholics in the United Kingdom, Armenians and Lithuanians in the former Soviet Union, Hutus and Tutsis in Burundi and Rwanda, and Kurds in various countries. In the case of national states, war may often be causally prior to nationalism. In the case of internal nations, civil war is typically caused at least in part by the domestic nationalism.

For the first phenomenon, to say that war is causally prior to nationalism is not, of course, to say that nationalism develops only after a particular war starts. Rather, nationalism is often used *as a means to mobilize* a population for war, both during war and, often, in preparation for war. For example, the Nazi leadership first used nationalist appeals to mobilize the German people and then went to war. During that war, of course, they continued to use nationalist appeals. The Nazi leaders were presumably themselves acting from nationalist concerns, in which case the war was therefore partly caused by nationalism. But one may still suppose that the popular nationalist intensity was heightened by national leaders as a means to mobilize for war.[15] Such mobilization makes sense because coordination of a large population is a form of power. The ideal level of coordination for a government interested in fighting a war is likely to be at or near the whole-nation level.

In the case of subnationalisms, members of a subnational group may believe they can benefit individually if the group gains at the expense of some other group. Then they may respond to nationalist, ethnic, or religious appeals that come up spontaneously or through the deliberate efforts of potential leaders. *The possibility of coordination of an ethnic group entails the possibility of intergroup conflict.* If coordination were not possible, so that a particular group could not gain ascendancy in government, there would be no ground for conflict. Or, if there were nothing to gain from another group or from ascendancy over it, there would be little incentive for coordination of one's own group. But often there are ready advantages from coordinated action to gain political power.

At least in part, the role of nationalism in war is opportunistic. It can be the great coordinator not for collective action by the population so much as for charismatic power for mobilization of a kind that is especially needed for war. It is simply available as a focus for such coordination and therefore it is used. Other possible motivations, especially universalistic ones, may not be as effectively available as such foci. Woodrow Wilson's appeal to universalistic ideals after World War I foundered both at home and abroad on nationalist opposition. Stalin mobilized the Soviet people with nationalist and not merely communist rhetoric. The power and immediate success of Sergei Eisenstein's movie, *Alexander Nevsky* (1938), lay in its ethnic and nationalist portrayal of Germans versus Russians as the rising power of Hitler's Germany seemed to threaten the Soviet Union.[16] Class, religion, and even humanitarianism could all work to mobilize people under relevant circumstances, and the first two of these might be used to coordinate peoples for war, as religion has been used during the Crusades and in other times and places. But nationalist and ethnocentric identities seem especially suitable for warlike manipulation.

There need be nothing inherently warlike in nationalism itself. There may be instances of "pure" nationalism in the sense that individuals merely identify with a particular nation or subgroup without having an out-group against which to direct hostility and without having a goal that could be better achieved through massive coordination, as ethnic goals may be. As noted earlier (in chap. 4), Melville Herskovits supposes that much of the ethnocentrism of anthropological peoples is benign in this way.[17] The eighteenth-century German poet, Johann Gottfried Herder, defended a nonaggressive nationalism on the claim that, as Isaiah Berlin argues, to be human means something like having the epistemological comforts of home, of being among your own kind.[18] There might even be a psychology of nationalist commitment that is not motivated by interest in any central way. (The account of norms of exclusion in chapter 4 would not encompass such disinterested nationalism, although it might help to focus discussion even of such a case by helping to differentiate it from cases of coordination for group interest.) But, again, a leadership bent on war can take advantage of Herskovits's simple reasoning from the is-ought fallacy to amass popular support and to turn the nationalist sentiment militant.

Finally, note that if there are interests in group fates, as outlined above, then it may be virtually impossible to resolve many ethnic and nationalist conflicts directly. If a particular ethnic group or nation is to benefit from some policy, the benefit may be purchased at the cost of another group or nation. The conflict between two groups may not be resolvable through compromise that implies mutual gain over the status quo. Such conflicts might be finally trumped by dramatic economic benefits of cooperation, as in the West European community since sometime in the 1950s when the benefits of trade and open economies may finally have swamped the benefits of nationalist separatism. Québécois business leaders in the 1970s seem to have concluded that cooperative gains from staying in the Canadian federation outweighed potential gains from separation (see further discussion below, under "Québécois Nationalism"). The woeful irony of the current upsurge of ethnic conflict in the former Soviet Union is that the Soviet economy failed to lead people past the possibility of gaining at each other's expense. It failed to make the prospect of mutual gain better than that of conflictual gain. If we run up against severe limits to growth around the world, we may expect ethnic conflicts over limited opportunities to become harsher. In part this is for merely opportunistic reasons: Because a supposed ethnic group can proclaim its identity and take action against others, it may do so for the benefit of its members.

Unfortunately, if a group can benefit from gaining ascendancy over another, then the other has incentive to deter the first group. David Hume argued that there were two ways in which the ancient Anglo-Saxons under King Edgar deterred the Danes. They deterred the foreign Danes, who sometimes attacked from the sea, by maintaining navies to destroy them wherever they attacked. And they deterred the domestic Danes by suppressing them where they lived. "The foreign Danes dared not to approach a country which appeared in such a posture of defense:

The domestic Danes saw inevitable destruction to be the consequence of their tumults and insurrections."[19] In the jargon of modern deterrence theory, they practiced deterrence by denial against the foreign Danes and deterrence by punishment against the domestic Danes.

The chief form of deterrence that conflicting ethnic groups in the same state have against each other is yet a third variety: They deter through preemptive attack. They strive to suppress members of an opposing group where they are in order to prevent their eventual rise. Against the foreign Danes the Anglo-Saxons needed only to be strong to ward off violent conflict. Against the domestic Danes they had to engage in violence in order to retaliate for violence against themselves. Ethnic groups in almost all quarters of the globe seem deliberately to engage in violence in order to preempt violence against themselves. In this, they are like Mafia leaders, who strive to murder rivals for the leadership in order to preempt suffering further themselves.

TERRITORIAL CONSIDERATIONS

In many contexts, it is clear that peoples are better off joining together; in others, perhaps they are better off going their separate ways. Canada, Mexico, and the United States recently adopted the North American Free Trade Agreement (NAFTA) in order that their peoples might gain from the greater efficiencies of a larger North American market; the nations of the European Union (EU) have done likewise; the original United States Constitution was virtually a customs union to improve the American market; and many nations of the world have joined the General Agreement on Trade and Tariffs (GATT) to benefit from freer markets. But at the same time, Québécois have been debating secession from Canada, numerous former Soviet Republics have left the former Soviet Union, the Czech Republic and Slovakia have split, Slovenia and Croatia have seceded from Yugoslavia, and parts of Bosnia have been carved away to join Croatia and Serbia. Even in the midst of the cases of fragmentation, greater integration of the partial markets with larger, even world, markets would be beneficial to many of the relevant people. Hence, they are trading some presumed benefit from smaller national scale or greater homogeneity against the more readily assessable benefit of greater economic productivity from larger national scale. For example, an instant casualty of the Yugoslav wars was the near demise of the economical Yugo car and its corporation, whose parts were scattered among the parts of Yugoslavia.[20]

There appear to be two classes of fragmenting nations. The first, as in Slovakia, Slovenia, and Quebec, involves nations in which regions seemingly expect to gain merely from autonomy. The second, as in the de-

struction of Bosnia and the conflict in Northern Ireland, involves gains
to one region or people at the direct expense of another people. These
might be seen as noninvidious and invidious cases, respectively. Even in
the noninvidious cases of secession, there might be losses to the people
left over after the secession. For example, Czechs might lose from the
reduced scale of their market caused by the Slovakian secession. But the
supposed gains to the Slovakians do not come from these losses to the
Czechs, which are net losses to the joint community.

What, then, are the gains from homogeneity? From Herder forward,
supporters of noninvidious nationalism and ethnic identification have
struggled to define the gains beyond the epistemological comforts of
home. Their case remains largely metaphorical. True believers may not
need more than metaphor and rhetoric. But if others are to understand,
they will have to be given more than rhetoric. Moreover, the case for
noninvidious nationalism and ethnic identification must be balanced by
having them go sour when, in Eric Hobsbawm's words, the nationalist
or ethnic booster concludes, "We are different from and better than the
Others."[21]

In the invidious cases, it may not be difficult to imagine the benefits of
conquest. The Tutsis would clearly benefit economically from gaining
control over the lands of Rwanda if they could only expel the Hutus as
the Hutus earlier expelled many of them. (In the actual event, Tutsis of
the current generation might not gain, because their rebellion might be
too costly even if it succeeds.) Serbians can easily enough imagine gains
from squeezing Muslims off much of the land of Bosnia and Croatians
out of the Krajina district (formerly part of Croatia but now annexed to
Serbia). And Northern Irish Catholics and Protestants might easily imagine themselves as respective losers if Northern Ireland stays English or
reverts to Ireland.

Finally, there may be cases of internal conflict between well-defined
groups that do not involve substantial group claims against each other.
The Somali conflict discussed below might be such a case, in which the
only potential beneficiaries are the warlords who hope eventually to gain
control of the nation. The loyalists of one of these might be motivated to
support him not because they expect to gain from the whole enterprise
but because they can only lose even more from the defeat of their clans-
man than from his victory.

Analytically, the most difficult question in all the cases is what the
secessionists gain in the noninvidious cases, such as Slovakia and Quebec. Apart from the fact that many Slovakians and Québécois think they
stand to gain, it is hard to specify what the gains can be, and they have
done a poor job of explaining themselves. There are, of course, likely to

be career gains to particular political leaders who back the fragmentation from the larger nation.

All three of these types of conflict are represented in the cases surveyed below. Northern Ireland, Burundi and Rwanda, and Yugoslavia all involve invidious conflicts in which there must be grand losers to enable the winners to gain. Quebec is most likely a noninvidious conflict in which (at least some) Québécois think they would gain from secession but in which their presumptive gains would not be taken from other Canadians. And Somalia may be a nearly pure case of mere leadership struggles. The conflict in Yugoslavia has also been spurred by leadership struggles as has, apparently, that in Quebec. Canadian Prime Minister Jean Chrétien, a federalist from Quebec, notes that Lucien Bouchard, a leader of the separatist movement in the nineties, had earlier belonged to the Liberals, the Parti Québécois, the New Democratic Party, and the Tories. "That man has a certain flexibility," Chrétien says.[22] One might say the same of Slobodan Milosevic, Gerry Adams, and many other ethnic separatists. But in this respect, they are not unusual, they are merely politicians with eyes on their careers.

Contemporary Cases of Violent Conflict

Conflict between ethnic groups is commonplace. Extensive violence between such groups is far less common. Hence, it follows that the incidence of violence requires something beyond merely the fact of ethnic conflict for its explanation. What leads to conflict is fairly systematic considerations, as outlined here, especially in chapters 3 and 4. What turns a conflict violent may be far less systematic, because violence is commonly a tipping phenomenon.[23] That is to say, when violence goes beyond some level, mechanisms for maintaining order may break down enough that violence can flare out of control and fuel itself. While tipping may occur from systematic accumulation of similar events, it can also occur from more or less random shocks. Violence is a tipping phenomenon because, once it begins or reaches a high enough level, it is often self-reinforcing. Violence can provoke reprisals and preemptive attacks. Very quickly, the general stability of expectations of reasonable behavior can collapse, making preemption seem to be a compelling interest, thereby insuring further violence.

One can see how diverse the events that tip conflicts into violence are from the survey of several cases below. These cases will be presented very briefly. In some respects, greater detail would not help substantially in our understanding of them, although it might well help to determine the points at which the events began to spiral out of control and into violence. But all of the cases have the quality that, to a large extent, they could have gone in many ways. The greater detail that would tell us why one case tipped the way it did rather than another way can often—perhaps usually—be treated as essentially accidental. For example, British intelligence might have penetrated and destroyed the Irish Republican Army as it revived around 1970. Tito might have died a decade or more earlier when the Yugoslavian economy was doing well and could have driven the successor regime to maintain the mixed society. The United Nations might have intervened in the Horn of Africa before mayhem had a chance to destroy much of the institutional and economic structure of its nations.

Some of these things are worthy topics for explanation, but not all of them are, at least not for social scientists, although, for example, Tito's longevity might be of interest to medical gerontologists. But one may proceed with trying to explain the range of violence in the ethnic conflicts of the era without explaining all the details. Indeed, it is inherent in typical coordination interactions that they could go more than one way, as in left or right, or perhaps in many ways, as in the plausible slang constructions for any notion. For example, the driving convention has gone left in some regions and right in others. There might be interesting explanations for why North America spontaneously adopted the convention of driving on the right while Sweden and England originally adopted the opposite convention—but not very interesting. The convention on the use of "nigger" as a black term of approbation may have depended on millions of accidental choices (as discussed in chap. 4). We need not explain those individual choices in order to have a compelling understanding of the final result of them. And what we want to understand may include only that final result.

If history had gone only slightly otherwise, the ethnic groups, languages, religions, and, therefore, borders of the regions of Yugoslavia might have been radically different. Primordialists would then be telling us that there was something natural about this radically different Yugoslavia. And communitarians would be telling us there was something right about the values of its various ethnic communities. What would be natural and what would be right would be essentially accidental.

Yugoslavia

Until recently, Yugoslavia was often seen as an example of a multi-ethnic state that worked. Its population, according to the most recent and presumably final national census of 1981 was 36 percent Serbian, 20 percent Croatian, 9 percent Muslim (meaning exclusively Muslim Slavs, and not including Turks or Albanians, who are not Slavs), 8 percent each Slovenes and Albanians, 6 percent Macedonians, 5 percent "Yugo-slavs," 3 percent Montenegrins, and 2 percent Hungarians, with sprin-klings of several other groups.[24] It was federally organized into six re-publics and two provinces (Vojvodina and Kosovo). Three of these eight federal units had relatively homogeneous populations: Slovenia, Kosovo, and Montenegro. Bosnia was by far the least homogeneous.[25] Serbia has absorbed Vojvodina and Kosovo, which bring it concentrated ethnic minorities, and it appears likely to absorb much of Bosnia. The unraveling of Yugoslavia might be thought to have begun with Serbian suppression in 1981 of Kosovo agitation for elevation to republic status. This signaled other groups about possible futures.

Although there are also other conflicts, including the simmering Al-banian Kosovo unease in the new Serbian world, the violent conflicts centrally at issue in Yugoslavia since 1991 are between Serbs, Croats, and Muslims. Most of the Muslims are in Bosnia but, because they are a minority of the Bosnian population, it is misleading to think of them as "the" Bosnians as one might think of Croats as the Croatians and Serbs as the Serbians. The three peoples are essentially the same people—much more so than are, for example, the Swiss with their several languages, diverse ethnic backgrounds, and religious differences. They are south Slavs who speak the same language, Serbo-Croatian, although this lan-guage is written in the Roman alphabet in Croatia and in Cyrillic in Serbia and Bosnia. Dialect differences are said by some linguists to be less significant than dialect differences between English in the United Kingdom and English in the United States. In any case, they are regional rather than ethnic—for example, Serbs, Croats, and Muslims of Mostar speak the same dialect. As though to counter or ridicule their own claim that their language encapsulates their history, Croatian leaders set about trying to separate Croatian from Serbian and from its own regional dia-lects in Bosnia.[26] Further evidence that the ethnic purists stand on air is that two-thirds of the half million people of Montenegro believe that Montenegrins are indistinct from Serbs, while the other third claim there are irreconcilable differences.[27] Whichever definition a Montenegrin ac-cepts, the implicit nation—greater Serbia or Montenegro—is surely an instance of what Benedict Anderson calls imagined communities.[28]

The Muslims of Bosnia are merely the descendants of those Slavs who converted to Islam during the Ottoman hegemony or later. For example, the builder of the now-destroyed Ferhadiya Mosque in Banja Luka was Ferhad Pasha Sokolovic, whose Serbian uncle converted to Islam after the Ottoman invasion.[29] Many of the Muslims must descend from the Protestant Bogomils, who may also be the origin of the Huguenot and Bohemian Protestant sects. No doubt there are people who today count as Croats and Serbs who converted back from Islam or who descend from such reconverts. Both the conversions and reconversions must commonly have been spontaneous and individual and must therefore have split families and neighborhoods. In a sense, Bosnia was converted into its multi-cultural status.

The chief standard difference between the three peoples is religion, although it is not an important concern to large numbers of Yugoslavs, who were among the least religious people in the world when their society turned bloody. Bogdan Denitch reports attempting to do a survey in Yugoslavia some years ago and encountering a subject who, when asked his religion, wanted first to know Denitch's religion. "I'm an atheist," Denitch said. His subject retorted, "I know all you damn intellectuals are atheists, but are you a Catholic, Orthodox, or Muslim atheist?"[30] For him, the religious label was merely a nationality label. There is symbolic emptiness in this move. It says there is nothing of religious importance in the label. But if there is nothing of religious importance, there is nothing of *any* importance in the label. It is merely a vacuous signal for coordination on exclusion and even murder. In any case, the three-way conflict between Muslims, Croats, and Serbs is not marked by the kind of definition that separates, say, Armenians from Azeris on coincident lines of language, religion, and genetic lineage.

There has, of course, been a history of conflict and even violence between the groups, but the versions of that history declaimed by the leaders of the current conflict are debased and largely false. These versions are a clear instance of Renan's dictum that nationalists get their history wrong.[31] A thesis of comparative politics in earlier decades was that cross-cutting cleavages (for example, you and I share religion but differ in class) lead to pluralistic stability, while overlapping cleavages lead to divisive conflict. That thesis once seemed to be supported by Yugoslavia; it now seems belied by that country.

The current Yugoslav disaster is similar to 1917 in Russia, 1945–49 in China, and the late 1970s in Iran in an important strategic respect. The disaster began at a time of tottering weakness of the central regime that fell under the sway of a Serbian jingoist, and that enabled a similarly jingoist Croatian leader to think it possible to secede from Yugoslavia and even preemptively to suppress Croatian Serbs.[32] The earlier Russian and Chinese regimes had been mortally weakened by war and the Iranian regime had been broken by the death agony of the Shah. All three were therefore relatively easily pushed aside by modest revolutionary organizations. The Yugoslav federation was severely weakened by internal political conflicts over the succession of Marshal Tito, who died in 1980 after keeping potential successors weak lest they try to succeed him before he was ready and after leading the economy into stagnation after earlier decades of impressive growth and development.

There were many important events along the way from 1980 to the early 1990s.[33] With the death of Tito and an economy that would not perform well, discredited Communist leaders used nationalist appeals to cling to power. Milosevic proposed as early as 1986 to make Serbia the dominant nation of the Yugoslav federation—if necessary, by inciting large Serbian minorities in other republics to demand Serbian protection. Serbia was the strongest part of Yugoslavia and Serbs dominated the military. But Serbs were also large minorities in Croatia, Kosovo, and Bosnia-Hercegovina. In the face of these seeming threats, Croatia moved for independence in 1990. Plausibly the Croatian leaders assumed that they would never see a better moment for success, but their move threatened the 600–700,000 Serbs in Croatia. As though to exacerbate the threat to the Croatian Serbs, the new Croatian constitution declared them a "protected minority" (not a promising term) and the Croatian government began to remove them from the police. The dismissed police officers re-formed as paramilitary units in opposition to the new state. Serbia intervened on their side and Yugoslavia tipped into disaster.

Preemptive moves are often made because the other side cannot credibly commit to act in certain cooperative ways. Restate the previous story of Croatia. The Croatian Serbs cannot commit themselves to be loyal to Croatia. Croatia therefore preempts the possibility that the Croatian Serbs will be a fifth column in the Croatian police and military by removing them from those bodies. Once the Croatians have done that, there is no way they can commit themselves to be fair in their further treatment of Croatian Serbs, who therefore rebel and seek help from Serbia.

If relevant commitments to cooperation were difficult in Croatia, they were virtually impossible in Bosnia. With Croatia gone from the federation, in the words of Robert J. Myers, Bosnia may have become a no longer avoidable tragedy.[34] Even at the outset, its prospects looked relatively bleak. The population of Bosnia was about two million Slavic Muslims, one and a half million Serbs, and just under a million Croats. The Muslims were not even a majority and were only slightly more numerous than the Serbs. Bosnia was the very image of Yugoslavia and its existence at all depended on its being only a part of Yugoslavia. But, with Slovenia and Croatia out of Yugoslavia, it—or at least its Muslim population—seemed likely to be reduced to subordinate status.

Given its mix of peoples, Bosnians should have viewed independence as impractical. When their government, under President Alija Izetbegovic, a one-time champion of an Islamic state in Bosnia, chose independence in December 1991, their ruin was secured.[35] Because of the difficult mix of populations in Bosnia-Hercegovina, Tito had established the principle that the three constituent "nations," Muslims, Serbs, and Croats, were to coexist in the governing of Bosnia and that all three would have to agree before constitutional changes could be made.[36] Bosnian secession from Yugoslavia violated that principle because the Bosnian Serbs (or, rather, their representatives) opposed it. But, arguably, the principle had died with the secession of Slovenia and Croatia and the implicit death of Yugoslavia.

Through all of this development, the principal leaders seem scurrilous. But they may also seem to have been relatively rational in their sequenced reactions to various turns in the mounting violence. People of good will, forced to choose in some of these moments, might have done as badly. Even people of good will can be panicked into escalating moves by the fear of failing to respond to an aggressive adversary, especially when preemptive responses might be vastly more beneficial than later responses. As Misha Glenny writes, "In order to understand the atrocities, we must understand the politics, and not the other way around."[37] He thinks the politics is that of territorial-acquisition and, evidently, personal political power. A partial exception might be Izetbegovic, who was earlier sentenced to prison for publishing his theses on an Islamic state, and whose beliefs may have weighed at least as heavily as his own career interests.[38]

Kaplan argues on the contrary that Communism suppressed and magnified millennial conflicts that, once given normal room to play, exploded with all the fantastic hatred and suspicion of the seemingly insane Yugoslavs of all ethnicities.[39] "The Balkans," he writes, "are a region of pure memory."[40] Evil memories turn to bullets, atrocities are the natural response to myth, hatred is the stuff of every group. It is all fate and doom, inescapable and endlessly repeated throughout history. Eric Hobsbawm eloquently excoriates such perversions of history.[41] But, on Kaplan's account, the recent explosions and especially the atrocities could as well have been spontaneous upheavals from below. Indeed, they were merely the expectable further expression of the long history of violent hatreds among the peoples of Yugoslavia. Those hatreds have become primordial, almost mystical. They have become poetic and transhistorical and even beyond meaning: "Today's events are nothing more than the sum total of everything that has gone before."[42] The most grandiloquent, florid metaphor evidently cannot suffice to capture their spirit.

Kaplan's view is flatly contradicted by the simplest facts of the history of the conflicts, which have been led and enflamed from above, with rabidly distorted national control of almost all television and information on the conflicts. The hatred had to be mobilized. It took a year of war in Bosnia to produce expulsions and mass atrocities. Glenny aptly calls this history a paradox for the thesis of ethnic hatred.[43] Kaplan is as guilty as the most rabid Yugoslav leaders of getting the history wrong. Against his view, the distorted past events have been seen as means, not ends. They are principally means to hold onto political leadership in grim times. The leadership of these groups is often purely opportunistic. As the Belgrade actor Boro Todorovic noted in 1991, the Serbian nationalist leaders "until yesterday were champions of the League of Communists, fighters for brotherhood and unity."[44] They were, to be consistent over their political careers, champions only of themselves and their own personal opportunities.

Hence, as Michael Ignatieff says, "It is not how the past dictates to the present, but how the present manipulates the past that is decisive." To mobilize for war, "nationalists had to convince neighbors and friends that in reality they had been massacring each other since time immemorial. But history has no such lesson to teach . . . [T]he Balkan peoples had to be transformed from neighbors into enemies, just as the whole region had to be turned from a model of interethnic peace into a nightmare from the pages of Thomas Hobbes."[45] The reporter, Slavenka Drakulic, had "always defined herself by her education, profession, gender, and personality," but in 1991 she found herself "stripped of all defining marks of identity other than simply being a Croatian."[46]

Some of the worst, most violent political leaders in a century of dreadful political leaders have engineered the violence and the ethnic hatred, most of which has, of course, been carried out by armies under higher orders.[47] Moreover, the leaders have seized on enflaming so-called ethnic hatred in part merely out of opportunism—the grim and often cruel deaths of tens of thousands are no more than a means for them to gain and hold office. Large percentages of all the major groups were so far from hating each other at the outset of the conflagrations that they were heavily intermarried. There may be no society that has enjoyed a broader mixing of ethnicities in the past four or five decades. In the United States there is massive intermarriage between some groups, such as those of varied European national origin, but relatively little between other groups, such as blacks and Asians, blacks and whites, and Asians and whites.

Many of the intermarried Yugoslavs may have had their lives wrecked even more thoroughly and hatefully than have the typical Bosnian, Croatian, and Serbian nationals who have not intermarried. Recall the epigraph of chapter 4 of the Serbian refugee from Sarajevo who was impressed into military service in one of the Serbian units besieging the Muslim-majority city. To make up for his remaining eighteen months with the Muslims of Sarajevo, he was invited to kill a Muslim to prove his loyalty to Serbia.[48] If a Serb of Sarajevo could not be trusted, how much less a Serb married to a Croat or Bosnian could be trusted. And how about a Serb whose cousin is a convert to Islam?

Perhaps the most striking act that is taken to represent hatred in the Yugoslav disaster is the seemingly deliberate destruction of the most beautiful towns and cities, including Bosnia's capital, Sarajevo, and Croatian Vukovar, which was completely and methodically leveled or, as Serbs declared, liberated.[49] Hitler in defeat wanted to burn Paris. Hitler and the Serbian leaders want the destruction not merely of people and government, but of civilization. Bogdan Bogdanovic, an architect and former mayor of Belgrade, detects "a malicious animus against everything urban, everything urbane, that is, against a complex semantic cluster that includes spirituality, morality, language, taste, and style. From the fourteenth century onward the word 'urbanity' in most European languages has stood for dignity, sophistication, the unity of thought and word, word and feeling, feeling and action. People who cannot meet its demands find it easier to do away with it altogether."[50]

But, again, the animus in the architectural and urban destruction is preemptive and future-oriented. The Serbs wish to secure their hold by eliminating centers and institutions of potential opposition. Much of the intermarriage in Yugoslavia has been in the cities. In destroying Sarajevo, the Serbians do not destroy a Muslim city, they destroy a multicultural city, which may be far more offensive to them than a Muslim city would be. Similarly, Vukovar was a multicultural city, with 43 percent Croats, 37 percent Serbs, and 20 percent Hungarians and others.[51] The Serbian warmongers do not value the Serbs in such cities. The mobilizers of ethnicity want ignorance first and foremost. They want woefully restricted horizons in order to induce the lowest denominator of the epistemological comforts of the ethnic home, in order to induce blinkered loyalty. Evidently, they find people who fit their mold more readily in rural areas than in cities.[52] Ignorance and urbanity have gone to war, and urbanity has been the instant loser in Yugoslavia.

Some of the destruction is more precisely targeted. Large numbers of Mosques and Muslim libraries have been selectively destroyed. The destruction has not merely been by mortar fire, as much of what we have seen in Sarajevo has been. Rather, the Serbian forces have dynamited mosques, then bulldozed the rubble to leave empty fields where weeds might grow. They may have destroyed half the mosques of Bosnia. And they have executed or deported hundreds of Muslim clerics.[53] They specifically wish to destroy anything that smacks of Muslim community just as they wish to destroy anything that smacks of cosmopolitan transcendence of narrow community.

Note a peculiarity of the Yugoslav disaster. Insofar as its motivations are those of Milosevic and rabid nationalists, with their recollections of conflicts from World War II and from many centuries earlier, their present attacks have the character of the Corsican *vendetta transversale*, which is revenge visited upon a relative of the perpetrator. *Vendetta transversale* had some point in a society, such as that of Iceland or Corsica, in which family members might be induced by the threat of their own collateral murder to take responsibility for policing their fellow family members' actions. It has no point in the context of Yugoslavia. There can be no *vendetta transversale* defense of ethnic groups against one another. The only defense must be the preemptive one that makes reference to future threats, in which past threats are merely evidence of the range of possibilities. That defense is strictly a defense of pure conflict, not of moral rightness based on retribution. The latter can apply to living Yugoslavs only with respect to their current atrocities.

Northern Ireland

People who write about and work on ethnic conflicts often note that, while they can make sense of many of them, they can make little sense of that in Northern Ireland. For a quarter-century, it has been fought by paramilitary groups, beginning with the revived Irish Republican Army (IRA), and followed by similarly violent Protestant groups such as the Ulster Defense Association and the Ulster Volunteer Force. The violence began soon after the rise of an impressive, but peaceful, civil rights movement in defense of the personal rights of Catholics in Northern Ireland in 1968. (There was still a property qualification for voting in local elections—this discriminated against Catholics, who were poorer and less likely to own property. Hence, the civil rights movement was demanding, among other things, "one man, one vote.")

Local Protestant police forces failed to protect Catholic civil rights activists and even, while off-duty, participated in attacking a civil rights march in January 1969. British troops were dispatched to protect the demonstrators. The entry of British troops was, hence, initially an analog of the use of federal troops in the civil rights struggles in the American South. But the government of Ted Heath ended home rule in Northern Ireland and put its six counties under direct government from London. British soldiers soon turned to ferreting out and arresting republican activists and they have lingered to fight a quasi-war. Their presence, the revival of the IRA, and the re-creation of Protestant paramilitary terror squads, have made the past quarter-century a bloody era, with more than three thousand deaths (one person in about five hundred) and other brutalities from sectarian violence.[54]

The conflict in Northern Ireland is similar to the chiliastic movement of the Lubavitchers in Crown Heights, New York (discussed in chap. 7), in that it embroils a society that is well-educated and relatively prosperous. It seems difficult therefore to see it as in the interest of those involved in it. How then does it succeed? Let us canvass two possible answers.

First, another way to frame the problem of the IRA is to say that, for it to work, it must do a remarkably thorough and pervasive job of distorting the understanding of its recruits to get them to identify sufficiently strongly with the group as virtually to surrender the normal identities of their time and place. They require not merely the epistemological comforts of home to motivate them. They require the suppression of ordinary understandings, the imposition of an astonishing degree of ignorance in a society in which such ignorance must be hard to achieve.

How is such unusual ignorance in the midst of a modern society maintained? Plausibly, it is the product of the move to a defensive structure for the IRA in its fight for Irish independence from English rule earlier this century. That move was to decentralize its organization into individual cells with little or no connection between them. With this structure, similar to that analyzed by Philip Selznick for the American Communist Party,[55] successful police infiltration could do little harm to the movement beyond a single cell. Similarly, a traitor could do little harm because he or she had little information to share with the enemy. Evidently, even prison offers a more enlightened society than these cells, and radicals might often come out of prison opposed to continuation of the violence for which they were convicted.[56]

Unfortunately, the cellular structure leaves the IRA out of control. If individual cells can consistently recruit new, young members and can consistently isolate them from influences of the larger society, they can sustain lives of their own. And over time they may tend toward the most extreme positions through exclusion of the less committed and the urge to declare and display total commitment (see further, chap. 4, under "Functional Explanation" and "The Epistemology of Norms"). In recent years, they seem often to strive deliberately to embarrass Gerry Adams (the head of Sinn Féin, the political wing of the republican movement) in his claims that they are really reasonable and that they want peace. They are like Serbian General Mladic in Bosnia—they have no superior to whom to answer for their actions and they confound the politicians by cavalierly violating agreements.

Hence, the conflict in Northern Ireland may largely be a historical residue. It may once have made some sense at the level of individual participants in it, but now it makes sense at that level only as the product of the past mobilization of the IRA. The past mobilization created cells with autonomous power to recruit members and to indoctrinate them, producing, one may suppose, a combination of moral commitment and epistemological ignorance that guarantees actions that, in the abstract, seem contrary to self-interest. As though to match the IRA, Protestant terrorist cells work the other side of this atavism. The remarkable result is an ethnic-religious mobilization in a society that is relatively well-off by world standards and that might be still better off if it were not disrupted by extremist actions of terrorism.

Second, the remarkable intensity of the IRA activists is, *even in Northern Ireland*, extraordinary. There are only a few hundred active participants in a population of about half a million Catholics, and some of the activists are probably from the Republic of Ireland. The average long-term member has been responsible for several murders. There may soon be more movies and novels about the IRA than it has members. They are a fringe, more of a fringe even than the activists in many other contemporary cases of ethnic violence. Nor do they have broad support. In the elections of 1992, Gerry Adams could not hold his Parliamentary seat even in a predominantly Catholic district. The party itself won only about 11 percent of the Northern Irish vote—a third of the voters are Catholic, so that Sinn Féin won a third of the Catholic vote—and less than 2 percent in the Republic of Ireland. Most of the Catholics of Northern Ireland are said to support John Hume, who renounces the use of violence.[57] A distressing tone of Sinn Féin's political program finds resonance in the party's name, which means "we, ourselves" and therefore seems to say, "not yours, get out," to the Protestants. The party labels itself with a norm of exclusion as clear and antagonistic as any in the annals of ethnic conflict short of genocidal norms.[58] Yet, seen from the side of those attempting to mobilize the Irish, it may sound like a positive name, a name that rallies "us" to the cause.

According to an apparently sensitive and articulate Protestant doctor—who served in the emergency room of a West Belfast hospital, where he treated many bomb and gunshot victims, including Gerry Adams, and who supports union of the two Irelands—the Protestants of Northern Ireland fear "communal death."[59] "We would be lost," they say.[60] It is in some ways an odd fear, in other ways an obvious fear. It is odd in that most of the Protestants of Northern Ireland must think that their majority government provides the possibility of communal life to minority Catholics. For some reason, however, they doubt that the Catholic majority government of the Republic of Ireland would provide Protestants any possibility of communal life. Evidently, they think Protestants are decent and fair, Catholics vicious and partisan. But the fear is obvious in that shifting from being part of a Protestant nation (the United Kingdom) to being part of a Catholic nation involves risks. (At the moment, however, every choice involves risks; the status quo brings the risk of long-term violence and the slow degradation of the life and economy of Northern Ireland for both Catholics and Protestants.)

The Protestant extremists are accused of particularly vile policies in that they seem to attack ordinary people rather than soldiers, police, or political leaders. In part, this difference might be merely one of opportunity. There are no alternative army or police forces and there are few political leaders for Protestants to attack. In actual fact, of course, the Protestants attack leaders when they can, as they attempted to assassinate Bernadette and Michael McAliskey in 1981. Bernadette was formerly Bernadette Devlin, an internationally renowned civil rights activist, once very popular in the United States, who had since become a militant republican. In any case, the IRA also attacks and often kills relative innocents, such as shoppers or bus riders. Moreover, both Catholic and Protestant paramilitary groups shoot up their own communities. The IRA is said to have pumped more bullets into fellow Irish Catholics than they did into the British Army in 1993.[61] This might make sense for an organization that is hardly an organization but is merely a collection of independent cells, each of which might use its deadly capacities for its own particular purposes as well as for the republican cause. Such narrowing of interests may be the way of all groups.

Somalia

Hobbes's vision of the anomic, individualized state of nature may be fundamentally refuted by the recent quasi-order of Somalia. Hobbes feared individual-to-individual warfare. But somewhere between his so-called state of nature and the well-governed national state there is the possibility of spontaneously organized subgroups. So long as there are other societies wealthy and organized enough to produce modern weaponry, especially assault rifles, armored cars, light artillery, and portable rockets, a state of nature will be subject to anarchically organized warfare between relatively large but unstable groups. It will not be a Hobbesian war of all against all in which each individual must fear *every* other individual. Philosophical anarchists are generally right in their central claim: Anarchy need not mean chaos. There is at least sub-order in the anarchy of Somalia. And sub-order may be far more destructive than any likely more complete order would be and possibly more destructive than a Hobbesian state of nature just because the destruction is somewhat organized and not merely spontaneous.

In a society torn into sub-orders, any line of identification may be seized upon to define loyalties, so that any merely personal conflict over leadership might turn willy-nilly into an ethnic or tribal conflict. As it happens, the actual Somali conflict of the early 1990s has been between two powerful leaders within the powerful Hawiya clan. Mohammed Ali Mahdi and Mohammed Farah Aidid are fighting over the succession to Mohammed Siad Barre, who was overthrown in January 1991. Hence, the violence shares central features with the violence in Yugoslavia. It is largely the engineered product of ambitious leaders.

Barre had been, in the view of some, a Somali nationalist who appealed over the clans to national unity. As was Tito, he was of mixed descent and perhaps therefore naturally a nationalist. He declared himself a Somali, and, David Laitin says, "most of his followers accepted this as honest."[62] Many in the Mageertayn and Isaaq clans called him a Marehan, after his father's but not his mother's clan. This was intended as a put-down, as though to call him bush league. He attacked Ethiopia in 1977 in the hope of annexing the part of it that was populated by Somalis, and his war made him nationally popular. He allied with clan leaders and armed the clans as support for the national army. When the Soviet Union switched from backing him to backing Ethiopia, his army was crushed.

The newly armed clan leaders then turned on Barre, calling his dictatorship the MOD government—for Marehan, Ogaadeen, and Dulbahante, the three clans of his family. In self-defense, Barre also resorted to recruiting clan followings. The former nationalist turned to opportunistically playing on groupism in order to maintain his position. Both Barre and his opponents attempted (successfully, alas) to mobilize clan loyalties in order to top each other in the national conflict. In essence, the defeat and consequent weakness of the national government gave opportunity for alternatives, and these fastened on clan identifications, which exacerbated the incipient anarchy.

Somalia is an accidental state whose borders could as well have been drawn radically differently but were drawn more coherently than those of many other African nations. It comprises many clans that, in 1993, were divided into at least fourteen warring factions. The then chief of United Nations forces, Major General Imtiaz Shaheen, said, "It is just a geographical land mass called Somalia,"[63] apparently meaning that it had no government. In one sense, Shaheen was wrong. Somalia the state coincides remarkably well with the distribution of Somalis, with the exception of those in Ethiopia. But in another sense, he was right. Civil warfare reduced Somalia to such poverty and starvation that the United Nations and the United States intervened primarily in the attempt to feed the starving. Foodstuffs could not simply be directed to the central authorities—there were no longer any central authorities. Shaheen was talking about the Somalia in which the UN has intervened. *That* Somalia *is* merely a geographical land mass fought over by many groups, especially the two Hawiya leaders.

Many people might idealize civil-war Somalia as somehow just the old Somalia in a moment of duress. But anyone hoping to see order come to it cannot so trivially idealize it. The prospects for peace in the longer run are dismal if the warlords cannot be brought together or be brought under control because several of them have enormous power based in their huge caches of arms, and they could perhaps maintain the destructiveness of their quasi-order indefinitely. Re-coordinating civil-war Somalia on order will be very difficult.

A well-educated Somali of the Hawiya clan of Aidid and Mahdi suggested that the best thing foreigners could do would be to buy assault rifles from individual Somalis.[64] He may have had a clearer sense of the nature of the Somali problem than do western political leaders, who betray almost no ideas. The *New Yorker* reporter who quoted the Somali's suggestion seemed to think it simplistic as though the bloodiness of the feud between Aidid and Mahdi were not related to the availability of deadly weapons. It is not simplistic nor is the violence and destructiveness of the feud somehow determined in its own right independently of structural constraints and masses of cheap weapons.

Hutus vs. Tutsis

Ethnic differences in Burundi and Rwanda may be like those in Bosnia in the sense that they now seem to pose an inevitable tragedy. The Tutsis comprise a relatively small minority—10 to 15 percent according to stylized statistics not founded on recent censuses—of the populations of these nations. (Despite the supposed 15 percent Tutsi representation in Burundi, in the national election of June 1993, the Hutu candidate for president won 65 percent of the vote and the Tutsi candidate won 33 percent.[65] Many Tutsis supposedly boycotted that election, calling it an ethnic census.) But they have historically been in the position of political and military domination over the majority Hutus. Both nations now have Hutu-dominated governments, but Tutsis still dominate the military in Burundi. There is a very small third group, the pygmy Twa, who are said to be less than 1 percent of the populations. (They are near relatives of Ota Benga, who suffered mortally from his loss of identification after going to America.[66])

There is, however, on the accounts of many journalists and scholars, a striking difference between the various Bosnians, on the one hand, and the Hutus and Tutsis, on the other. An outsider in Bosnia might have to work to determine who is Muslim, Croatian, or Serbian. No one, it is often implied, typically has to work at distinguishing most of the Hutus from most of the Tutsis. The Tutsis, descendants of Nilotic or Ethiopian interlopers, are typically lighter and taller. In their attacks on Tutsis, the Hutus hack off their lower legs, as though symbolically to cut them down to size and to eliminate a source of their political power.

On this view, the Hutus and the Tutsis are typically unlikely to be mistaken about *identity* in an objective sense. In this instance, *identification* might readily go with identity, so readily that each might assume the most likely identification of anyone is with that person's ethnic group. Unlike most cases of ethnic conflict discussed here, this one involves visually compelling differences. It is therefore easy to coordinate on the group identifications and hard to break the coordination.

Suppose these descriptive claims were true, or roughly true. There is still the difficult question of *why the designations Tutsi and Hutu have become ethnic labels*. Lucy Mair asserts that the distinction between Tutsi and Hutu depends on the possibility of owning cattle.[67] René Le-marchand argues further that the very terms, Tutsi, Hutu, Twa, the *ganwa* or princely elite, and king identified positions that individuals held, not the ineradicable features of the individuals. A *ganwa* could be demoted to Tutsi status, while Hutus and Twa could rise to Tutsi status. Moreover, under another set of meanings, the status terms were strictly relative: A *ganwa* was Hutu to the king, and a Tutsi was Hutu to a *ganwa*. Tutsis used their daughters to marry into important Hutu families.[68] All of these were social, not ethnic categories.

Clearly then, the division of the Tutsis and Hutus into *hostile* ethnic groups is not an inescapable primordial fact but a social construction, a very recent one at that. The social construction comes from more than three decades of nearly constant ethnic strife in which many have been periodically killed and brutalized. Unlike the Yugoslavians, who lived amicably with each other for forty-five years before their recent atrocities, the Hutus and Tutsis have living memories of recent, murderous confrontations. Like the Yugoslavians who have been subjected to the racist tirades of Milosevic, Tudjman, and other venal leaders, Rwandan ethnic animosities were, for seventeen years, cultivated by a corrupt, failed domestic leader, President Juvénal Habyarimana. A Hutu at the head of a Hutu-dominated government, Habyarimana evidently thought he needed the distractions of racism to maintain his personal control.[69]

State-controlled Rwanda radio continued to incite hatred of Tutsis during the violence after Habyarimana's death.[70] A radical Hutu station called on Hutus to kill Tutsis. "When you are killing the wives, don't spare those who are pregnant," the station urged. "The mistake we made in 1959 was not to kill the children. Now they have come back to fight us."[71] These Hutus perhaps share with the Croatian killer of

Mostar the recognition that their cause is merely to secure their interests. As did the Athenians at Mílos and Julius Caesar in Gaul, they slaughtered thousands to preempt future conflict.

Monique Mujawamariya, a Rwandan peace activist, blamed the initial violence after the president's death on "small bands of young men who'd been systematically transformed by the regime into killing machines . . . and then unleashed upon the population."[72] Although Tutsi rebels contributed to the slaughter in April 1994, the United Nations Security Council attributed the worst of the massacres to Rwandan government forces.[73] Hence, Mujawamariya and the Security Council concur in judging that the horrors result from central organization rather than from spontaneous displays of supposed ethnic hatred.

In part, the confrontations have been partly about class or economic issues, just as the group labels originally were. Tutsis are cattle owners who control a disproportionate share of the national land; Hutus till the soil. Indeed, even the relative physical differences may depend in part on diet, with the Tutsis benefiting from a high protein diet that includes drinking fresh blood and milk from their cattle.[74] There is therefore evidently a significant correlation of ethnicity and economic position that defines the conflict between Tutsis and Hutus. But, as they have living memories of violence, so also they have living memories of cooperation, including the rise of Hutus to the status of Tutsi when they have been successful first as clients of Tutsis, then as peers.[75] In attacking Tutsis, the Hutus also attack their Hutu clients. In the recent chaos in Rwanda after the death of President Habyarimana, marauding Hutus evidently killed opponents of Habyarimana, including both Hutus and Tutsis. During the subsequent attacks by Tutsi rebels, Hutus fled into Tanzania in vast numbers just as, earlier, Tutsis had fled Rwanda. The difficult, rugged terrain of Burundi and Rwanda, which lie in the mountainous continental divide between the Nile and the Congo watersheds, often keeps local populations separated from those in neighboring valleys. These countries have very high rates of population growth and the highest population densities in Africa.[76] Hence, good agricultural land is in short supply in both Burundi and Rwanda and the land is getting more strained each year.

But, finally, one might not wish to call the conflict between Hutus and Tutsis a class conflict because the two "classes" are virtually unrelated to each other—they are not in complementary roles. Tutsis raise cattle primarily for their own use, while Hutus raise crops primarily for their own consumption, and both Rwanda and Burundi are organized primarily in agricultural subsistence units that spread over the land. The two groups do have an economic conflict—but it is merely a conflict for alternative uses of limited resources. They are like the warring kings of France and

Spain, who, the French king said, were in complete agreement: They both wanted the same thing.

Recent violence began in 1959 when Ruanda-Urundi was on the eve of independence as two separate nations. In colonial and pre-colonial times, the Tutsis had been in dominant positions despite their far lesser numbers and, with post-colonial independence, the Hutus wanted to change the relationship. By 1963 they had driven large numbers of Tutsis from Rwanda and killed many others,[77] leaving Tutsis as only about 10 percent of the population. There have been periodic excesses since, although none as grim as the recent mayhem in Rwanda. Before colonial times, there had been frequent civil wars of succession, although too little is known of these to assess whether they involved ethnic conflict.[78]

In newly independent Burundi, politics was initially not centrally about ethnic conflict but about legislative versus monarchical powers, with Tutsis and Hutus together in a majority party against the Tutsi king. Ethnic Hutu and Tutsi parties, the latter evidently fueled by refugees from Rwanda, soon sealed the conflict. A Hutu uprising in 1965 led to massive slaughter and another in 1972 was even bloodier when Tutsis retaliated by targeting educated Hutus.[79] The army deposed the last king in 1966 and replaced the monarchy with a republic. The first democratically elected and first Hutu leader of Burundi, President Melchior Ndadaye, came to office when the Tutsi president Pierre Buyoya arranged for a democratic election in June 1993 under a constitution with consociational protections of the Tutsi minority. Ndadaye was killed in a military (hence, Tutsi-led) coup in October 1993, setting off an immediate round of violence that soon engulfed Rwanda as well after an airplane crash—perhaps deliberately caused by Tutsi rebels or by Hutus who feared Habyarimana was about to settle with mostly Tutsi rebels—killed the leaders of both nations (including the new Hutu president of Burundi, Cyprien Ntaryamira). The transition to democracy via election was seemingly handled with remarkably good sense, extensive planning, and little or no ethnic conflict between the two candidates for president. Yet, it was disastrous.[80]

If Hobbes is right that any effort to upset the state will only bring harm on all, then the Hutus of Burundi were bound to suffer either from the unequal coordination on order as it existed upon independence or from the bloody disruptions of civil war. Burundi might have worked, but its colonial history under Germany and then Belgium did not prepare its peoples and its economy for self-governance. And splits among the Tutsi tribes enhanced the prospects for anti-democratic government, as did, presumably, the fact of the overwhelming Hutu majority.

In the grim economics of black Africa, where per capita income is steadily falling over recent decades while populations are growing rapidly, the main hope many people have for changing their personal positions is through a change in the position of their group. This is true even though economic differences within groups are likely larger than modal differences between groups. In Rwanda and Burundi, this problem was exacerbated from before independence by the shortage of good land and the combined ethnic-economic conflict over the use of land for cattle and crops. But conditions are so desperate in both countries that the prevalence of one ethnic group over the other would merely bring most of its members, at best, to a slightly less destitute status.

If it were possible to create governments that could turn the national economy around, ethnic conflict might subside. Otherwise, it seems unstoppable. It is too well defined and transparently evident in both Rwanda and Burundi. Here, despite some intermarriage, especially in Burundi, primordial differences in physique provide signals that cannot be overlooked—a military squad on the rampage can choose whom to kill on sight based on these characteristics. If Yugoslavia can turn to barbarism, Rwanda and Burundi seem hopeless. But note, oddly, that if ethnicity were to regulate relations between them heavily enough, Tutsis and Hutus might view each other as they would view marauding animals, not as people sufficiently like themselves as to be worthy of hatred. Even in this case, in which ethnic *identity* may seem more clearly primordial than in most of the other violent cases in our time, it does not make sense to say that ethnic *identification* is primordial—what brings out identification is grievous conflict over pathetically limited resources, especially if identification is helped along by venal and bestial political leaders.

Québécois Nationalism

Finally, consider a case that has not involved much violence. Quebec is a peaceful, prosperous province of Canada. French Canadians, most of whom live in Quebec, have evidently long thought they suffered under discriminatory policies and under the general hegemony of the English language in the Canadian government and economy. During the 1970s, there was great agitation and the election of a separatist government for the province. That government was merely a plurality government in that, as is commonly possible in first-past-the-post multiple-party elections, the winning Parti Québécois received only 41 percent of the total vote cast. Despite this tenuous hold on the electorate, the party called a referendum on separation. Not surprisingly, 60 percent voted against independence, and the separatist movement calmed down.

One reason for the popular failure of both the Parti Québécois and the move to separation was apparently that Quebec business leaders feared the consequences of separation for economic prosperity.[81] In the October 1993 Canadian parliamentary elections, with less than half the Quebec vote, the Parti Québécois captured fifty-four of Quebec's seventy-five seats in the parliament. Although it received fewer total votes (14 percent of the national vote) than either the outgoing Tory Party or the upstart Reform Party, it had the second largest number of seats behind the majority Liberals, making party leader Lucien Bouchard officially leader of Her Majesty's Loyal Opposition. Bouchard promised a referendum on separation as soon as his party gained control of the Quebec provincial parliament, presumably in an election during 1995.

A striking difference between this account and the accounts of conflicts in Yugoslavia, Northern Ireland, Somalia, and Burundi and Rwanda is that it is largely about peaceful elections. This is a difference that is not merely about the lack of violence. Once a government is in place to handle conflicts through electoral and legislative devices, the problem of collective action that a reform group faces is much milder in two important respects.

First, the group need motivate little more than voting the right way among people who would mostly be voting anyway. It requires little commitment other than the risked commitment implicit in the outcome of the vote. Even for that, however, I can generally suppose my own vote is virtually irrelevant, so that I personally risk nothing and incur almost no costs for my action. I therefore need not be mobilized through the sanctions of a norm of exclusion—although such mobilization might help to get me to vote one way rather than another. If I do vote, however, I may tend to vote in a way that matches my interests or my values.

Second, the apparent costs of mobilizing a group may become potential benefits for leaders, who therefore have very strong incentive to lead and who may even be financially supported by holding public office during their years of leadership. Bouchard has a solid income, very good support for his leadership activities, and the hope of even greater rewards in the future.

Apparently the urge for Quebec secession is genuinely a noninvidious nationalist urge. The Quebec separatists do not wish to carve off some piece of anglophone Canada; they merely wish to replace their national government in Ottawa with one in Montreal. What is the interest of Québécois in seeking separate nationhood for Quebec? The individual Québécois could reasonably expect more nearly equitable chances under French ethnic government. This might well be a reasonable expectation both in the historic past and still now. That is to say, the typical Québécois would rank higher in the smaller society of independent Quebec than in the larger society of Canada. But, while relative opportunities within the society might have been better, gross opportunities would have been poorer if the business leaders' view was correct at the time of the 1980 referendum.

What has happened since 1980? Now there are substantial constitutional guarantees for equity, so that the average Québécois might expect to do as well in dual-language Canada as in a separate French Quebec. Unfortunately, this expectation cannot yet be a confident one because two centuries of actual experience weigh against the very recent promise of protection. Hence, we might still expect the average Québécois to be relatively better off in an independent Quebec.

Would the average Québécois still be absolutely worse off in an independent Quebec than in Canada? Possibly not. The conditions of international capital today, the likelihood of economic deals with the United States, France, and other nations, the—perhaps shaky—establishment of NAFTA, and the growing accomplishments of native business leadership may now have quieted the earlier worries, so that Quebec might now be economically free to go its own way without economic injury to the typical Québécois.[82] Indeed, part of the worry in the late seventies may have been the threat of losing anglophone Québécois from important managerial positions in Montreal. But the election of the Parti Québécois already drove many anglophones out,[83] and francophones now fill far more managerial positions than before. No matter which choice they finally make, however, Québécois may face relative assimilation into a larger culture if they want the fullest benefits of economic prosperity.

The interests of the typical Québécois in Quebec secession might be economic, non-economic, or a combination. Suppose first that their interests are essentially economic. What might be the gain from being part of Canada? Clearly, there is the plausible gain that comes from the greater productive efficiency of a larger market—the overall Canadian market is four times the size of Quebec's. Trade between Quebec and Ontario is about $50 billion U.S. annually.[84] *Before NAFTA, Quebec got the benefits of free trade in a larger market than its own by being part of Canada*—although it probably got these benefits at a lower level of supply from union with Canada than it would from a full union with all of North America.[85] Therefore, the Parti Québécois originally sought *souveraineté-association*—political sovereignty combined with economic association with Canada.

Conceivably, economic association has been the only great benefit of being in Canada (apart from the elimination of the threat of war between Quebec and Canada). Actual debate in Canada partly trivializes the issues by focusing on the net flow of revenues between Quebec and the national government. Bouchard claims Ottawa gets 23 percent of its revenue from Quebec and returns only 19 percent. Official data from Statistics Canada say that Quebec enjoyed a net revenue gain from Ottawa of $73 billion Canadian in the decade 1981–91.[86] Bouchard's data seem likely false; the official data are misleading. Against the supposed implication of the official figures that other provinces have been supporting Quebec, note that Quebec's share of the increase in the national debt during the period was near the same amount. (At separation, Quebec would have to assume some share of the national debt, largely canceling its revenue-flow benefits.) In an era of such deficit spending, Bouchard's figures seem implausible. Both sets of figures are rhetorical, not meaningful.

If NAFTA is secure, then perhaps Quebec can drop out of Canada without cost in economic efficiency, because NAFTA could protect Québécois economic interests even better than *souveraineté-association* would have done. As Québécois say, "Canada is useless now."[87] But it does not follow that Quebec can *gain* from dropping out. Even to argue that it can requires defining a good that would be better served at the regional level. There are some Herder-like claims about the benefits of a homogeneous society in international economic competition—but these claims are ungrounded and very murky. In all the rhetoric over Quebec there has not been a convincing account of what a relevant benefit or good could be.

This is not to deny that there could be such a good. There may be. For example, Canadians can easily claim that there is at least one public good of great value that Canada can seemingly provide its citizens better than a grand government of North America could do. That good is law and order. Canada and the United States seem to be radically different in their success in providing such a good and Canadians could probably only lose by merging the two systems of law and order. Since the costs and benefits of the Canadian system are likely to be largely internalized, there cannot be an easy argument for merger to capture externalities. (Quebec seems unlikely to be able to make a parallel claim with respect to Canada.) Hence, Canadians could readily conclude that they would benefit from greater market integration with the United States and Mexico but not from legal integration.

The claim that it is in the interests of Québécois to be governed by Québécois might be an instance of the general insistence on "passive representation" in government agencies and legislative bodies. It is said, for example, that blacks in the United States can expect government agencies to understand their concerns better if there are blacks in the agencies. It may not be enough merely to have active representation by white advocates of black interests, because the white advocates may not be adequately attuned to the finer aspects of the black experience in a multiracial society. Recall white man John Howard Griffin's disconcerting discovery of what it meant to be black in the American South in 1959 in his book, *Black Like Me*.[88] He was a wonderfully equitable man who, however, lacked full understanding of the problems of blacks until he had his skin darkened and his head shaved to travel through black quarters of the Deep South. Having passive representation of minorities and of women in political bodies is therefore in the interests of these groups and their individual members. It is not merely a symbolic concern. Indeed, even when it is referred to as a symbolic concern, the symbol is commonly thought important for its causal effect on motivating others in the affected group to seek public positions and on motivating those outside the group to treat the group's members more equitably.

This account is still strictly from interests. But many must suppose what really drives the French Canadians and other ethnic and nationalist groups is more nearly a desire for popular sovereignty, for control over their own destiny. No doubt, that is part of the story. How much? Unfortunately, it may be a much larger part of the story in the vision of academics and of occasional politicians than of most of the actual people whose identities are at stake. The voters of Quebec split into several groups at all recent elections and the victors have not always represented majorities. Which Québécois will be sovereign in an independent Quebec? They are apt to share the fate of democratic systems everywhere, in which individuals count for little and in which even groups count only so long as they focus on single issues (such as abortion or war with country X) while submerging their disagreements on all else. That my nation is headed by a fellow Québécois is likely to be little consolation if her policies are miserable. Indeed, the whole Canadian government has been led by Québécois for twenty-nine of the past thirty years—and that may not be the least of the reasons some Québécois now want out of Canada.

The problems of Quebec, some of the East European regions, and many others are the problems of ethnic and cultural groups that ostensibly wish to protect so-called noneconomic interests. For example, when earlier Izetbegovic wanted to create an Islamic state in Bosnia, perhaps he merely wanted to protect Muslim interests. But it seems plausible that he primarily wanted to support Muslim beliefs. (In either case, his apparent belief that the large minority of Muslims in Bosnia should run the state was roughly as stupid and provocative as Milosevic's view that the 36 percent of Serbs should run all of Yugoslavia. Perhaps even more provocative was that the governments of Yugoslavia and Bosnia would put men with such views at their heads, thereby frightening others into preemptive moves.)

Many Québécois think their opportunities in Canada are limited by their use of the French language; and they think that autonomy would give French the proper stature. But their opportunities in a North American economy may be no more favored than their opportunities in predominantly anglophone Canada. Perhaps what they want is not economic but purely cultural. They want survival of the French language and its cultural residues in Quebec. Quebec political scientist Stéphane Dion argues that fear of loss of language is the main force behind the separatist movement.[89] The French of France also worry about their language and culture, but they have been fighting a losing battle since the fall of Napoleon. That battle is so badly lost that the French enact laws to enforce the priority of French film in French theaters and the use of the French language, even though that may mean they cannot have safe sex.[90] It is not at all clear that Quebec in the maelstrom of North America can do any better than Quebec in Canada because, in moving from Canada to North America it moves its French population from about 25 percent to about 2 percent of the whole. The effect of NAFTA is to supply one public good at a very high level—the good of market efficiency. But this effect is accompanied by the even more compelling need to coordinate on the predominant English language (perhaps eventually to be Spanish—then Gringos may cavil as francophones do now).

Still, perhaps what is at issue in Quebec and many other subnational regions is cultural survival. This concern might be a less shallow variant of the is-ought fallacy: It is ours, therefore it is good *for us*. But here the claim of goodness may be grounded in interests of Québécois. If French Canada gets rolled over by the Anglo-Saxon cultural and linguistic juggernaut that dominates much of the world, French Canadians of current generations will become virtual immigrants in the larger Canadian culture. Their opportunities in that culture will, on average, be poorer than those of native Anglo-Saxons of the same generations. *Per se*, this is not a final defense of the goodness of a separate linguistic culture. A very small subnational community of people who speak a different language might sensibly elect to have their children educated in the national language in order to give them better opportunities in life. Cultural survival would be a net good for Québécois if, as supposed above, they could do at least as well in a separate political community while escaping their relatively second-class status in greater Canada.

MORAL RESPONSIBILITY FOR CONTEMPORARY VIOLENCE

Kaplan's thesis that Yugoslavia is merely predictable history replaying itself through the horrid psychology of singularly wretched people is potentially harmful. Suppose we accept it as true. Then we must conclude that there is not much we can do to resolve the conflicts in Yugoslavia. We might help to stabilize borders and move people, but this would merely fuel future violence. If Kaplan is wrong, and the problems are essentially failures of political structures rather than of his mass psychology that is incredibly focused on grotesque fantasies, then we might suppose that political structures were the difference during the period of Tito's reign and that they could be made to be the difference again in the future.

Americans and non-Yugoslav Europeans might prefer to believe Kaplan's thesis, because it lets them off the moral hook. They cannot be responsible for making things better if all that matters is the perverse and even idiotic psychology of the peculiar peoples of Yugoslavia, who are evidently radically defective as people in comparison to generally amicable Americans and non-Yugoslav Europeans. Against this thesis, one might be bothered by the memory of German behavior in its genocidal policies fifty years ago or by the memory of the brutality of European-Americans slaughtering unarmed women and children of harmless Indian tribes such as the Yahi.[91] We are lacking in a primordialist account of the hunting parties casually organized for the sporting murder of these Indians.

There may be good arguments that the United Nations, the United States, and others should not intervene militarily in Yugoslavia, but this is not a good argument. There might be compelling pragmatic reasons for not intervening. For example, it might seem utterly implausible that an intervention could make things better.[92] The primordialists and racists salve our conscience when we watch the carnage on the news, when we see cameras pan the shattered, sometimes smoking buildings of once idyllic Sarajevo. That it had taken centuries to build that once wonderful, beautiful city counts for almost nothing in the primordialist assessment. All that really counts is that, in eighteen months, the city was virtually destroyed.[93] It is that spasm of destruction that supposedly reveals the character of the Yugoslav peoples. This belief seems inconceivable—except that it seems to be the dominant view of contemporary observers. It is generally presented with metaphor rather than with data.

As noted in chapter 5, universalistic norms commonly are weak in comparison to group norms of exclusion. These latter norms are very strongly held when they are strongly reinforced by self-interest. But the weakness of universal norms may be evident not only in, say, Yugoslavia where ethnic conflict rages, but also in the United States and in other nations, whose people and leaders are reluctant to bear any costs to alleviate or control deadly conflicts. They are motivated, if at all, only by painfully weak universalistic norms—and these give not enough motivation to act.

CONCLUSION

Revolutions happen in a vacuum. So too do many violent outbursts of ethnic conflict. Rising prosperity seems generally to happen only under the conditions of functioning political order, so that political weakness is typically associated with economic malaise. Hence, one of the two seeming correlations of ethnic hostility, one with economic malaise and the other with political disarray, may be spurious. But it seems likely that both correlations are direct, not spurious. Economic malaise elevates the significance of group conflicts by making individual prosperity more tightly dependent on group prosperity. And political disarray makes it easier for groups to seize control or to mobilize against each other.

The role of political disarray in letting conflict become manifest is presumably clear. Economic prosperity may have a more complex role. Prosperity alone is not sufficient to reduce the interest in group success. Rather, it is the tighter connection between individual actions and prosperity that matters. Anomic capitalism, while it is successful, may pose a natural bulwark against the manifestation of ethnic conflict. It creates incentives at the individual level that largely run counter to the incentives for group identification and commitment.

Adam Smith held a sanguine view of the effects of the introduction of self-interest incentives that accompany the market. He supposed that the striving for self-interest would undercut motivations from religion and culture, which might otherwise destroy societies.[94] We might generalize for him to say it would especially undercut motivations to act on behalf of one's group. On its surface, this may sound like a pernicious change—we would surely prefer to have people behave morally enough to trump their self-interest, at least much of the time. But, in the experience of ethnic-group conflict, Smith's view seems compelling. We make a better world by ignoring what kind of world we make and living for ourselves than if we concentrate first on the ethnic political structure of our world.

It is hard to imagine a worse scenario for potential ethnic violence than that in Yugoslavia and much of the former Soviet Union from about 1991. The collapse of political power has been associated there not merely with an ordinary bout of economic malaise but with the deliberate transition from command to market economy. In such a transition, the initial steps destroy the productivity of hordes of bureaucrats who were facilitators in the former economic order, immediately reducing economic production and distribution before the new organization of the economy can take hold. It would already have been treacherous merely to have weakened government. The Chinese gerontocracy chose to maintain strong government through the period of making the transition to the market and thereby reduced the chances of retrograde group mobilization. Much of the Hungarian economic transition was accomplished under the pre-1989 autocratic government. The Yugoslav problem was heightened by the fact that Serbia was an economic laggard behind Slovenia, Croatia, and parts of Bosnia, including the now destroyed city of Sarajevo. Croatia could plausibly have prospered under independence. Serbia has less chance of immediate economic success as an independent nation—it faces a very difficult transition. Wars of national aggrandizement distract national attention from the looming internal conflicts.

In our time there is massive mobilization of groups, especially ethnic groups, for ostensibly group-level purposes. Individuals have identified with groups so strongly that they seem to forgo their personal interests while seeking their groups' interests. The common understanding of the logic of collective action suggests that these group-oriented actions cannot be rational in the sense of being individually self-interested. Instead, seemingly, they must be irrational (people are foolish or crazy) or extra-rational (people are motivated by moral or group commitments). The latter inference is, however, wrong—because the former suggestion is wrong. There may be foolishness, craziness, morality, and extra-rational group identification at work for many participants in violent ethnic conflict. But these are given their field of play by the individually rational tendencies to group identification. Unfortunately, in these conflicts group-oriented activity is often contrary to group interests.

When a group's members suffer discrimination as members of the group, as in the case of blacks in the United States and South Africa, action on behalf of the group may be virtually necessary to remove the shackles on individuals. In the United States after the Civil War and Reconstruction, blacks were second-class citizens at best under the law; in South Africa they have been no citizens at all. In such cases, the urge for group action can in fact be a universalistic, not an exclusionary, urge. It can be an urge for individual equality. The urge in most of the violent ethnic conflicts of our time is not universalistic but is particularistic and exclusionary. It is an urge for superiority, not equality. It is typically an urge to benefit at considerable cost to others, and therefore there is such great opportunity for violence. But, as in many real-world situations of pure conflict, if ethnic conflicts do not remain latent but become manifest, they typically entail losses on all sides, not gains. The love of the group can be a disaster even for its own members.

Still, one might think that group assertion ought somehow to be respected, that groups ought to be able to choose for themselves. Unfortunately, we now know too much to make such claims as that various peoples have "chosen for themselves." We might claim to want self-governance by our group. What can this mean? Few of us will be the governors. Do we think our ethnic peers will, other things being equal, do a better job of securing our interests? Or do we merely feel good to know a Texan or Armenian or Catholic is in charge—not because it matters for our results but purely and simply because we like that fact?

Democratic theory cannot ground any claim for genuine support of any but virtually pure coordination interests, such as in driving conventions, time conventions, and other such important but politically minor matters.[95] These matters have often been settled without democratic procedures at all because each could be handled by genuine coordination over repeated opportunities for resolution until finally one of various possible coordination conventions is established.

Beyond such matters, it would be perverse and incoherent for a political theorist to claim that, as a United Nations official claimed of war-torn Somalia, "Whatever Somalia becomes will be what the Somali people want it to be."[96] There will be an outcome in Somalia and Somalis will be in the thick of the conflicts over what it turns out to be, but it is absurd and meaningless to say that anybody will control what happens or that "the Somali people" will do anything. Many of them will contribute efforts and these efforts will result in something that no one need have wanted or even imagined. If it is plausible to say Somalis *will* control their outcome, then it is as plausible to say they have controlled it so far—no one should want any more of such control.

Again, the Somalis, Yugoslavs, various ethnic groups, and we can do little about controlling our destiny except for matters on which we all agree enough to coordinate on relevant leadership or policy. Oddly, beyond such matters as the driving and time conventions, there are few such matters. We can purge our society or at least our polity of certain other groups; we can enforce the use and teaching of our language; and we can impose our religion and its strictures on everyone. But imposing these strictures is unlikely to be lexicographically prior to all other matters in our preferences. Most of us do not want the separation of our group and its elevation to power first and then all else. Rather, we want prosperity, safety, and other things and in part therefore we might want group hegemony. If group hegemony were sure to lead to disaster, its achievement would not dominate concern with achievement of these other things. After a small number of coordination matters, we will face the usual problems of government, in which there may be too little consensus for coordination. When we get beyond initial spleen, we are likely to find that *we* can control nothing in our destiny. Some of us will be lucky enough to have our favored policies adopted; most of the time most of us will not be so lucky. Controlling our own destiny will then be merely rhetoric, not a plan for action.

These issues raise the question whether group mobilization is good. Obviously, the successful mobilizing of groups for collective purposes can be a wonderful and beautiful achievement. But it has also brought about some of the worst disasters in the history of humanity. Yet, there is a widely held view that communitarian commitment is a good thing and, indeed, there is a recent movement in political and legal philosophy in support of communitarianism. The epistemological and moral status of communitarianism is the subject of chapter 7.

CHAPTER SEVEN

Einstein's Dictum and Communitarianism

> The important thing is not to stop questioning.
> —Albert Einstein

PORTIA'S JUSTICE

In the penultimate scene of *The Merchant of Venice*, which is uneasily bracketed among Shakespeare's comedies, Shylock wins his case for exacting a pound of flesh from the merchant Antonio, who has defaulted on a loan. Antonio had gladly accepted the default condition, so urgently had he needed the money. Portia, in disguise as a young judge from Rome, rules that Shylock may take his pound of flesh. But, on penalty of death, he may not shed a single drop of Christian blood nor take even a tiny fraction more or less than a pound of flesh.

Shylock surrenders and then Portia turns the civil trial into a criminal trial of Shylock, convicting him of a crime with which he had not been charged. To top that, she invokes as his punishment the liquidation of his fortune and, hence, his destruction as a money-lender. He must turn half his holdings over to the Venetian state and half to Antonio. Antonio proposes instead that he, Antonio, merely have use of the other half until Shylock dies, when the assets go to his (Shylock's) daughter and her Christian husband.

Why does otherwise lovable Portia do such harsh things, all with lively wit and seemingly great relish? One might suppose she was merely invoking natural law where positive law had run out to punish Shylock for his awful demand of a pound of flesh. But would she have done the same if the positions of Shylock and Antonio (a close friend of her new husband, Bassanio) had been reversed? It is brazen to say what a fictional character would have done if her fictional circumstances had been otherwise. But in this case, it seems overwhelmingly clear that Portia's justice is communal justice, not natural justice that applies equally to all.

Shylock is a Jew and a money-lender—a non-Christian and, in the vocabulary of his time, a usurer (recall the complicity of the two religions in creating the role of Jewish money-lender, as discussed in chap. 4). He is outside the community of Antonio, Bassanio, and Portia, and she crushes him for that fact in what is one of the ugliest scenes in all of

Shakespeare. Portia says to Shylock, "Thou shalt have justice, more than thou desir'st"—the justice of her powerful community's will—and the actress who can say that line without venom may never yet have walked the stage as Portia. Her community declares Shylock the Jew an outsider who must pay grievous penalties for intending harm to an insider that might result in the insider's death.

One might suppose this is merely literature and not our world. But the world has at least as ugly scenes for us. Consider one particularly grim but perhaps representative example. According to Amnesty International, village councils, or salish, often preempt Bangladeshi law and impose local justice on people. In August 1992 a fourteen-year-old girl was sentenced by salish to a hundred lashes after her rape by an influential villager. "The salish acquitted the rapist but took [the girl's] pregnancy resulting from the rape as evidence of illicit sexual intercourse."[1]

More generally, the original notion of a trial by a jury of one's peers was essentially a communal notion—but more nearly with respect to knowledge than to value judgments. My peers from my own community would know me and the community well enough to judge whether I had committed a crime of which I stood accused. The medieval English jury was self-informing and the only speakers at a criminal trial were the defendant and the judge—the jurors were "the witnesses for good or ill," both from prior knowledge and from the limited trial.[2] But if jurors have the power of judgment over me, they might soon choose to judge my values or my fit with the community rather than my actions. Then they might act toward me as the communities in some of Tennessee Williams's plays act toward interlopers or communal misfits, as many European and American communities acted toward those women whom they disliked and called witches, or as Portia acted toward Shylock.

The notion of trial by a jury of one's peers has been transformed over the centuries into a universalistic rather than communal principle. Now jurors should not come to judgment with their own private knowledge but should rely entirely on the knowledge presented to them in the trial. The move to a fully universalistic principle of jury selection came in England in 1856 with the policy of allowing changes of venue to escape the accused's perhaps prejudiced community.[3]

Universalistic principles date back more than two millennia in philosophy, but they are a recent innovation in practice. When they have been defended, they have often been posed against the vagaries of communal justice and abuse. Against them, however, there is a current movement in political philosophy to elevate the anti-universalism of what has been much of the practice over the universalism of the philosophers. There has almost always been some concern with communal definition of how things should be done. For example, David Hume yielded to communal devices in establishing legal and social conventions. But the anti-universalism of communitarian political theorists today cuts much deeper than this.

COMMUNITARIAN STRANDS

The communitarian label is applied to several distinctively different theses, some of them considered together, but some of them contrary to others. Two very broad categories that are quite different can be called *particularistic* and *philosophical communitarianism*, as already noted in chapter 3.[4] Actual, practicing communitarians, such as the Amish, the Lubavitchers, some of the original Anti Federalists, and seemingly countless other groups around the world, are particularistic communitarians. Their central beliefs are those of the group-level analog of solipsism: They think *their* community is right. Very often, they also think some other group or groups are wrong, perhaps even that they should be excluded, suppressed, or exterminated.

Philosophical communitarians hold, rather, that community is right, or that community defines the person, or that community defines what is right for its members, or that individuals not grounded in community are likely to be morally unmoored. Philosophical communitarians make claims about community in general, not about a single particularistic community. Philosophical communitarians are morally appalled by some of the most atrocious actions of particularistic communities, just as traditional universalistic moral theorists are. Philosophical communitarianism is, perversely, a universalistic movement in its focus on community rather than on any particular community. Particularistic communitarianism is an anti-universalistic movement—or, rather, an array of many such movements.

These two strands sometimes come together in philosophical communitarian arguments that are about the ordinary or street-level epistemology of individuals. What anyone knows is very heavily socially determined. An epistemological account of individuals' knowledge of facts and of moral principles must therefore be at least partly grounded in communities. Philosophical communitarianism is often discussed as though it were a normative theory. It makes better sense to view it as an epistemological theory that might have normative implications. At the very least it has descriptive and explanatory implications for what individuals' normative judgments are. As a normative theory about what is right or wrong, good or bad in a given community, communitarianism is easily dismissed and is of little interest, although it may be as persuasive to individuals as particularistic communitarianism can be. As merely an epistemological theory about how people come to believe what they do and have the interests or preferences that they have, philosophical communitarianism is a less audacious and innovative theory but also a much more plausible theory.

Epistemological Communitarianism

Communitarianism poses two epistemological issues for moral and political philosophy. The first issue is the communitarian answer to the question of personal identity, of how we have become who we are.[5] Despite normative and even metaphysical arguments by both its defenders and its critics, this is seemingly a straightforward epistemological problem of the way we come to know anything at all, including our identities. This is a problem that has had a central place in philosophical debate over the centuries. The second epistemological issue is the implication that the only or, at least, a chief source of the knowledge that we have of what is right and what is good comes from our community. Sometimes this seems to be treated as a constitutive issue, as though right could only mean what a community thinks is right. But it is as an epistemological thesis that it offers communitarianism's most compelling claim on moral and political theorists. These two epistemological issues are conceptually distinct, although one might suppose that the second issue depends causally on the first to some extent.

Much of the literature on communitarianism, both by its defenders and by its critics, has largely focused on the communal determination or construction of personal identity. I wish to focus on the second issue, whether our knowledge of the right and the good must come principally from our community. If community determination does not matter, normative communitarianism is of little interest for moral and political theory about the right and the good.

One might argue further that different communities' values are right for them. But it would be sufficient for much of the import of communitarianism to argue merely that individuals cannot typically know anything other than what they get from communities. Community A says that X is right; community B says that not X but Y is right. Each conclusion is morally right in the following sense. People in A and B are making what they deem to be correct statements. Moreover, on their actual understanding of the truth of the matter they could not readily conclude otherwise. It might be possible for them to come to know otherwise, but, forced to decide here and now, they must decide from their knowledge as now available and that knowledge is likely to favor their community's value.

On this view of the issue of communitarianism, any debate over what is "really" right is, practically speaking, misguided. From the perspective of my knowledge and understanding, the morality of my community may be right. Similarly, from the perspective of your knowledge and understanding, the morality of your community may be right. To conclude that this is the whole story, however, requires one of two moves. First, we might suppose that no one could believe other than what her community believes, a possibility that Richard Rorty suggests.[6] But this is empirically false, not to say preposterous. It is, ironically, false even of the communitarian theorists. Their actual theoretical position is not the position of any of the communities they revere. The theorists suppose that these various communities have different but still right values. But the actual communities typically believe nothing of the sort; rather, they believe they are right simpliciter and others are wrong. If philosophical communitarians could only come by their knowledge and beliefs communally, they would not have their relatively abstract views about communities in general.

Second, we might suppose that one could not find an alternative grounding for moral claims. This, too, seems to be false, as is suggested by the communitarians' own writings. Communitarians began their contribution to contemporary moral and political theory as an assault on universalistic, highly intellectualized, non-communitarian theories. Perhaps most people could not produce a Kantian, Millian, or Rawlsian theory (although seemingly anyone can produce a rights theory). Still, it is conspicuously false that one cannot ground a moral or political theory in elements that are not communitarian unless this term is inflated to cover so much that it loses its force.

Throughout the following discussion, I will refer to the two general forms of communitarianism: philosophical and particularistic. When I refer to communitarians, I will generally mean theorists, philosophical communitarians, not such people as the believers in a particular community's values, who would not generally call themselves communitarians. I wish to connect particularistic and philosophical communitarianisms by arguing for an account of communitarianism that is grounded on a relatively simple, commonsense epistemology. I will refer to this variant of philosophical communitarianism as *epistemological communitarianism*. Epistemological communitarianism is pragmatic. If this vision is properly limited, it should be shared by all pragmatic moral theorists, including utilitarians. Its defender argues that, to understand a community's values and its reasons for acting, we must see them from the perspective of the community. As roughly a Humean in epistemology, I agree. What we typically need for understanding moral and rational choice are not theories or stipulations of what is objectively right but understandings of what reasons people have to think something right.

Philosophical communitarianism must be a claim about perspective and the rationality of *seeing a community's values from the perspective of a member of the community.* Epistemological communitarianism is grounded in a particular form of the claim for rationality within a perspective. From the perspective of my knowledge, your community's values may seem wrong. From your own perspective, they naturally seem right. But more than this can be said about your perspective. It is plausible, at least in many particularistic communitarian positions, that it is rational for you to act from your perspective. It may be rational even in the very strong, narrow sense that it is in your interest, which is partly determined by your communitarian beliefs.

To say that one is rational or moral from within a communal view might be merely a circular claim. But note how it could be true in a non-trivial sense. If I argue with you about the sensibleness of your beliefs and get you to act against them, you might come to think you have lost as a result of my good services. There might, after all, be substantial costs and disruptions of changing your beliefs. Hence, you might eventually come to think that the costs of transition from your earlier beliefs to beliefs encouraged by me outweigh any advantage gained by acting from the "better" beliefs. This could be true even though you come to agree with my perspective and therefore to reject your community's beliefs.

Throughout the argument below, I will presume that there is a strong rational case for the particularistic communitarian guidance of actions by members of the communities under discussion. For example, given their beliefs, many of the Lubavitchers, discussed below, will be presumed to have a clear interest in the preservation of their community. They may also have other, conflicting interests. But, otherwise, I will presume many of them are well served by following their communal norms.

In addition to the utilitarian reading of communitarian epistemology implicit in much of my discussion, one might give a deontological reading with a claim that autonomy is enhanced by cultural membership in a community. Will Kymlicka holds this view and he ascribes it as well to earlier liberal thinkers from John Stuart Mill to John Dewey.[7] As the doleful stories of the wild boy of Aveyron, France, last century and of the two wolf children found in India in 1920 and as developmental, ethological theories in psychology suggest, however, there is prior need for some degree of social grounding for an individual to have a self at all or even to have language and other capacities.[8] Apart from this concern, I do not know what to make of the claim that autonomy is enhanced by strong, monocultural ties—perhaps merely because I do not find the foundational concern with autonomy compelling.[9] Moreover, communitarians in a sense actually argue for autonomy, but at the level of the group, not the individual. Group autonomy need not contradict the possibility of individual autonomy, but it seems to fit uneasily with it.

FROM KNOWLEDGE TO GOOD

In essence, communitarians argue from the epistemology of ordinary people growing up and living in communities to what it is right for them to do. Roughly, the argument could be filled out as follows. Most knowledge is socially created and reinforced. As Howard Margolis writes, "By and large the easiest and even the most reliable reason for believing X is to be aware that everyone else believes X."[10] Cognition is intrinsically a-logical.[11] Rorty, perhaps the most epistemologically minded communitarian, evidently shares this vision of the social grounding of our knowledge. He says, "rational behavior is just adaptive behavior of a sort which roughly parallels the behavior, in similar circumstances, of the other members of some relevant community."[12] We build our cognitions from patterns and from society and we could no more justify many of them than most of us could prove (or even state) laws of physics. At some point, most of our knowledge is grounded in sand. My ordinary knowledge is to a large extent what my society has given me. Someone in a different society may have quite different knowledge.

This account of knowledge formation, or some variant of it, might be accepted by virtually every political philosopher. But communitarians seem illicitly to transpose this into an argument about the overall rightness of what communities do. A community value or moral rule may be right with respect to the community's received wisdom and understanding. It need not be right according to any general theory of the right. Of course, communitarians often argue against such theories that they can have no compelling ground, that they are trumped by communal values.

Much of the history of moral theory is de facto argument against the position of the solipsist, for whom X is right just because she says it is, and against pure egoism. If solipsism were counted among moral theories, it would be in contention for recognition as the most debased and the silliest of the lot. Evidently no one defends solipsism. Egoism, however, is a sufficiently articulate position that it is often taken as the central problem for moral theory. Henry Sidgwick even counts it as one of the major plausible moral theories.[13] Throughout the history of western moral theory, at least from Socrates forward, however, the question "Why be moral?" is primarily the question why not simply seek one's own interest and ignore the interests of others. On some statements for it, communitarianism is merely the group-level analog of solipsism. Immediately one may wonder, why should group-level solipsism somehow be appealing when individual-level solipsism is so odious? This is not a question I can answer. And the major communitarians do not answer it. Group-solipsist views could be appealing if group interests were generally worthy of satisfaction and if they did not harmfully conflict with other groups' interests—but these are contingent matters.

A more credible claim for communitarianism might be that it is a group-level analog of egoism. But this is also a perverse claim. Egoism at the individual level makes clear enough sense. The analogous groupism makes much less sense. It is, after all, individuals who must act according to group values. The group "acts" only by aggregation of individual actions. Groupism requires that individuals sometimes submerge their own individual interests in order to support group values. They could avoid such a conflict if they have somehow adopted the group's values as their own individual values. Groupism becomes a coherent position if we can give an account of that "somehow." It seems plausible that the only way to do that is to go through epistemological motors for how an individual might come to believe a group's values.

A frequent objection to utilitarianism is that it elevates whatever preferences an individual has to the status of—almost unquestioned—value. Communitarianism does likewise. John Stuart Mill defended communities' rights to their own norms on utilitarian grounds, largely by leaving it to individuals to follow their own values even when these seem to be capriciously determined.[14] But his argument did not elevate the values of such communities as Mormons to the status of being right for the relevant people. Rather, he merely supposed that the harm of the state's trying to override their values would be greater than the harm of letting those values reign. This is an epistemological account whose force depends on the motivating power of beliefs and on Mill's pessimism about uses of the power of the state.

The claim that a community's values are right for it is essentially a functional claim. But it is typically under-argued. What is the function that is being served when the community follows its norms and moral rules? If it is any of the standard functions that crop up in moral and political theory, then communitarianism reduces merely to an epistemological gloss on the possibility of instantiating one of these theories. If the function is not one of these, must it then be reduced to community rule-following for the sake of community rule-following or for the sake of survival as a community? Are communitarians subject to a variant of the ridicule that Arthur Schopenhauer heaped on Immanuel Kant for their apparent claim that the community's rules are right because they are right? Or, worse, merely because they are the community's rules?

Communitarians can avoid making claims about the rightness per se of a community's rules or values and merely argue that acting according to these values serves the members of the community. If it could be shown that acting from the community's values serves the interests of the members, then, in essence, communitarianism is utilitarian. Or if acting from community values serves the autonomy of the community's members, then communitarianism might be construed as an autonomy theory. None of the major communitarian philosophers would find these to be congenial resolutions of the problem of the rightness of community values. In these resolutions, a community's values are right only as a means, not as an end.

Some of the argument of pragmatic, policy-oriented communitarians, such as Amitai Etzioni, is with the workability of a moral system that can make a society function well for its members.[15] In this concern, they are welfarist communitarians. There is a quality of community-based morality that may seem to give it strong epistemological appeal to these communitarians. Particularistic communitarianism may be the only genuine case of seat-of-the-pants ethics for the individual actor. Pilots of small airplanes often claim to fly by the seat of their pants. They feel what the aircraft is doing and they react accordingly. One can also master many other pragmatic activities, such as riding a bicycle or playing a sport, with seat-of-the-pants techniques. These activities give more or less instant, continuous feedback on how well they're being done. There is an objective world with actual laws governing functionally right and wrong actions. In such an objective world, seat-of-the-pants techniques can work very well.

We cannot normally do ethics by the seat of our pants. Ethics shares the liability of knowledge more generally that is captured in Wittgenstein's remark that you cannot check your memory of the train schedule by looking up the schedule in your mind. Your—possibly mistaken—memory is just what you invoked to get the schedule in the first place. There is no further feedback, as variations in gravity and torque might feed back through your seat in the airplane. But for the communitarian, there is the possibility of further feedback. The community is the storehouse of moral knowledge, the equivalent of the printed schedule of departures and arrivals. You act and then relatively quickly get feedback from the community on whether you have gone astray or aright. Particularistic communitarians can act as though there were objective determinations of the right and wrong, as though moral realism were acting on the seats of their pants. Despite a recent flood of work on moral realism, there is no comparable feedback in standard moral theories.

In utilitarianism, of course, one may get feedback on whether a particular action has good consequences in certain circumstances, but one cannot get feedback of a relevant kind about whether the principle of enhancing welfare is itself moral. With communitarian ethics, feedback is entirely social and conventional and in principle it is neither right nor wrong in general except insofar as the communitarian morality is right or wrong.

A standard move of the communitarian, whether particularist or theorist, is to stipulate up front that the community's values are right, because they are the community's. If the community vision is right, at least for its members, then checking one's actions against the community schedule of rights and wrongs settles the issue of the rightness or wrongness of one's actions. Critics of communitarianism want to check rightness against some more nearly abstract universalistic schedule. Unfortunately, their schedules are often too abstruse for the typical person to be consciously following them or even to be held accountable to them. If the communitarian position is essentially epistemological, it must be about why it is that people hold their community views and why their actions are, by their own lights, moral if they fit those views and immoral if they violate those views. Then the critic has no ground on which to criticize—although some critics might attempt to stand on a cloud of idealism and argue from how idealized people ought to behave.

The chief epistemological problem with particularistic communitarianism is that it violates the dictum of the epigraph of this chapter: The important thing is not to stop questioning. The dictum is attributed to Einstein, who presumably directed his remark to beliefs in scientific matters. To question such beliefs is to increase the chance of bettering them. Communitarianism and other command theories of ethics and politics violate Einstein's dictum. They assume that some important truths are perfectly known and not subject to improvement.

One might suppose that, because values are not matters of truth or falsity, Einstein's dictum does not apply to them. But such a supposition is wrong. One might better a community's values, for example, if they happen to be inconsistent or to conflict with their supposed purpose or if they are grounded in factual beliefs that could be subject to challenge.[16] To question values that a community has established often means, inherently, to go outside the community's values to judge them. But this is not the whole story. Under some variant of Kant's dictum that "ought" implies "can," the last of these considerations covers virtually all stipulations of what one should do. Questioning merely the empirical judgments in practical implications of a community's values opens up the wider likelihood of questioning everything. One cannot typically blinker oneself against theoretical or foundational issues while ostensibly focusing only on empirical issues. Even the praticularistic communitarian must agree with Einstein's dictum for empirical matters (the Catholic Church once thought otherwise and sullied itself in trying to suppress Galileo and other scientists). Hence, the particularistic communitarian's values are at risk.

The communitarian dictum that my community's values are right for me effectively stipulates that I not go outside or pass judgment on our values. My only standard is those values. In essence, communitarian ethics is an ethics of command, as religious ethics often is.[17] If particularistic communitarianism violates Einstein's dictum, we must conclude that the *truth* of the relevant community's values is not an issue. The values cannot be shown to be true without questioning, without arguing them against alternatives. But this means that it is perverse to go on to say that those values are right. Rightness is not an external attribute of particularistic communitarian values.

Values are right only within a theory or from a defined perspective. Philosophical communitarians seem often or even typically to suppose only the latter, that values are right only from a defined perspective. Values derived from a theory do not count. In his critique of deontological liberalism, Michael Sandel essentially argues against the intelligibility of Kantian and Rawlsian liberalism because of its transcendental grounding in what certain kinds of ideal or abstract "persons" would think.[18] People in real communities are not ideal or abstract in the relevant ways. For example, they are not the "unencumbered" selves who can go behind John Rawls's veil of ignorance and strip themselves of almost all their particular attributes while somehow remaining people who have choices to make. But these criticisms, while plausibly pointed, are directed at the particular cases of Rawlsian and Kantian liberalism, not at the coherence of any theory whatever. The commonsense utilitarianism of John Stuart Mill and many others does not fall to Sandel's kind of criticism.

One could argue against Sandel's criticism that Rawls's theory of justice does not really depend on his veil of ignorance argument. That argument is more nearly a metaphorical device than a conceptually necessary part of the derivation of his theory. Without this device, Rawls's theory would still be rationalist in a less intimidating sense than that in which Kant's views are rationalist. The theory would not be the product of any standard kind of traditional community. If one could argue for such a rationalist theory without making the supposedly metaphysical moves that upset the communitarians, that theory would then yield judgments of right and wrong. We could say that X is right within the theory even though there might be no extant traditional community in which X is held to be right or in which X is what people do.

Some of the communitarians go so far as to say that when we say something is wrong, what we are saying is that *we* (members of our community) do not do it.[19] But this is so patently false that it seems absurd to ground a moral theory in it. To suppose that this is the meaning of a claim that something is wrong is to suppose that, for example, in 1860 no plantation southerner, white or black, could have held that slavery was wrong.

One might also read Rorty to suppose that one cannot hold views outside some community.[20] Either this is so vague that it has no implication for communitarianism, or it is trivially false. The issue turns on the meaning of "some." Suppose "some" is various for a given individual. My belief that the world is roughly spherical and not flat may come from one or more communities, my belief that ethics cannot be objectively true may come from others, my view that human welfare trumps concern with so-called rights of individuals and communities may come from others still, and so on. I am not the product of "my community" but of many communities, some of which may seem ill-fit together. Such diversity of attachments and sources evidently fits Rorty's view. This ostensibly communitarian concern is too vague for political and moral philosophers to bother with it. Sandel's concern with my identity as the product of my community seems to shred before the number of my effective communities. Moreover, if I have my values and knowledge from many communities, no one of which stipulates what values and knowledge I am to follow overall, then there seems to be a very large residual role for something like autonomous judgment, perhaps even for abstract judgment that is not itself communal, even, heaven forbid, for rationalist deduction. I adopt (or adapt to) new communities by my own choice and judgment.

Suppose "some" is a particular community for a given individual. The apparently intended reference for communitarianism often seems implicitly to be more nearly such communities as the Crown Heights Lubavitchers. Such communities produce people who supposedly are similar in their beliefs. Yet, unless a community is completely sheltered against intrusive ideas from others and has no experience contrary to its values, it cannot seriously be expected to turn out people with uniform values. There will be variety even among the relatively isolated Amish of Lancaster County, Pennsylvania, who therefore find it necessary to engage in harsh shunning and excommunication to keep the community separate. Indeed, there was enough variety among the seventeenth-century Mennonites that Jacob Ammann led the formation of the strict

Amish sect. They and many other religious groups came into existence at a roughly specifiable time. Hence, particularistic communitarian values are at best likely to be modal for a group, not uniform. Those within a group who push for revisions, as did Ammann, must appeal intellectually to some kind of truth claim that rests on foundations outside current practice. Such claims are special cases of the claim that *this* community is the one we should adhere to—but this claim cannot be strictly communitarian for anyone who needs to be convinced of it. Imagine the pointlessness of the debate between followers of Ammann and the other Mennonites: "Ours is the community." "No, ours is." Presumably, what they thought they were arguing was that certain views were correct and that they formed their community around those views.

COMMUNAL GOOD

Clearly, one kernel of truth in communitarian moral theory is that successful coordination on ways of doing things well and even on tastes then makes those ways of doing things and those tastes good—so long as they do not have perverse incidental effects. This is the group-level analog of the economists' principle that, to satisfy your tastes or preferences, we need only know what they are—we do not need to inquire into how you came by them. The development of musical instruments and musical styles seems to be the result of cultural accident. Yet, most of us would grant that the different musics are all good for the relevant listeners and in apparently the same way: They give pleasure. Some large part of a culture's values may have this coordination structure. Yet, these values are not called into question by their happenstance origins.

It might happen that some cultural products sweep through other cultures, displacing other products from those cultures. For example, the violin and piano have become internationalized and have partly driven out native instruments in many cultures. Such a result suggests that in some sense the internationalized cultural product is better at meeting some demand than is the displaced product. In the case of the piano and violin, they may have prevailed in part not because of their own superiority in making music (although that might be the chief story); they may also have prevailed because they brought with them a vast literature of music and greater opportunities for access to the world.

Such coordination products seem not to be at the core of concern in communitarianism. Rather, there are values that seem somehow collective in a stronger sense. According to Daniel Bell,

> The core of Puritanism . . . was an intense moral zeal for the regulation of everyday conduct, not because the Puritans were harsh or prurient, but be-

cause they had founded their community as a covenant in which all individuals were in compact with each other. Given the external dangers and psychological strains of living in a closed world, the individual had to be concerned not only with his own behavior but with the community. One's own sins imperiled not just oneself but the group; by failing to observe the demands of the covenant, one could bring down God's wrath on the community.[21]

As in the vendetta, the community must police the individual for its own protection.

With its implication of inherently joint survival or demise, Bell's characterization makes adherence to communal values good in this case. But this implication may sound odd even for the Puritan community. Consider a vision of the maintenance of a group good that might tip into steady decline from individual withdrawals. As reported by David Remnick, Menachem Schneerson, the Rebbe of the Lubavitcher community in Crown Heights, Brooklyn, admonished his people in 1969:

> "In recent times, a plague has spread among our brethren—the wholesale migration from Jewish neighborhoods," the Rebbe said. "One result of this phenomenon is the sale of houses in these neighborhoods to non-Jewish people. Even synagogues and places of Torah study are sold." Citing Talmudic sources, the Rebbe said that it was prohibited for Jews to sell their houses to Gentiles when the sale would have negative consequences for the community. "Such stringent prohibitions of Torah law would apply if the sale of the house to a non-Jew caused damages to only one person," he declared. "How much more so does it apply when, as in our case, the damage is suffered by all neighborhood residents."[22]

The damage that all residents of the neighborhood would suffer, of course, was the loss of their existence as a community and thereby perhaps of their culture and values.

The Rebbe's concern raises questions about the wholeness and permanence of a community and its culture. The Lubavitchers have a specific origin elsewhere in the world. Most of the European Lubavitcher community was destroyed by the Nazis. But a smaller part of it was in the Soviet Union and survived the Holocaust. The settlement of a fairly extensive community in Brooklyn was relatively recent, beginning in 1940. In 1992 the Lubavitcher community in Crown Heights numbered about twenty thousand. Many of the community have, as suggested by the Rebbe's invocation of prohibitions on selling out, moved on to suburban areas around New York.[23] If all of them had scattered, the Rebbe might have thought it urgent to re-create the community somewhere, as much of the European community of Lubavitchers had earlier been recreated in Brooklyn.

The earlier re-creation evidently served the interests and satisfied the yearnings of the earlier generation of Lubavitchers. If this generation has scattered, perhaps scattering served their interests and satisfied their yearnings. What of the seeming group good of the community is left? If anything, it must be something that transcends the interests of the potential members of the community. Or perhaps maintenance of a relevant community is a real and strong interest of the present generation, but it does not trump their interests in other things, such as safety and prosperity for their children. The collective good of community falls victim to the private goods of safety and prosperity. Now the Rebbe says that my leaving our community would be wrong because it would harm others who stay behind, who thereafter see non-Jews moving into my abandoned home. I could retort—rightly by my understanding—that my staying in the community would harm my family. Whose harm trumps whose? The collective's or the individual's?

One could imagine that almost everyone in the community would rather move. Their interests begin to sound like a trump. And one can imagine that some would very strongly prefer to move, so that their personal gains would far outweigh the losses of those who stay. We might then see the community unravel, as in Albert Hirschman's argument for "exit."[24] Indeed, Hirschman's most compelling example of exit is the exit by the upper middle class from city schools in the United States to put their children in suburban schools. As they moved out, quality often deteriorated so that the next lower level of quality demanders moved out, and so on until the city school system collapsed into a state of disastrous quality, as in Chicago, Detroit, Washington, and other cities. In this model, those who demand most from their community are the first to leave because they are the first to be dissatisfied.

Part of Hirschman's account of the decline of city schools does not fit the Lubavitcher case. The Lubavitcher community of Crown Heights seems likely to lose people who weigh individual benefits above collective values. Hence, those who stay behind are likely to be higher demanders for certain of their community values than are those who depart. Nevertheless, it may be true that as the community dwindles in size the personal costs of staying in it rise. Members might stay intensely committed and even active in defense of the community almost up to the moment when they leave.

We could resolve the case if either of two extreme conditions were met. First, it might be true that everyone in the community, or even everyone after a certain incidence of departures, would rather stay than depart on the condition that everyone else do likewise. Second, it might be true that everyone would rather depart for the individual benefits of life elsewhere. It seems very unlikely that either of these conditions is met in Crown Heights, although there is no adequate test. The first condition might require something like contractual guarantees to prevent strategic planning for contingencies that might lead some to depart preemptively—for example, when a good job opportunity in a distant suburb became available. The second condition seems likely false in fact for the Crown Heights Lubavitchers.

A third extreme—but perhaps grimly possible—condition is that almost everyone is worse off after the community unravels even though each departure made someone better off. In this case, the Rebbe's view would be compelling. Was this the Rebbe's analysis? Plausibly not. He may simply have held that the community and its values are right and should—morally—be maintained. He may not have been a philosophical communitarian, as Alasdair MacIntyre, Richard Rorty, and Charles Taylor are, but a particularistic communitarian, for whom the only community of interest was the Lubavitcher community.[25]

The Moshiach of Crown Heights

Schneerson was, after all, held to be the Messiah, the Moshiach, by many in his community. An outsider can only reject this view and must be astonished that anyone held it. There is no room for discussion of such a claim. People who believe it surely are, given their belief, fully justified to hold their community as special, as right in ways that other communities are not.

Those of us not in the Rebbe's community may find the claims that he was the Messiah no more solid than the many claims throughout history that religious resolution was at hand through some person of the moment. That the Rebbe was alive in our own time does not rescue claims for his being the Moshiach from the disbelieving curiosity we have for past claims of others, such as Sabbatai Sevi, whose career as a charismatic leader ended when he was offered a choice between the sword and conversion to Islam in the seventeenth century and who came to be ridiculed as "the false messiah" after his conversion.[26] There is only the difference that telling the story of the Rebbe with the kind of irony or humor one might use on Sabbatai Sevi's story would seem inappropriately rude to the Rebbe's followers.

From my epistemology, it seems easier to explain how a group of people could have come to believe the Rebbe is the Messiah than to come to believe it myself.[27] From my epistemology, it is absurd to suppose there is a Moshiach in Crown Heights—or anywhere else. I must be like most of those who have followed the story in greeting it with astonished disbelief. It is yet another in the long, demoralizing line of millenarian movements. But, wonder of wonders, this one happened in Brooklyn, New

York, in a well-educated community near the end of the twentieth century. It could well have been the best-educated millenarian movement in history. The Rebbe's followers were not isolated stone age primitives falling for a cargo cult. Every philosophical communitarian must be troubled by their movement, because it represents how perverse a community might be even when it is not primarily driven by hostility toward an outside group. It is the latter kind of community, such as a vicious Nazi community, that is often seen as the bugbear of philosophical communitarianism. But one need not have vicious views to produce distressing results.

Must the philosophical communitarian give any honor to the Lubavitcher community's self-conception and its beliefs?[28] The philosophical communitarian could say, what all could say, that, *given their beliefs*, the members of the community have views of right and wrong that are justified. Or the communitarian may go further to say that the views of the community entail or even constitute the rightness of the community. But this is patently false because no one outside the community can plausibly hold that a member of the community is somehow morally bound to hold to the community's beliefs and values. As John Locke argued, beliefs are not fully willed, they are not tractable to our wishes.[29] Rather, they largely happen to us, although we may do a lot of work to get them to happen. A member of the Lubavitcher community could well come to believe that a failing old man, no longer able to speak, was not a plausible candidate to be the Moshiach, no matter how righteous he may have seemed throughout his life as the Rebbe. And a member could go much further and come to believe that the community's values are destructive of its people and their lives. Such a belief entails a claim that one can go outside the community's values to criticize or even merely to understand them.

Now note what the first move of the philosophical communitarian is. It borders on a de facto utilitarian defense of community. It says that a member of a community may have no better grounds for judging rightness of things than what is given in the principles or values of the community. For epistemological reasons, the individual community member is justified in holding views that may be clearly unwarranted from some other perspective. It might be disruptive in the short run to attempt to change the community's ways, as a government might attempt to do. Hence, the welfare of the members of the community, once they hold their particular values, may be best served by their living according to their values. This says absolutely nothing about the inherent rightness or wrongness of their values. It says only that for perhaps psychological reasons, once they have their values, they will be happiest or best off or whatever if they live by them.

It is possible that some Crown Heights Lubavitchers are repelled by the fanaticism of their fellows in the community, especially by incredible claims that Schneerson, even when ninety years old and infirm after a stroke, was "King, Messiah, forever and ever!"[30] Hence, the intensity of the community's values may tend to drive the non-fanatics out. Oddly, Schneerson's 1969 argument might still apply to the non-fanatics in a way he presumably did not intend. Perhaps many of them have already left, thereby leaving the more intense, fanatic communalists behind, thus making life worse for the remaining non-fanatics. The non-fanatics who leave harm the non-fanatics who stay. Hence, on Schneerson's argument, it is wrong of them to leave. Despite Schneerson's argument, however, it may not seem wrong for the non-fanatic to leave rather than defer to the interests of other non-fanatics. Part of what is at stake is lives of further generations.

FUTURE GENERATIONS

Unfortunately, we may object even to the seemingly weak conclusion that a community's members may be best served if they adhere to the communal values they happen to have. True, the current generation may be best off merely following out their values to the end of their days. They (and I sympathize—more fully by the year) are too set in their ways and norms to change without great trauma. But their children and grandchildren may be the terrible losers of being dragged along for the ride. The Inuit who wish to re-create or maintain their native ways, constructing their village life around fishing and sealing in Hudson Bay, wish to revive their past ways not merely for themselves *but also for their children*. The present generation does not wish to take the losses of making the transition from one to another culture. Something like that transition may be almost inevitable for their descendants, however, who may pay more dearly for the transition than the present generation would have done. The claim that it is a culture rather than the group of individuals of the present generation that is being protected when their village life is maintained through the reduction of their children's prospects is hollow.

One of the changes that communities—in order to have a more specific term, let us speak of traditional communities—must endure in modern times is the overpowering effects of technological developments. The Luddites in industrializing England objected to the radical change in their lives brought on by changing from traditional modes of manufacturing cloth to gigantic water-powered looms. In one sense, no one could object to the change, because it meant enormous cost savings that could make cloth cheaper and more abundant. But in another sense, the traditional workers were instant losers from the new technology, because they lost jobs of modest skill and, if they got jobs in the new mills, got lower-skill jobs. The benefits of the change were relatively universal. The costs were borne by select groups. But there was no hope of the Luddites' maintaining their traditional industry once water and then steam power drove massive looms. A nation that today attempted to cut itself off from such disruptive technological developments would soon find itself in relative poverty.[31] Maybe there are good things about having 80 percent of a population on the land. But there are bad things about it too, not least of which is that, with 80 percent of the population producing only raw food, there cannot be much else produced or consumed, so that life must be impoverished.

The epistemological communitarian argument may apply with considerable force to a protected or isolated community. For example, it might apply to the Amish or even to the Crown Heights Lubavitchers. Or it might come to apply to Iran if the Ayatollahs suppress all unbelievers and certain foreign influences for a generation or so.[32] But it falters in a more nearly pluralist society in which individual members of any community may readily find ways to criticize and revise their communal values. Even such communities as the Amish and the Lubavitchers, as successful as they may be in creating the possibility for the kind of life they value, fail to hold their members against the blandishments of the larger pluralist society in which they are embedded. Their communal epistemology is challenged by other epistemologies, and their members, who must finally apply epistemological insights to their own actions, frequently opt for the extra-communal epistemologies.

Outsiders, such as epistemological liberals, cannot say the next generation should accept current communal beliefs in order then to benefit from fulfilling them—they might as well accept relevant *extra*-communal beliefs in order to benefit from them. On their own epistemology, it is likely that liberal outsiders must hold that the next generation be allowed considerable freedom to adopt whatever beliefs. From this view, it seems likely that the outsiders' account of comparative benefits from staying in and leaving the community tend to favor leaving, because leaving gives better opportunities to the next generation. Schneerson and his fellow Lubavitchers would presumably have weighed this consideration negatively and therefore they concluded all the more strongly that leaving the community is harmful and in violation of the Torah. Who was right, the outsiders or the Rebbe? From their own perspectives, they were both right.

Consider a celebrated case. It is a sad fact for certain communitarians that many young males very often leave the Amish, Hutterite, and other such communal, religious societies, usually not to return. They follow

Einstein's dictum right out of their communities. Although the rigidities and stultifying qualities of these societies might put off even the most enthusiastic academic communitarian, some of the communal qualities of these societies are impressive. Nevertheless, these communities might have been facing steady demise that was slowed and maybe even stalled altogether by the Supreme Court decision in *Wisconsin v. Yoder et al.* In this case, the members of the Old Order Amish religion and the Conservative Amish Mennonite Church appealed their conviction of violating the Wisconsin state law requiring education through age sixteen—that is, approximately through tenth grade, or half of high school.

The Supreme Court ruled, oddly, that the Amish community had the right to restrict its children's education to lower levels of schooling than were legally required in the larger community. The Court noted the view of the Amish that secondary school education (beyond eighth grade) was "an impermissible exposure of their children to a 'worldly' influence in conflict with their beliefs."[33] In its decision, the Court found for the sentiments of the Anti-Federalist communitarians who originally opposed the U.S. Constitution, to allow the Amish their own communal standard on education. The instructive fact of this decision is that it was directed at children. Typically, government is thought to have the power to intervene on behalf of children against their parents' wishes. In this instance, the Court arguably intervened against children on behalf of their parents. A young Amish who now wishes to try a broader canvass can still do so, but at the great handicap of qualifying only for jobs requiring no more than an eighth-grade education, less than typical impoverished ghetto youths get, and these youths are commonly unemployable.

A standard reading of this decision is that it was entirely a matter of the Constitution's religion clause that protects religion and religious belief from regulation by the state. The actual opinion, however, blurs this reading severely by giving other reasons for the decision. The opinion of the Court says, "It is one thing to say that compulsory education for a year or two beyond the eighth grade may be necessary when its goal is the preparation of the child for *life in modern society* as the majority live, but it is quite another if the goal of education be viewed as the *preparation of the child for life in the separated agrarian community that is the keystone of the Amish faith.*"[34]

The Court might have thought even more sociologically about the issues at stake in *Yoder*. Suppose a fourth of Amish youth leave the community and seek work in the larger society. They come ill prepared. The question for the Amish parents and Church is how many additional young people will depart if they take another two years of public school, and perhaps how much harm to the beliefs even of those who do not leave will be caused by the extra years of education. It seems plausible that the Court should have weighed the interests of all those directly concerned in the decision, including, of course, *those who would be leaving the community*. Instead, the Court essentially weighed only the interests of parents and perhaps "the community," somehow defined, against the usual interest of the state in having citizens be minimally educated. It could conclude that the latter was outweighed by the former in large part because it ignored the interests of the children who leave the community of the Amish. As do virtually all practicing communitarians, *the Court failed to justify the impositions of a particular culture on children*. Ordinarily, parents are constitutionally free to attempt to educate their children in a particular faith in the United States. But some parents are now entitled to go further and attempt to handicap their children enough to make them less able to leave the community of the faith.

In this case, the Court did not merely deal with preferences and interests. Rather, it affected identity and identification. It would be hard to defend a community's practices on the demeaning claim that the community requires enforced ignorance to keep itself intact—although the Court openly accepted this awkward, demoralizing defense in *Yoder*. Communitarianism requires the use of future generations, use that is likely to be abuse. This is the crux of the clash between liberalism and communitarianism. One might give *Yoder* a false liberal gloss by treating it as a decision about the liberties of adult Amish then living in the community. But the decision was fundamentally illiberal in its manipulation of future generations in the (potentially conflicting) interest of those adult Amish.

RESPECT FOR CULTURES

In moral and political philosophy over the past few decades, so-called respect for persons is a frequent concern. Any but a command theory of morality must, virtually by definition, be based in some kind of respect for persons. For example, the universalist theories of utilitarianism and of Rawlsian justice start from an accounting of each and every person's interests, somehow defined. The final theories then may abstract from actual individuals.[35] Communitarianism seems distinctively different from these theories in that it gives substantial priority to community over individuals. According to Rorty, "the naturalized Hegelian analog of 'intrinsic human dignity' is the comparative dignity of a group with which a person identifies herself."[36] There can likely be no universal sense in which individuals must be respected. Does respect for cultures, however, make sense?

Strangely, this may still be a universalistic question. At issue is obviously not the respect of individuals within a culture for that culture, but the respect of individuals outside the culture for the culture. That seemingly is a question to which there should be a universal answer for all the outsiders even if the question is specifically about one culture. To what extent should an outsider respect a culture or its norms? I respect Einstein or a relevant expert, Mother Teresa or other especially honorable person. But another culture may seem perverse and harmful to its members and others. For example—very nearly the standard example—the culture may require that its widows immolate themselves on the funeral pyres of their husbands. It would be absurd to say I do or should respect that culture or, at least, that aspect of the culture.

Perhaps I could say the *preferences* of members of the culture now merit consideration as, after all, their individual preferences. But then I do not substantively respect the beliefs and norms of their culture, I only respect the persons whose beliefs these are. Perhaps I could go a bit further and say I respect or at least accord consideration to culturally determined actions of members of the community. But this is a peculiar move if I think those preferences were formed in perverse ways or are harmful. It might even be a reprehensible move if those preferences are being inculcated in others, such as the next generation.

We are not finally morally bound to deal with people exclusively at the level of their beliefs. We may deal with them at the level of their possibilities. And the epistemological defender of communal beliefs must grant the similar epistemological claims for my belief in what their possibilities are and for my acting as well as I can toward others even if this means going against their culture's beliefs.

Communitarian Consent or Agreement

One of the most widely supported principles for political justification in our time is some variant of consent. The standard, and possibly strongest, moral defense of the duel was that duelers consented to their risks. Consent seems so compelling that one of the most implausible of all political theories, contractarianism, has a strong following. Much of the writing by its advocates makes communitarianism seem also to be a consent theory. We honor what a community wants because that is what the members of the community want.

Against such views there is a transparent objection that has often been raised and just about as often ignored. Agreement is not right-making. Therefore, consent and its variant theories—contractarianism and much of communitarianism—are not genuine moral theories. We can contract or commune for evil, as the Mafia, the Croatian killers of Mostar, and the Hutu *interahamwe* (those who think together and attack together) militia in Rwanda do. Indeed, when consent theorists justify contracting and communing, they typically base their justifications only on the service of the contractual or communal arrangements to the interests of the contractors or communers, not by the service to good of whatever kind, such as the more general interest or the interests of others. Even if the so-called Aryan community of Germany in the late 1930s and early 1940s had unanimously contracted for it, the Holocaust was not moral. Even if all Serbs share in the outrageous bile of Milosevic and Karadzic, their murder of Muslims is not moral.[37]

Communitarianism does entail agreement or contract by convention even if there is nothing vaguely like a contract or election.[38] Actual agreement by convention is typically achieved with a bit of coercion at the fringes of the group, or even a lot of coercion, as in the analysis of norms of exclusion in chapter 4. If agreement per se is not right-making, then surely *agreement through coercion* is not right-making.

It is implausible to assert the rightness or goodness of communitarian commitments per se. The ugly side of particularistic communitarianism in practice often make it one of the most grotesque and immoral movements of human history. Among the consequences of such commitments are distressingly many of the worst manifestations of social organization, including, in living memory, ethnic cleansing and the final solution. Too many of the greatest communitarians of history number among the greatest criminals. The bland, arid defense of communitarianism palls before its historical practice.

The strength of many norms of group adhesion and of exclusion is virtual testimony to their harm. There would be no point in such norms if they were not applied to suppress, coerce, or exclude those at the margins of group identification. There is nothing inherently good or bad in group loyalty. My loyalty to the Azeris or the Tutsis, for example, would be pointless, foolish, and of no interest to them except insofar as they might be able to put me to use in their cause. The loyalty of a particular Azeri or Tutsi to her group is also not inherently right or wrong. But contingently it is also likely to be good for the Azeri or the Tutsi primarily to the extent it helps them prevail against the Armenians or the Hutus.

The more individuals become focused on the norms, interests, and demands of their groups, the more they may be capable of turning into destructive forces such as the brutal Croatian killers whose task is the elimination of Muslims in Mostar now and forevermore (chap. 6). In the United States and in many other nations with long histories of racial and ethnic discrimination, concern with discrimination against individuals on ethnic grounds has often been transmuted into an assertion of the elemental and (implicitly) enduring rightness of each ethnic group's identity and of identification with the group. But the latter focus has great potential to harden ethnic divisions and to exacerbate ethnic conflict over the long run, and it is likely to shackle the next generation.

The Rationality of Communitarian Commitment

We might carelessly say of the commitment to furthering communal interests that it is individually rational if it furthers individual interests. For example, we could rationally defend commitment to a community if we could defend protectionism of any kind for that community. This would be a self-interest, not a distinctively moral, defense. We could go further and defend community as answering already established preferences. But this latter claim does not yield a defense of exclusive education of the young in the norms and preferences of the community. And, in any event, this self-interest defense must be strategically complete or it may be invalid. The communities that defend their values to such an extent that they wage war with other communities may make virtually all members of their own community worse off, not better off, as in the initial result of 1990s violence in Yugoslavia and elsewhere.

Note, however, that the definition of individually rational in this view is not that of the literature on collective action. In that literature, my individual action on behalf of our group must itself benefit me more than it costs me. It is not enough to say that such actions by all of us generally do benefit all of us. We can, however, trick up the latter concern to yield the former association if we suppose that our group must vote on its benefit. In voting, each of us can now look on the provision of the group good as effectively (legally) tied to contributions to its supply. I do not contribute my taxes and then hope others do likewise. I contribute my taxes only if our vote carries, in which case all contribute their taxes as well. If communitarianism is a form of agreement by convention, each of us effectively votes for the communal package.

Hence, our major concern is with the epistemology of what we agree to. In a sense, our communal agreement will be some form of aggregation from our individual values, which are our individual bits of knowledge. What are the odds that we will get a relevant aggregation? This is, interestingly, merely a variant of a question that the Marquis de Condorcet tried to answer before the Red Terror of the French Revolution put an end to his thoughts. On matters of truth versus falsity, such as in a trial to determine whether someone is guilty of a particular crime, the average person has a view that is some fraction guilty and the remaining fraction innocent. Condorcet's *jury theorem* says that, if each person is more likely to be right than wrong, a larger jury is more likely to reach the truth than is a smaller jury. Having only a judge yields the worst error rate. With a very large jury, the odds of error are vanishingly small.

Insofar as a community's norms are defined and enforced by the whole community and not by a single governor or small body of governors, its norms might therefore seem to be privileged. But this conclusion is wrong for two reasons. First, there is no need that the community's members must be more likely right than wrong about anything of much significance. Second, it need not typically be true that communal norms are a matter of getting it right or wrong—they may be a matter of selecting good norms from some number more than two, perhaps much more than two.

Consider the first problem. If community members are less likely to be right than wrong, then leaving choice to the whole community maximizes the likelihood of error. In part, it is perhaps their sense of this difficulty that drives the Ayatollah Khomeinis of the world to insist on autocratic rule in their communitarian visions. There is a huge literature, especially in the twentieth century, on the problems of so-called mass society that largely assumes that the typical citizen is more likely to get important matters wrong than right. This view arguably underlies much of the analysis in William Kornhauser's *The Politics of Mass Society*.[39] Indeed, ethnic mobilization may constitute a variant of his notion of mass society, one in which more diverse pluralism is destroyed by fixation on the preferred group. Hence, strong ethnic politics tends to reduce connections of other kinds, including, in Yugoslavia, as earlier in Nazi Germany, familial connections from intermarriage. The view also partially underlies the work of the racist and elitist French social psychologist, Gustave Le Bon, author of *The Crowd*.[40] It is a common theme for many of the opponents of democracy.

Should we be optimistic with Condorcet (who eventually committed suicide) or pessimistic with Kornhauser? That depends on what the facts of the matter are. In ethnic politics, the facts are often conspicuously wrong. Again, as Renan said, it is characteristic of nationalists to get their national history wrong, even stupidly wrong. Where the facts are so tendentiously wrong, one may reasonably suspect the principles that partly turn on them and the justifications that are impossible without them. This is not just a problem for communitarian views. Commonsense epistemology may produce agreement by convention on some putative fact or principle about, say, the physical world. That fact may nevertheless be wrong. Intensity and unanimity of belief need not correlate well with truth.

Now consider the second problem above, that our choices of norms are unlikely to be restricted to choices over mutually exclusive dyadic alternatives, such as guilty and innocent. In the face of this problem, the jury theorem fails to apply unless all possibilities could be weighed in paired comparisons. Condorcet's theory of voting, especially as later developed by Kenneth Arrow, suggests that there cannot generally be a successful resolution of this problem.[41] Moreover, larger, more diverse societies are more likely to fail to have communitarian norms than are smaller, less diverse societies. The desire for community is implicitly therefore a desire for small community, which is what the Anti-Federalists wanted.

Ostensibly communitarian criticisms of national politics are often beside any conceivable point. Those who wish to restore community in large, modern nations should face their problem more squarely, acknowledge that community can come only at the small and restrictive scale where there is the potential for all of the ugliness of the norms of exclusion of chapter 4, with their enforced sterility of thought. And they should ask whether a world of thousands of tiny, commonly exclusive communities could be an attractive world at all. It might be the group-level equivalent of the failure of collective action: Each group seeks its own, and all groups suffer. For example, it is all too obvious in many contexts that strong community at the local level does not translate into strong community at the larger national level.[42] There, the aggregation of strong local norms is as likely to produce fratricide, destruction, and the deliberate cultivation of ignorance as to produce community or general agreement.

Concluding Remarks

The claim that groups and individuals have varying epistemological stances is of general importance in normative social theory. It is, of course, central to philosophical communitarianism. Kymlicka implicitly puts it at the center of his argument for protecting minority communities in a liberal political theory.[43] It is also at the core of arguments over rule- and other utilitarianisms. It is because of the differing epistemological positions of individuals and institutions that we should want to augment moral choice by individuals with regulation by institutions.[44] Many debates in moral and social philosophy seem to be thinly veiled epistemological arguments. Indeed, words such as "true" and "false" often appear in these debates. Yet, the debaters often do not display a clear, frontal recognition of the epistemological bases of their various disagreements. One of the most common confusions from failing to deal carefully with epistemological considerations is to argue from theoretical grounds what individuals ought to do without giving adequate attention to what the individuals could know they ought to do. This confusion clouds debates over whether one ought to obey the law and, as mentioned, debates over rule-utilitarianism.[45] It is also at the core of current debates over communitarianism.

Why do people fear that their communities are threatened by pluralism? Because they are, of course. But they are threatened primarily through the varied epistemologies of pluralism. Pluralism works its corrosion of traditional community by giving members of the community alternative visions, especially alternative visions of values. Younger members, whose life patterns are not yet well established, may be particularly open to alternative visions. Hence, a community may tend to fail intergenerationally in the face of pluralist exposure in a variant of the problems faced by cultures in which very small numbers speak a rare language (as discussed in chap. 3). The young may think of failure as liberation. Certain values of life on the land in advanced industrial states were displaced by ordinary welfare concerns over a few generations, as the returns from life on the land were swamped by opportunities elsewhere. (Even when those opportunities were poor, as in the ramshackle communities on the outskirts of Latin American cities such as Caracas or as in the dust-bowl thirties in the United States, they were evidently better than what the land offered.)

In the end, we who stand outside some community, many of whose epistemological principles and insights we reject, can only do as Mill does. Insofar as our actions matter, as they commonly do if we share a government with the community, we can support the members of the community in seeking their own values—but only within the limits implied by conflicts with other communities and with future generations. This makes us epistemological communitarians, perhaps, or merely, like Mill, utilitarians willing to take psychological and social constraints fully into account. We can recognize that, given their epistemologies, the Rebbe in Crown Heights and his followers can be particularistic communitarians. But *we* cannot in any stronger sense be normative communitarians. To argue that we should be is oddly to argue that, although we should respect the epistemologies of other communities, we should not respect our own. That is an incoherent and unphilosophical position.

The antagonism communitarians have to liberalism is motivated by two contrasting positions. Liberals—must one speak of traditional liberals?—seem to presume that their liberal conclusions are right simpliciter and are not merely the result of their community's way of thinking. Communitarians suppose that all knowledge is embedded and therefore cannot be judged from an outside, over-arching system. Commonsense epistemologists, in the tradition of David Hume, can agree fairly extensively with the communitarian position, but they likely reject its most rigid assertions. In particular, the epistemological liberal must suppose that exposure to more ideas, as commended in Einstein's dictum, is likely to give one a better chance at reaching correct conclusions about many factual and quasi-factual matters. For example, someone with historical knowledge of millenarian movements and their often disastrous results for their followers must think it implausible that such movements are good for people and must view the prospects of the Lubavitchers of Crown Heights with sadness.

Even if *what* we know is culturally determined in large part, as philosophical communitarians typically contend, it does not follow that our knowledge of it is culturally biased. We seem fairly confident of the objective knowledge of many things, such as the woefully objective fact that a small number of physicists and others put together novel bombs that performed roughly as intended and theoretically expected in destroying Hiroshima and Nagasaki. Those bombs were an implication of Einstein's audacious theoretical equation of mass and energy—theory massively affected reality.

Commonsense epistemology allows for variations in our confidence of our knowledge. My belief that concern for human welfare dominates concern for various community values or even for community survival is radically different from my belief that certain rough physical laws hold sway over us. The latter views are so compelling that, if I meet someone from a culture that blocks her belief in them, my epistemological communitarianism will turn out to be little more than charity toward her for her ignorance. It will not be respect for her views as I might have respected the views of the Jew who believed in the Lubavitcher community and its putative Moshiach. The brunt of my charity might be to attempt to teach her better or to support putting institutions in place to overcome such ignorance. It may be true that I can hold my views only from within a (rather amorphous and loose) community and that she cannot hold my views from within her community. But it would be false to conclude that my understanding of physical laws does not apply to her even in her ignorance of those laws. In this sense, it would be perverse to say I am no more right about these matters than she is even though the explanation of my holding my views while she holds hers may be overwhelmingly cultural.

A community embedded in an open, pluralist society may not be able to sustain the narrowest communitarian vision, because its members may too often run up against articulate and credible challenges to their particularistic communitarian norms. When an individual in a particular community gains additional epistemological perspective, she may accordingly have to revise her own views of what is right. While the Lubavitchers successfully maintain their values against such revision, the only resources they have to defend themselves against the encroachments of the broader society are the resources of their communal values and motivations. Invoking these probably heightens conflicts with their neighbors. If they were more resilient, more open to experiment and to other values, they might be more successful at living at peace with their neighbors. It may be false to infer from a group's exclusive identification with its own members that others are held to be not only different, but also wrong. But it may also be very natural to do so and to read hostility from the desire for separatism. Those may be lethal inferences.

Perversely, survival in the long run may require less commitment and a bit of diversity, not austere homogeneity. The American Indians died at horrendous rates from infections brought in by Europeans. Plausibly, the chief reason for their staggeringly high rates of mortality was their lack of genetic diversity, since such diversity slows contagion.[46] One might suppose that similarly dismal results follow from lack of *social* diversity for groups that face competition from others. Alas, such considerations argue against group survival in any case if the group is defined by its homogeneity. Individual and group survival may conflict. As Francis Black remarks of the virulence of epidemics in homogeneous populations, "Intermarriage between populations reduces the problem, but an unfortunate consequence of intermarriage is often the loss of indigenous culture."[47]

Again, *philosophical communitarians do not share the views of any particularistic communitarian: they are not themselves communitarians of the kind about whom they theorize.* Rather they share the views of the community of philosophers who have similar epistemological stances. But if this is their community, the universalistic (inherently anti-communitarian) philosophers who have dominated western ethics for several centuries can also appeal to their own community in support of their universalistic values, such as general welfare or autonomy. If we are epistemological communitarians, as I am and as some other universalistic moral philosophers could coherently be, we recognize simply that knowledge comes not only from historical experience, but also from theory and reflection. We are in such great need of better knowledge in much of our lives individually and communally that it would be silly and self-abnegating to reject such knowledge. Indeed, it would be silly not to pay heed to Einstein's dictum even in moral and political philosophy, as in practical life. That dictum is a supremely pragmatic principle. To reverse Ashis Nandy's claim (in chap. 1), any particularistic communitarian society that rejects Einstein's dictum likely does so at its long-run peril, although it may be epistemologically damned in any event.

Rorty, Sandel, and other contemporary writers in the new communitarian tradition tend to direct their arguments explicitly or implicitly to deontological, rationalist moral and political theory, especially Kantian and Rawlsian theory. In their emphasis on community as the source of knowledge and rightness, however, they often conclude against universalist views. It is not only Kantians who are universalist, however. Until the rise of communitarianism one might have said that the one principle shared by *all* the major schools of western ethics is universalism. For example, Rorty says that, for many people, the Vietnam War "betrayed America's hopes and interests and self-image," but that they went further to argue that the war was immoral. Rorty thinks they had no ground on which to make the universalist judgment. He says, "Dewey would have thought such attempts at further self-castigation pointless."[48]

Rorty, generally a pragmatist, puts John Dewey high on the list of earlier philosophers who share many of his own views.[49] But Dewey openly made utilitarian universalistic arguments and could surely have countenanced a claim that, say, the American war on Vietnam was immoral if he supposed, as many critics of that war do suppose, that it did more harm than good. Dewey did not oppose all universalistic moral claims but only those that were supposedly grounded in certainty deduced from abstract theory—Dewey was committed to Einstein's dictum.

In implicitly lumping rationalist certainty and universalism into a single category, Rorty seems to make the mistake of Hayek, who opposed Cartesian constructivism as Rorty opposes Kantian constructivism. Hayek supposed utilitarianism is disqualified as a moral theory because he mistakenly thought it must be rationalist and constructivist.[50] Perhaps Rawls's constructivism is misguided, but his universalism is not, and the rejection of the former does not require rejection of the latter. Dewey clearly held that phrases such as "better than" and "worse than" have meaning without our having to infer them from spurious notions of the "best."[51] Although the comparative referent in a claim that one state is better than another might typically be the state we are in, one's capacity to make the judgment need not depend on one's being in the referent state.

John Locke and Adam Smith saw group motivations as pernicious, as they often were in their personal contexts.[52] In the time of Hobbes and Locke in England, religious groups were murderously intolerant of each other. In Smith's time, mercantilist groups severely damaged the prospects for economic progress. For all three, focusing political and economic effort on the self and the family would contribute to a world of individual opportunity whose benefits in civility, liberty, and prosperity would swamp those of the oddly narrower world of group opportunity. Locke also supposed there were epistemological barriers to concluding that one religious faith is more nearly right than another in its beliefs.

Whatever we may have learned from theory and history since their times, we have only learned even more forcefully why their views were compelling.

In sum, communitarianism cannot be taken seriously as a moral or political theory. It is a serious matter only to the extent its epistemological vision is a problem for moral and political theories. Epistemological communitarianism is merely the thesis that what it is rational to do depends on who one is because, principally, it depends on what knowledge and desires one has. Since one's knowledge comes primarily through social learning, rather than direct learning of the facts or deduction of the ideas themselves, one must choose and act under the substantial constraint of what some community has taught. But our knowledge comes from varied communities, even many communities, and we are individually creative in choosing and packaging our bits and ranges of knowledge. In large societies we pick and choose from many communities—we do not suffer the dictates of only one.

Some of what we learn, or conclude, is that some conclusions or principles are universal in their ranges of application, as are arithmetic, the concern for welfare or autonomy, and, oddly, the universalistic view that communities make right. Hence, the impulse of communitarian moral and political theory is internally inconsistent if it goes beyond the limited thesis of epistemological communitarianism. That limited thesis is not only consistent with full-blown communitarianism. It is consistent with all moral and political theories that are at all practical and not purely ideal. It is even required for the reasonableness of all such theories.

The epistemological communitarian who is aware of the diversity of communities must embrace Einstein's dictum and be open to learning from other cultures. This runs against the hallmark of the particularistic communitarian's vision of her society, a vision that is closed to revision. The epistemological communitarian might be able to understand that—and even how—people of a given culture think there is something morally right about that culture and accept its norms as though by command. But the epistemological communitarian cannot share their group-solipsist view. Group-centric morality and group-centric politics are not subject to *a priori* claims of their rightness. Devices for mobilizing individuals for group purposes are often the invidious devices of norms of exclusion and imposed ignorance. The norms and values of groups can be right only by contingent chance and not merely by inference from their origins in a community.

Oddly, epistemological communitarianism implies two striking realizations. First, we should give consideration to community members. In particular, we should acknowledge the extent to which communities can constrain knowledge to produce behavior that we might otherwise wrongly attribute to especially evil or vicious personal character. Second, we should give strong consideration to the contingent sources of support for various communal values and norms. Often we will find we can explain these in ways that lead us to conclude they have no moral standing. These two implications together imply that normative communitarianism is misguided.

More generally, we should conclude that group organization and individual commitment to group purposes are not proof of the rightness or goodness of what the group wants or achieves. Indeed, we should often become suspicious of group success in mobilizing individuals just because individual incentives typically run counter to group action. We should look to the incentives that produce group commitment to determine what their character is. As in the norms of exclusion canvassed in chapter 4 and the distorted universalistic norms canvassed in chapter 5, the incentives for group commitment may be perverse and destructive. Successful collective action can sometimes be a wonderful achievement. But it can also be a dreadful one, the source of great harm, even to those who succeed in the collective action. In the widespread mobilization of the imagined communities of the ethnic groups of our time, the harms seem grotesquely to outweigh any plausible benefits. Despite the occasional good that it may do, group-solipsist ethnic assertion is one of the great disasters of modern civilization.

CHAPTER EIGHT

Whither Difference?

> Alone, I was afraid of the world and insecure. But I felt cockier
> and surer of myself when hanging with my boys. . . . We did
> things in groups that we'd never try alone.
>
> —Nathan McCall, *Makes Me Wanna Holler:*
> *A Young Black Man in America*

KAFKA'S FAILURE AT MARRIAGE

Franz Kafka was a notorious failure at marriage, indeed, a preemptive
failure who repeatedly failed even to *get* married. The issue evidently
bothered him enormously and sparked many entries in his diary. The
most telling of these is his observation that he did not envy any particular married couple. He only envied "the whole of marital happiness in its
endless variety," not its instances. Even in the most favorable case, he
believed he would probably have doubted the happiness of a particular
couple.[1] The idea of marriage is simply not matched by the reality.

I will not speak of marriage, but when I was growing up I had the view
that communities were wonderful things and I probably even envied
many people that they belonged to this or that seeming community. This
is apparently the experience of many people. Years later I came to think
of strong communities as Kafka thought of marriage: I doubt that any
particular community lives up to the ideal of community. Communities
turn exclusive even when there is no point, plausibly merely because it is
easier to maintain loyalty through the discipline of norms of exclusion.
We are like the woeful commander in Vietnam, who found that he had
to destroy a village in order to save it. We strengthen our community by
turning it into something we would never have wanted to join.

This view should not be misread as even more pessimistic than it is.
There are many benign and perhaps wholly beneficial "communities" of
importance in our lives. Typically, however, these are not central to our
commitments, they do not occupy a major part of our lives, and they
need not turn on us to keep us loyal. There are support groups, neighborhood groups, extended family groups, work groups, religious
groups, play groups, and many others that may be significant in our
lives, but they do not generate their own moralities—they do not attain
the status of anything the communitarian philosophers would call a

community. No doubt, there are even ethnic communities that are relatively central to their members' lives that are also benign because they have not become the focus of politics and conflict with alternative groups.

Moreover, some communal mobilizations are good even on universalistic principles. When, contrary to universalistic principles, injustice is being done against a group by a counter-group or by a state, then group organization and identification may be rationally and morally justified for the first group if such organization can help overcome the injustice. For example, the NAACP, in its long history of working to undo Jim Crow practices and laws, was justified on universalistic principles to work for the group. The alternative to universalistic justice is the communal justice of *The Merchant of Venice*, the Jim Crow laws of the American South, the salish of Bangladesh, and witch hunts everywhere. The distressing message of our era is that the universalistic pursuit of, say, equality is less well reinforced by self-interest than is the communal pursuit of inequality and special status, and that the latter is degrading and destructive.

Unfortunately, even benign groups may go sour. The dream of an Israeli homeland has produced grotesque excesses, such as Baruch Goldstein's murderous rampage killing twenty-nine Palestinians in a mosque in Hebron in February 1994. Most Israelis must be appalled at the distortion of their ideal of an independent, liberal, decent Jewish state. In a 1981 letter, the late Harold Isaacs, a professor of political science at M.I.T., wrote that his beloved Israel had become "a bleak place, falling into the hands of nationalist-tribal zealots hand-in-hand with medieval-religious-fanatic zealots."[2] Similarly, the successes of the Civil Rights movements in the United States and in Northern Ireland in mobilizing relevant populations set up the subsequent successes of separatist movements that are not benign, that at their worst are malign.

In the face of these experiences and the grotesque experiences of Yugoslavia, Rwanda and Burundi, Sri Lanka, and many other places, it is untenable to claim that community is simply good. When it is good, it is good; but it can be bad, and when it is, it can be horrid beyond measure. In many times and places, people would be better off if they could individually break the hold of malignant community over them, but all too often communities are too spiteful to let them go easily. Community per se does not define the good or the bad. It is community in contingent contexts that is either good or bad.

A large part of the reason for the sometime horrors of community is that the urge for communal identification is unhappily subject to great distortion from the corrosions of self-interest mechanisms, such as those that feed norms of exclusion. What holds members to a community is often personal benefits of membership rather than the program or ideals of the community. Even when the personal benefits are benign, they often have malign correlates, as is true of what seem to be the two chief individual benefits.

The first individual benefit of belonging to a group, the epistemological comforts of home, seems harmless and sweet. But these comforts typically require exclusion of those who make for discomfort—often hateful exclusion. There may be a tendency for the selection of extremists, as results from the emigration from Crown Heights of Jews not fervently attached to the Lubavitcher movement, or from the self-selection of the most radical Irish Catholics into the IRA and the most radical Zionists into the Israeli West Bank settlements.

The second individual benefit is straightforwardly economic: access to jobs and position. The state itself directly controls many jobs. In some societies, the fraction is well over half. In many societies, the best jobs that most people could get are state jobs of the officialdom or the military. Most jobs in health, education, and public services in many nations are controlled by the state. Indeed, in such impoverished, subsistence societies as Somalia, Burundi, and Rwanda, the most valuable resource may be government itself. Land runs a poor second, especially if the government can tax the product of land. If my group is in control of government in such a society, I am likely to be much better off than I would otherwise be. Even in Yugoslavia, Serbs benefited from Serbian dominance of the military and the government. With the fragmentation of Yugoslavia, they will lose. The harsh turn to war came after Croatia, upon declaring independence, replaced Serbs with Croats in the police force in Krajina.[3] Again, there might be a strictly benign economic benefit from homogencity—perhaps Iceland, Japan, and Sweden prosper because the people in any of these societies all share similar values and expectations that are culturally learned. But the initial destruction that is necessary to create homogencity where it does not exist, as in Yugoslavia and Rwanda and Burundi, heavily mortgages whatever future benefits might come from it.

Because the achievement of community has potentially malign correlates of exclusion, the fundamental problem of community is that it is easily subject to excess. It is like law enforcement in that enforcement of the law can be made more rigorously effective in bringing miscreants to justice only at the risk of mistakenly bringing more innocents to injustice. More convictions means more convictions of both the guilty and the innocent. That is the statistically inescapable trade-off. If we have a regime of law enforcement at all, we accept some level of abuse of the innocent. Analogously, the development of communal loyalties and norms that can support many individuals in their lives can obstruct the lives of many others. Stronger community may mean richer support for some things while it means stronger intrusion and control for others, so that there is a trade-off of good and bad effects. At some point, the bad effects may outweigh the good. It is therefore incoherent to claim that community is inherently good. It is sometimes no doubt good, and it is sometimes clearly bad. Moreover, for some individuals, such as Thomas Wolfe, the good of even benign small-town community might be outweighed by its bad.

A seemingly plausible communitarian response to the atrocities of communal conflict in, for example, Yugoslavia is that these are the result of a breakdown of community and its civilizing constraints on behavior. Unfortunately, the response is overtly wrong-headed. It is not a breakdown of community that entices Serbs from small, homogeneous communities to join in the attack on cosmopolitan Sarajevo. Moreover, the universalism that characterized Sarajevo before its descent into hell continued to grace the lives of its severally entangled ethnic groups even after the city was attacked and shelled into poverty. Community, not its failure, is the mainstay of the atrocities of Yugoslavia. Community has been harnessed to the state and to the self-aggrandizing purposes of political leadership, and it is being abused. But its abuse is facilitated by the incentive structure of group identification, an incentive structure that is strengthened by exclusion and the seeming rewards of intense inclusion.

In the communitarian vision of a community, there is no problem of responsibility. Individual community members must merely act according to the standards of the community or be held accountable. In the politics of community, one's chief responsibility is to act on behalf of the community. Oddly, if one accepts it, individual responsibility is therefore replaced by license. One can then do things one would never have done without the urging of the community, as in the epigraph for this chapter. As do the Croatian killers of Mostar, one can murder former neighbors with impunity. As do the Serbian soldiers in Bosnia, one can rape former neighbors for the greater good of Greater Serbia. Communal morality turns into a variant of the doctrine of realism in international relations: Anything is acceptable in defense of one's community.

One of the great communitarian thinkers before the latter end of the twentieth century was Edmund Burke, who extolled tradition. Part of his defense of tradition is that it has already survived the distortions of unintended consequences that tend to overwhelm the effort to reform institutions or to create them de novo, as in the French Revolution. We know our traditional devices work—we cannot be so sure of proposed alternatives. But even a Burkean in our world cannot justify complete stasis. If other communities are making economic progress, my community might soon be destroyed if it stays out of the changes. For example, even without internecine warfare, the people of Rwanda and Burundi would likely aspire to the wealth achieved in other societies. But that aspiration requires radical changes in traditional ways of doing things. Community is not the key to progress, prosperity, or merely decent lives in black Africa.

PLURALISM

Isaiah Berlin calls himself a pluralist in the strong sense that he not only thinks different cultures must be tolerant of each others' members but he also thinks the world is a better place for us just because there are many different cultures and groups in it. I agree. Thomas Wolfe realized he could not go home again. Many people would not want to go home again—there are too many places of greater interest. Berlin, of course, is a migrant across cultures, and his identity depends on his migrations and his multiple roots. There is, however, an even stronger position on pluralism that many communitarians seem to take. It is that, in some sense, each culture's own values, whatever these happen to be, are right for it. Bernard Williams once called such relativism the anthropologist's heresy, but it has now become the political philosopher's communitarian heresy.[4]

Berlin's pluralism is about the facts of the world. Communitarians—especially particularistic communitarians—have a vision about the good of each community. In the politics of ethnicity, the facts fit Berlin's pluralist view. But it would be perverse to fit the communitarian vision to these facts of diversity. For example, as discussed in chapter 3, there are vastly many languages in the world, most of them culturally poor and giving access to none of the world beyond a very small community. In particular, most of them provide relatively limited access to modern life or to positions in a modern economy or polity and virtually no protection against the modern world around them. Nevertheless, their speakers might rightly conclude that they are better off being allowed to live out their lives in these languages rather than being forced to enter civic and economic life at the disadvantage of using what to them is a foreign language. Much of the discussion of this matter in communitarian political philosophy and in popular accounts treats the issue as though this were the whole story.[5] Unfortunately, the most important part of the story is not the fate of the small number of people in the single generation or two who now speak some isolated language. Rather, the most important part of the story is the future generations of these people and the opportunities they might have opened to them if they convert to a regional or world language rather than a narrow, communal one.[6]

Similarly, the protection of the current generations of North American and other aboriginal populations' prerogative of maintaining their primitive economic existence and their sometimes coercive communal organization with, in Canada, state enforcement of communal property arrangements, the recent establishment of a legal right for Amish parents to keep their children uneducated, the forceful institutionalization of minor languages as required for official and business transactions, and other such communally motivated policies often have as their sad consequence the fettering of the lives of future generations, who, in a sense, are used by the present generations merely to make life a bit more comfortable for themselves.

These are not knock-down moral issues to which the answer is obvious. Defenders of communal "rights" are, implicitly, opponents of individuals' opportunities. Many populations around the world face this awful trade-off. It is probably adults speaking largely for themselves who make the political decisions, and the future generations are without voice in the matter. It behooves serious students of these matters to recognize the brutality of policies that either enforce or block such communal rights and not to treat the policies as merely blandly beneficial to someone.

The world of pluralism is a world in which such trade-offs must be taken seriously and not discounted merely because they are the problem of a different group or community whose good is not my community's concern. The world of pluralism is the world in which the vast number of particularistic communitarian communities are embedded. Except for the occasional Iceland, no community is an island. And even Iceland has plausibly prospered as it has in large part because it is an open, cosmopolitan society—not a narrowly communal society.[7]

UNIVERSALISM

Universalistic norms are not naturally reinforced by self-interest, and they therefore lack the additional force that such interest gives to norms of exclusion. Indeed, they are often so weakly motivated that they are distorted into forms that can be reinforced by self-interest, as, for example, in vendetta and Catholic guilt. There might never have been a society regulated by a genuine vendetta norm of retaliation only for particular wrongs, but if that was the origin of recorded practices, vendetta turns into feud. Feud has a substantially different incentive structure and tends to lead to a different epistemology of the actions of others. Feud pits the interests of one group (such as a family) against that of another over generations. It is only incidentally driven by particular wrongs. But it may be exacerbated and even driven by the mutual ignorance that the feud produces.

Similar distortions afflict other universalistic norms. For example, the universalistic norm of Catholic guilt may be especially strong in Latin communities in which guilt becomes associated with the intrafamilial norm of maternal respect. In such communities it may even survive the decline of its religious backing. There are noninvidious groups, but the force of self-interest reinforcement of group identification often distorts even these, driving them to invidious norms of exclusion.

The universalistic norm of honesty breaks down into a strongly reinforced norm of honesty in iterated small-number dealings and a very weakly reinforced norm of honesty in broader relationships to the large community of all citizens, all taxpayers, or large firms, such as department stores or banks. Even in an iterated small-number context, the norm may be corroded if there is a prospect of the end of the relationship.[8] While many people may be consistently honest or dishonest across all dealings, others are honest with associates and dishonest in any more nearly anonymous context, because their behavior is well monitored in the first context and poorly monitored in the latter. Hence, interest correlates with honesty, and for many people there may be little or no moral motivation in their sometime honesty.

Despite the power of norms that are driven by incentives of exclusion, there has often been a struggle for universalism, or at least for a more nearly inclusive principle. That struggle has been engaged by religious, political, and intellectual leaders and no doubt by millions in their own daily lives. The struggle for universalism has taken many centuries and has often been opposed by narrower interests. One of the earliest struggles on record was Antigone's effort to get a decent burial for her brother. Her two brothers, Eteocles and Polynices, killed each other in battle, one fighting for and the other against Thebes. Creon, king of Thebes, ordered communal justice: burial for Eteocles and rotting on the field where he lay for Polynices. When Antigone defied Creon and performed the funeral service for Polynices, Creon had her buried alive. Universalism lost to communalism.[9]

There have often been strong anti-universalistic political movements. For example, there were the Anti-Federalists at the time of the United States constitutional debates, virulent, warlike nationalism in nineteenth-century Europe, and Nazism and fascism in the 1920s and 1930s. But not until recently has universalism been opposed by an articulate, philosophically erudite movement. Indeed, until recently, all philosophical discussion of ethics (excepting some theological ethics) in the western tradition has been in agreement on a single issue: universalism. It has taken two and a half millennia for western philosophy to generate a program of anti-universalistic particularism, a program that threatens metaphorical, and perhaps real, burial for the Antigones of our time.

Kantians, libertarians, natural law theorists, virtue theorists, utilitarians, and others have differed on many central issues, but they have all typically assumed that whatever their principles were, they must apply universally and without prejudice to all. Communitarians have raised an issue that formerly elicited no argument. In part they seem to have done so merely from the observation that, after all, ordinary people reason from communal standards and communal understandings, not from the ethereal universalistic principles of moral philosophers. But this would be a radical and defective move—it virtually says that the way people *do* reason is the way they *should* reason. Communitarians conclude to an "ought" from an "is." We have long ridiculed Voltaire's Pangloss for thinking this is the best of all possible worlds. How much more should we ridicule someone who says that whatever world exists is *eo ipso* good?

The practicing communitarian shares the perverse idea of the medieval European that "what has been has *ipso facto* the right to be."[10] Of course, practicing communitarians, like medieval Europeans, typically hold this view only with respect to what has been in their own communities, not in other communities. They are group solipsists. There is perhaps no part of the medieval mentality that we should more avoid than this commitment to the *ipso facto* rightness of whatever is.

Some people are not merely utilitarian or Kantian moral theorists, they are plausibly utilitarians or Kantians in their actual lives (we should hope that the correlation is not perfect, because there are proportionately few moral theorists). André Trocmé, the Protestant minister of Le Chambon, France, who spent several years risking his life to rescue Jews from the Nazis, was evidently morally motivated.[11] And some people, such as Colomba and the Jewish castaway in chapter 5, may hold to odd norms after leaving the communities that gave the norms their meaning and their backing, so that they finally seem to be strictly normatively motivated. But much of the motivation in the world that ostensibly is normative may be like norms of exclusion—it is grounded in strong personal incentives with effective reinforcement. In the politics of ethnicity and in the politics of other kinds of groups as well, norms of exclusion are powerful, and we do not need recourse to strictly normative claims to explain them.

DESTRUCTION AND CONSTRUCTION

The groups of interest in this book are those that generally depend on spontaneous, internal incentives for mobilization and identification. They are especially interesting because they organize and accomplish collective purposes without the benefit of a hierarchical state's enforcement power. Groups, such as ethnic groups, that depend on coordination power can accomplish things that are very different from what groups and institutions, such as established governments, that depend more heavily on resource or exchange power commonly accomplish. Coordination power is inherently less flexible just because it depends on the commitments of individual group members. And it must be quite focused if it is to maintain commitments. Typically, this means it can be more readily mobilized by hostilities to extant institutions, practices, or statuses than by commitment to practical programs or policies for development. It is more likely to be important in times of crisis and loss than in times of relative prosperity and progress.

Hobbes's generalization from the revolutionary times through which he lived in England is that rebellion makes the present generation worse off. This is perhaps merely an instance of the implication that spontaneously organized groups are more likely able to focus their coordination if they have an antagonistic institution to attack. This means that, initially, their goal is destructive. It is then not a necessary but nevertheless a plausible conclusion that those who fight government are worse off even if they win their fight. The contemporary histories of Northern Ireland, Yugoslavia, Burundi and Rwanda, Somalia, India, and many others seem to support Hobbes's thesis, while the cases of Czechoslovakia, Romania, and others seem contrary to Hobbes's conclusion—that is, they will seem contrary if they succeed economically. But even in a successful Czech Republic, the older citizens may be worse off in the transition.

Just because "collective interest" is a potentially confused notion, we may doubt the reasonableness of empowering collectivities to act for their members if the ground for membership in the collectivity is narrowly conceived and unrelated to most policy issues of interest to various members. For example, Milosevic may successfully mobilize a relevant fraction of Serbs behind his Serbian nationalist program. But it is unlikely that the same people will concur on other major policy matters that will eventually arise, especially once there is no war in Croatia or Bosnia and no further territory to annex to greater Serbia.[12]

One might think the Yugoslav wars will end from the exhaustion of all parties, including finally even the Serbs. But Milosevic has demonstrated no talent for managing an economy, or for domestic government more generally. His chief talent has been in mobilizing people and resources for war and genocide. The changed demands that would follow the end of war might bring him down quickly, and he might recognize that threat. Hence, he might think it in his interest to sustain the war as long as possible, perhaps by spreading it to Kosovo. Ethnic war is the one policy that has so far unified his backers.

The politics of ethnicity, however, entails yet another loss that is seldom noted. It is the loss that Thomas Wolfe might have borne if he had *not* gone to Harvard. As Henry Louis Gates says of the identification with fellow blacks, "It means that your tale is never completely your own—that the particularity of your tale is subordinated to an overarching narrative."[13] Identification with the group means substantial loss of one's personal identity. The preachers of ethnic identity mask this loss with the crude implication that personal and ethnic identity are somehow the same.

Such a personal loss through the blending of the self into a larger social whole is the project of many thinkers and leaders, good and bad. The project has been special to Germans such as Hegel, Herder, Hitler, and many others. It has been special to Zionists and pan-Arabists, and to nationalists of many other stripes. The project often has been honorable, even sweet, and it has often been genocidal. It is difficult to believe that the genocides have been outweighed by the good that the project has brought in the twentieth century.

The communal project seems to have risen to political prominence with the rise of the modern nation-state in Europe. It is often phrased as a project for a people, but in the era of state capacity to reach all the corners within the state's boundaries, it has also been associated with territorial claims. The union of a people and a territory is typically an accident, an accident that almost never happens in the world today. It takes extraordinary conditions, such as those of Iceland, to produce a state from a single people. Hence, the project becomes contradictory or violent. For example, Croatia at its recent independence was a contradictory nation. It was both territorial and ethnic, despite the overt fact that ethnicity and territory did not coincide. By implication, the new state invited Serbs to leave the territory, as many have done, and it asserted its hegemony over Croatian communities elsewhere, especially in Bosnia-Hercegovina.

Strangely contrary to the actual history of the rise of the communal project, it is often called tribalism. It is true that some of the conflicts today are seemingly associated with tribal identities. But tribalism may have been relatively benign before the era of the modern state. When groups must obtain much of what they want through a state, they are far more likely to come into overt conflict over limited resources. The reciprocal genocide of Rwanda and Burundi is largely a product of state organization, as is the carnage in Yugoslavia.

RESOLUTIONS OF CONTEMPORARY VIOLENCE

A part of the problem in the five conflicts discussed in chapter 6 is that there are rabid leaders with programs that are inherently exclusive, even violently so. This is least true, perhaps, in the case of Somalia, where the conflict may be primarily about which individual gets power. In the other cases, the presence of people such as Ian Paisley, the late Juvénal Habyarimana, Slobodan Milosevic, and the like almost guarantees that the conflicts will be hard to forget and transcend because such people will make it their program to intensify them.

A part of the problem in Somalia, Rwanda, and Burundi is that there is no solid structure of government extant. Restoring order, as the United Nations and the United States have attempted to do in Somalia and France in Rwanda, is extremely difficult if the first task is to create institutions that are almost wholly missing. The earlier colonial government in Rwanda and Burundi failed to create a semblance of native institutions. In Somalia, war destroyed the cohesion of the government of Siad Barre. In none of these countries is there a credible institutional structure for governing. To some extent this is even a problem in Bosnia, where the Serbian forces ostensibly are spontaneously organized by a rump political group that withdrew from the Bosnian government.

In these conditions, even the most benign intervention would have to be massive to be effective, and it might have to run the equivalent of a benign colonial government for many years before native institutions could be created and repaired. In Rwanda and Burundi, indeed, it might require a full generation or so of guarantees by external powers to bridge from the thirty-year era of genocide to an era of life without frequent violence. Understanding the problems in these nations is no guarantee of finding resolutions to them.

In both the Yugoslav and Somali cases, intervention early might have stopped the process of building coordinations behind the warmongers. There were voices for quick measures,[14] but intervention at early stages was not expedient (the United States was in a hotly contested presidential election). And intervention early would have seemed wrong to many because it would not have been justified by actual, but only by potential, events. This is a perverse analog of the problem that rebellious groups can more readily focus on destructive than on constructive projects (as discussed above). The United Nations might be moved by carnage to think intervention justified, but it might never be moved to intervene in order to prevent potential carnage unless it is invited to station its troops between conflicting sides.[15]

Migration—a spontaneous analog of ethnic cleansing—may change the future directions of some of these conflicts. For example, most of the Serbs of Croatia are no longer there—from a total of 766,000 in 1948, the number had fallen to about 70,000 in 1992.[16] But part of the change followed the secession of territory from Croatia to Serbia, and this might eventually be the focus of irredentist conflict. Tutsis may tend to go to Burundi, Hutus to Rwanda. Tutsis then might not face ratios of six or seven to one against them in Burundi and might finally be able to live with consociational arrangements. In Rwanda, Hutus might finally have such a clearly dominant position that churning up ethnic hostilities would no longer be a successful device for distracting the populace from seeing the extensiveness of government failure. The ratios in the two nations must already have shifted significantly in these directions and away from the stylized, outdated claim that the populations of both countries include about 15 percent Tutsis.

One of the most important of all changes, however, in all of these and many other cases, is to reduce the sway of ethnicity. This can happen naturally with certain economic and social changes. As many of the next generation move off the land and go to the city, the communal ignorance that creates such people as Radovan Karadzic and, apparently, many of the members of the Irish Republican Army will have less impact. Rural enclaves of minorities may decline intergenerationally, as they have done throughout the developed and developing world.

These two effects may be compounded. As the young go off to cities in these days of relatively easy emigration, they might commonly go to cities in the nation which is dominated by their ethnic group. For example, Hungarians in Serbian Vojvodina may often go to Hungary; Turks in Serbian Kosovo may go to Turkey.[17] A perverse implication for Serbia will be greater incentive for Serbs to stay on the land and not to migrate to cities, with the result that the Serbian economic transformation may be slowed, so that Serbia may be more backward a generation from now than it would have been had Serbian leadership struggled to keep Yugoslavia together.

THE FUTURE OF ETHNIC NATIONALISM

Readers of Daniel Patrick Moynihan's *Pandaemonium* and Eric Hobsbawm's *Nations and Nationalism since 1780* know there is an apparently deep disagreement about the significance of ethnic nationalist mobilization in our time. Hobsbawm thinks nationalism is no longer a main agent for global progress and emancipation as it once arguably was.[18] Moynihan thinks it the dominant issue of our era in international politics.[19] Their authors might find me perverse, but I find both these books compelling and often brilliant. They are two of the best books ever written on the topic. Oddly, moreover, I think both books are generally correct in their conclusions. Nationalism and ethnic mobilization today bring more degradation and ruin than emancipation and progress, but they nevertheless dominate politics in much of the world.

Improvement of the lives of most people in the world does not depend on successful ethnic mobilization. For some who are subjugated or virtually so, the first step to a better life may well be successful ethnic mobilization, as in the Civil Rights movement in the United States and in the black freedom struggle in South Africa. But this should be a short-term transitional effect. At some point—long ago reached by many peoples, including the unfortunate Serbian, Muslim, and Croatian peoples—successful ethnic mobilization is likely to bring more harm than good, both for those who mobilize and for those against whom they mobilize. For the longer term, economics and not rabid politics is the route to better lives for South African blacks, as for everyone else.

Despite the fact that rabid mobilization is not likely to be beneficial to groups, it happens nevertheless. Group mobilizations that might have benign purposes of mutual benefit to members of the group but that can benefit from the use of self-interest devices are apt to be distorted in adapting themselves to those devices. There are many wonderful groups in the world, groups whose purposes are to benefit themselves or particular others without invidious harm to anyone else. But groups whose success depends on defeating some other group tend to mobilize commitments through self-interest. And groups with ostensibly benign goals may be strengthened by the distortions of group-solipsism. In particular, groups often resort to the functional creation of norms of exclusion that define conflicts on which people can be coordinated, conflicts that then can lead to violence. This is true in many and varied contexts, of which the most important today is ethnic conflict.

Will the incidence of ethnic conflict subside? Perhaps, but if the account here is roughly right, the future does not look promising. If ethnic conflict is grounded in interests in position, it may therefore be worse today than in the past. Today the role of politically determined position looms very large in the lives of many people—proportionately far, far more people than a century ago. Opportunity for position may be the biggest lure to identification in Rwanda and Burundi and to loyalty in Somalia. The trouble with government is that it can discriminate on jobs and other opportunities according to group membership. It need not, but it can. Therefore, groups wish to control government—either of the present nation or of a rump one.

Economic boom could reduce the appeal of ethnic identification and the politics of ethnicity. In China today one could even conclude that economic boom has helped to reduce the appeal of intensive politics.[20] Of course, that appeal was first brutally reduced by the use of tanks to crush the pro-democracy movement. It might be a distressing conclusion, but perhaps the boom has been helped by the foreclosure of political alternatives. Because group activity does not pay, individuals seek their own personal fortunes, with the Smithian result that the society generally benefits. That conclusion is consistent with the recognition that, not least among the reasons to prefer smaller government, is to reduce the value of gaining control of it. Without the urge to control government, ethnic politics would be of little note in many nations. Multiethnic states in which the state controls most employment face a constant threat of ethnic politics unless they can crush opposition or can enforce universalistic principles for selection into employment.

FAREWELL TO COMMUNITY?

What is the appeal of strong, exclusive community that lies behind much of the politics of ethnicity? Perhaps it is little more, in principle, than the appeal of a simplicity that may no longer be possible, a simplicity that stands behind the epistemological comforts of home. Dorothy Osborne (later Lady Temple) wrote in a seventeenth-century letter of the "young wenches" who "keep Sheep and Cow's and sitt in the shades singing of Ballads; I goe to them and compare their voyces and Beauty's to some Ancient Shepherdesses that I have read of and finde a vaste difference there, but trust mee I think these are as innocent as those could bee. I talke to them, and finde they want nothing to make them the happiest People in the world, *but the knoledge that they are soe.*"[21] Alas, Osborne's lovely wenches could not have such knowledge without wrecking it. They were happy only in the state of ignorance of alternatives, some of which—the more opulent life of the manor—they knew to some degree. They would have had to take someone else's assessment of their happiness on faith, for which they could have no ground. It is distressing that only an external judge can say they were happiest in the world.

Again, one cannot have such knowledge without wrecking it. Even to engage in the politics of ethnicity is already to grant that the knowledge has been wrecked. The politics of ethnicity has little or no residue of the beauty of simplicity that Osborne observed in the local wenches who tended sheep and cows. The politics of ethnicity is waged in a context of knowledge that transcends the comfortable epistemology of the community. If it does not universalistically appeal to equality of treatment for a particular group, it is apt to be harsh and demoralizing. For a strong community to succeed politically would require that it destroy much of what surrounds it and barricade itself against much of the world—perhaps even to purge itself of the weakly committed and to tear down cities where cosmopolitan values might fester, as Pol Pot sought to destroy Phnom Penh and as Milosevic might wish he could destroy Belgrade.

The community of Osborne's wenches has long since been swept away by economic, technological, and—not least—political changes. That is, its epistemology has been swamped by other epistemologies, and no one in developed societies can be ignorant as Osborne's wenches were. There may be almost no one left other than one who has been reared in ignorance in an Old Order Amish or similar community who today would honestly wish themselves back into the life of Osborne's wenches or any near equivalent.

In Osborne's time, life was more decentralized and anarchic for most people than it is today. A century after Osborne, the Anti-Federalists' program of strong communities, weak states, and an even weaker national federation was still a plausible program. But it would soon have been doomed to implausibility if the Anti-Federalists had got the constitution they wanted. In a radically decentralized world, it was possible for people even to get by with varied languages, because they did not depend on each other in daily relations. The only large centralized organization through much of European history was the Catholic Church, whose "employees" shared the common Church Latin language. When French leaders chose to pull the polyglot peoples of France into a single nation, they introduced standardized French to enable individuals to be drawn more successfully into national political and military service.[22] In our time it is almost impossible to imagine a state that does not reach out to all citizens, and language is a central factor in its reach. Formerly, individuals dealt with linguistic disadvantages individually. Now they insist on collectively dealing with them by establishing language rights.

The appeal of the simplicity of life in past communities, however, is only an in-principle appeal because such simplicity is not available to the professors who write on communitarianism or to the peoples of Yugoslavia, Quebec, Northern Ireland, or most other hotbeds of communal agitation. The actual appeal on the ground is very heavily a matter of individual self-interest. The principal interest is inclusion versus exclusion. This is of great importance when the epistemological comforts of home and other rewards of group membership are especially significant. Naturally, these may weigh less heavily for some than for other potential members of any given community. Those for whom they do not weigh heavily or for whom contrary interests balance or outweigh these interests will be at the fringe of a community.

If the community has a strenuous leadership, or if it coordinates very forcefully on strong commitment to the group, or if the lower commitment of the fringe members makes them less comfortable to be around, the fringe members may be pushed out of the group. It is the degree of tolerance of fringe members that defines the group's boundaries. Periods of harsh conflict, such as in Yugoslavia, Rwanda, and Burundi during their internecine wars, can lead to far stronger commitments and to grim intolerance. That intolerance may then be retrospectively misinterpreted as the source of the violence that has caused it. The politics of ethnicity is the politics of group effort to prevail against others, often in what is seen as a zero-sum world. Under the rigors of conflict, that effort may even be turned on many of one's own.

FINAL REMARKS

Julius Moravcsik, a philosopher at Stanford, states four criteria for communal ties that, taken together, are so demanding that community can seldom, if ever, be relevant to political communitarianism. The criteria are that members (1) have respect for each other, (2) have concern for each other's welfare, (3) trust each other on communal issues, and (4) care for each other.[23] Any community substantial enough to be of political significance would turn these conditions into abstract, quasi-universal principles—or into blind commitments unfounded in knowledge of each other beyond closest relations. These criteria are among the normative constraints that make Moravcsik's communitarianism morally universalistic—for him, communities do not define the right or the good; rather, they must live up to it.

Many observers of actual communities (Moravcsik's "de facto" communities) would likely add a fifth criterion: that members exclude those not deemed to fit in the community. Edward Said says that Michael Walzer's book, *Exodus and Revolution*, "may be a tragic book in that it teaches that you cannot both 'belong' and concern yourself with [others] who do not belong."[24] The 1990s behavior of Rwandans, Burundans, Serbs, Croats, Catholic and Protestant Northern Irish militants, and many others teach a similar lesson. The striking character of a community that is too large to fit Moravcsik's criteria is that it may nevertheless be supported by strong norms of exclusion that give it life and force.

Exclusion can be motivated by strain for epistemological comfort, economic advantage, or religious beliefs, which might themselves fit well with an urge for epistemological comfort. Religious beliefs have played a role in the Middle East, Northern Ireland, Quebec, and in the Amish and Lubavitcher communities, but little or none in Rwanda and Burundi, Somalia, or Yugoslavia. In Somalia, economic advantage may be the principal motor of the violence, especially the economic advantage of whoever finally wins control and of his supporters.

In all of these cases, to belong means to dampen concern with those who are excluded or, worse, to be overtly hostile to them. The dreadful lesson of these conflicts seems to be that individuals have an immediate interest in doing things that lead to their own shackling and to the suppression of others. They can have an interest in reducing themselves to something less than human, to a standard pawn in a large strategic game, plausibly played by thugs. They give up their claim to personal identity by giving themselves over fully to trivializing identification, in which, as Gates wrote, "your tale is subordinated to an overarching narrative." Individuals acting in groups bolstered by norms of exclusion can transcend the negative logic of collective action—but all too often only at the cost of degradation of self and other.

Notes

CHAPTER ONE
INDIVIDUALS AND GROUPS

1. *New York Times* (12 December 1993), p. 4.2.

2. There are, of course, misfits who are the result of ethnic mixing. Indeed, in certain societies, virtually everyone might actually be a misfit. For example, many, perhaps most, American racists are merely second, third, or later generation misfits.

3. Philips Verner Bradford and Harvey Blume, *Ota Benga: The Pygmy in the Zoo* (New York: St. Martin's, 1992).

4. Mancur Olson, Jr., *The Logic of Collective Action* (Cambridge, Mass.: Harvard University Press, 1965); Russell Hardin, *Collective Action* (Baltimore: Johns Hopkins University Press, 1982).

5. Erik H. Erikson, *Insight and Responsibility* (New York: Norton, 1964), p. 91.

6. Oral remarks at the Transcultura Conference on "The Conditions of Reciprocal Understanding: 100 Years of International and Cross Cultural Understanding," University of Chicago, September 12–17, 1992.

7. Benedict Anderson, *Imagined Communities: Reflections on the Origin and Spread of Nationalism* (London: Verso, rev. ed., 1991 [1983]).

8. Noted by John Gumperz at the Transcultura Conference.

9. At the Transcultura Conference.

10. Theodora Kroeber, *Ishi in Two Worlds: A Biography of the Last Wild Indian in North America* (Berkeley: University of California Press, 1976 [1961]).

11. As summarized by James Strachey, ed., Sigmund Freud, *The Ego and the Id* (New York: Norton, 1962), p. xvi.

12. See, e.g., John Finley Scott, *Internalization of Norms: A Sociological Theory of Moral Commitment* (Englewood Cliffs, N.J.: Prentice-Hall, 1971), pp. 146–54.

13. See related discussion under "Intention and behavior" in chap. 6.

14. Anatol Rapoport, *Fights, Games, and Debates* (Ann Arbor: University of Michigan Press, 1960), pp. 47–59.

15. Jon Elster, *Sour Grapes: Studies in the Subversion of Rationality* (Cambridge: Cambridge University Press, 1983). Kierkegaard is supposed to have said genius never desires what does not exist—sour grapes is the consolation of those less than genius.

16. Michael Polanyi, *The Tacit Dimension* (Garden City, N.Y.: Anchor, 1967 [1966]), pp. 9–10.

17. Quoted in Polanyi, *The Tacit Dimension*, p. 95.

18. Kazuo Ishiguro, *The Remains of the Day* (New York: Knopf, 1989), p. 42.

19. Jessica Anderson, *Tirra Lirra by the River* (Penguin 1984 [1978]), p. 119.

20. Kurt Tucholsky, *Politische Briefe* (Reinbek bei Hamburg: Rowohlt, 1969), letter of March 4, 1933 to Walter Hasenclever, pp. 11–14, at p. 12.

21. For Samuel Johnson, see James Boswell, *Life Of Johnson* (London: Oxford University Press, 1976 [1791]), pp. 947–48; John Stuart Mill, *Principles of Political Economy* (Toronto: University of Toronto Press, 1965 [1871], 7th edition, ed. J. M. Robson), bk. 5, chap. 11, sect. 13, p. 960; Joseph Townsend, *A Dissertation on the Poor Laws, By a Well-Wisher to Mankind* (Berkeley, Calif.: University of California Press, 1971 [1786]); Alexis de Tocqueville, "Memoir on Pauperism," in Seymour Drescher, *Tocqueville and Beaumont on Social Reform* (New York: Harper, 1968 [1835]), pp. 1–2. See further, Russell Hardin, "Altruism and Mutual Advantage," *Social Service Review* 67 (September 1993): 358–73.

22. At the Transcultura Conference, for which meals were served at Woodward Court, an undergraduate dormitory at the University of Chicago.

23. Another growing literature, including work on Gramsci's notion of hegemony, asserts that there is too little attention to the state.

24. Russell Hardin, "Acting Together, Contributing Together," *Rationality and Society* 3 (July 1991): 365–80.

25. Anthony Heath, *Rational Choice and Social Exchange* (Cambridge: Cambridge University Press, 1976), pp. 59–60.

26. David Hume, *A Treatise of Human Nature*, 2d edition, ed. L. A. Selby-Bigge and P. H. Nidditch (Oxford: Oxford University Press, 1978 [1739–40]), bk. 3, pt. 3, sect. 1, p. 523; Russell Hardin, *Morality within the Limits of Reason* (Chicago: University of Chicago Press, 1988), pp. 42–44.

27. Anderson, *Imagined Communities*, p. 7.

CHAPTER TWO
GROUP POWER

1. David Hume, *A Treatise of Human Nature*, any edition, especially bk. 3, pt. 2, sect. 8, "Of the Source of Allegiance"; David K. Lewis, *Convention* (Cambridge, Mass.: Harvard University Press, 1969).

2. Ian R. Bartky and Elizabeth Harrison, "Standard and Daylight Saving Time," *Scientific American* 240 (May 1979): 46–53.

3. Ibid., p. 49.

4. Charles Taylor, "What's Wrong with Negative Liberty," in Taylor, *Philosophy and the Human Sciences, Philosophical Papers*, vol. 2, pp. 211–29, at p. 218.

5. This is related to a general problem of strategic interaction. In an interactive context, my action is typically not merely to choose to do X rather than Y. It is to choose the strategy of doing X with all of its possible range of outcomes depending on what others do. Hence, a simple action theory is beside the point of such strategic choices. See further, Russell Hardin, *Morality within the Limits of Reason* (Chicago: University of Chicago Press, 1988), pp. 68–70.

6. Adam Smith, *An Inquiry into the Nature and Causes of the Wealth of Nations* (Oxford: Oxford University Press, 1976; Indianapolis, Ind.: Liberty Classics, 1981, reprint), bk. 5, chap. 1, pt. 2, pp. 711–15.

7. William James remarks, "This tendency of organic unities to accumulate when once they are formed is absolutely all the truth I can distill from Spencer's unwieldy account of evolution" (William James, "Herbert Spencer," pp. 107–22 in James, *Essays in Philosophy* [Cambridge, Mass.: Harvard University Press, 1978; essay first pub. 1904], p. 119).

8. Of course, there may be some conflict in our group. I may wish I were leader in your stead. To become leader, however, I will need to gain a sufficient following to make it the interest of others to recoordinate behind me.

9. John Austin, *The Province of Jurisprudence Determined* (New York: Noonday Press, 1954 [1832]).

10. This theory is severely criticized by H.L.A. Hart, *The Concept of Law* (Oxford: Oxford University Press, 1961).

11. David Hume, "Of the First Principles of Government," pp. 32–36 in Hume, *Essays Moral, Political and Literary*, ed. by Eugene F. Miller (Indianapolis, Ind.: Liberty Press, 1985; essay first pub. 1741), p. 34. Many philosophers have followed Hume's view. Although he seems to know better in other places, Hume here fails to note that "the presumed opinion of others" need be only the opinion that they are themselves at risk if they do not support the tyrant. They can take that risk with impunity only if they are relatively sure others will join with them, that is, will coordinate on redefining power. See further, Gregory S. Kavka, *Hobbesian Moral and Political Theory* (Princeton: Princeton University Press, 1986), pp. 254–66. Kavka cites several references (p. 257n).

12. Anthony D'Amato, "Is International Law Really 'Law'?" *Northwestern Law Review* 79 (1984–85): 1293–1314, p. 1295.

13. Talcott Parsons, "Power and the Social System," pp. 94–143 in Steven Lukes, ed., *Power* (New York: New York University Press, 1986 [1963]), at p. 121.

14. Gaetano Mosca, *The Ruling Class* (New York: McGraw-Hill, 1939), p. 53.

15. Pavel Campeanu, "The Revolt of the Romanians," *New York Review of Books* (1 February 1990), pp. 30–31.

16. Campeanu, "The Revolt of the Romanians."

17. The unnamed Prisoner's Dilemma is reported in Merrill Flood, "Some Experimental Games," *Management Science* 5 (October 1958): 5–26, esp. pp. 11–17. It was less accessibly published in "Some Experimental Games," Rand Corporation Research Memorandum RM-789 1, 20 June 1952. To my knowledge, this is the first instance of the appearance of the Prisoner's Dilemma.

18. Merrill Flood, private communication, February 25, 1975, reports that Tucker gave the game its present name.

19. Arthur Stinchcombe captures this growing sense in his sly review of work by Jon Elster, "Is the Prisoner's Dilemma All of Sociology?" *Inquiry* 23 (1980): 187–92.

20. Mancur Olson, Jr., *The Logic of Collective Action* (Cambridge, Mass.: Harvard University Press, 1965).

21. Xenophon, *The Persian Expedition*, bk. 1, chaps. 8–10; bk. 2, chap. 1.

22. Max Gluckman, *Politics, Law and Ritual in Tribal Society* (Chicago: Aldine 1965; reprinted New York: New American Library, 1968), p. 181.

23. Parsons, "Power and the Social System," pp. 97, 101.

24. Brian Barry, "Is It Better To Be Powerful or Lucky?" *Political Studies* 28 (June and September 1980): 183–94, 338–52.

25. Russell Hardin, "Hobbesian Political Order," *Political Theory* 19 (May 1991): 156–80.

26. Adam Smith, *An Inquiry into the Nature and Causes of the Wealth of Nations*, bk. 5, chap. 1, pt. 2, p. 709. See also Smith, *Lectures on Jurisprudence* (Oxford: Oxford University Press, 1978; Indianapolis, Ind.: Liberty Classics, 1982, reprint), p. 16.

27. Plato, *The Republic*, bk. 2, 360b–c.

28. Olson, *The Logic*, p. 105, emphasis in original.

29. A survey of some of the literature on this issue is in Scott Lash and John Urry, "The New Marxism of Collective Action: A Critical Analysis," *Sociology* 18 (February 1984): 33–50. To escape the difficulties of basing a theory of revolution on individual interests, Lash and Urry want to focus on the "causal powers" of social classes.

30. Marx called the February 1848 Revolution "a surprise attack, a *taking* of the old society *unawares*" (Karl Marx, *The 18th Brumaire of Louis Bonaparte* [New York: International Publishers, 1963], p. 18). Alas, it was also notice to the old society that it could be taken if it did not become more aware in the future.

31. Richard J. Arneson, "Marxism and Secular Faith," *American Political Science Review* 79 (September 1985): 627–40, quote on p. 633.

32. Marx, *18th Brumaire*, p. 19.

33. Arneson, "Marxism and Secular Faith," p. 633.

34. Marx, *18th Brumaire*, p. 18.

35. For surveys of this field see Jules Coleman, "Law and Economics," chap. 5 of Jeffrie Murphy and Jules Coleman, *The Philosophy of Law* (Boulder, Colo.: Westview, 1990, rev. ed.); Richard A. Posner, "The Ethical and Political Basis of Wealth Maximization," pp. 88–115 in Posner, *The Economics of Justice* (Cambridge, Mass.: Harvard University Press, 1981); and Russell Hardin, "The Morality of Law and Economics," *Law and Philosophy* 11 (November 1992): 331–84.

36. Richard A. Posner is, of course, not oblivious of strategic considerations in the common law. See his brief discussion of *stare decisis*, the doctrine of decision according to precedent, in Posner, *Economic Analysis of Law* (Boston: Little, Brown, 1992, 4th ed.), pp. 547–48.

37. Bernard Williams, *Ethics and the Limits of Philosophy* (Cambridge, Mass.: Harvard University Press, 1985), p. 44.

38. See further, Russell Hardin, "Does Might Make Right?," pp. 201–17 in J. Roland Pennock and John W. Chapman, eds., NOMOS 29: *Authority Revisited* (New York: New York University Press, 1987).

39. This is obviously a contingent claim that depends on what coordination opportunities there are.

40. Smith, *Wealth of Nations*, bk. 5, chap. 1, pt. 2, p. 716.

CHAPTER THREE
GROUP IDENTIFICATION

1. E. J. Hobsbawm canvasses difficulties in the definition of nationalities and ethnic groups. Hobsbawm, *Nations and Nationalism since 1780: Programme, Myth, Reality* (Cambridge: Cambridge University Press, 1990), pp. 1–13.

2. Among others, see Thorstein Veblen, *An Inquiry into the Nature of Peace and the Terms of Its Perpetuation* (New York: Augustus M. Kelley, 1964 reprint [1917]).

3. Mancur Olson, Jr., *The Logic of Collective Action* (Cambridge, Mass.: Harvard University Press, 1965); Russell Hardin, *Collective Action* (Baltimore: Johns Hopkins University Press for Resources for the Future, 1982).

4. Olson, *The Logic of Collective Action.*

5. Cf., Hobsbawm, *Nations and Nationalism*, p. 8.

6. Thomas C. Schelling, *The Strategy of Conflict* (Cambridge, Mass.: Harvard University Press, 1960).

7. Russell Hardin, "Acting Together, Contributing Together," *Rationality and Society* 3 (July 1991): 365–80.

8. William Rees-Mogg, "The Sheriff Fiddles while the Town Burns," *Independent*, 4 May 1992, p. 17. Quoted in Daniel Patrick Moynihan, *Pandaemonium: Ethnicity in International Politics* (Oxford: Oxford University Press, 1993), p. 24.

9. Russell Hardin, "Hobbesian Political Order," *Political Theory* 19 (1991): 156–80.

10. Robert Axelrod, "An Evolutionary Approach to Norms," *American Political Science Review* 80 (1986): 1095–1112.

11. Hardin, "Acting Together, Contributing Together," esp. pp. 374–77.

12. Karl Marx, *The 18th Brumaire of Napoleon Bonaparte* (New York: International Publishers, 1963 [1852]), pp. 123–24.

13. Marysa Navarro, "The Personal Is Political: Las Madres de Plaza de Mayo," in Susan Eckstein, ed., *Power and Popular Protest* (Berkeley: University of California Press, 1989), pp. 241–58, esp. p. 250; John Simpson and Jana Bennett, *The Disappeared and the Mothers of the Plaza* (New York: St. Martin's Press, 1985), pp. 156–57.

14. Stéphane Dion, "The Importance of the Language Issue in the Constitutional Crisis," in Douglas Brown and Robert Young, eds., *Canada: The State of the Federation 1992* (Kingston: Institute of Intergovernmental Relations, 1992). See further discussion in chap. 6.

15. Fred Hirsch distinguishes between positional and material goods and their interaction in a growing economy. Hirsch, *Social Limits to Growth* (Cambridge, Mass.: Harvard University Press, 1976), esp. chap. 3. The roles of positional and distributional goods in ethnic conflicts were analyzed earlier by Daniel Bell in "Nationalism or Class?—Some Questions on the Potency of Political Symbols," *The Student Zionist*, May 1947 (cited in Moynihan, *Pandaemonium*, p. 59).

16. See further cases in Donald Horowitz, *Ethnic Groups in Conflict* (Berkeley: University of California Press, 1985).

17. David D. Laitin, *Hegemony and Culture: Politics and Religious Change among the Yoruba* (Chicago: University of Chicago Press, 1986), pp. 133–34.

18. See further, chap. 6.

19. Moynihan, *Pandaemonium*, p. 37.

20. Gary S. Becker, *The Economics of Discrimination* (Chicago: University of Chicago Press, 1971, 2d ed. [1957]).

21. *New Yorker* (7 March 1988), p. 83.

22. James W. Fernandez, "Tolerance in a Repugnant World and Other Dilemmas in the Cultural Relativism of Melville J. Herskovits," *Ethos* 18 (June 1990): 140–64, p. 144.

23. Bernard Williams, *Morality : An Introduction to Ethics* (New York: Harper, 1972), p. 21.

24. Fernandez, "Tolerance in a Repugnant World," pp. 143–46. In the vocabulary of chap. 7, Herskovits is an epistemological communitarian but not a normative communitarian.

25. David Hume, *A Treatise of Human Nature*, ed. L. A. Selby-Bigge and P. H. Nidditch (Oxford: Oxford University Press, 1978, 2d ed.; first pub. 1739–40), bk. 3, pt. 1, sect. 1, pp. 469–70.

26. Melville J. Herskovits, *Cultural Relativism: Perspectives in Cultural Pluralism*, ed. Frances S. Herskovits (New York: Vintage, 1972), p. 21. See also Fernandez, "Tolerance in a Repugnant World," pp. 155–56.

27. Herskovits, *Cultural Relativism*, pp. 102–3.

28. Vladimir Reznichenko, "Anti-Semitism on Trial," *Soviet Life* (February 1991): 14–17, esp. p. 15.

29. Hobsbawm, *Nations and Nationalism*, p. 12. Hobsbawm quotes Ernest Renan's rueful comment: "Getting its history wrong is part of being a nation." For the Northern Irish equivalent, see Roy Foster, "Anglo-Irish Relations and Northern Ireland: Historical Perspectives," in Dermot Keogh and Michael H. Haltzel, eds., *Northern Ireland and the Politics of Reconciliation* (Cambridge: Cambridge University Press, 1993), pp. 13–32. For France, see Herman Lebovics, *True France: The Wars over Cultural Identity, 1900–1945* (Ithaca, N.Y.: Cornell University Press, 1992). A—perhaps apocryphal—fundamentalist preacher in Texas campaigned against the teaching of languages in the local public schools. Why? Well, if English was good enough for Jesus, it is good enough for our children.

30. Consider, for comparison, why loyalty to a sports team rises as it wins. Perhaps loyalty rises because the team seems therefore to justify loyalty but perhaps it rises also and more so because the team therefore repays loyalty with greater pleasure.

31. See further, Russell Hardin, "Common Sense at the Foundations," in Bart Schultz, ed., *Henry Sidgwick As Philosopher and Historian* (New York: Cambridge University Press, 1992), pp. 143–60.

32. As if there were not enough problems with such knowledge, Mark Monmonier warns us against too great credence in maps (*How to Lie with Maps* [Chicago: University of Chicago Press, 1991]).

33. See Hobsbawm, *Nations*, p. 6.

34. Lord Acton, *Essays in the History of Liberty*, ed. J. Rufus Fears (Indianapolis, Ind.: Liberty Classics, 1985, essay on "Nationality," first pub. 1862), p. 411. Hobsbawm's remark is quoted in the text at n. 29.

35. Some, however, argue against it. Michael Sandel argues against John Rawls's theory of justice that it is grounded on what idealized individuals without cultural knowledge would choose. But such socially unencumbered people cannot exist and it is unclear how a theory based on their choices should be compelling to people as they actually occur. Michael J. Sandel, *Liberalism and the Limits of Justice* (Cambridge: Cambridge University Press, 1982).

36. Charles Taylor, "Irreducibly Social Goods," in Geoffrey Brennan and Cliff Walsh, eds., *Rationality, Individualism and Public Policy* (Canberra: Centre for Research on Federal Financial Relations, 1990), pp. 45–63. Also see accompanying comments by Robert E. Goodin, John Broome, Frank Jackson, and Peter Gärdenfors. Taylor speaks of public goods, but this is a terminology that leads to confusion for those who understand it in its technical sense in economics. Few if any goods are genuinely public, but many goods are collectively provided.

37. Taylor, "Irreducibly Social Goods," p. 55.

38. Theodora Kroeber, *Ishi in Two Worlds: A Biography of the Last Wild Indian in North America* (Berkeley: University of California Press, 1976 [1961]).

39. Taylor, "Irreducibly Social Goods," p. 55. Julius Moravcsik makes a similar claim for the intrinsic value of certain communities in "Communal Ties," *Supplement to Proceedings and Addresses of the American Philosophical Association* 62 (September 1988): 211–25.

40. *Science* 251 (11 January 1991): 159. Only about 5 percent of extant languages—about three hundred—are safe from extinction. Some linguists question the significance of their colleagues' claims because they question the way languages are counted.

41. Kurt Tucholsky, *Politische Briefe*, ed. by Fritz J. Raddatz (Reinbek bei Hamburg: Rowohlt, 1969), letter of 15 December 1934 to Walter Hasenclever, pp. 58–60, at p. 58.

42. Ibid., letter of 29 November 1935 to Hasenclever, pp. 71–74, at p. 72.

43. Ibid., letter of 20 April 1933 to Hasenclever, pp. 19–21, at p. 20. He added, "When abroad, one can do that."

CHAPTER FOUR
NORMS OF EXCLUSION

1. David K. Lewis, *Convention* (Cambridge, Mass.: Harvard University Press, 1969); Russell Hardin, *Morality within the Limits of Reason* (Chicago: University of Chicago Press, 1988), pp. 47–53.

2. As should become clear below, this means the norm cannot be given a functional explanation, as many other norms can be.

3. Peter Steinfels, "Debating Intermarriage and Jewish Survival," *New York Times* (18 October 1992), p. 1.

4. For the relationship of prisoner's dilemma to coordination and convention

in ongoing contexts, see Russell Hardin, *Collective Action* (Baltimore: Johns Hopkins University Press for Resources for the Future, 1982), chaps. 9–12.

5. Edna Ullmann-Margalit, *The Emergence of Norms* (Oxford: Oxford University Press, 1977). As will become evident in the discussion of the prisoner's dilemma fringe of norms of exclusion, these norms govern relations that can be coordination for many but prisoner's dilemma for others. These norms get their backing from coordination, but they are invoked against the prisoner's dilemma fringes.

6. Virginia Woolf supposes the norms of male dominance over women that degrade our lives function to give males a sense of confidence in their own superiority, because, under these norms of exclusion, every male is automatically superior to more than half the race. Woolf, *A Room of One's Own* (Harmondsworth, Middlesex: 1945 [1928]), pp. 36–38.

7. V. G. Kiernan, *The Duel in European History: Honour and the Reign of Aristocracy* (Oxford: Oxford University Press, 1986), p. 277. There is a fine summary of this work in the review by Christopher Hill, "Touché!," *New York Review of Books* (14 June 1990), pp. 55–57.

8. Deuteronomy 23:19.

9. Thomas Aquinas, *Summa Theologiae* II-II. Question 78 ("On the Sin of Usury"). Even with the backing of the Church, however, the injunction against Christian lending was commonly broken. See Robert S. Lopez and Irving W. Raymond, eds., *Medieval Trade in the Mediterranean World* (New York: Columbia University Press, 1955), pp. 156–61.

10. See further, chap. 3.

11. See Hardin, *Morality within the Limits of Reason*, chap. 2.

12. Russell Hardin, "The Street-Level Epistemology of Trust," *Analyse und Kritik* 14 (Winter 1992): 152–76; repr. *Politics and Society* 21 (December 1993): pp. 505–29.

13. Hardin, *Collective Action*, pp. 153–54.

14. Ibid., pp. 173–205.

15. The discussion that follows here is a response to a challenge from Robert K. Merton to make sense of the use of negative terms as markers of self-approbation. Incidentally, despite its very large vocabulary, the spell checker on my computer does not know the word "nigger." Presumably, it is a very bourgeois, perhaps white spell checker. Even at this late date, most whites have difficulty reinserting nigger into their vocabulary. Ironically, a chief obstacle to reinserting it may be black opposition.

16. From the album *Midnight Marauders* (1994), distributed by RCA Records.

17. John Camper, "Loyola Struggling to Handle New Racial Tensions: Professor's Remark Sets Off Firestorm," *Chicago Tribune*, 15 April 1990, sect. 2, pp. 1ff.; Jim Bowman, "Watch More Than P's and Q's," *Chicago Tribune*, 21 April 1990, sect. 1, p. 12. For further discussion, see Michael Davis, "Wild Professors, Sensitive Students: A Preface to Academic Ethics," *Social Theory and Practice* 18 (Summer 1992): 117–41.

18. Robert K. Merton, "Insiders and Outsiders: A Chapter in the Sociology of Knowledge," *American Journal of Sociology* 28 (July 1972): 9–47, at p. 20.

19. Recall that both supporters and opponents of Clarence Thomas's appointment to the U.S. Supreme Court were bothered by the fact that some of the accusations against him were that he made overt and sexually suggestive comments, just as many blacks, both men and women, commonly do in bantering conversations among themselves.

20. Janet Mancini Billson and Richard Majors, *Cool Pose: The Dilemmas of Black Manhood in America* (Lexington, Mass.: Lexington, 1992).

21. This is a modified version of the account of Jon Elster, *Ulysses and the Sirens* (Cambridge: Cambridge University Press, 1979), p. 28. See also Russell Hardin, "Rationality, Irrationality, and Functionalist Explanation," *Social Science Information* 19 (September 1980): 755–72. In this earlier work I spoke of "functionalist explanation." That terminology is misleading because it tends to invoke the specter of functionalism. Functional explanation does not entail functionalism. In functionalist theories it is supposed that some behaviors are functional for the survival or good of the society. Racism, which is a norm of exclusion, is not likely functional for the survival or good of a society. But it can be given a functional explanation in that it may be supported through its contribution to the interests of racists.

22. This potential benefit may be offset by the potential cost of reduced access to jobs and resources controlled by other groups and by the larger society, as noted below.

23. See further, chap. 3.

24. Sara Rimer, "Shawn, 17: Running Past Many Obstacles," *New York Times* (25 April 1993), pp. 1, 47.

25. Kristin Hunter Lattany, "Off-Timing: Stepping to the Different Drummer," in Gerald Early, ed., *Lure and Loathing: Essays on Race, Identity, and the Ambivalence of Assimilation* (New York: Penguin, 1993), pp. 163–74, at p. 168. Edmund Morgan, who briefly replaced Leonard Jeffries as head of the Black Studies Department of the City College of New York, reputedly said to a class, "I fear that I gave up a good deal of my blackness in the course of moving into a mixed world." One of his students reacted harshly: "My feeling is that if you have your identity, that's sacred." James Traub, "The Hearts and Minds of City College," *New Yorker* (7 June 1993), pp. 42–53, at p. 52.

26. Jervis Anderson, "The Public Intellectual," *New Yorker* (17 January 1994), 39–48, at pp. 45–48.

27. Michael Hechter, "The Attainment of Solidarity in Intentional Communities," *Rationality and Society* 2 (April 1990): 142–55.

28. *New York Times* (14 November 1993), p. I.8.

29. See further, Robert K. Merton, "Our Sociological Vernacular," *Columbia* (the magazine of Columbia University), November 1981.

30. For example, many aristocrats might have come to grasp the effect of the dueling norm on the exclusion of others from the aristocratic status, while many others might never have appreciated the impact of dueling on aristocratic identification. For the first group, Elster's additional conditions were not met; for the latter group they were.

31. Robert K. Merton, *Social Theory and Social Structure* (New York: Macmillan, 1968, enlarged ed.), pp. 114–18; Hardin, "Rationality, Irrationality,

and Functionalist Explanation," pp. 757–60. Elster's own primary concern with the difference between intentional and non-intentional explanations of behavior may have led him to focus on latent, non-intentional patterns as functionally to be explained. But the defining characteristic of functional explanation is feedback, not lack of intention.

32. Irving Lewis Allen, *The City in Slang* (Oxford: Oxford University Press, 1993), pp. 217–18.

33. Allen says that "to name Us with an ironic epithet given to Us by Them . . . implicitly names Them" (Allen, *The City in Slang*, p. 218). It seems unlikely that young blacks who call one another nigger are centrally motivated by the intention to name Them.

34. I came of age during the civil rights era in Texas and I have many memories of Toms being quoted, but I have no published source. Similarly, I have memories, possibly exaggerated, of people such as Stokely Carmichael challenging blacks with their racial identity. Carmichael urged abandonment of the term Negro (Stokely Carmichael and Charles V. Hamilton, *Black Power: The Politics of Liberation in America* [New York: Random House, 1967]). For capsule histories of the changes in self-designations of American blacks, see Tom W. Smith, "Changing Racial Labels: From 'Colored' to 'Negro' to 'Black' to 'African American,' " *Public Opinion Quarterly* 56 (1992): 496–514. The last of Smith's changes is seemingly underway now, but only time will tell whether usage will tip.

35. Arthur Hertzberg says that "anti-Semitism is used by people who want to show they are the truly loyal and pure representatives of their ethnic group or nation" (Hertzberg, "Is Anti-Semitism Dying Out?" *New York Review of Books* [24 June 1993], pp. 51–57, at p. 51).

36. The use of the term "bad nigger," applied, for example, to a violent criminal, may have separate origins. It may be more nearly a Sartrean or Nietzschean declaration of self. See further, Jack Katz, *Seductions of Crime: Moral and Sensual Attractions in Doing Evil* (New York: Basic Books, 1988), pp. 263–64.

37. See Edna Ullmann-Margalit and Sidney Morgenbesser, "Picking and Choosing," *Social Research* 44 (Winter 1977): 757–85.

38. I owe this example to Fritz Stern. See "Gueux," *New Encyclopedia Britannica, Micropaedia* vol. 4, 15th ed. (1978), p. 78.

39. John Howard Griffin, *Black Like Me* (New York: New American Library, 1976 [1961]).

40. Thomas Wolfe, *You Can't Go Home Again* (1940); *Look Homeward, Angel* (New York: Scribner's, 1929).

41. Thomas Wolfe, *The Web and the Rock* (New York: Harper, 1939). In his 1988 presidential campaign, George Bush evidently borrowed and distorted Wolfe's "thousand points of . . . light."

42. Herman Melville put this concern more generally: "In the soul of man there lies one insular Tahiti, full of peace and joy, but encompassed by all the horrors of the half-known life. God keep thee! Push not off from that isle, thou canst never return!" (Melville, *Moby Dick* [published in 1851 as *The Whale*], any complete edition, chap. 58).

43. One might nevertheless suppose that, before the Civil Rights movement, many whites in the South were responsible as individuals for what the larger

society did insofar as many of them actively participated in Jim Crow practices. Dwight Macdonald supposed that typical Germans were less culpable of Nazi actions than typical white southerners were of racial exclusion and subjugation. Dwight Macdonald, *The Responsibility of Peoples and Other Essays in Political Criticism* (London: Victor Gollancz, 1957), pp. 19–24.

44. Griffin, *Black Like Me*, p. 153.

45. See further, the discussion of tipping below, under "Stability and Fragility of Norms."

46. There were exceptions, such as the notable bias against Jews and, no doubt, a general bias in favor of Russians.

47. Ian Gilmour, *Riot, Risings and Revolution: Governance and Violence in Eighteenth-Century England* (London: Hutchinson, 1992), pp. 265, 279.

48. Kiernan, *The Duel in European History*, p. 159.

49. Ibid., p. 152.

50. Francis Bacon, *The Charge of Sir Francis Bacon Knight, His Majesties Attourney generall, touching Duells, upon an information in the Star-chamber against Priest and Wright* (London: 1614; New York: Da Capo Press, facsimile reprint, 1968), pp. 22–23.

51. Adam Smith, *Lectures on Jurisprudence* (Oxford: Oxford University Press, 1978; Indianapolis, Ind.: Liberty Press, 1982 [from lecture notes dated 1762–1763]), p. 123.

52. For a typical statement, see Cesare Beccaria, *On Crimes and Punishments* (Indianapolis, Ind.: Hackett, 1986 [1764]; trans. from the Italian by David Young), p. 21.

53. Bacon, *The Charge of Sir Francis Bacon*, pp. 28–30 (pp. 28 and 29 are misnumbered as 20 and 21).

54. Cited in Kiernan, *The Duel in European History*, p. 282.

55. Bacon, *The Charge of Sir Francis Bacon*, pp. 16–19, 31–32 (the last page is misnumbered as 24).

56. Ibid., pp. 12, 6.

57. Thomas Hobbes, *Leviathan* (Harmondsworth, Middlesex: Penguin, 1968 [1651]), chap. 10, p. 157 [45].

58. Kiernan, *The Duel in European History*, p. 160.

59. Ibid., p. 159; see also pp. 16, 111, 329. Kiernan's view of the individual irrationality of dueling might be roughly Bacon's point that the duel was too grievous a response to such trivia as insults.

60. Warren F. Schwartz, Keith Baxter, and David Ryan, "The Duel: Can These Gentlemen Be Acting Efficiently?" *Journal of Legal Studies* 13 (June 1984): 321–55, at p. 333.

61. Cited in Kiernan, *The Duel in European History*, p. 171. See also pp. 16, 52, and 77. Smith also shared Montesquieu's view of the high cost of failing to duel (Smith, *Lectures in Jurisprudence*, p. 123).

62. Bacon, *The Charge of Sir Francis Bacon*, pp. 9–10.

63. Kiernan, *The Duel in European History*, p. 208, emphasis added. The victim of the duel was Sir Alexander Boswell, son of James Boswell.

64. Ibid., p. 27.

65. Ibid., pp. 15, 77, 137, 156–57, 213, 328; Smith, *Lectures on Jurisprudence*, p. 123. J.C.D. Clark cites English gentlemen's handbooks of the time that

note that failing to duel is, in the words of one of them, "worse than being buried alive" (Clark, *English Society 1688–1832: Ideology, Social Structure and Political Practice during the Ancien Regime* [Cambridge: Cambridge University Press, 1985], p. 109).

66. Kiernan, *The Duel in European History*, p. 160.

67. Quoted in Robert Irving Warshow, *Alexander Hamilton: First American Businessman* (New York: Greenberg, 1931), p. 216.

68. Kiernan, *The Duel in European History*, pp. 265, 273, 274, 281–82, 101; see also pp. 113–15.

69. As cited in Schwartz et al., "The Duel," p. 324.

70. Kiernan, *The Duel in European History*, pp. 144, 272, 269, 138. Kiernan's imputation of general concern to vindicate the standards of the class may involve great license. Presumably, the chief, perhaps often even the only, motivation was personal, not collective. The role of the collective, of the class as such, was merely to set constraints on and incentives for individual action. Elsewhere, Kiernan suggests that most duels were "meaningless scrimmages" (p. 329).

71. Ibid., pp. 117, 265, 271, 283.

72. Aristocrats accounted for about 2 percent of the population of France in the early eighteenth century (Roland Mousnier, *The Institutions of France under the Absolute Monarchy 1598–1789* [Chicago: University of Chicago Press, 1979, from 1974 French ed.], p. 147).

73. Kiernan, *The Duel in European History*, p. 11.

74. Ibid., pp. 63, 317.

75. As happens at the conclusion of the duel in Turgenev's *Spring Torrents* described below. See also Kiernan, *The Duel in European History*, pp. 149–51.

76. Kiernan, *The Duel in European History*, p. 111.

77. Women evidently did duel, but rarely (Kiernan, *The Duel in European History*, pp. 132–33, 203, 327).

78. Ivan Turgenev, *Spring Torrents* (Baltimore: Penguin, 1980 [1872]; trans. Leonard Schapiro), pp. 71–77.

79. Ivan Turgenev, *Fathers and Sons*, trans. Rosemary Edmonds (Baltimore: Penguin, 1965 [1861]), p. 235.

80. Fyodor Dostoevsky, *The Brothers Karamazov* (Penguin, 1958, in one vol. 1982 [1880]), p. 352.

81. Anton Chekhov, "The Duel," in Chekhov, *The Duel and Other Stories* (New York: Ecco Press, 1984 [1891]; trans. Constance Garnett), p. 133. Earlier, Laevsky, Von Koren's adversary, thinks that dueling is "stupid and senseless . . . but that it [is] sometimes impossible to get on without it" (p. 126). Again, the impossibility is merely personal costs of defying the norm of the exclusive group of frivolous aristocrats and arrivistes.

82. Dostoevsky, *The Brothers Karamazov*, p. 349.

83. Theodore Caplow presents data from many kinds of organizations that suggest a strong tendency for members to distort upward the prestige of their organizations. He calls this tendency the aggrandizement effect. (Theodore Caplow, *Principles of Organization* [New York: Harcourt Brace Jovanovich, 1964], pp. 213–16.) We might suppose that tendency afflicted the aristocracy of Europe.

84. Leo Tolstoy, *War and Peace* (London: Everyman, 1911 [1864–1869]), pt. 1, chaps. 73–74. In an apparently petty moment the future pacifist Tolstoy challenged Turgenev to a duel, but later had the sense to back down. Kiernan, *The Duel in European History*, pp. 288–89.

85. Neither Burr nor Hamilton would qualify as an aristocrat by birth. The dueling norm was probably more weakly grounded in their wider community than was the norm of European aristocrats.

86. Kiernan, *The Duel in European History*, p. 326. It died sooner in England, Dominic Lieven argues, because in England it lacked military backing. There was not the same, separate military class that there was in France and Germany, and military officers had civilian lives in civilian dress and even entered politics. Dominic Lieven, *The Aristocracy in Europe 1815–1914* (New York: Columbia University Press, 1992), p. 195.

87. Kiernan, *The Duel in European History*, p. 112. In our time, the parvenu can buy a coat of arms from the College of Heralds in the United Kingdom for a modest sum—less than a thousand pounds in 1984 (p. 326). The trend in the price matches the trend in the value. Alternatively, for $149 one may buy a square foot of land in Caithness in the Scottish Highlands, and thereby become a Laird of Camster (advertisement, *Scientific American*, December 1992, p. 163).

88. This was the view of Algernon West (Kiernan, *The Duel in European History*, p. 218).

89. Ibid., pp. 6, 62, 119; Gilmour, *Riot, Risings and Revolution*, p. 267.

90. Pierre de Bourdielle Brantôme, quoted in Kiernan, *The Duel in European History*, p. 64.

91. Prosper Mérimée, "The Etruscan Vase," pp. 93–115 in Mérimée, *Carmen and Other Stories*, trans. Nicholas Jotcham (Oxford: Oxford University Press, 1989 [1830]). His adversary had ignored a worse offense in public the evening before.

92. Bernard de Mandeville, *An Inquiry into the Origin of Honour and the Usefulness of Christianity in War* (London: 1836), p. 64 (cited in Kiernan, *The Duel in European History*, p. 75).

93. T. V. Smith, "Honor," *Encyclopaedia of the Social Sciences* (New York: Macmillan, 1932), vol. 7, pp. 456–58, at p. 458.

94. Walter Scott, *Count Robert of Paris* (Edinburgh, 1831), chap. 2; quoted in Kiernan, *The Duel in European History*, p. 237.

95. See further, chap. 7.

96. This is discussed more fully in chap. 7.

97. Hardin, *Collective Action*, p. 218.

98. See Margaret Levi and Steven DeTray, "A Weapon Against War: Conscientious Objection in the United States, Australia, and France," *Politics and Society* 21 (December 1993): 425–64.

99. See further, chap. 5.

100. Kiernan, *The Duel in European History*, p. 326.

101. *New York Times* (5 September 1967), p. 24.

102. Jane Austen, *Emma* (London: Penguin 1985, first pub. 1816), chap. 55, p. 464.

103. Tolstoy in his gloomy later years had a grimmer view: "The people perish, they are accustomed to the process of perishing, customs and attitudes to life have appeared which accord with the process." Leo Tolstoy, *Resurrection* (London: Penguin, 1966, trans. Rosemary Edmonds; first pub. 1899), p. 286.

CHAPTER FIVE
UNIVERSALISTIC NORMS

1. Anthony Downs, *An Economic Theory of Democracy* (New York: Harper and Row, 1957).

2. David Hume, *A Treatise of Human Nature*, any edition, bk. 3, pt. 2, sect. 5. Russell Hardin, *Morality within the Limits of Reason* (Chicago: University of Chicago Press, 1988), pp. 41–44, 59–65.

3. Jon Elster, *The Cement of Society: A Study of Social Order* (Cambridge: Cambridge University Press, 1989), p. 98.

4. For the defining accounts of the distinction between consequentialist and non-consequentialist views, see C. D. Broad, "The Doctrine of Consequences in Ethics," *International Journal of Ethics* 24 (April 1914): 293–320; and G.E.M. Anscombe, "Modern Moral Philosophy," pp. 26–42 in Anscombe, *Ethics, Religion and Politics* (Minneapolis: University of Minnesota Press, 1981, essay first pub. 1958).

5. See further, Russell Hardin, "The Economics of Knowledge and Utilitarian Morality," in Brad Hooker, ed., *Rationality, Rules, and Utility: Essays on Richard Brandt's Moral Philosophy* (Boulder, Colo.: Westview Press, 1993), pp. 127–47.

6. V. G. Kiernan , *The Duel in European History: Honour and the Reign of Aristocracy* (Oxford: Oxford University Press, 1986), p. 161.

7. Chap. 4, under "The Epistemology of Norms." Hereward was an intuitionist in the sense that he simply intuited the rightness of his norm, as though, his conspicuous stupidity notwithstanding, he had relevant mental powers for such intuition.

8. Elster, *Cement of Society*, p. 97.

9. T. V. Smith, "Honor," in *Encyclopaedia of the Social Sciences* (New York: Macmillan, 1932), vol. 7, pp. 456–58, at p. 457.

10. *Ernani* (1844), with a libretto by Francesco Maria Piave, was based on the play *Hernani* (1830), by Victor Hugo.

11. Smith, "Honor," p. 456.

12. Quoted in Charles Osborne, *The Complete Operas of Verdi* (New York: Da Capo, 1969), p. 91.

13. William Ian Miller, *Bloodtaking and Peacemaking: Feud, Law, and Society in Saga Iceland* (Chicago: University of Chicago Press, 1990), esp. chap. 6.

14. Marc Bloch, *Feudal Society* (Chicago: University of Chicago Press, 1961, trans. by L. A. Manyon), vol. 1, p. 129.

15. In Iceland, feuds did not cross social strata (Miller, *Bloodtaking and Peacemaking*, p. 185), although they might involve killing across social strata, as when one farmer kills another's slave in retaliation for a harm done by the other farmer.

16. Max Gluckman, *Custom and Conflict in Africa* (Oxford: Blackwell, 1956), pp. 18, 13.

17. Ibid., p. 22.

18. For Albania, see Margaret Hasluck, *The Unwritten Law in Albania*, ed. by J. H. Hutton (Cambridge: Cambridge University Press, 1954), esp. pp. 219–60.

19. See further, Sally Falk Moore, *Law As Process: An Anthropological Approach* (London: Routledge & Kegan Paul, 1978), pp. 130–31; Miller, *Bloodtaking and Peacemaking*, pp. 198–206.

20. Miller, *Bloodtaking and Peacemaking*, pp. 205, 217.

21. Prosper Mérimée, "Colomba," pp. 162–290 in Mérimée, *Carmen and Other Stories* (Oxford: Oxford University Press 1989 [story from 1840]), p. 289.

22. Ibid., p. 218.

23. Ibid., p. 177.

24. Ibid., pp. 174–75. Icelandic culture similarly had contempt for one too quick to give up on vengeance and to settle for compensation (Miller, *Bloodtaking and Peacemaking*, p. 189).

25. Mérimée, "Colomba," p. 190.

26. Miller, *Bloodtaking and Peacemaking*, pp. 188–202.

27. Ibid., pp. 204–5. Mere animus was not, however, a proper ground for vengeance (p. 216).

28. Ibid., p. 215.

29. Ibid., pp. 182–84.

30. Ibid., p. 30.

31. Ibid., pp. 1–2.

32. Ibid., p. 200.

33. Anatole France, *Le Livre de mon ami* (New York: Holt, Rinehart and Winston, 1905 [1885]), chap. 8.

34. For an example of the norm of responsibility to the community, see Rabbi Schneerson's challenge to those Jews who might leave Crown Heights, as discussed in chap. 7.

35. G.E.M. Anscombe, "On Transubstantiation," pp. 107–12 in Anscombe, *Ethics, Religion and Politics* (Minneapolis: University of Minnesota Press, 1981, essay first pub. 1974).

36. This problem is partially analogous to many others. For example, the enduring symptoms of grief may result from the fact that the departed person occupies many places in one's mind as a living presence in experiences or stories not yet revised by death. The simple knowledge of death need not be imprinted on all these memories as soon as it becomes available (Hardin, *Morality within the Limits of Reason,* pp. 181–82).

37. Diego Gambetta, "Mafia: The Price of Distrust," in Gambetta, ed., *Trust: Making and Breaking Cooperative Relations* (New York: Basil Blackwell, 1988), pp. 158–75.

38. Anton Blok, *The Mafia of a Sicilian Village 1860–1960: A Study of Violent Peasant Entrepreneurs* (New York: Harper, 1974), pp. 211–12.

39. In Elster's terminology, we have a filter explanation for *omertà*, though not a functional explanation, because the relationship between the Mafia's

power and the norm of *omertà* is likely recognized by members of the Mafia subject to the norm. See chap. 4, "Explaining Norms of Exclusion."

40. Prosper Mérimée, "Mateo Falcone," in Mérimée, *Carmen and Other Stories* [story from 1829], pp. 54–66.

41. See further, chap. 2, under "Coordination and Power."

42. See chap. 2, under "Leviathan."

43. Mérimée, "Colomba," p. 273.

44. See further, Russell Hardin, "Blackmailing for Mutual Good," *University of Pennsylvania Law Review* 41 (April 1993): 1787–1816.

45. Earlier discussion in chap. 4, under "Norms of Difference and Universalistic Norms."

46. This essentially libertarian view was articulated in the early nineteenth century by William Hazlitt (cited in Kiernan, *The Duel in European History*, p. 227; see also p. 209).

47. Prosper Mérimée, "The Etruscan Vase," in Mérimée, *Carmen and Other Stories* [story from 1830], pp. 93–115, at p. 115.

48. The presence of others was not necessary. If I challenged you in private and you failed to accept the challenge, I could say so in public and thereby put you in a position in which you had to challenge me on the ground that I was lying, or you would lose face. The norm was brutally thorough for anyone who wished to invoke it.

49. See Kiernan, *The Duel in European History*, pp. 137, 156.

50. Hardin, *Morality within the Limits of Reason*, chaps. 4 and 5.

51. This seems to be the implication of Robert Nozick's position in *Anarchy, State, and Utopia* (New York: Basic Books, 1974). In essence, something that comes into place through actions that are individually or dyadically voluntary in context is morally acceptable. Something that comes into place only by violating someone's preferences is morally wrong.

52. Giacomo Puccini, *Tosca* (New York: G. Schirmer, 1956 [1900]), libretto by Luigi Illica and Giuseppe Giacosa, act 2, p. 30.

53. In *Jean de Florette* and *Manon of the Spring*, respectively.

54. For southern Italy, see Edward C. Banfield, *The Moral Basis of a Backward Society* (New York: Free Press, 1958).

55. Gambetta, "Mafia: The Price of Distrust."

56. *Science* 258 (16 October 1992): 487.

57. William Butler Yeats, "The Second Coming," first stanza, in Yeats, *The Collected Poems of W. B. Yeats* (New York: Macmillan, 1956, definitive ed.), p. 185.

58. Elster's norms of revenge include both the vendetta and idiosyncratic revenge. See Jon Elster, "Norms of Revenge," *Ethics* 100 (1990): 862–85.

59. Emily Brontë, *Wuthering Heights* (Oxford: Oxford University Press, World's Classics, 1981[1847], ed. Ian Jack). Heathcliff married Isabella to gain her heirs' control of the family property (his commitments were long-term). Formerly sweet and trusting, she remarks upon leaving him: "What misery laid on Heathcliff could content me, unless I have a hand in it? I'd rather he suffered *less*, if I might cause his sufferings, and he might *know* that I was the cause" (ibid., p. 179). Heathcliff was perhaps a fictional exaggeration, but only an exaggeration

within human bounds. Malcolm Roland Schlette waited thirty-one years to kill the man who was the prosecutor in the trial that sent Schlette to jail for twenty years (*New York Times* [20 November 1986]).

60. Yasunari Kawabata, *Beauty and Sadness* (New York: Knopf, 1975 [1965]; trans. Howard S. Hibbett).

61. Elster, *The Cement of Society*, p. 98.

62. Smith, "Honor," p. 457.

63. Gananath Obeyesekere, *The Work of Culture: Symbolic Transformation in Psychoanalysis and Anthropology* (Chicago: University of Chicago Press, 1990), p. 274.

CHAPTER SIX
VIOLENT CONFLICTS

1. Robert D. Kaplan, *Balkan Ghosts: A Journey through History* (New York: St. Martin's, 1993), p. 75.

2. Belgrade, the capital of Serbia, is far from the war zones of Yugoslavia, but many of its people have been brought to poverty by the wars and the collapse of the economy. In December 1993, there was a bread line that stretched three miles through the city (*New York Times* [19 December 1993], p. I.20). Part of the problem is the imposition of economic sanctions against Serbia by other nations. But Serbia's economy likely could not support free-market importation of necessities of life even without sanctions—rather, it would have to rely on charity from abroad. And its economic hardships had begun well before the war with a slow slide into severe crisis.

3. Faoud Ajami, "The Summoning," *Foreign Affairs* 72 (September–October 1993): 2–9, at p. 9.

4. See, e.g., the essays of Walker Connor, *Ethnonationalism: The Quest for Understanding* (Princeton: Princeton University Press, 1994).

5. Connor (*Ethnonationalism*, p. 203) quotes a Ukrainian nationalist who believes his people are chosen by god:

> I know that all people are equal.
> My reason tells me that.
> But at the same time I know that my nation is unique . . .
> My heart tells me so.

Living with contradictions may be especially common for rabid nationalists. Greek nationalists think it only natural that the Greek part of Albania should be made autonomous or part of Greece, but also natural that minorities inside Greece should have no recognition. Hugh Poulton, *The Balkans: Minorities and States in Conflict* (London: Minority Rights Publications, 1993 new ed. [1991]), p. 225.

6. Connor, *Ethnonationalism*, p. 146.

7. Thomas C. Schelling, *Micromotives and Macrobehavior* (New York: Norton, 1978, pp. 101–2. It was the threat of Jewish tipping out of Crown Heights that worried Rabbi Schneerson—see further, chap. 7.

8. Connor, *Ethnonationalism*, pp. 202, 212.

9. Quoted in Robert D. Kaplan, "A Reader's Guide to the Balkans," *New York Times Book Review* (18 April 1993), pp. 1, 30–33, at p. 31. Kaplan quotes Andric in order to refute the common claim that Bosnians could not hate so much if they were so thoroughly intermarried and so neighborly as in Sarajevo.

10. The quoted phrases come from the ordinarily sane *Economist* in a survey of current ethnic conflicts. *The Economist*, 21 December, 1991, p. 45.

11. See, e.g., Bogdan Denitch, *Ethnic Nationalism: The Tragic Death of Yugoslavia* (Minneapolis: University of Minnesota Press, 1994).

12. Robert Block, "Killers," *New York Review of Books* (18 November 1993), pp. 9–10, at p. 10.

13. Block, "Killers," p. 9.

14. Émile Durkheim, *The Rules of Sociological Method* (New York: Free Press, 1964 [1895]), p. 33. Darmesteter goes on to include childhood memories of religious ceremonies in the list of things a competent scholar of religion needs.

15. This is the general form of nationalism of concern in some of the best recent literature. See, e.g., E. J. Hobsbawm, *Nations and Nationalism since 1780: Programme, Myth, Reality* (Cambridge: Cambridge University Press, 1990), and John Breuilly, *Nationalism and the State* (Chicago: University of Chicago Press, 1985 [1982]).

16. It was also, no doubt, that nationalist portrayal which forced the withdrawal of the film after the German-Soviet Pact of 1939. See Ephraim Katz, *The Film Encyclopedia* (New York: Putnam, 1982 [1979]), p. 383.

17. Herskovits, *Cultural Relativism*, pp. 102–3.

18. Isaiah Berlin, *Vico and Herder: Two Studies in the History of Ideas* (New York: Viking, 1976). Also see Berlin's more recent views in the light of the new nationalisms of Eastern Europe and the former Soviet Union in Nathan Gardels, "Two Concepts of Nationalism: An Interview with Isaiah Berlin," *New York Review of Books* (21 November 1991), pp. 19–23.

19. David Hume, *The History of England*, vol. 1 (Indianapolis, Ind.: Liberty Press, 1983 [1778]), p. 97.

20. *New York Times* (18 October 1992), p. 4.3.

21. Eric Hobsbawm, "The New Threat to History," *New York Review of Books* (16 December 1993), pp. 62–64, at p. 64.

22. Mordecai Richler, "O Quebec," *New Yorker* (30 May 1994), pp. 50–57, at p. 56.

23. Schelling, *Micromotives and Macrobehavior*, pp. 101–2.

24. Denitch, *Ethnic Nationalism: The Tragic Death of Yugoslavia*, p. 29. Connor (*Ethnonationalism*, pp. 214, 225 n. 15) thinks at least some of these data fraudulently underrepresent some minorities.

25. See map in Branka Magas, *The Destruction of Yugoslavia: Tracking the Break-up 1980–92* (London: Verso, 1993), p. 178.

26. *New York Times* (26 December 1993), p. I.3. At this writing, the Croatian government is attempting to sever the Croatian language from the virtually identical Serbian. "The language preserves the nation's history and

culture," the head of Croatian television said. "The language is the womb." If we accept the hyperbole, we must wonder: Why the violent conflict with Serbia? Just over the alphabet?

27. Misha Glenny, *The Fall of Yugoslavia: The Third Balkan War* (New York: Penguin, 1994, rev. [1992]), p. 131.

28. Benedict Anderson, *Imagined Communities: Reflections on the Origin and Spread of Nationalism* (London: Verso, 1991 rev. [1983]).

29. *New York Times* (27 February 1994), p. 4.6.

30. Denitch, *Ethnic Nationalism: The Tragic Death of Yugoslavia*, p. 29.

31. Quoted in Hobsbawm, *Nations and Nationalism since 1780*, p. 12. See further, chap. 3 under "The Is-Ought Fallacy."

32. James Fearon, "Ethnic War as a Commitment Problem," paper presented at the 1994 meeting of the American Political Science Association, 2–5 Sept., New York.

33. Glenny, *The Fall of Yugoslavia*, surveys the events.

34. Robert J. Myers, "The Moral Menace of Intervention," unpublished paper, Carnegie Council on Ethics and International Affairs, New York, 1994.

35. Misha Glenny, "What Is To Be Done?" *New York Review of Books* (27 May 1993), pp. 14–16, at p. 14.

36. John C. Calhoun, who wanted rule by "concurrent majorities" in the South and North in the United States before the Civil War, would have approved.

37. Glenny, *The Fall of Yugoslavia*, p. 184.

38. Ibid., pp. 183 (territorial-acquisition), 126 (Milosevic's apparent lack of nationalist or ethnic feeling), 148 (Izetbegovic's theses).

39. Kaplan writes that Communism kept the processes of history and memory on hold for forty-five years, "thereby creating a kind of multiplier effect for violence" (Kaplan, "A Reader's Guide to the Balkans," p. 30).

40. Ibid., p. 1. Glenny also sometimes falls into making such claims (e.g., *The Fall of Yugoslavia*, p. 148). Elsewhere, Kaplan calls the past his own personal obsession: "On the road, when I met people, I asked them always about the past. Only in this way could the present become comprehensible." (Kaplan, *Balkan Ghosts*, p. xxi.)

41. See Hobsbawm, "The New Threat to History."

42. Kaplan, "A Reader's Guide to the Balkans," p. 30.

43. Glenny, *The Fall of Yugoslavia*, p. 187.

44. Ibid., p. xiii.

45. Michael Ignatieff, "The Balkan Tragedy," *New York Review of Books* (13 May 1993), pp. 3–5, at p. 3.

46. Ibid., p. 4; see Slavenka Drakulic, *The Balkan Express: Fragments from the Other Side of War* (New York: Norton, 1992).

47. As may also be true of ethnic conflicts in Sri Lanka, Thailand, and Myanmar, in all of which Buddhist majorities rule and evidently participate in attacks on various minorities. See, e.g., S. J. Tambiah, *Sri Lanka: Ethnic Fratricide and the Dismantling of Democracy* (Chicago: University of Chicago Press, 1986), pp. 138–40.

48. *New York Times* (14 November 1993), p. I.8; previously cited in chap. 4. Despite its brutality, the commander's challenge made some sense. Consider the related rule on those banished permanently from medieval Icelandic society. A permanent outlaw could be reinstated if he declared he would kill three other outlaws and could subsequently prove he had done so (Birgir T. R. Solvason, "Institutional Evolution in the Icelandic Commonwealth," *Constitutional Political Economy* 4 [1993]: 97–125, at p. 112).

49. Glenny, *The Fall of Yugoslavia*, p. 115. Vukovar was of no military significance. It was isolated from other Croatian enclaves in a predominantly Serbian region just inside the original Croatian border from Vojvodina. It fell to methodical, trivially easy shelling from all directions at once. No wonder that a Macedonian deserter from the Serbian onslaught against Croatians in then-Croatian Krajina described the action thus: "This is not a war, this is extermination" (p. 126).

50. Bogdan Bogdanovic, "Murder of the City," *New York Review of Books* (27 May 1993), p. 20. Bogdanovic's view is widely shared. See, e.g., Poulton, *The Balkans: Minorities and States in Conflict*, pp. 212–13.

51. Magas, *The Destruction of Yugoslavia*, p. 356.

52. Glenny, *The Fall of Yugoslavia*, p. 3.

53. Roy Gutman, *A Witness to Genocide* (New York: Macmillan, 1993), esp. pp. 77–83.

54. Dermot Keogh and Michael H. Haltzel, "Introduction," in Keogh and Haltzel, eds., *Northern Ireland and the Politics of Reconciliation* (Cambridge: Cambridge University Press, 1993), pp. 1–10.

55. Philip Selznick, *The Organizational Weapon: A Study of Bolshevik Strategy and Tactics* (New York: McGraw-Hill, 1952).

56. David Remnick, "Belfast Confetti," *New Yorker* (25 April 1994), 38–77, at pp. 71–72, 75. Milovan Djilas supposes, on the contrary, that jailing radicals often reinforces their epistemological blinders, and he cites the examples of Stalin, Hitler, Tudjman, and Izetbegovic (*New York Times* [26 December 1993], p. 4.7).

57. For his views, see John Hume, "A New Ireland in a New Europe," in Keogh and Haltzel, *Northern Ireland and the Politics of Reconciliation*, pp. 226–33.

58. See further the views of the 1970s Sinn Féin leader, Daithí Ó Conaill in Keogh and Haltzel, "Introduction," p. 4.

59. Remnick, "Belfast Confetti," p. 77.

60. *New York Times* (5 December 1993), p. I.3.

61. Remnick, "Belfast Confetti," pp. 72–74.

62. Letter of 7 February 1994. The account of Barre's role here is from Laitin.

63. *New York Times* (21 February 1993), p. I.3.

64. *New Yorker* (6 January 1992), p. 24. The weapons the United States might buy are largely those that the U.S. and the Soviet Union earlier gave to Mohammed Siad Barre during his twenty-one years of dictatorship. If nations may be held responsible for their actions, the U.S. bears heavy responsibility for the current carnage in Somalia.

65. René Lemarchand, *Burundi: Ethnocide as Discourse and Practice* (Cambridge: Cambridge University Press, 1994), p. 178.

66. See chap. 1.

67. Lucy Mair, *African Societies* (Cambridge: Cambridge University Press, 1974), p. 167. Were she writing today, she might weaken this claim somewhat. See also Alex Shoumatoff, "Rwanda's Aristocratic Guerrillas," *New York Times Magazine* (13 December 1992), pp. 42–48.

68. Lemarchand, *Burundi*, pp. 1–16. Against his view of the fluidity of the labels with respect to ethnic background, Lemarchand notes that Tutsis cannot be demoted to Hutu or Twa.

69. For a brief account, informed by Monique Mujawamariya, a Rwandan human rights activist of mixed-ethnic parentage, see Lawrence Weschler, "Lost in Rwanda," *New Yorker* (25 April 1994), pp. 42–45.

70. *New York Times* (8 May 1994), p. 1.10.

71. Alex Shoumatoff, "Flight from Death," *New Yorker* (20 June 1994), pp. 44–55, at p. 53.

72. Weschler, "Lost in Rwanda," p. 45.

73. *New York Times* (1 May 1994), pp. 1.1, 16.

74. Tutsis who have grown up in refugee camps after the exodus from Rwanda in the early 1960s have not had the high-protein diet of their parents, and they are said to be shorter. (Shoumatoff, "Rwanda's Aristocratic Guerrillas," p. 44.)

75. Mair, *African Societies*, pp. 166–81.

76. Rwanda may have achieved the highest fertility rate on record, at 8.3 live births per woman (Shoumatoff, "Rwanda's Aristocratic Guerrillas," p. 48).

77. Mair, *African Societies*, p. 180.

78. Max Gluckman, *Politics, Law and Ritual in Tribal Society* (Chicago: Aldine, 1965; New York: New American Library repr., 1968), p. 189.

79. Mair, *African Societies*, p. 181.

80. Lemarchand, *Burundi*, pp. 178–87, xvi–xix.

81. Stéphane Dion, "The Quebec Challenge to Canadian Unity," *PS: Political Science and Politics* (March 1993), pp. 38–43, at p. 38.

82. Dion, "The Quebec Challenge to Canadian Unity," p. 41.

83. About 15 percent—129,705—of anglophone native Québécois have left since the 1976 election of the Parti Québécois. Richler, "O Quebec," pp. 54, 57.

84. *New York Times* (27 February 1994), p. 1.19.

85. Canada also is in a new position after NAFTA. It too should lose nothing from the smaller market that follows from having Quebec go its own way. John Hume notes the same change in the position of the United Kingdom with respect to Northern Ireland. In the grand market of the European Union, the advantage to Britain of holding Northern Ireland in the general British economy is now gone. See John Hume, "A New Ireland in a New Europe," pp. 228–29.

86. Richler, "O Quebec," p. 54.

87. Dion, "The Quebec Challenge to Canadian Unity," p. 41.

88. John Howard Griffin, *Black Like Me* (New York: New American Library, 1976 [1961]).

89. Stéphane Dion, "The Importance of the Language Issue in the Constitutional Crisis," in Douglas Brown and Robert Young, eds., *Canada: The State of the Federation 1992* (Kingston: Institute of Intergovernmental Relations, 1992); "The Quebec Challenge to Canadian Unity," pp. 39–40.

90. Annie Cohen-Solal, a former French cultural attaché in New York who now teaches at New York University, explains the use of English words in French as the result of the rigidity of French and the flexibility of English, in which safe sex, however unglamorous it may be, is at least linguistically possible. *New York Times* (20 March 1994), p. 4.2.

91. For an account of the atrocities against the Yahi, see Theodora Kroeber, *Ishi in Two Worlds* (Berkeley: University of California Press, 1976 deluxe ed. [1961]), pp. 56–100.

92. Glenny, "What Is To Be Done?" p. 16.

93. Sarajevo presents an easily comprehended example of the possibility that the cost of delivering some massive harm may be radically less than the cost of achieving the reverse good. A company of jerks with mortars and a week to use them can do more harm to a magnificent cathedral or mosque than can be repaired by hundreds of world-class craftsmen laboring for several years. See further, the discussion of chap. 3 under "Group Identification from Coordination."

94. Albert O. Hirschman, *The Passions and the Interests: Political Arguments for Capitalism before Its Triumph* (Princeton: Princeton University Press, 1977; Stephen Holmes, "The Secret History of Self Interest," pp. 267–86 in Jane J. Mansbridge, ed., *Beyond Self Interest* (Chicago: University Of Chicago Press, 1990); and Istvan Hont and Michael Ignatieff, "Needs and justice in the *Wealth of Nations*: an introductory essay," pp. 1–44 in Hont and Ignatieff, eds., *Wealth and Virtue: The Shaping of Political Economy in the Scottish Enlightenment* (Cambridge: Cambridge University Press, 1983).

95. Russell Hardin, "Public Choice vs. Democracy," in John W. Chapman, ed., NOMOS 32: *Majorities and Minorities* (New York: New York University Press, 1990), pp. 184–203.

96. *New York Times* (21 February 1993), p. I.3.

CHAPTER SEVEN
EINSTEIN'S DICTUM AND COMMUNITARIANISM

1. *New York Times* (26 June 1994), p. 4.5. There is a problem with such a report—we, the readers of the *Times* report, do not know how the claim that there was a rape has been established.

2. Thomas Andrew Green, *Verdict According to Conscience: Perspectives on the English Criminal Trial Jury, 1200–1800* (Chicago: University of Chicago Press, 1985), pp. 14, 16.

3. Theodore F. T. Plucknett, *A Concise History of Common Law* (Boston: Little, Brown, 1956, 5th ed. [1929]), pp. 127–28.

4. Julius Moravcsik distinguishes between "de facto" and "normative" communitarianism. He uses the latter term in a largely universalistic way to apply to communities that meet certain normative standards. Moravcsik, "Communal

Ties," *Proceedings and Addresses of the American Philosophical Association* (September 1988), supplement to vol. 62, no. 1, pp. 211–25, at pp. 212–13.

5. As represented in the title of Charles Taylor's book, *Sources of the Self: The Making of the Modern Identity* (Cambridge, Mass.: Harvard University Press, 1989).

6. Richard Rorty, "Postmodernist Bourgeois Liberalism," in Rorty, *Objectivity, Relativism, and Truth: Philosophical Papers*, vol. 1 (Cambridge: Cambridge University Press, [1985]), pp. 197–203.

7. Will Kymlicka, *Liberalism, Community, and Culture* (Oxford: Oxford University Press, 1989), p. 207.

8. Harlan Lane, *The Wild Boy of Aveyron* (Cambridge, Mass.: Harvard University Press, 1976; reprinted New York: Bantam, 1977); Robert M. Zingg, "India's Wolf Children: Two Human Infants Reared by Wolves," *Scientific American* (March 1941): 135–37; Inge Bretherton, "The Origins of Attachment Theory: John Bowlby and Mary Ainsworth," *Developmental Psychology* 28 (1992): 759–75.

9. See further, Russell Hardin, "Autonomy, Identity, and Welfare," in John Christman, ed., *The Inner Citadel: Essays on Individual Autonomy* (New York: Oxford University Press, 1989), pp. 189–99.

10. Howard Margolis, *Patterns, Thinking, and Cognition* (Chicago: University of Chicago Press, 1987), p. 135.

11. Ibid., p. 45.

12. Rorty, "Post modernist Bourgeois Liberalism," p. 199. Rorty attributes this view to W. V. Quine. See further, Will Kymlicka, *Liberalism, Community, and Culture* (Oxford: Oxford University Press, 1991), p. 65.

13. Henry Sidgwick, *The Methods of Ethics* (London: Macmillan, 1907 [1874], 7th ed.), pp. 6–11.

14. John Stuart Mill, *On Liberty*, any standard edition.

15. Amitai Etzioni, *The Spirit of Community: Rights, Responsibilities, and the Communitarian Agenda* (New York: Crown, 1993).

16. Even in the arts one might think Einstein's dictum should apply. The values of, say, painting are not merely a deontological commitment to certain forms or styles or subject matters. Rather, painting must find much of its value in the development and expression of artists and their communities and in the esthetic appreciation of those who sponsor and view it. These latter considerations are subject to empirical testing to find better forms, styles, and subject matters for their achievement.

17. Alan Donagan, "Moral Dilemmas, Genuine and Spurious: A Comparative Anatomy," *Ethics* 104 (October 1993): 7–21, at p. 14.

18. Michael J. Sandel, *Liberalism and the Limits of Justice* (Cambridge: Cambridge University Press, 1982).When Sandel speaks of deontological liberalism, one suspects he means or at least feels the term as a curse. Kymlicka dismisses Sandel's criticisms (Kymlicka, *Liberalism, Community, and Culture*, pp. 52–58).

19. Rorty, "Postmodernist Bourgeois Liberalism," p. 200.

20. See further, Kymlicka, *Liberalism, Community, and Culture*, pp. 63–70.

21. Daniel Bell, *The Cultural Contradictions of Capitalism* (London: Heinemann, 1976), p. 59.

22. David Remnick, "Waiting for the Apocalypse in Crown Heights," *New Yorker* (21 December 1992), pp. 52–57, p. 54.

23. Ibid., pp. 52–54.

24. Albert O. Hirschman, *Exit, Voice, and Loyalty* (Cambridge, Mass.: Harvard University Press, 1970).

25. The current Lubavitchers pose an odd problem for the thesis, noted earlier, that autonomy is enhanced by strong, monocultural ties. Maintenance of the Lubavitcher community may be sponsored by outsiders, who contribute to its religious operations of providing cultural services and proselytizing for conservative Judaism. Outside donations help to fund a substantial organization that employs many Lubavitchers, thus presumably helping to secure their loyalty.

26. Gershom Scholem, *Sabbatai Sevi: The Mystical Messiah* (Princeton: Princeton University Press, 1973).

27. See further, chap. 3.

28. For further discussion, see below, under "Respect for Cultures."

29. John Locke, *Letter on Toleration*, any standard edition.

30. Remnick, "Waiting for the Apocalypse," p. 53.

31. This is arguably the brunt of the failure of Soviet socialism. See Russell Hardin, "Efficiency vs. Equality and the Demise of Socialism," *Canadian Journal of Philosophy* 22 (June 1992): 149–61.

32. If it does come to apply to Iran, then might will perversely have made right. See further, "Does Might Make Right?" in J. Roland Pennock and John W. Chapman, eds., NOMOS 29: *Authority Revisited* (New York: New York University Press, 1987), pp. 201–17.

33. *Wisconsin v. Yoder et al.*, 406 U. S., pp. 205–49, at p. 211.

34. Ibid., p. 222; emphases added.

35. "Respect for persons" is either a complex or a vacuous notion whose implications cannot be as transparent as its users typically assume. Many people claim that it differentiates some theories, especially rights theories, from others. The work (or definition) to show such a conclusion is yet to be done.

36. Rorty, "Postmodernist Bourgeois Liberalism," p. 200.

37. The term, "murder," is not used in a hyperbolic sense here. It does not refer to the killing of Muslim defenders in military actions but, rather, to the deliberate murder of Muslim women, children, and civilian men.

38. Russell Hardin, *Collective Action* (Baltimore: Johns Hopkins University Press, 1982), chaps. 10–13, discussion of contract by convention.

39. William A. Kornhauser, *The Politics of Mass Society* (New York: Free Press, 1959).

40. Gustave Le Bon, *The Crowd* (London: 1922 [1895]).

41. For a brief account, see Brian Barry and Russell Hardin, *Rational Man and Irrational Society?* (Beverly Hills, Calif.: Sage Publications, 1982), pp. 213–28.

42. For an apparently contrary and strongly felt view, see Wendell Berry, *Sex, Economy, Freedom, and Community: Eight Essays* (New York: Pantheon, 1993), especially the title essay. Berry, incidentally, thinks community is inherently associated with place. It is interesting to note that medieval law in much of Europe applied to the person as a representative of a community, irrespective of

place. "Hence the celebrated remark of an archbishop of Lyons, that when in Frankish Gaul five persons happened to be gathered together it was no occasion for surprise if each of them—a Roman perhaps, a Salian Frank, a Ripaurian Frank, a Visigoth, and a Burgundian—obeyed a different law" (Marc Bloch, *Feudal Society* [Chicago: University of Chicago Press: 1961], vol. 1, p. 111). In the morass of Italian states, it was sometimes the burden of the individual, before entering a contract, to stipulate to which law he was bound in this case (ibid., pp. 111–12).

43. Kymlicka, *Liberalism, Community, and Culture.*

44. Russell Hardin, "The Economics of Knowledge and Utilitarian Morality," in Brad Hooker, ed., *Rationality, Rules, and Utility: Essays on Richard Brandt's Moral Philosophy* (Boulder, Colo.: Westview Press, forthcoming).

45. Russell Hardin, "My University's Yacht: Morality and the Rule of Law," in Randy E. Barnett and Ian Shapiro, eds., NOMOS 26, *The Rule of Law* (New York: New York University Press, 1993), pp. 127–47. See also Hardin, "The Street-Level Epistemology of Trust," *Analyse und Kritik* 14 (December 1992): 152–76; reprinted in *Politics and Society* 21 (December 1993): 505–29.

46. Francis L. Black, "Why Did They Die?" *Science* 258 (11 December 1992): 1739–40.

47. Ibid., p. 1740.

48. Rorty, "Postmodernist Bourgeois Liberalism," p. 201.

49. Charles Peirce, arguably the most aggressively pragmatist philosopher, outdid Einstein's dictum: "The scientific man is above all things desirous of learning the truth and, in order to do so, ardently desires to have his present provisional beliefs (and all his beliefs are merely provisional) swept away, and will work hard to accomplish that object." Charles Sanders Peirce, "Preface" to *Scientific Metaphysics*, in *Collected Works of Charles Sanders Peirce* (Cambridge, Mass.: Harvard University Press, 1935), vol. 6, p. 3. Rorty's pragmatism cannot fit well with normative communitarianism, which commands without questions.

50. F. A. Hayek, *The Mirage of Social Justice*, vol. 2 of *Law, Legislation, and Liberty* (Chicago: University of Chicago Press, 1976), pp. 17–23; and *Rules and Order*, vol. 1 of *Law, Legislation, and Liberty* (Chicago: University of Chicago Press, 1973), pp. 8–54.

51. John Dewey, *The Quest for Certainty: A Study of the Relation of Knowledge and Action* (New York: G. P. Putnam's Sons, 1960 [1929]).

52. Locke, with his usual inconsistency, was nonetheless contractarian.

CHAPTER EIGHT
WHITHER DIFFERENCE?

1. Franz Kafka, *Tagebücher* (Diaries) (Frankfurt: Fischer, 1967), p. 391, entry for 17 October 1921.

2. Quoted in Daniel Patrick Moynihan, *Pandaemonium: Ethnicity in International Politics* (Oxford: Oxford University Press, 1993), p. 165.

3. Earlier, the Serbs who dominate Kosovo, with its 90 percent Albanian population, began to remove Albanians from public service jobs. Some lost their

jobs when the local court system was abolished by Milosevic; some when they refused to write in the cyrillic alphabet; many struck in sympathy with those who were dismissed. Aryeh Neier, "Kosovo Survives!" *New York Review of Books* (3 February 1994), pp. 26–28. Even if there is not ethnic cleansing more generally, ethnic purging from office is the threat of virtually all the ethnic group mobilizations.

4. Bernard Williams, *Morality: An Introduction to Ethics* (New York: Harper and Row, 1972), p. 20. Williams's view is discussed more fully in chap. 7 here.

5. The communitarians have evidently been remarkably successful popularizers, who can reach people who have never heard of Rawls, Mill, or Kant. Perhaps, as in the contrast between norms of exclusion and universalistic norms, their anti-universalism has resonances that universalism cannot match. See William A. Galston, "Clinton and the Promise of Communitarianism," *Chronicle of Higher Education*, 2 December 1992, p. A52, and Peter Steinfels, "A Political Movement Blends Its Ideas from Left and Right," *New York Times* (24 May 1994), p. 4.6.

6. The movement to restore dead or moribund regional languages in Europe also has desultory implications for future generations. Hobsbawm remarks of this movement that "the sort of provincial middle classes who once hoped to benefit from linguistic nationalism can rarely expect more than provincial advantages from it today." E. J. Hobsbawm, *Nations and Nationalism since 1780: Programme, Myth, Reality* (Cambridge: Cambridge University Press, 1990), p. 178.

7. *New York Times* (26 June 1994), p. 4.5.

8. Russell Hardin, "Trusting Persons, Trusting Institutions," in Richard J. Zeckhauser, ed., *The Strategy of Choice* (Cambridge, Mass.: MIT Press, 1991), pp. 185–209.

9. Antigone's views are often seen as forerunners of natural law. Independently of the supposed truth of natural law, it was generally universalistic in conception.

10. Marc Bloch, *Feudal Society* (Chicago: University of Chicago Press, 1961), vol. 1, p. 113.

11. Philip P. Hallie, *Lest Innocent Blood Be Shed* (New York: Harper, 1979).

12. Hobbes notes the possibility that a community without government might coordinate on joint action in the general interest in the face of a particular crisis, such as attack from outside. But this, he says, is not enough for security because, afterwards, when they no longer have a common enemy, "they must needs by the difference of their interests dissolve, and fall again into a Warre amongst themselves." Thomas Hobbes, *Leviathan* (Harmondsworth, Middlesex: Penguin, 1968 [1651]), chap. 17, p. 225 [86].

13. Henry Louis Gates, Jr., "Bad Influence," *New Yorker* (7 March 1994), pp. 94–98, at p. 94 (a review of Nathan McCall, *Makes Me Wanna Holler: A Young Black Man in America* [New York: Random House, 1994]).

14. For example, George Kenney resigned from the U.S. State Department in protest over American policy toward the early fighting in Yugoslavia. *New York Times* (27 August 1994), p. A7.

15. Similarly, recall that South Carolina's John C. Calhoun wanted southern secession from the United States before it was made too late by the relative increase in northern power and the number of states that supported a constitutional amendment against slavery. Secession only came when prospects turned considerably worse.

16. The 1948 number had been reduced by about a third well before the Serbo-Croatian war, and most of the remainder were taken away from Croatia in the Republic of Serbian Krajina, leaving only about seventy thousand in April 1993. Stevan K. Pavlowitch, "Who is 'Balkanizing Whom? The Misunderstandings between the Debris of Yugoslavia and an Unprepared West," *Daedalus* (Spring 1994), pp. 203–23, at p. 223n.

17. Hugh Poulton, *The Balkans* (London: Minority Rights Group, 1993, new ed. [1991]), p. 226.

18. Hobsbawm, *Nations and Nationalism*, pp. 163–65.

19. Moynihan, *Pandaemonium*, p. 125.

20. Sanyuan Li, "Hazards of Democratization in China" (Chicago: University of Chicago diss. in Political Science, 1994).

21. Quoted in Virginia Woolf, *A Room of One's Own* (Harmondsworth, Middlesex: Penguin, 1945 [1928]), p. 63, emphasis added.

22. Eugen Weber, *Peasants into Frenchmen: The Modernization of Rural France, 1870–1914* (Stanford, Calif.: Stanford University Press, 1976).

23. Julius Moravcsik, "Communal Ties," *Proceedings and Addresses of the American Philosophical Association* (September 1988), supplement to vol. 62, no. 1, pp. 211–25, at pp. 212–13.

24. Edward W. Said, "Michael Walzer's *Exodus and Revolution*: A Canaanite Reading," in Edward W. Said and Christopher Hitchens, eds., *Blaming the Victims: Spurious Scholarship and the Palestinian Question* (London: Verso, 1988), pp. 161–78, at p. 178; Michael Walzer, *Exodus and Revolution* (New York: Basic Books, 1985).

References

Acton, Lord. *Essays in the History of Liberty*. Ed. by J. Rufus Fears. Indianapolis, Ind.: Liberty Classics, 1985, essay on "Nationality" first pub. 1862.

Ajami, Faoud. "The Summoning," *Foreign Affairs* 72 (September–October 1993): 2–9.

Allen, Irving Lewis. *The City in Slang*. Oxford: Oxford University Press, 1993.

Anderson, Benedict. *Imagined Communities: Reflections on the Origin and Spread of Nationalism*. London: Verso, rev. ed., 1991 (1983).

Anderson, Jervis. "The Public Intellectual," *New Yorker*, 17 January 1994, 39–48.

Anderson, Jessica. *Tirra Lirra by the River*. Penguin, 1984 (1978).

Anscombe, G.E.M. "Modern Moral Philosophy," pp. 26–42 in Anscombe, *Ethics, Religion and Politics*. Minneapolis: University of Minnesota Press, 1981, essay first pub. 1958.

————. "On Transubstantiation," pp. 107–12 in Anscombe, *Ethics, Religion and Politics*. Minneapolis: University of Minnesota Press, 1981, essay first pub. 1974.

Arneson, Richard J. "Marxism and Secular Faith," *American Political Science Review* 79 (September 1985): 627–40.

Austen, Jane. *Emma*. London: Penguin 1985, first pub. 1816.

Austin, John. *The Province of Jurisprudence Determined*. New York: Noonday Press, 1954 (1832).

Axelrod, Robert. "An Evolutionary Approach to Norms," *American Political Science Review* 80 (1986): 1095–1112.

Bacon, Francis. *The Charge of Sir Francis Bacon Knight, His Majesties Attourney generall, touching Duells, upon an information in the Star-chamber against Priest and Wright*. London: 1614; New York: Da Capo Press, facsimile repr., 1968.

Barry, Brian. "Is It Better To Be Powerful or Lucky?" *Political Studies* 28 (June and September 1980): 183–94, 338–52.

Barry, Brian, and Russell Hardin. *Rational Man and Irrational Society?* Beverly Hills, Calif.: Sage Publications, 1982.

Bartky, Ian R., and Elizabeth Harrison. "Standard and Daylight Saving Time," *Scientific American* 240 (May 1979): 46–53.

Banfield, Edward C. *The Moral Basis of a Backward Society*. New York: Free Press, 1958.

Beccaria, Cesare. *On Crimes and Punishments*. Trans. from the Italian by David Young. Indianapolis, Ind.: Hackett, 1986 (1764).

Becker, Gary S. *The Economics of Discrimination*. Chicago: University of Chicago Press, 1971 2d ed. (1957).

Bell, Daniel. "Nationalism or Class?—Some Questions on the Potency of Political Symbols," *The Student Zionist*, May 1947.

Bell, Daniel. *The Cultural Contradictions of Capitalism*. London: Heinemann, 1976.

Berlin, Isaiah. *Vico and Herder: Two Studies in the History of Ideas*. New York: Viking, 1976.

Berry, Wendell. *Sex, Economy, Freedom, and Community: Eight Essays*. New York: Pantheon, 1993.

Black, Francis L. "Why Did They Die?" *Science* 258 (11 December 1992): 1739–40.

Bloch, Marc. *Feudal Society*. vol. 1. Trans. by L. A. Manyon. Chicago: University of Chicago Press, 1961, (1939–40).

Block, Robert. "Killers," *New York Review of Books*, 18 November 1993, pp. 9–10.

Blok, Anton. *The Mafia of a Sicilian Village 1860–1960: A Study of Violent Peasant Entrepreneurs*. New York: Harper, 1974.

Bogdanovic, Bogdan. "Murder of the City," *New York Review of Books*, 27 May 1993, p. 20.

Boswell, James. *Life Of Johnson*. London: Oxford University Press, 1976 (1791).

Bradford, Philips Verner, and Harvey Blume. *Ota Benga: The Pygmy in the Zoo*. New York: St. Martin's, 1992.

Bretherton, Inge. "The Origins of Attachment Theory: John Bowlby and Mary Ainsworth," *Developmental Psychology* 28 (1992): 759–75.

Breuilly, John. *Nationalism and the State*. Chicago: University of Chicago Press, 1985 (1982).

Broad, C. D. "The Doctrine of Consequences in Ethics," *International Journal of Ethics* 24 (April 1914): 293–320.

Brontë, Emily. *Wuthering Heights*. Ed. by Ian Jack. Oxford: Oxford University Press, World's Classics, 1981 (1847).

Campeanu, Pavel. "The Revolt of the Romanians," *New York Review of Books*, 1 February 1990, pp. 30–31.

Caplow, Theodore. *Principles of Organization*. New York: Harcourt Brace Jovanovich, 1964.

Chekhov, Anton. "The Duel," in Chekhov, *The Duel and Other Stories*. Trans. by Constance Garnett. New York: Ecco Press, 1984 (1891).

Clark, J.C.D. *English Society 1688–1832: Ideology, Social Structure and Political Practice during the Ancien Regime*. Cambridge: Cambridge University Press, 1985.

Connor, Walker. *Ethnonationalism: The Quest for Understanding*. Princeton: Princeton University Press, 1994.

D'Amato, Anthony. "Is International Law Really 'Law'?" *Northwestern Law Review* 79 (1984–85): 1293–1314.

Denitch, Bogdan. *Ethnic Nationalism: The Tragic Death of Yugoslavia*. Minneapolis: University of Minnesota Press, 1994.

Dewey, John. *The Quest for Certainty: A Study of the Relation of Knowledge and Action*. New York: G. P. Putnam's Sons, 1960 (1929).

Dion, Stéphane. "The Importance of the Language Issue in the Constitutional Crisis," in Douglas Brown and Robert Young, eds., *Canada: The State of the Federation 1992*. Kingston: Institute of Intergovernmental Relations, 1992.

————. "The Quebec Challenge to Canadian Unity," *PS: Political Science and Politics* (March 1993), pp. 38–43.

Donagan, Alan. "Moral Dilemmas, Genuine and Spurious: A Comparative Anatomy," *Ethics* 104 (October 1993): 7–21.

Dostoevsky, Fyodor. *The Brothers Karamazov*. Penguin, 1958, in one vol. 1982 (1880).

Downs, Anthony. *An Economic Theory of Democracy*. New York: Harper and Row, 1957.

Durkheim, Émile. *The Rules of Sociological Method*. New York: Free Press, 1964 (1895).

Elster, Jon. *Ulysses and the Sirens*. Cambridge: Cambridge University Press, 1979.

————. *Sour Grapes: Studies in the Subversion of Rationality*. Cambridge: Cambridge University Press, 1983.

————. *The Cement of Society: A Study of Social Order*. Cambridge: Cambridge University Press, 1989.

————. "Norms of Revenge," *Ethics* 100 (1990): 862–85.

Erikson, Erik H. *Insight and Responsibility*. New York: Norton, 1964.

Etzioni, Amitai. *The Spirit of Community: Rights, Responsibilities, and the Communitarian Agenda*. New York: Crown, 1993.

Fearon, James. "Ethnic War As a Commitment Problem." Paper presented at the 1994 American Political Science Association meeting, 2–5 September, New York.

Fernandez, James W. "Tolerance in a Repugnant World and Other Dilemmas in the Cultural Relativism of Melville J. Herskovits," *Ethos* 18 (June 1990): 140–64.

Flood, Merrill. "Some Experimental Games," Rand Corporation Research Memorandum RM-789-1, 20 June 1952.

————. "Some Experimental Games," *Management Science* 5 (October 1958): 5–26.

————. Private communication, 25 February 1975.

Foster, Roy. "Anglo-Irish Relations and Northern Ireland: Historical Perspectives," in Dermot Keogh and Michael H. Haltzel, eds., *Northern Ireland and the Politics of Reconciliation*. Cambridge: Cambridge University Press, 1993.

France, Anatole. *Le Livre de mon ami*. New York: Holt, Rinehart and Winston, 1905 (1885).

Freud, Sigmund. *The Ego and the Id*. Ed. by James Strachey. New York: Norton, 1962.

Galston, William A. "Clinton and the Promise of Communitarianism," *Chronicle of Higher Education*, 2 December 1992, p. A52.

Gambetta, Diego. "Mafia: The Price of Distrust," in Gambetta, ed., *Trust: Making and Breaking Cooperative Relations*. New York: Basil Blackwell, 1988.

Gardels, Nathan. "Two Concepts of Nationalism: An Interview with Isaiah Berlin," *New York Review of Books*, 21 November 1991, pp. 19–23.

Gates, Henry Louis, Jr. "Bad Influence," *New Yorker*, 7 March 1994, pp. 94–98.

Gilmour, Ian. *Riot, Risings and Revolution: Governance and Violence in Eighteenth-Century England*. London: Hutchinson, 1992.

Glenny, Misha. "What Is To Be Done?" *New York Review of Books*, 27 May 1993, pp. 14–16.

———. *The Fall of Yugoslavia: The Third Balkan War*. New York: Penguin, 1994, rev. (1992).

Gluckman, Max. *Custom and Conflict in Africa*. Oxford: Blackwell, 1956.

———. *Politics, Law and Ritual in Tribal Society*. Chicago: Aldine 1965; repr., New York: New American Library, 1968.

Green, Thomas Andrew. *Verdict According to Conscience: Perspectives on the English Criminal Trial Jury, 1200–1800*. Chicago: University of Chicago Press, 1985.

Griffin, John Howard. *Black Like Me*. New York: New American Library, 1976 (1961).

"Gueux," *New Encyclopedia Britannica, Micropaedia* vol. 4, 15th ed. (1978), p. 78.

Gutman, Roy. *A Witness to Genocide*. New York: Macmillan, 1993.

Hallie, Philip P. *Lest Innocent Blood Be Shed*. New York: Harper, 1979.

Hardin, Russell. "Rationality, Irrationality, and Functionalist Explanation," *Social Science Information* 19 (September 1980): 755–72.

———. *Collective Action*. Baltimore: Johns Hopkins University Press for Resources for the Future, 1982.

———. "Does Might Make Right?" pp. 201–17 in J. Roland Pennock and John W. Chapman, eds., NOMOS 29: *Authority Revisited*. New York: New York University Press, 1987.

———. *Morality within the Limits of Reason*. Chicago: University of Chicago Press, 1988.

———. "Autonomy, Identity, and Welfare," in John Christman, ed., *The Inner Citadel: Essays on Individual Autonomy*. New York: Oxford University Press, 1989.

———. "Public Choice vs. Democracy," in John W. Chapman, ed., NOMOS 32: *Majorities and Minorities*. New York: New York University Press, 1990.

———. "Acting Together, Contributing Together," *Rationality and Society* 3 (July 1991): 365–80.

———. "Hobbesian Political Order," *Political Theory* 19 (May 1991): 156–80.

———. "Trusting Persons, Trusting Institutions," in Richard J. Zeckhauser, ed., *The Strategy of Choice*. Cambridge, Mass.: MIT Press, 1991.

———. "Common Sense at the Foundations," in Bart Schultz, ed., *Henry Sidgwick As Philosopher and Historian*. New York: Cambridge University Press, 1992.

———. "Efficiency vs. Equality and the Demise of Socialism," *Canadian Journal of Philosophy* 22 (June 1992): 149–61.

———. "The Morality of Law and Economics," *Law and Philosophy* 11 (November 1992): 331–84.

———. "The Street-Level Epistemology of Trust," *Analyse und Kritik* 14 (Winter 1992): 152–76; reprinted *Politics and Society* 21 (December 1993): pp. 505–29.

————. "Blackmailing for Mutual Good," *University of Pennsylvania Law Review* 41 (April 1993): 1787–1816.

————. "Altruism and Mutual Advantage," *Social Service Review* 67 (September 1993): 358–73.

————. "The Economics of Knowledge and Utilitarian Morality," in Brad Hooker, ed., *Rationality, Rules, and Utility: Essays on Richard Brandt's Moral Philosophy*. Boulder, Colo.: Westview Press, 1993.

————. "My University's Yacht: Morality and the Rule of Law," in Randy E. Barnett and Ian Shapiro, eds., NOMOS 26, *The Rule of Law*. New York: New York University Press, 1994.

Hart, H.L.A. *The Concept of Law*. Oxford: Oxford University Press, 1961.

Hasluck, Margaret. *The Unwritten Law in Albania*. Ed. by J. H. Hutton. Cambridge: Cambridge University Press, 1954.

Hayek, F. A. *Rules and Order*. Vol. 1 of *Law, Legislation, and Liberty*. Chicago: University of Chicago Press, 1973.

————. *The Mirage of Social Justice*. Vol. 2 of *Law, Legislation, and Liberty*. Chicago: University of Chicago Press, 1976.

Heath, Anthony. *Rational Choice and Social Exchange*. Cambridge: Cambridge University Press, 1976.

Hechter, Michael. "The Attainment of Solidarity in Intentional Communities," *Rationality and Society* 2 (April 1990): 142–55.

Herskovits, Melville J. *Cultural Relativism: Perspectives in Cultural Pluralism*. Ed. by Frances S. Herskovits. New York: Vintage, 1972.

Hertzberg, Arthur. "Is Anti-Semitism Dying Out?" *New York Review of Books*, 24 June 1993, pp. 51–57.

Hirsch, Fred. *Social Limits to Growth*. Cambridge, Mass.: Harvard University Press, 1976.

Hirschman, Albert O. *Exit, Voice, and Loyalty*. Cambridge, Mass.: Harvard University Press, 1970.

————. *The Passions and the Interests: Political Arguments for Capitalism before Its Triumph*. Princeton: Princeton University Press, 1977.

Hobbes, Thomas. *Leviathan*. Harmondsworth, Middlesex: Penguin, 1968 (1651).

Hobsbawm, E. J. *Nations and Nationalism since 1780: Programme, Myth, Reality*. Cambridge: Cambridge University Press, 1990.

————. "The New Threat to History," *New York Review of Books*, 16 December 1993, pp. 62–64.

Holmes, Stephen. "The Secret History of Self Interest," in Jane J. Mansbridge, ed., *Beyond Self Interest*. Chicago: University of Chicago Press, 1990.

Hont, Istvan, and Michael Ignatieff. "Needs and justice in the *Wealth of Nations*: an introductory essay," in Hont and Ignatieff, eds., *Wealth and Virtue: The Shaping of Political Economy in the Scottish Enlightenment*. Cambridge: Cambridge University Press, 1983.

Horowitz, Donald. *Ethnic Groups in Conflict*. Berkeley: University of California Press, 1985.

Hume, David. *A Treatise of Human Nature*. Ed. by L. A. Selby-Bigge and P. H. Nidditch. Oxford: Oxford University Press, 1978 2d ed.; first pub. 1739–40.

Hume, David. "Of the First Principles of Government," pp. 32–36 in Hume, *Essays Moral, Political and Literary.* Ed. by Eugene F. Miller. Indianapolis, Ind.: Liberty Press, 1985; essay first pub. 1741.

———. *The History of England.* Vol. 1. Indianapolis, Ind.: Liberty Press, 1983 (1778).

Hume, John. "A New Ireland in a New Europe," in Dermot Keogh and Michael H. Haltzel, eds., *Northern Ireland and the Politics of Reconciliation.* Cambridge: Cambridge University Press, 1993, pp. 226–33.

Ignatieff, Michael. "The Balkan Tragedy," *New York Review of Books*, 13 May 1993, pp. 3–5.

Ishiguro, Kazuo. *The Remains of the Day.* New York: Knopf, 1989.

James, William. "Herbert Spencer," in James, *Essays in Philosophy.* Cambridge, Mass.: Harvard University Press, 1978; essay first pub. 1904.

Kafka, Franz. *Tagebücher* (Diaries). Frankfurt: Fischer, 1967.

Kaplan, Robert D. *Balkan Ghosts: A Journey through History.* New York: St. Martin's, 1993.

———. "A Reader's Guide to the Balkans," *New York Times Book Review*, 18 April 1993, pp. 1, 30–33.

Katz, Ephraim. *The Film Encyclopedia.* New York: Putnam, 1982 (1979).

Katz, Jack. *Seductions of Crime: Moral and Sensual Attractions in Doing Evil.* New York: Basic Books, 1988.

Kavka, Gregory S. *Hobbesian Moral and Political Theory.* Princeton: Princeton University Press, 1986.

Kawabata, Yasunari. *Beauty and Sadness.* Trans. by Howard S. Hibbett. New York: Knopf, 1975 (1965).

Keogh, Dermot, and Michael H. Haltzel. "Introduction," in Keogh and Haltzel, eds., *Northern Ireland and the Politics of Reconciliation.* Cambridge: Cambridge University Press, 1993.

Kiernan, V. G. *The Duel in European History: Honour and the Reign of Aristocracy.* Oxford: Oxford University Press, 1986.

Kornhauser, William A. *The Politics of Mass Society.* New York: Free Press, 1959.

Kroeber, Theodora. *Ishi in Two Worlds: A Biography of the Last Wild Indian in North America.* Berkeley: University of California Press, 1976 (1961).

Kymlicka, Will. *Liberalism, Community, and Culture.* Oxford: Oxford University Press, 1989.

Laitin, David D. *Hegemony and Culture: Politics and Religious Change among the Yoruba.* Chicago: University of Chicago Press, 1986.

Lane, Harlan. *The Wild Boy of Aveyron.* Cambridge, Mass.: Harvard University Press, 1976; repr. New York: Bantam, 1977.

Lash , Scott, and John Urry. "The New Marxism of Collective Action: A Critical Analysis," *Sociology* 18 (February 1984): 33–50.

Le Bon, Gustave. *The Crowd.* London: 1922 (1895).

Lebovics, Herman. *True France: The Wars over Cultural Identity, 1900–1945.* Ithaca, N.Y.: Cornell University Press, 1992.

Lemarchand, René. *Burundi: Ethnocide as Discourse and Practice.* Cambridge: Cambridge University Press, 1994.

Levi, Margaret, and Stephen DeTray. "A Weapon Against War: Conscientious Objection in the United States, Australia, and France," *Politics and Society* 21 (December 1993): 425–64.

Lewis, David K. *Convention*. Cambridge, Mass.: Harvard University Press, 1969.

Li, Sanyuan. "Hazards of Democratization in China." Chicago: University of Chicago diss. in Political Science, 1994.

Lieven, Dominic. *The Aristocracy in Europe 1815–1914*. New York: Columbia University Press, 1992.

Locke, John. *Letter on Toleration*. Any standard edition.

Macdonald, Dwight. *The Responsibility of Peoples and Other Essays in Political Criticism*. London: Victor Gollancz, 1957.

Magas, Branka. *The Destruction of Yugoslavia: Tracking the Break-up 1980–92*. London: Verso, 1993.

Mair, Lucy. *African Societies*. Cambridge: Cambridge University Press, 1974.

Mandeville, Bernard. *An Inquiry into the Origin of Honour and the Usefulness of Christianity in War*. London, 1836.

Margolis, Howard. *Patterns, Thinking, and Cognition*. Chicago: University of Chicago Press, 1987.

Marx, Karl. *The 18th Brumaire of Louis Bonaparte*. New York: International Publishers, 1963 (1852).

McCall, Nathan. *Makes Me Wanna Holler: A Young Black Man in America*. New York: Random House, 1994.

Melville, Herman. *Moby Dick* (published in 1851 as *The Whale*, any complete edition).

Mérimée, Prosper. "Colomba," in Mérimée, *Carmen and Other Stories*. Oxford: Oxford University Press, 1989 (story from 1840).

———. "The Etruscan Vase," in Mérimée, *Carmen and Other Stories*, pp. 93–115.

———. "Mateo Falcone," in Mérimée, *Carmen and Other Stories*, pp. 54–66.

Merton, Robert K. *Social Theory and Social Structure*. New York: Macmillan, 1968 enlarged ed.

———. "Insiders and Outsiders: A Chapter in the Sociology of Knowledge," *American Journal of Sociology* 28 (July 1972).

———. "Our Sociological Vernacular," *Columbia* (the magazine of Columbia University), November 1981.

Mill, John Stuart. *On Liberty*. Any standard edition.

———. *Principles of Political Economy*. Ed. by J. M. Robson. Toronto: University of Toronto Press, 1965 (1871), 7th ed.

Miller, William Ian. *Bloodtaking and Peacemaking: Feud, Law, and Society in Saga Iceland*. Chicago: University of Chicago Press, 1990.

Monmonier, Mark. *How to Lie with Maps*. Chicago: University of Chicago Press, 1991.

Moravcsik, Julius. "Communal Ties," *Proceedings and Addresses of the American Philosophical Association* (September 1988), supplement to vol. 62, no. 1, pp. 211–25.

Moore, Sally Falk. *Law As Process: An Anthropological Approach*. London: Routledge & Kegan Paul, 1978.

Mousnier, Roland. *The Institutions of France under the Absolute Monarchy 1598–1789*. Chicago: University of Chicago Press, 1979, from 1974 French ed.

Moynihan, Daniel Patrick. *Pandaemonium: Ethnicity in International Politics*. Oxford: Oxford University Press, 1993.

Murphy, Jeffrie, and Jules Coleman. *The Philosophy of Law*. Boulder, Colo.: Westview, 1990, rev. ed.

Myers, Robert J. "The Moral Menace of Intervention." Unpublished paper, Carnegie Council on Ethics and International Affairs, New York, 1994.

Navarro, Marysa. "The Personal Is Political: Las Madres de Plaza de Mayo," in Susan Eckstein, ed., *Power and Popular Protest*. Berkeley: University of California Press, 1989.

Neier, Aryeh. "Kosovo Survives!" *New York Review of Books*, 3 February 1994, pp. 26–28.

Nozick, Robert. *Anarchy, State, and Utopia*. New York: Basic Books, 1974.

Obeyesekere, Gananath. *The Work of Culture: Symbolic Transformation in Psychoanalysis and Anthropology*. Chicago: University of Chicago Press, 1990.

Olson, Mancur, Jr. *The Logic of Collective Action*. Cambridge, Mass.: Harvard University Press, 1965.

Osborne, Charles. *The Complete Operas of Verdi*. New York: Da Capo, 1969.

Parsons, Talcott. "Power and the Social System," pp. 94–143 in Steven Lukes, ed., *Power*. New York: New York University Press, 1986 (1963).

Pavlowitch, Stevan K. "Who is 'Balkanizing' Whom? The Misunderstandings between the Debris of Yugoslavia and an Unprepared West," *Daedalus* (Spring 1994), 203–23.

Peirce, Charles Sanders. "Preface" to *Scientific Metaphysics*, in *Collected Works of Charles Sanders Peirce*. Cambridge, Mass.: Harvard University Press, 1935, vol. 6.

Plato. *The Republic*. Any edition.

Plucknett, Theodore F. T. *A Concise History of Common Law*. Boston: Little, Brown, 1956, 5th ed. (1929).

Polanyi, Michael. *The Tacit Dimension*. Garden City, N.Y.: Anchor, 1967 (1966).

Posner, Richard A. "The Ethical and Political Basis of Wealth Maximization," in Posner, *The Economics of Justice*. Cambridge, Mass.: Harvard University Press, 1981.

———. *Economic Analysis of Law*. Boston: Little, Brown, 1992, 4th ed.

Poulton, Hugh. *The Balkans: Minorities and States in Conflict*. London: Minority Rights Group, 1993, new ed. (1991).

Puccini, Giacomo. *Tosca*. New York: G. Schirmer, 1956 (1900), libretto by Luigi Illica and Giuseppe Giacosa.

Rapoport, Anatol. *Fights, Games, and Debates*. Ann Arbor, Mich.: University of Michigan Press, 1960.

Remnick, David. "Waiting for the Apocalypse in Crown Heights," *New Yorker*, 21 December 1992, pp. 52–57, p. 54.

———. "Belfast Confetti," *New Yorker*, 25 April 1994, pp. 38–77.

Reznichenko, Vladimir. "Anti-Semitism on Trial," *Soviet Life* (February 1991): 14–17.

Richler, Mordecai. "O Quebec," *New Yorker*, 30 May 1994, pp. 50–57.

Rorty, Richard. "Postmodernist Bourgeois Liberalism," in Rorty, *Objectivity, Relativism, and Truth: Philosophical Papers*. Vol. 1. Cambridge: Cambridge University Press, 1991 (essay from 1985).

Said, Edward W. "Michael Walzer's *Exodus and Revolution*: A Canaanite Reading," in Edward W. Said and Christopher Hitchens, eds., *Blaming the Victims: Spurious Scholarship and the Palestinian Question*. London: Verso, 1988.

Sandel, Michael J. *Liberalism and the Limits of Justice*. Cambridge: Cambridge University Press, 1982.

Schelling, Thomas C. *The Strategy of Conflict*. Cambridge, Mass.: Harvard University Press, 1960.

———. *Micromotives and Macrobehavior*. New York: Norton, 1978.

Scholem, Gershom. *Sabbatai Sevi: The Mystical Messiah*. Princeton: Princeton University Press, 1973.

Schwartz, Warren F., Keith Baxter, and David Ryan. "The Duel: Can These Gentlemen Be Acting Efficiently?" *Journal of Legal Studies* 13 (June 1984): 321–55.

Scott, John Finley. *Internalization of Norms: A Sociological Theory of Moral Commitment*. Englewood Cliffs, N.J.: Prentice-Hall, 1971.

Scott, Walter. *Count Robert of Paris*. Edinburgh, 1831.

Selznick, Philip. *The Organizational Weapon: A Study of Bolshevik Strategy and Tactics*. New York: McGraw-Hill, 1952.

Shoumatoff, Alex. "Rwanda's Aristocratic Guerrillas," *New York Times Magazine*, 13 December 1992, pp. 42–48.

———. "Flight from Death." *New Yorker*, 20 June 1994, pp. 44–55, at p. 53.

Sidgwick, Henry. *The Methods of Ethics*. London: Macmillan, 1907 (1874), 7th ed.

Simpson, John, and Jana Bennett. *The Disappeared and the Mothers of the Plaza*. New York: St. Martin's Press, 1985.

Smith, Adam. *An Inquiry into the Nature and Causes of the Wealth of Nations*. Oxford: Oxford University Press, 1976; Indianapolis, Ind.: Liberty Classics, 1981, rcpr.

———. *Lectures on Jurisprudence*. Oxford: Oxford University Press, 1978; Indianapolis, Ind.: Liberty Classics, 1982, reprint (from lecture notes dated 1762–1763).

Smith, T. V. "Honor," *Encyclopaedia of the Social Sciences*. Vol. 7. New York: Macmillan, 1932, pp. 456–58.

Solvason, Birgir T. R. "Institutional Evolution in the Icelandic Commonwealth," *Constitutional Political Economy* 4 (1993): 97–125.

Steinfels, Peter. "A Political Movement Blends Its Ideas from Left and Right," *New York Times*, 24 May 1994, p. 4.6.

Stinchcombe, Arthur. "Is the Prisoner's Dilemma All of Sociology?" *Inquiry* 23 (1980): 187–92.

Tambiah, S. J. *Sri Lanka: Ethnic Fratricide and the Dismantling of Democracy*. Chicago: University of Chicago Press, 1986.

Taylor, Charles. *Sources of the Self: The Making of the Modern Identity*. Cambridge, Mass.: Harvard University Press, 1989.

———. "Irreducibly Social Goods," in Geoffrey Brennan and Cliff Walsh, eds., *Rationality, Individualism and Public Policy* (Canberra: Centre for Research on Federal Financial Relations, 1990), pp. 45–63.

Tocqueville, Alexis de. "Memoir on Pauperism," in Seymour Drescher, *Tocqueville and Beaumont on Social Reform*. New York: Harper, 1968 (1835).

Tolstoy, Leo. *War and Peace*. London: Everyman, 1911 (1864–1869).

———. *Resurrection*. Trans. by Rosemary Edmonds. London: Penguin, 1966; first pub. 1899.

Townsend, Joseph. *A Dissertation on the Poor Laws, By a Well-Wisher to Mankind*. Berkeley, Calif.: University of California Press, 1971 (1786).

Tucholsky, Kurt. *Politische Briefe*. Ed. by Fritz J. Raddatz. Reinbek bei Hamburg: Rowohlt, 1969.

Turgenev, Ivan. *Fathers and Sons*. Trans. by Rosemary Edmonds. Baltimore: Penguin, 1965 (1861).

———. *Spring Torrents*. Trans. by Leonard Schapiro. Baltimore: Penguin, 1980 (1872).

Veblen, Thorstein. *An Inquiry into the Nature of Peace and the Terms of Its Perpetuation*. New York: Augustus M. Kelley, 1964 repr. (1917).

Verdi, Giuseppe. *Ernani* (1844), with a libretto by Francesco Maria Piave, based on the play *Hernani* (1830), by Victor Hugo.

Walzer, Michael. *Exodus and Revolution*. New York: Basic Books, 1985.

Warshow, Robert Irving. *Alexander Hamilton: First American Businessman*. New York: Greenberg, 1931.

Weber, Eugen. *Peasants into Frenchmen: The Modernization of Rural France, 1870–1914*. Stanford, Calif.: Stanford University Press, 1976.

Weschler, Lawrence. "Lost in Rwanda," *New Yorker*, 25 April 1994, pp. 42–45.

Williams, Bernard. *Morality: An Introduction to Ethics*. New York: Harper and Row, 1972.

———. *Ethics and the Limits of Philosophy*. Cambridge, Mass.: Harvard University Press, 1985.

Wisconsin v. Yoder et al., 406 U. S., pp. 205–49.

Wolfe, Thomas. *Look Homeward, Angel*. New York: Scribner's, 1929.

———. *The Web and the Rock*. New York: Harper, 1939.

———. *You Can't Go Home Again* (1940).

Woolf, Virginia. *A Room of One's Own*. Harmondsworth, Middlesex: Penguin, 1945 (1928).

Xenophon. *The Persian Expedition* (or *Anabasis*). Any edition.

Yeats, William Butler. *The Collected Poems of W. B. Yeats*. New York: Macmillan, 1956, definitive edition.

Zingg, Robert M. "India's Wolf Children: Two Human Infants Reared by Wolves," *Scientific American* (March 1941): 135–37.

Index

Russell Hardin, Professor of Politics at New York University, is the author of numerous works, including *Morality within the Limits of Reason* and *Collective Action*. He is a fellow of the American Academy of Arts and Sciences and the American Association for the Advancement of Science.